NEVER BEEN THIS CLOSE TO CRAZY

Alan Hardwick

Co-Creator

Kristen Martin

ISBN: 978-1-7339-746-2-2

Alan Hardwick

ISBN: 978-1-7339746-2-2

Library of Congress Control Number: 2019940319

Cover design by Logan Hardwick (www.repyoutate.com).
Illustrations by Lauren Trahan (www.facebook.com/ltatts6789/).

First Edition.

Introduction

Nikki

If you would have told me three years ago I'd be sitting on the shore of Puget Sound watching five children frolic in the surf with the love of my life by my side, I would have asked if you were on crack. I was a successful, attractive, divorced 40-year old woman with no children or desire to have any so late in life.

Not that I'm *against* children; I'm the youngest of two, the self-proclaimed Daddy's favorite. As a child (ok, and as an adult), nobody could say no to me. If they did, I'd do it anyway. Perceptive and adventurous, I skillfully terrorized my older sister and my parents with great satisfaction. We lived an upper middle-class lifestyle where tangible things were honestly more important than loving one another. I took the world head-on, becoming the youngest manager at my first real job. I married at age twenty and divorced for the first time at twenty-one. I remember waking up in the hospital wondering what the hell had happened to me. Looking in the mirror and reading the police report informed me that I had been beaten and left for dead by my first husband. Three years later, I was dating and living life again in Seattle, telling my friends how someday I'd write romance novels.

My motto has always been to aim high, tell no one, and take your time. Growing up, I quietly dreamt of living in Seattle, California and Texas. Every move I made throughout the years was made with these goals in mind. In 1994, I moved to California where I met my second future ex-husband. We married in 1998 and promptly hit the road for Austin with our cats and a U-Haul. During this 10-year marriage, I realized I was never going to have children. It saddened me but also put my life into perspective. In 2002, we moved to Seattle trying to make each other happy. My career was taking off

4

and I had become well-respected in my field of work. By early 2008, I filed for divorce, no longer able to continue in a loveless marriage. I moved north, he stayed in our house. I remember telling him, "One day you'll thank me for this but I know today is not that day." He had a few choice words for me. Imagine that.

The ink was on the divorce papers but not truly dry when I started dating again. I was looking for that elusive love of a lifetime. I wasn't sure I'd ever find it, but I was going to have a blast trying and would not settle for less. Like most single women, I had a mental picture of what my future soul mate should be, from his financial standing to his appearance. True to form, I had it precisely mapped out—a goal in mind. I found men everywhere (Starbucks, Whole Foods, the beach, the bars, work, parties, friends of friends, and even in traffic), but I soon came to the realization they were all missing something. Until I met Alex Hill.

I would later learn this man was, and will forever be, my soul mate, confidant, best friend, lover, advisor, Padawan learner, and partner in crime. His love of life, children, and God left such an impression on me. Alex was one man I couldn't shake and honestly didn't want to. His financial portfolio was a mess, he drove his parent's Buick station wagon, he claimed to have a crazy ex-wife, and he had full custody of five children. I realize that doesn't exactly match my aforementioned list, but I was drawn to this wonderful human in a very short period of time.

While I do believe in a higher power, I'm not a religious person. I wake up every morning with a goal to be the best person I can be while still having fun. I live my life within my own set of rules—I am a law-abiding citizen. Okay wait…I'm NOW a law-abiding citizen; let's not focus on my younger years, thank you.

My sense of humor may tend sarcastic but not to the point of offensive. More like…sassy. I find humor in everyday events. I've been known to be mischievous, seeking out fun with unsuspecting innocents, particularly when bored. At work I'm known as the Master Prankster, that coworker people love to hate. Styrofoam peanut-filled cube, office turned into the paper supply room while my coworker was on vacation, taking a parking space hostage—the list goes on.

I'm known as an expert interviewer; details do not get by me often and I have an enviable sixth sense. When Alex began to open up about his ex-wife, I quietly maintained the mindset that I could forge a relationship with her. That's what I do, I'm in human resources for crying out loud! Over time, I read the entire court case of their divorce, digested countless email and texts from her, and listened to her children as they spoke of their mother. Despite all that information, I held onto my belief. Or I did...until the day I was exposed first-hand to the crazy.

I've done a couple of things since meeting Alex that I'm not proud of, things which under normal circumstances, and maybe in hindsight, I would not recommend. While I won't attempt to excuse what I've done, my goal was never to hurt anyone or cause any sort of harm. Rather, it was always to provide insight into an unstable, often undecipherable mind while also making certain life events manageable and, yes, unexpectedly entertaining.

This book is about us. It's about our desire to make a wonderful life with each other despite the odds. It's about protecting a protector and helping a family at risk find peace. It's about navigating the craziness of my own growing love for Alex and his kids. The pages are in chronological order and told in alternating perspectives of Alex and me over the course of two years. The names and locations have been changed to protect the guilty, but it is essentially a true story. As you read this book, sit tight, get comfy, hold on, and don't worry too much when that little thought crosses your own mind like it did ours: *Maybe I'm the crazy one!*

# # #

Alex

If you would have told me twenty years ago I'd be a single father of five children living in a seaside town, I would have lost you at 'single.' Divorced? No way. Sure, I'm a cop, but that typical divorced-cop characteristic was not going to be part of *my* story; I'd lived through divorce as a child and was firmly dedicated to sticking it out through thick and thin, better or worse, sick and tired, poor or poorer and all that. I was a family man through and through: husband first, father second, and the rest could play catch up. Divorce was not an option. I only wanted enough money to make simple ends meet. I would never allow my job to take any sort of priority over the family.

That was a challenge when I became good, really good at my job. It was pretty unexpected, actually. Like many musicians, my music studies in college led me straight to law enforcement (naturally?), though not in the back seat of the patrol car. I never expected to be a police officer, or first in my academy class. I never expected to conduct organized crime investigations or start an intelligence unit, or to be the first guy to earn a detective badge in only 7 months. I've always loved working hard and having fun while seriously excelling in my work. But with my family as the priority, I figured accomplishments like these would remain well out of reach in my career.

A great way to make sure your job doesn't take priority over your family is to have five kids and simultaneously watch your wife lose her mind. We intended to have a large family compared to today's standards. Not sure why…it just seemed like the thing to do at the time, like church on Sundays or duty sex on important holidays. Might be why four of the five were born within a 4-week window. Maybe. Deduction powers at work here.

I was the youngest of three children to my adopted parents. I was born to a 17-year old girl who relinquished me at birth. By the time I was 3 years old, my parents figured out adding a boy to the family was insufficient to solve their marital problems. After they divorced, I lived with my mom and sisters for a few years until my dad won custody for reasons I still don't understand.

Dad was the local milkman. Not kidding. Even better, when the Darigold plant in Everett closed some of their facilities, Dad transferred to southwest Washington and took the coolest job any 5th grade boy could hope for.

My dad cut cheese. This was fun to explain to my friends.

Dad was intent on making a man out of me, requiring me to keep up. I have this image of the back of my dad's boots on a cattle trail walking briskly through a wet pasture on old man Bicknell's farm in Lewis County. It was never easy keeping up with him—he made sure of it. Dad was neither affectionate nor encouraging; he was demanding, hard, and bull-headed.

By the time I was 16, I found people who would fill my need for love and acceptance at a local church. These Presbyterians were brighter than I expected: my pastor soon realized the dysfunctional relations in my home and pushed me straight back to the kitchen table with an assignment: Love your dad. On purpose. I had been waiting for Dad to love me, to show me that he cared, to encourage me in my dreams. I wanted him to tell me *he* loved me. Wisely, my pastor showed me that love was something you give, not demand.

Those were the days I like to remember about my dad. He retired early and started his own business in the fur industry. Now think: my dad went from being the milkman, to cutting cheese, to chasing beaver. Boy, howdy.

Rather than follow all my father's footsteps, I became a non-profit music teacher while still attending college, then married a woman before I was 21. My roommate told me I really needed to catch her before she glommed on to someone else. Clue #1: 'glommed on.' We all had high opinions of Holly; she was summertime blonde, just shy of 5-8, pretty, entertaining, smart enough, loyal, openly devoted to her faith and strongly committed to marrying someone who had no thought of ever filing for divorce. Ever. Her parents and their parents all went through divorce, just like mine. We were both eager to stop the cycle.

We all want the happily-ever-after and hope like crazy that we are capable of achieving it. After 10 years of marriage, I made the conscious decision to remain in a troubled relationship, knowing it could bring harm to me and our children. Five years after that, the marriage was on life-support as I clung to our vows. She finally made her move, but in a way I never saw coming. On a rainy February night, Holly tearfully sat each of the children down, one by one, and knelt in front of them, forcing the choice on them before she walked out the door: "Do you want to leave with mommy, or do you want her to be all alone while you stay here with your father?" I watched, powerless, as the damage was being done.

When Holly drove away, alone, in a madly packed Suburban, I had finally reached that point of knowing I'd done all I could to save the marriage. That's when I became a quiet fan of Sarah McLachlan, repeating her perfectly depressing songs as I lay alone in bed at night, wondering if a deflated, abandoned father of five would have any hope of raising children with a positive impression of motherhood. Wondering if my children would resent my choice to divorce without having the facts of what really happened. Wondering if a musician-turned-cop could ever freely love someone again.

I had no idea of the amazing journey which lie ahead, a journey which began at a little coffee shop in Mill Creek.

1. SPEND ALL YOUR TIME LOOKING

September 19, 2008

Racing in my black 2007 Saturn Sky to meet up with Detective Alex Hill, the dashboard clock read 5:58. *Damn, I'm late!* I headed north on the Bothell-Everett Highway, slipping the convertible's tires a bit on the wet road when I hit second gear. Might have been a little on purpose. I hoped the weather would improve so we could take in a walk after coffee.

This promised to be an interesting first date with a man I'd barely met a few days before when he held the door for me at The Spotted Cow in Mill Creek. *He's got five kids, surely he'll understand being a few minutes late,* I thought. Not sure why I was so concerned; I'd nearly given up on the whole dating thing anyway.

At 6:02 pm I calmly walked into the coffee shop and looked around. Alex was not there. My sudden relief quickly converted to annoyance. *Oh great, he's not here—am I getting stood up?* That'd be a first. I ordered my drip coffee from the ditzy barista with the obstructive nose ring. I wondered how often she had to wash that thing. Turning from the counter to take a second look around, I saw Alex rushing through the front door, disheveled and as handsome as the first time we met. I giggled cutely at him.

"Nikki, sorry to keep you waiting!"

"No worries," I said. "I'll be over there," pointing to a table near the back window. I pretended not to watch him in my periphery as he collected his americano, added a dash of cream, and gingerly transported the oversized mug to our table with a big sigh. His relief told me some of his trips to the table didn't end in such a success. His large hands dwarfed the coffee mug.

"My 16-year old, Martin, got in an accident about an hour ago," he said. "He's ok, just a little shaken up and upset about his first car. I stopped to help him out on my way here."

I probed him for details on the accident down to the liability. Needing a visual aid, Alex scratched out a diagram of the accident scene on a paper napkin with a cheap pen he had in his pants pocket. Go figure...a cop scratching out a crime scene on a napkin. All I could think was how this man has full custody of five children and *oh boy is he cute*! I started to be glad I didn't hang up the whole dating thing.

Over the course of more than an hour, we talked about how we ended up in our chosen professions. Alex confessed his music education studies were interrupted when he began his family before finishing college. When he and his wife found out they were pregnant, he knew he needed a job that paid more than the $800/month he was making by teaching at a small private school. He looked in the classifieds and found the highest paying job listed that day—Police Officer—and applied.

Up to that moment, Alex had been fairly vague regarding his law enforcement job. It didn't take much to get him talking. Alex explained he had been out of uniform for 5 years, assigned to a multi-agency task force with the FBI for preventing terrorism.

"What exactly does *that* involve?" I asked.

"Can't say," he said, raising one eyebrow with a sly grin. "Ever seen the show *24* on TV? Sorta like that, without the jumper cables or helicopters."

I hadn't seen the show, but I knew about it. Alex didn't seem like the *Jack Bauer* type; he impressed me as a brilliant man who also knew how to be real. I never anticipated meeting a man who equaled me in common sense. It's a superpower possessed by very few.

I shared with Alex how my adult working life had evolved starting in retail and progressed to working with systems and processes for the human resources function. It wasn't nearly as sexy as the whole cops-n-robbers thing, or terrorists, whatever. He actually seemed interested, engaged.

"Do you know how to read music?" he asked.

"Not a note," I replied. I had tried playing the bass guitar for a short stint back in the day but it didn't last long. Neither did that relationship.

"It's pretty simple," he said, then began to geek out a little on another paper napkin, showing me the pattern of notes on a scale. "It's like a language, a code of sorts," he said. "What kind of music do like?"

"A wide array," I said, slightly worried now that he may not be my type. "Alice In Chains, maybe some Aerosmith, a little country, but I love some Jason Mraz."

"I kinda skipped the whole metal scene," he said.

As our meeting turned to evening, we talked about a group of diverse individuals that had slowly been gathering at a table next to us. We entertained ourselves with trying to figure out what exactly brought them all together. It was nice, being together. Much better than I anticipated.

We outlasted the neighbors and eventually got the not-so-subtle cue to leave when the barista started stacking chairs upside down on the tables. A light mist had settled in as Alex walked me out to my car. We made plans for the following evening, after which Alex leaned in for a hug. I reached my arms around his back and up to his shoulders for the tight embrace, wanting to relieve some of the responsibility I knew he was carrying. He has since reflected on that moment as the best hug he's ever had. We pulled apart and he gently leaned in for our first kiss. *That* was more than I ever expected.

Much more. In fact, despite the mist, we made-out in the parking lot until the landscaping sprinklers unnecessarily kicked on a few hours later.

# # #

September 20, 2008

A good way to ignore my twisted feelings was to take out the trash. Or, in this case, steal somebody else's, usually before dawn. Picking up the garbage of a suspected terrorism facilitator living in Mountlake Terrace at 4:30 am without being noticed had been a marginally successful bi-weekly operation, yielding an occasional hand-written sticky note (literally) or maybe some mail. This week, I had a pleasant task force partner to help sort through it in the dimly-lit loading bay of the nearby QFC grocery store. Today, however, the look on Detective Jim Richardson's face was anything but pleased.

"Does this guy eat anything other than fish?"

"God, I wish," I said. "You're a Scot, you should be used to rotting meat."

While quietly digging through a week's worth of refuse sorting for scraps of paper, I couldn't escape the repeating thought of Nikki. I hadn't even had a hint of infidelity in the 20 years of being with Holly, but despite how done my marriage was, it was still a marriage on paper. I felt very conflicted inside about my evening with Nikki, like I had broken a sacred rule or violated the very laws of God. The way she held me, her kiss—it had been a very long time since I felt anything like that. I wrestled with the guilt, wondering what my kids would think.

"Bingo!" Jim held up a ripped, dripping…thing. Looked like paper.

"Phone bill?"

"Through September 1st," he beamed. "Now we have his number."

I looked at the stained document. "And some of his friends. Good stuff, Jim. Now let's get the hell out of here before some early-morning dog walker realizes we aren't a couple of homeless guys."

"Right," he said, snapping off his nitrite gloves with a grin. "They might call the cops."

# # #

I knew I should get a to-do list written or I'd just wander aimlessly around the house all morning. I threw on a sweatshirt, shorts and tennis shoes, gathered my hair in a clip, and headed for Starbucks. It was a top-down kind of mild Saturday in my favorite season. Actually, I think that about every season in Seattle.

As I waited in line at Starbucks I made my to-do list on my phone.
- Laundry
- Vacuum and dust
- Clean out fridge
- Get nails done
- Wash car

I know there's more…what am I forgetting? I was leaving for a business trip to

Burbank Monday morning and I had a football game to attend on Sunday, leaving Saturday to get ready for my trip. Alex was coming over tonight. I was so excited I was finding it hard to focus.

A man in line behind me distracted me from my daydream trying to engage me in conversation. I did the unthinkable: I began to compare this complete stranger to Alex—another stranger. As I ordered my grande drip in a venti cup, he asked for my phone number. I graciously declined the advancement with a white lie. "I'm dating someone." Okay, it's not much of a white lie, I was actually dating three men. I'd never been able to date more than three at a time…it became a horrible circus act when I attempted it. Dating three men shouldn't imply I was sleeping with all of them, usually only one. Hoochie? Eh, it's really not that way, or, okay, whatever. I'd pretty much written off one of the guys. Intellectually, we were not a match. Number two was a Seattle fireman with all the proper equipment but without the emotional commitment, if you know what I mean.

Now there was Alex, the new man on the block, the one that continued to linger on my mind. Oh, a text!

Alex: Hey! What time tonight would you like to get together?

Nikki: 6-ish? I don't have anything fancy planned - Just a movie.

Alex: Sounds perfect. I'm looking forward to seeing you.

Nikki: Me too!

Get a movie! I knew I was forgetting something for my to-do list.

# # #

The shower was adequate to remove the odor of used seafood and curry from my body, but my clothes needed additional attention. I managed to stuff a load of laundry into the wash and start breakfast before the kids were awake. By 10 am, the kids were fed and ready for the weekly Saturday visit with their mom. As ready as they could be, anyway. I sat down to take a look at Facebook, the new social networking fad which seemed to have some investigative potential. At least that's how I talked myself into using it. After logging in, my favorite church lady, Terri Joyner, sent me a direct message.

Terri: Alex! Any trauma this week?

Alex: A little too quiet, although Holly keeps sending long hand-written letters to the kids in the mail.

Terri: Seriously? Like with stamps?

Alex: Yeah. I got a note or two from the GAL this week too.

Terri: What's a GAL?

Alex: A Guardian ad Litem. Ours is Ron Taylor. He's the person appointed by the court to watch out for the kids' interests. He included me in his response to Holly's texts.

Terri: Are the letters to tug at their hearts?

Alex: Yes.

Terri: Those texts of hers are crazy…I got a few more this week!

Alex: Ron just got assigned to our case 3 weeks ago and is already overwhelmed with her texting anger. I'll show you the texts at church tomorrow. Here's a sampling: "Holly, I of course take no exception to your right to be angry. I must however insist that you not subject your children to your 'righteous anger' in any way. Try to consider the idea that YOU might be at least a part of the reason limits on your time with the children are necessary."

Terri: Hmm - seems like he isn't THAT harsh to her.

Alex: "…Holly, the boundary re you contacting the children is based on your ongoing choices to villainize their father and to burden them with your feelings re case issues. You have done a lot of this, even after the court order. I would have to see radical change to justify dropping this boundary. I will remind Alex to put kids on phone to you, at least the young ones."

Terri: Wait, so she's claiming you refuse to put the kids on the phone to her?

Alex: Right. So untrue. I tell them almost every day to call mom. In the evenings if I'm not out doing my Secret Squirrel stuff I make sure they call. There are days it doesn't happen, but in the week, she talks to the kids several times. Anyway....I gotta get back to the salt mines.

Terri: Well, hang in...what else can you do?

Alex: Win the lottery, maybe find a sane girlfriend.

Terri: Keep dreaming, pal.

Alex: Thanks for your friendship and support, Terri. So appreciated. You've seen this whole thing from before it began, when you taught the kids their first piano lessons. I truly value your input and perspective.

Terri: We're all in this together, Alex. I just hope you can find some happiness when it's all done. You deserve that.

I knew Terri was the one I could trust to talk about Nikki. Eventually.

# # #

Much to my satisfaction, Alex arrived at 6:00 pm on the nose. I gave him a tour of my little shack and got him a run-of-the-mill beer. We began to chat about anything and everything—an even exchange. Something that had not happened for me in a very long time. The movie was playing but I honestly can't remember the name of the flick. I think I fell asleep well after midnight but that too is a blur. Another parking lot episode sorta took over.

After he left I found a pen on the floor. It was the same cheap pen he had at the coffee shop, a grey Paper Mate. I smiled as I put it on the counter thinking how much fun I was going to have with his little missing instrument.

September 21, 2008

Sunday is my favorite day of the week during the fall for one simple reason: football. Today's battle put my beloved Seattle Seahawks against the St. Louis Rams. I'd been a Seahawks season ticket holder since 2000 when Seattle built the stadium to replace the Kingdome. Just a mere three years ago, our team made it to the Super Bowl. Despite the rough start this year, I still believed we could do it again!

Elle, my perpetually tardy sister and cheering partner, was on her way over to pick me up. The down-side of Elle driving to the game was her insistence on obeying the speed limit. Seattle traffic literally flew past us as we held up the right lane. It made no sense to me how a woman with a 5.0 liter Mustang would drive it like a gutless hybrid. She was proud of her ticketless record. No fun at all.

In the first quarter, Elle was introduced to a rather rowdy and moderately intoxicated seat neighbor who thought it was a good idea to chest bump my sister after a great interception. It was the goofiest thing I think I'd ever seen.

She turned to me wide-eyed and gasped, "Did you see that? *Did you?* That was my first chest bump ever," she announced.

I couldn't stop laughing. "I think he got way more out of it than you did," I said.

We screamed, cheered, boo'd, and lost our voices like classic Seahawks fans. It's quite a feeling to be part of the 12th Man, those legendary fans who cause more false starts than any other fan base in the NFL.

Exhausted and delighted with our first win of the season, we drove back to my house. Elle had decided to stay the night because she was taking me to the airport early the following morning. To say she's not a morning person would be a gross understatement. After we got home from the game, I started to give her some vague info about Alex. During the conversation I received a text.

Alex: Really. You've got to stop taking about me...

Nikki: *What?* Are you here?

Alex: LOL Not anymore.

Nikki: Stalker! LOL! You should have poked in!

Alex: Is THAT what she said?

I flung open the front door and looked around. Indeed, he was gone, but on the railing of the porch lay a single red rose. *Wow…really?* It was quite a moment—my sister staring at me with a grin bigger than the one she had from the chest bump. *What a sweet thing for him to do*, I thought.

In eight hours, I would head to California again for two long weeks of work, unable to ride the momentum of this developing relationship. I showed Elle the pen Alex left behind after last night's escapade. We quickly devised a plan for the poor Paper Mate. Considering his profession, we went with the terrorism theme, especially since Elle's profession was in corporate security.

I was probably going to get in trouble for this.

2. RANSOM

September 22, 2008

While waiting for my flight from Seatac to sunny Burbank California, I began the fun with Paper Mate Ultra Medium Point.

> **Nikki**: We have your precious Paper Mate. The device will detonate on 10/2 @ 2100 if demands aren't met. Pen me a song convincing me to save the lil guy. Don't call the Pocket Protector Police (PPPD).

> **Alex**: I will not be threatened.

> **Nikki**: Originals only—no Milli Vanilli. PS, your Paper Mate screams like a girl. We've replaced your little writing instrument's innards with explosive material, making him a deadly PBIED (pen borne improvised explosive device). Parts are parts when your forgotten pen blows!

I looked around and thought to myself, *Self, you're in an airport sending texts with words like pen borne improvised explosive device. Probably shouldn't be doing this here. Eh, what the hell…just one more before I board the plane.*

> **Nikki**: By this time tomorrow, if Paper Mate is somehow conscious, he will be allowed to contact you directly. We have scrambled the signal, so don't even think about having your silly NSA friends trace the texts.

September 23, 2008

Working for Rove Aerospace has its perks, among them being the fact that I simply didn't have to work very hard. In my 20-year career in human resources and systems management, I've hired, fired, coached, mentored, and counseled thousands of people in corporate America. I've told off CEO's and their cronies, and lived to tell the tale. It's no stretch to say I'm a force to be reckoned with, and I usually get my way.

One time, at a Texas-based company during a final executive meeting prior to laying off 50% of their workforce, the executives all started to waffle and couldn't come to the obvious decision. Annoyed, I announced, "When all-y'all are done with this circle-jerk, I'll be in my office," then left the room with a hint of disgust. I respect true leaders, but I certainly don't fear them. I only fear the bad ones.

Probably number one on my list of perks is the ability to travel with the likes of Morna McMasters. While I don't typically befriend my subordinates, Morna became the exception to this rule. Brash yet sensitive, inappropriate yet professional, untrusting yet embracing. A unique woman for whom I am forever thankful to be able to call my friend. She is a single, 5'10" blonde bombshell. And to top it off…she's Irish. Very Irish.

On this trip to Burbank, my team was in the throes of a company initiative which most in the industry said could not be done. Many before had tried and ultimately given up. Not us! Today, I planned to lay off Rove's payroll department in Burbank, thereby accomplishing the unthinkable: Centralization of the payroll function! It would have been simpler to figure out how to live on the moon. Payroll is the only function in most organizations that can bring a company completely to its knees. In addition to centralization, we also tackled a new timekeeping system with integration to the manufacturing platform. Again, something others had attempted and failed.

Over breakfast, I updated Morna on my love life. She was excited to hear about Alex and encouraged me to kick the other guys to the curb. I showed her my ransom texts and shared my plan for poor Paper Mate.

During the next several meetings, I continued sending ransom texts to Alex.

10:03 am

> **Nikki**: Pen Master, they are threatening to leak me. They showed me what they did to Sharpie. I don't think he'll ever write again. Help me…I'm very afraid! I'm uncontrollably clicking.
>
> Fondly Yours, Paper Mate Ultra Medium Point

12:00 pm

Nikki: Its getting bad Pen Master! I'm trying to remember my training but they've taken my cartridge out! I have no guts!

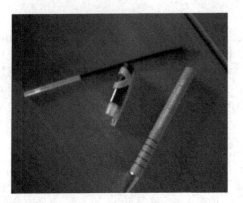

2:00 pm

    Nikki: I'm so scared I have writer's block.

With no answers from Alex, I was starting to wonder if I'd gone too far with my crass sense of humor, so I asked Morna. Probably not the right person to ask (she's off the crassness charts), but while talking it over we got our answer.

    Alex: When they tell you you're an expendable member, DON'T BELIEVE IT!

"Lad may be just as crazy as you, aye?" she smirked.

"That would be fitting," I replied.

September 24, 2008

Taking a cue from the interrogation methods in *Hogan's Heroes*, I sent a picture of Paper Mate resting blissfully during a late afternoon break against a plush pillow on the hotel room bed.

    Nikki: Pen Master, I may have been too quick to judge the situation. I think I'll hang out here awhile...

Rest assured I will 'escape' and return to you in due time. Fondly enjoying my cigarette, Paper Mate Ultra Medium Point.

Alex: Whoa—he looks comfy. Can we consider a prisoner swap?

In an effort to avoid getting sucked in to real work, Morna and I finished the work day at the bar. We often found ourselves spending $10 on a decent appetizer and $30 each on liquid nutrition. Maybe it was the booze, or maybe not, but somehow Morna was struck with another moment of brilliance. We gathered some publicly available props (coffee stir sticks, dental floss) for our next wave of torture. I said goodnight to Morna, took the props back to the hotel room, and with the extra encouragement of vodka, texted Alex at around 9.

Nikki: Hey. Whatchya wearing?

Alex: Um…you first.

Nikki: Hummmmmmmm.

Alex: Is this a recorded channel?

Nikki: You'd be the one to know! Don't you work for the government?

Alex: Close enough. Call?

He picked up immediately. "Hey there."

"Are you in bed?"

"Yep. Not bad for a Wednesday."

I laughed. "Well, aren't you the life of the party!"

"No, that sounds like you. Have you been out with Morna again?"

"Of course!" I was getting the giggles again. "It's her fault—she forced me to drink my dinner again. She had to have her beer-tini."

"Her…what?"

"Oh, she's from the Midwest," I explained. "It's a beer with olives—a beer TINI. You know, like a MAR-TINI??"

"New to me," Alex said. "But that's no surprise—five kids and a crazy ex hasn't exactly provided lots of time for me to explore the bar scene. Hell, I was married before I could legally drink."

"Then I clearly have a job to do," I said. "You live in downtown Edmonds, right? Have you been to the Taki Tiki?"

"Not yet," said Alex in a hopeful tone.

Alex explained he had moved into the house on Daley Street in April. He had planned to purchase a house in Edmonds, but Holly sabotaged the deal the day after she abandoned the family, resulting in the loss of their earnest money. Alex had four days to find a place for he and the kids to live since they had already given notice to vacate their Snohomish rental. Alex said he was thrilled to find a house only three blocks from the police station in downtown Edmonds for $1,700 a month, which barely fit into his budget. That is, until he had to pay spousal support.

"Are you kidding me? You pay $1,000 a month to her and you have the kids—How is that fair?" I couldn't believe it.

"My attorney explained to me that $1,000 a month was the minimum the court would expect for a divorce involving a stay-at-home mom of 20 years," he said. "I'm told to expect to pay this for at least three years unless she marries someone else before then."

Brilliance struck me. "I'd be happy to introduce Holly to my ex-husband. He's bi-polar...they'd get along great!"

Back to the giggles. These late-night conversations not only gave me a lot of insight into Alex's family situation, they also validated our intellectual compatibility. This was super important to me.

As the chuckles subsided, I learned how Holly was never content at any of the homes where the family lived. Alex explained how Holly's lack of contentment collided with his lack of enormous income, and we all know who wins in that crash. The family became routinely debt-poor, often including the massive amounts of spending by Holly at thrift stores for those amazing deals. *"Look Alex, I saved 40% on all this!"*

Alex and Holly owned three houses in under six years, capturing equity from the inflated housing market to buy down their debt with the sale. Each time, Alex said he hoped it was the last. They finally moved in with his parents the last time after Holly was certain the house was making her sick.

"That must have been hard for the kids, always changing schools and such," I said. I couldn't really relate; I lived in the same house for my entire childhood. My parents, despite their own issues, were definitely stable.

"Homeschooling had its benefits," he replied.

We chatted a bit more and said goodnight. Before drifting off to sleep, I wondered why I wasn't running away from this. Like hard and fast. Maybe it's my love for the underdog.

September 25, 2008

> **Nikki**: Paper Mate is getting a bit unruly. We've had to go to extreme measures to keep him contained and, well, under control. We need to see some progress on our demands or the torture will continue.

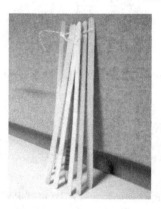

September 26, 2008

Nikki: We've been successful with our information extraction. Your little PM not only screams like a girl, he talks like one too, with a bit of motivation. Never mind the recent national discomfort with our methods. He's given up your last name, first name and now we're on to more personal information such as a birthdate...He's begging you to help him.

Alex: Water boarding? Really? OMG.

Nikki: LOL! Yeah, the cover for his face kept washing down the drain.

Alex: That deserves a call. Stand by to stand by.

I answered his call on the first ring. "Well, hello there…how's your day been?"

"Unreal. I gotta say, this ransom thing is pretty good. It's seriously been the high point of my day."

"Glad I could help," I replied. "So what's up? More crazy from the ex?"

He let out a notable sigh. "Yeah, that's sort of a norm around here. Today, I learned Martin may have to end up testifying against her in court. It sucks—a couple months ago, Holly invited herself into my house when I wasn't there. She claimed she was coming by to deliver something one of the kids had left at her apartment and took the opportunity to just waltz straight into the house. She started wandering around, saying what a nice place we had and how it needed a "woman's touch" to be just right. Martin and our oldest daughter, Katherine, both told her, "Uh…mom, pretty sure you shouldn't be inside here." She lingered a little longer, taking a good look around before she left. It sucked, mostly because our home was the one place the kids had found they didn't have to worry about Holly coming in and disrupting their space."

"Holy shit!" I said, trying not to stop the flow.

"When Holly left us last spring, she had been making all kinds of threats to scoop the kids up and take them with her to new ventures in North Carolina, or Denver, or North Dakota, or California…whatever the crazy plan was that day, she always included the kids. It's one of the main reasons I still worry for them. Before she went totally south, she took the kids on a couple of surprise trips to Leavenworth with little to no notice. So her threats to leave the state with them on a moment's notice aren't just wild ideas—they are plans that she very well may act upon. It's one of the reasons for the driving restrictions. Well, that plus the cars she keeps crashing."

"So did she go to jail for coming into your home? That's illegal, right? I mean with the restraining order?" I asked.

"You'd think so," Alex said. "It's like the department is afraid to do something to set her off. The restraining order clearly states she cannot enter our residence or grounds, but the most they would do is refer the case to the prosecutor. Thankfully, the prosecutor did file a charge on her finally, but

Martin is the primary witness since he's the oldest and saw the whole thing. He also wrote a statement to the officer who responded to the 911 call."

This was amazing to me. I couldn't fathom why Holly wasn't being held accountable on this and so many other things I was learning about. "She pleaded not guilty? It's clearly a violation, right? How does she think she's going to get away with this?"

"Holly doesn't seem to have the capability to take responsibility for anything," he said. "Everything is someone else's fault. She's great at pointing out the deficiencies of others, especially when they reflect her own shortcomings."

"I get the sense she deflects a lot," I said.

"Oh like crazy," said Alex. "I fell into the target zone of her blame-thrower for years and didn't even realize it. I was pretty certain I was a horrible husband, even though I worked my ass off and was constantly apologizing for something. When our counsellors started pointing out how I was 'damned if you do, damned if you don't,' things began to clarify for me. I still walked on eggshells most of the time just to appease her, and felt like I was taking the high road to minimize the impact of her wrath on the children. This meant I took the heat for lots of errors the kids made. Sad part is, I did the same thing to cover Holly's mistakes in public. Now that I've stopped doing that, Holly is starting to become known in public. Did I tell you about her getting tossed out of a biker bar?"

I couldn't wait. "Do tell!"

"According to the police report…"

"Wait—did she get arrested that time? This is better than daytime TV!"

"No, just trespassed," Alex said.

"Have you called Jerry Springer yet?" I said laughing. "I'm sorry, that was really insensitive of me. But seriously, have you called him?" I couldn't help giggling while apologizing, which didn't lend to my credibility. I made a quick attempt to gather myself. "Ok, really, I'm sorry, but at some point you gotta see the humor in this!"

Alex interrupted, laughing. "Oh trust me, if I didn't laugh about this stuff half of the time, I'd have eaten my gun years ago. Or I'd be just as nutty as she is. Ok, maybe not."

It took some time for both of us to calm down and stop giggling.

# # #

Wow. I never expected a woman to stick around after learning about Holly, let alone share a much needed laugh about the whole thing. She's pretty amazing, this Nikki. Still, I wondered if I should even be thinking about dating at this point. I barely had time to take care of the kids and the job.

Falling asleep that night after the phone call, I didn't need to soak myself in Sarah McLaughlin songs. A glass of Cabernet Sauvignon and lingering thoughts of Nikki did just fine.

September 27, 2008

> **Nikki**: We've not heard back from you regarding our demands. We've been generous in allowing your little Paper Mate to contact you. Do you miss him? Remember the fate of your beloved decapitated Sharpie? Yeah…that's what we thought. Get busy on complying with the demands or a similar fate will occur to PM. If you recall, the Sharpie suffered a painfully slow leakage and analysis of ink spatter patterns revealed nothing. Is this the destiny you wish for PM?

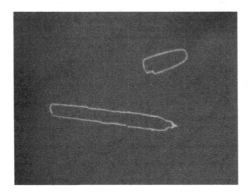

September 28, 2008

With school now well under way, Holly's behavior suddenly ramped back up.

I needed to advise the Guardian ad Litem with the hope he could provide some direction.

From: Alex
To: Ron Taylor, GAL
Subject: Friday incident

Ron, I need to let you know about an incident what occurred on Friday. I'd hoped the recent lack of bitter communication toward me was reflective of a trend toward stability for Holly. It was anything but that.

On Friday, our daughters Katherine and Evelyn went to spend the night at friends' homes who live in the same Bothell cul-de-sac. Katherine stayed at the Joyners, Evelyn at the Bauers. Both are good family friends.

At 5:45 pm, Holly texted me asking if she could take Evelyn on a date. I said no, she was having an overnight at the Bauers. Instead, Holly drove to the Bauers and told the parents she wanted to see Evelyn. Because the parents have been subjected to Holly's difficult behavior many times, they asked her to leave since they were headed out while their oldest son took care of the girls. Holly stormed next door and repeated the scene at Terri Joyner's house where Katherine and her friend were babysitting. After pounding on the door for 5 minutes, an 8-year old child answered, telling Holly that Katherine and her friend were hiding from her. Holly stormed into the cul-de-sac and yelled to anyone in earshot that she was not leaving until she got what she wanted: a music CD Holly had given Terri and now, suddenly, wanted back.

Holly eventually left after screaming how nobody can stop her from going anywhere she wants or from being with the children any time she wants. It was horribly disturbing to the girls. Terri Joyner received numerous threatening messages into the night.

Not knowing any of this was happening, Holly then texted me asking me to lift the driving restriction so she could take take Justin to a theater. I said I hoped in the future this would be fine; restrictions were primarily up to the GAL but her recent accident with the Prius gave me additional concern for now. Holly was very upset that I knew about the accident with the Prius and demanded to know how I found out. I didn't respond.

The accident was a rear-ender caused by Holly dropping her phone and slipping off the brake at an intersection. I had learned of it when I received a call from our insurance company asking me for details of a collision I didn't know about.

Holly then sent more messages blaming her past accidents on "critical kids who only love their dad," my "policing her again," and my "viewing her as a criminal and encouraging the kids to see her that way." Holly had stated that her driving record "proves" that she is a good driver. Yet the Prius accident plus others which have gone unreported, not to mention the very record itself, all speak to her ongoing elevated risk.

Ron, I mention this because it is another attempt by Holly to manufacture extra time with the kids, but this time by means of deceit, making up a story to cover her reason for being nearby. I'm concerned that she will combine these efforts: showing up unexpectedly and convincing the kids it's okay for her to drive them to some exciting destination. Coupled with her previous goals of taking them out of state, this could quickly become a dangerous situation.

If you need additional information, you are always welcome to talk to the children or others involved.

Alex

11:10 am

Nikki: Pen Master, I think the end may be near. I've been bitten, poked, almost drowned and sharpened to a fine point. They're threatening to remove my clip. I have to admit I kind of like the biting, but please send help pretty soon. Your Ever Faithful, Paper Mate Ultra Fine Point.

11:48 am

Alex: You there?

Terri: Yes. I got more texts from Holly today. She's nasty!

Alex: Ugh....Thank you for sending me the texts from yesterday; so ugly and untrue.

Terri: I will forward any more I get from her...and then I may block her.

Alex: Let me know. The GAL and my attorney both want to know if anyone gets a restraining or anti-harassment order...which would be the step that followed. It's very troubling the way she came over to your neighborhood.

Terri: Oh she texted me about that this morning...let me type them all up.

Alex: Thanks.

Terri: She is so mean. I may tell her that my text allowance is used up. She sent dozens this morning without me responding. Then she went back through my old texts and responded again!

Alex: She's obsessed. You don't need a reason to ask her to stop texting...if you ask and it continues, it can be considered cyberstalking. There I go again, thinking she is a criminal.

Terri: Bad, bad, bad cop! I feel violated by her. Abused. Emotionally molested. I should tell her.

Alex: She'd only respond by one-upping regardless of reality.

Terri: Grrrrrrrrrrr!

September 30, 2008

Nikki: The analysis of ink spatter patterns will reveal nothing. There won't be much for the forensics geeks to analyze. And don't think a pocket protector will prevent his slow painful leakage.

# # #

October 1, 2008

On Wednesday night, I flew back to Seattle from Burbank. On the way home, I called Alex and reminded him that his ransom payment was due. Alex came through by coming over for dinner and, let's just say, paying in full.

October 2, 2008

Nikki: Morning, Alex! I hope you slept well. I'm sending a pic of what PM's fate would have been had you not been so charming last night. Have a great day!

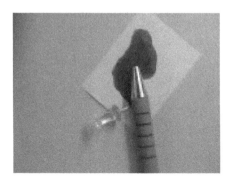

# # #

Have a great day. That hadn't been an easy option for a while. I had intended on staying a little on the cautious side revealing the layers of my life to Nikki, someone who lives her life so clear and straight-forward. Having a great day is something I had to chose intentionally despite the regular input to the contrary. I took her words to heart. *I'm going to have a great day. Period.*

It helped that last night was remarkably rewarding after paying her ransom. I had to go with an alternative to the cunning extortionist's demands since I didn't have a pen, so I covered Chris Rice's *Here Come Those Eyes*. I thought it appropriate, given Nikki's beautiful and unique blue-green eyes.

I fumbled a bit in the third verse when the dreaded L-word showed up:

> *If this is what they call love*
> *I can't believe I'm in it*
> *Thanking heaven every minute*
> *I'm the luckiest boy in this town.*

Pretty sure I added a few polychords in that phrase, might have even said something about not being sure of the words…okay, it was a classic dork moment. Still, her response was encouraging, and I managed to finish without making a total fool of myself.

So, with pen in pocket and a solid determination to have a great day, off I went. It started like most days, something like this:

- 5:00 am: Alarm. "Sleep is overrated," I think to myself. So is lying to yourself. Get up anyway.
- Shower, shave, suit & tie.
- Retrieve weapon from safe, press-check, secure in high-rise holster.
- Let the dog out.
- Unload remaining groceries from car.
- Go find Copper, the world's most distracted dog, in the dark; convince him to return with loud whispers
- Feed Copper.
- Start bowl of raisin bran.
- Move someone's laundry to start my load.
- Cut & stuff dinner into crock pot: meat, onions, celery, carrots, pepper, leftover wine.
- Make sandwiches for kids.
- Brush teeth.
- Finish soggy raisin bran (yes, in that order).
- Self talk about order of morning events.
- Try to ignore the set of texts and/or emails that came in overnight

from Holly.

- 5:45 am: Get Martin, Justin, Katherine, Kevin, and Evelyn out of bed.
- Give Martin bus money and charge of remaining morning tasks.
- Brush girls' hair.
- Take trash to curb.
- Remind the kids they have to go to mom's after school since it's Thursday.
- Hide frustration about indecipherable messages from Holly.
- Scrape windshield.
- Blow kiss to Evelyn, sweetly waving her 8-year old hand in the window as I drive away.
- 6:00 am: Wave back. Retain game face. Don't let yourself wish it were different. Pray and drive.

3. BENEFIT OF THE DOUBT

October 6, 2008

The drive to the FBI Resident Agency in Everett prepared me for the next 10 hours of daily non-stop pressure at the Joint Terrorism Task Force (JTTF). The daily grind at the JTTF involved digesting copious amounts of situational reports on loosely focused threat streams, managing resident and foreign human sources, integrating local information into the international scope of things, then prioritizing leads and ensuring the rest of the team was utilizing tools they hardly knew existed to do the job they hardly knew how to define.

Seven years after 9/11, the intelligence community was still evolving with every Tom, Dick, and Harry trying to make sense of three-letter agencies and figure out who oversaw what. FBI agents who had signed up to take down bank robbers and drug dealers found themselves thrust into terrorism or counter-espionage squads without a clue of how to function in a classified environment. The Bureau turned to any fort in the storm, including offers of help from local law enforcement agencies like my own. The Edmonds Police Department hired me in 2001 knowing my knack for intelligence work, so like all risky ideas, it made sense at the time.

In the midst of this chaos, I wound up taking lead on many of the major cases in our area of responsibility, everything north of Seattle to the Canadian border. Many of these cases involved targets who lived and operated in our footprint, but most of them were just associated to a bigger target somewhere else in the world. My case load was focused under one of two International Terrorism Operations Sections, which meant anything other than Hezbollah or Al Qaeda core leadership. I needed to be up to speed on a dozen other radical Islamic groups, most of whom spawned from the Muslim Brotherhood or some faction of the Taliban. And while the Patriot Act is widely touted as the most invasive piece of legislation ever invented, I can tell you first hand that it still takes way more than an act of Congress to listen to a suspected terrorist's phone calls in a timely manner. It's ridiculous.

Suffice it to say, I learned a lot during this time and it beat the hell out of writing speeding tickets to soccer moms. Besides, it's what every musician dreams of doing, right?

Mostly, my work was a welcome distraction from the stress of my home life, at least to the degree I could focus on it. The magnitude of my responsibilities didn't prevent Holly from inserting herself into an already convoluted day, making it even more...exciting. The running joke in the office was how easy counterterrorism was compared to living Alex's life on a Thursday.

Arriving at work, I entered the secure garage and proceeded through seven security barriers that would impress James Bond and Maxwell Smart, just to enter the nondescript FBI office housed in a former retirement home. The building was pink. Not making that up. For the next three hours, the adrenaline pump was at full tilt for the mad scramble. That is, until it all came to an abrupt halt when Holly tossed a few choice texts my way in a 10-minute period threatening to send the Edmonds Police to my house to retrieve property that didn't exist. *What?* Something told me that could cause some grief with my employer.

> **Holly:** I will be asking for a civil assist if you do not get my requested items to me by 6 pm today. Trusting you are "here to help."

> **Holly:** Do what you must. I have been asking since March. I have saved all your responses that state you would be doing it. No longer letting you be irresponsible. You are teaching our children to not follow thru with what you promise.

> **Holly:** I expect you to go back to emails and texts. Give me what you have stated you would. Rise up and be the man God created you to be. I believe in you, Alex. Love you always.

> **Holly:** I will be at your home at 5 pm to get ALL requested and personal items. If you can take off work to file wicked divorce papers, surely you can take time to bless me. I will have a civil standby.

I moved counterterrorism to the back burner where it didn't belong, then quickly pounded out a note to the GAL and my attorney. Given the complexities of our case (I thought she was an impossible psycho; she thought I was a dirty cop with who smuggled drugs in coffee shipments through Canada while using federal resources to spy on her idiot boyfriends), I was fortunate the court had appointed Ron Taylor as the GAL to oversee the needs and safety of the children. He just happened to have been voted "Father of the Year" by the local paper. What were the odds Holly would go bat-shit crazy on the Father of the Year? I should have known better.

I sorted through the last couple days' messages and copied some over to my note to give the GAL a full picture.

> **From: Alex**
> **To: Ron Taylor**
> **CC: Rachel Townsend**
> **Subject: Standby**
>
> Ron, the items below are for your information. Critical issue at hand: Holly is threatening again to have the police come to my house for a "civil standby" to get property she believes is there and is hers. I will be going through my boxes again today to see if there is anything that would make sense to send her way, but the things she wants are just not there, except for some Christmas photo-ornaments the kids used to use.
>
> Also: Holly sent an envelope home with the children after her visit with them. Kevin reluctantly delivered it to me; it was stuffed with material from what appears to be a seminar for wives of abusive police officer husbands and information on Parental Alienation Syndrome. She made many notes on the printed material about how I have been abusive to her. This was very disturbing to both Kevin and me—the warnings to Holly about disturbing the peace continue to go ignored. To that point, here's a sampling of her one-way communication activity from the weekend:
>
> Friday, October 3:
> - More than 30 instructional and unwanted text messages from Holly, including, "teach them to love their mom. It is the polar opposite of your own heart, so you will need the Spirit's strength.
> - In her ongoing quest for more time with the kids outside of the parenting plan, Holly made a doctor's appointment with the family physician consecutive to the time Justin and Kevin had an appointment with him. She came to the doctor's office, saw the boys in the office, then canceled her appointment and went to their football game.
> - During the football game, Holly sent repeated text requests

for me to have the boys find her in the stands to give her a hug.

- Holly offered the Suburban back to me for Homecoming dance on Saturday, then withdrew the offer after demanding to be present in the car if I was driving it.

Saturday, October 4: Text messages from Holly:

- "Cherish the woman who drew you into her whole being. You became like God. Your seed became life inside her. Martin, Justin, Katherine, Kevin, & Evelyn are the hand of God."
- "Want to know why I wanted to shoot for 10 children? I wanted you to have two handfuls of the jewels of God to love their daddy that does not know his mom."
- "You are intensely loved by a very profound woman."
- "Wanting to make this night very special for our boys. Hoping to do something together. Want them to know we care about their joy as a team."
- "Let's go to homecoming together. I want to share it with you. Since you are the driver, can we take them together? Shari's for pie after?"
- "No? Then you cannot take my car. No fudge either. Be nice or no benefits."
- "Divorce is the worst evil. I have no reason to be kind to you. It is my car, the car comes with the current owner. Martin can use it, you cannot anymore."
- "Still dreaming you are more of a Prince Charming than a Toad. You need Jesus to kiss you and change ur heart. Resemble your first love. He is the ONLY WAY."
- "If you want to use my car I have to be a passenger. WE are their parents. YOU are not the savior of our family. NO LONGER LETTING YOU WIN. SIDE BY SIDE OR NOT AT ALL."
- "I have not met Justin's date. We would not have let him go without meeting her. As his other parent, I would like to meet her before he holds her in his arms."
- "I deserve to be a part of this "first" for our sons."
- "A reasonable and wise way to approach this is...Your mom and I have always held to the premise that we will know your friends. Mom will go with us to meet your date."
- "Remember that when law enforcement officers are present

kiddos are prone to think person's request that is not granted is due to it being wrong. YOUR DISCOMFORT."

- "I am willing to walk home after boys are dropped off. YOUR Discomfort should be laid aside for the sake of the kiddos. Justin will only be uncomfortable if you are."

Sorting through it all, I changed plans after all this. Martin went along with her demands and drove his mom in the Suburban with his date to the homecoming dance.

I am being interviewed by Edmonds PD tomorrow for the internal investigation prompted by Holly's false allegations of domestic violence, drug running, and the like.

Alex

Pie? Are you kidding me? Okay, note sent, distraction over. I was glad it hadn't taken long for Ron Taylor to develop a sense of Holly's rapidly advancing mental instability. I've got to do something about her incessant texting to me. So frustrating! Now to nuke my cold coffee again and get focused. Phone buzzing…oh God what now?

Nikki: Hey! Whachya doin for lunch today?

Alex: Bored. Lonely. You?

Nikki: Let's fix it.

Alex: Ok…you like teriyaki?

Nikki: Love it. Noon?

Alex: Done. There's a place on 128th behind the McDonalds. See you there.

Meeting Nikki for lunch in 18 minutes would be a nice distraction from the drama Holly continues to drag into my already crazy day. Counterterrorism was a snap compared to keeping up with her rants. Despite my own horrible thoughts on how I might respond to her annoying badgering tirades (a Hellfire missile came to mind), I was determined to take the proverbial high road for the sake of the children.

#

I found the McDonalds parking lot Alex told me about and wondered, *isn't this a shady part of town?* The Home Depot just up the road had the largest theft-to-sales ratio of all Home Depot stores in the country last year. Not a great place. I found the suspicious looking teriyaki joint hidden in the strip mall behind Mickey-D's. *Hope he brings his gun.*

As we ordered at the counter, Alex reached for his wallet. "No, I asked you to lunch—I get to pay!" I knew that any guy going through a divorce with five kids probably didn't have lots of extra cash. This was later learned to be one of my more severe understatements.

As we sat down next to the window, I asked how his day was going. I knew he couldn't really talk about work since he'd have to find a good place for the body and all that. He instead mentioned he was distracted a little with his soon-to-be ex-wife.

"Is it amicable at all?" I asked.

"I wish. My ex is….Okay, so I know some guys are quick to say they have a 'crazy ex.' In my case, she's an actual bonafide certifiable crazy ex. The no-joking, seriously not well type."

"Ah. So, what does she do? Is she bi-polar or something?" I was grasping for something I could relate to. Everyone going through breakups deems their situation a little crazy. My ex-husband was actually diagnosed as bi-polar, so I guess I could say the same thing.

"Well," he said, "let's put it this way. Last weekend I learned she wanted to have ten children with me so I'd have two 'handfuls of the jewels of God' to love their daddy who does not know his mom. Then she offered to take me out for pie."

"Oh," I said. "Wait…what?" *Pie? Holy shit…what a crazy way to say that. Is that a code-word for sex?* I thought I'd take the easier path of the available conversations. "Okay, so you're adopted?" Alex followed suit and didn't seem to mind.

"Yes, from birth. My adopted parents had two daughters but also wanted a son. They were always open about the fact of my adoption, but the records were sealed so I have very little information about my birth parents.

We talked for a bit about Alex's hopes to learn more about his birth family, but this soon started to pale compared to the ten jewels thing which wouldn't go away from my brain. I circled back. "So, how are the kids taking all this? Does she have time with them?"

"It's not easy. The kids have dinner with her every Thursday and spend partial Saturdays with her every-other weekend. We used to have supervised visits, but the supervisors couldn't keep up with her weird demands so that didn't work out. It's difficult for the kids, but they are all trying to make the best of it."

"What kind of weird demands?" I asked. "Does she offend them or something?" I was trying to wrap my mind around it as I became more curious.

"It's more like Holly would get verbal with the supervisors when they would enforce a boundary. Then the kids would try to diffuse the situation, resulting in complete chaos with Holly yelling and the kids wanting out. The professional supervisors opted out due to her verbal abuse, which meant we were left with coordinating friends and family to be present during the visits since that was required by the court. Nobody could keep up with her, so eventually the court just ordered shorter time and no supervision. This made it better for the kids, but it's still a royal pain to manage, especially since she is not supposed to communicate with me except by text and email, and only for emergencies or coordinating visits."

I've been in the human resources business for a very long time. I've seen employees go through nearly every kind of life change one could imagine. But I just couldn't comprehend this—here's a woman who is, apparently, abusive to a child advocate during a visit. How is this even possible? She clearly could use a little counseling or something. Maybe some drugs.

"You know, I've been through a couple of divorces and never needed an attorney," I said. "But it sounds like you might need a good one. Is she on drugs? I mean, the prescribed kind." I still couldn't get past the whole pie thing.

"My boss recommended an attorney for me and she's wonderful," he said. "Rachel Townsend is super fair and keeps me on the high road. As for drugs, the best three weeks of the past three years was when Holly was on lithium. But then she though it was evil, so she stopped using it."

"So how are *you* doing in all of this? It sounds pretty stressful."

Alex remained a little vague in his answer, mentioning only that he sometimes has a hard time sorting through the messages Holly sends to him. He clearly wanted to take the high road amidst some pretty complicated circumstances, or at least it sounded that way. He seemed glad I had asked about him specifically, but he never really got to the thing I was looking for—how he was managing to handle it all.

After an hour and ten minutes, we both realized we'd better get back to work. It was easy to spend time with him. I couldn't wait to do it again. Truth be told, I wanted to know more about his soon-to-be-ex; maybe she's just misunderstood. Not sure I would understand her; sounded like she may have a bit of a religious bent that I'm not familiar with, too.

# # #

From: Ron Taylor, GAL
To: Alex
Subject: Re: Standby

Alex,

I need to run the content of your note by Holly for a response. If you don't want me to use your version, please provide one you are comfortable with me sharing with Holly; it is not necessary she be happy with what you say, but I don't want to set you up for any more trouble than necessary. Be sure not to allow any message or delivery processes to occur through the children.

Also, Holly is requesting individual time with the children and a return of her driving privilege. I will need to meet with the children and their counsellor, Dr. Jamil Maleek, before I can weigh in on this. A letter is going out today regarding the evaluation I have requested Holly do. Will copy to your attorney so she can set up the legal steps in the event Holly does not agree by tomorrow.

Later,

Ron

From: Rachel Townsend
To: Alex
Subject: Re: Standby

Hi Alex:

I don't see any reason why there should be any access to the house for a civil standby. You are fine to indicate there is no basis for access and that she should pursue her remedies through court.

I will want to know the status of the various claims Holly made against you as that information becomes available. I'm thinking I will be able to collect things and aim at filing something at the end of this week or beginning of next.

My sympathies to you and your children as you continue to experience this extremely difficult situation.

Rachel

From: Alex
To: Rachel Townsend
Subject: Re: Standby

Rachel, thank you for your kind note.

Status on the investigations against me from Holly's complaints:

1. Snohomish County Sheriff's Office, complaint made to 911 on March 1, 2008, alleging I was preventing Holly from removing children from home, engaging in emotional abuse and mental manipulation. Finding: NO ACTION by Patrol deputies.

2. Snohomish County Sheriff's office, complaint made in March 2008 (13-page handwritten statement) alleging domestic violence, abuse of police authority, etc. Finding by Snohomish County Detectives: UNFOUNDED. Prosecutorial review: DECLINED PROSECUTION.

3. Edmonds Police Department, complaint 08-127, abuse of authority by me and Sergeant Arancio. Finding: UNFOUNDED.

4. Edmonds Police Department, complaint involving domestic violence, abuse of authority, and various crimes. Status: PENDING INVESTIGATION. Should be resolved this week.

At the end of this current investigation, I will speak to our administrative assistant about releasing my personnel file to Ron Taylor and you, so you have original documents and not just my synopsis.

I can't thank you enough.

Alex

# # #

In the days that followed, Alex and I enjoyed late-night playful conversations with each other over the phone before falling asleep. Alex began to reveal more about the kids and their individual personalities. I learned they had been homeschooled off and on for a number of years and had only been in public school since the separation. They each had a strong protestant upbringing with a woman who never had an identity outside of religious motherhood. The children's future identities began to take shape for me in my mind and I soon realized what a massive challenge it would be for me to relate to them. If their mother was as screwed up as it appeared, these five kids would have major trouble coming in their teenage years. Was I even close to ready for this? *We're just dating*, I told myself.

Alex sometimes called me from his laundry room after his kids went to bed; he was clear that he wasn't going to let them know about me until much further down the road. This was actually a relief since I wasn't looking forward to presenting myself as some viable option for their replacement-mom just yet. Having not had children of my own, I felt a little ill-prepared.

Occasionally, Alex would slip out at night and come over for a little "adult time," as we called it. Alex cloaked these trips by stopping at the grocery store on his way home at around midnight or so and pick up cinnamon rolls or another box of cereal for the cupboard. He wound up with a LOT of cereal. Other nights I would come to his neighborhood and park down the street where the kids couldn't see us. Alex would tell the kids he was going for a walk, then meet me under the street lamp out of view just past the fence. It was like two kids sneaking out at night. We would walk the Edmonds waterfront, look at the boats in the marina, share our dreams and goals for the future, and invariably talk about some of the ongoing crazy developments with his ex. Since I didn't have to deal directly with the kids, I was more free to help Alex deal with Holly. This, over the course of time, became my personal mission. With a passion.

# # #

October 7, 2008

Alex: Hey. My cupboard is full. Wanna go for a walk tonight?

Nikki: In the rain? Wouldn't miss it.

Alex: Sweet. See you at the light post.

I felt weird meeting Nikki at the light post. How stupid; why can't I just be open about the whole thing? True, I was concerned the kids would be confused about me seeing someone when the divorce wasn't final, but the older ones had been bugging me about it already, egging me on, asking if I'd found a girlfriend yet. I remained playfully vague about the answer, avoiding the actual discussion. Nikki was certainly a different sort of woman compared to what they'd known; spiritual but not religious, straight forward with her intentions, could out-cuss a sailor before breakfast, and wasn't afraid of anything. Most refreshingly, she talked to me like an adult, about adult things; something I'd missed more than I ever realized.

I told the kids I was off for my evening walk and would be back in a bit. Nikki was under the light post at 8 pm sharp. The rain had lightened but left ample opportunities for Nikki to soak me with her puddle-jumping skills. Add that to the list.

We walked down Daley to 3rd Avenue, avoiding Bell Street where Holly had taken her latest residence. After we separated, Holly was legally restrained from coming to my workplace or residence, so in response she found an apartment across the street from the police station in the direct line between my house and Starbucks. She had the perfect vantage point for stalking me and for those "chance" or "accidental" run-ins where she could claim innocence.

Setting aside my internal frustration, I re-gripped Nikki's hand and continued to the waterfront. Somehow she managed to get both of my legs soaked. Nikki 2, Alex 0.

On the bluff above Puget Sound, we stopped to watch the well-lit Edmonds Ferry off-loading vehicles and passengers from the Olympic Peninsula. My phone buzzed with a text. I wanted to ignore it, but I knew it might be the kids. I pulled the phone out and saw the text was from Holly. I put it back into my pocket.

"Was that the kids?" asked Nikki.

"I wish. It's Holly again."

"What does she want?"

"I don't want to read it and ruin a nice walk," I said. Nikki was unmoved and somehow managed to splash me with yet another puddle. I didn't even see it coming.

"Gimme!" Nikki snatched the phone from my pocket and read out loud.

> **Holly**: "You did a gr8 job gathering my belongings yesterday, thank you. I would rather have you than anything else in the universe. I love you more than the most precious jewels. Do you think Obama is a terrorist? He is sure a gr8 debator. I am considering crossing my former line of always voting Republican. What do you think?"

"What the fuck! You're a Republican?"

I lost it. We laughed until it hurt. Nikki composed herself first.

"Hmm…says here she loves you more than the kids. Wow. And I gotta ask— is she serious about the Obama thing? Oh my God, she is messed up!"

Risky as it was, it seemed Nikki was starting to get it, giving me an overwhelming sense of relief. She saw directly into the mess of my existence and didn't run away. With my baggage, I kept wondering if the shoe was going to drop and she'd just disappear. Whatever her reason for staying the course, I was certainly glad. Her effect on my stress was truly beautiful.

Soaking wet, we made our way back to the lamp post. I scored a major puddle on the way back. And a long, long kiss.

# # #

October 8, 2008

To: Rachel Townsend, Ron Taylor
From: Alex Hill
Subject: Another Accident

I was informed today from Progressive Insurance that Holly had a collision on Tuesday, August 12, 2008 in a Toyota Yaris owned by Enterprise Rent-a-Car. Holly apparently promised to pay for damages, but failed to do so, prompting the claim made by Progressive yesterday. I don't know the amount, but this affects our insurance again with an "at-fault" accident on our policy. Holly has several of these, and I am concerned that our family will lose another auto insurance policy due to her accidents.

Tuesday, August 12 was one of the days Holly was with the children (4-8 pm).

Rachel, I can anticipate a need to have relief from insuring Holly for auto coverage. If we lose our policy based on this latest reported accident, am I able to then obtain a new policy without Holly as a listed driver? My cost now is over $1,000/month due to Holly's accidents.

Alex

To: Alex
From: Ron Taylor
Subject: Re: Another Accident

Alex,

I would like to determine whether or not the children were with Holly (in her care and/or in the car) when this accident happened.

I called Holly last night after speaking with Dr. Jamil Maleek to inquire if she had taken the police to your home or not. She cut me off, then texted me several more times, ultimately insisting I not phone her ever again as it is too upsetting for her.

Ron

To: Ron Taylor
From: Alex
Subject: Re: Another Accident

Ron, I don't know for sure if the kids were with Holly or not, but it seems that her great surprise at my learning of the Prius accident is suggestive that the kids were not there.

I'm sorry the communication with Holly is difficult and hope it improves. Good luck with that.

Alex

# # #

Decked out in Seahawks gear from their era of near-greatness, I headed out to pick up my sister for the second home game of the season. Season tickets in the club section came with perks: great seats, paid covered parking, bonus giveaways, and liquor. I had game day down to a science: leave home at 10:25, grab my grande drip in a venti cup, pick up my partner in crime, haul ass down Interstate 5 to the 4th Avenue exit, park on the 5th floor, east side, don my lanyard, grab my program at the door and walk directly to seats 5 and 6 in section 232 in time to watch the guys warm up. Clockwork.

Elle was ready when I arrived, complete with face paint and layers of blue and green. "Nice bling."

"Thanks," she replied. "Check out my new bracelet!"

I had seen that thing when she walked out of the house. I was fairly certain the crew on the International Space Station caught a glimpse of it too. "Wow...does it hurt?" The thing was somehow pointy and round at the same time.

"Na. You get used to it. So tell me tell me tell me! How are things with Alex?"

"You won't believe this. Elle, I think his ex is actually a horrible person. She's put that family through the ringer. And oh my god—the text messages from her are fucking crazy! I love you. I hate you. You're the best dad ever. You abuse my children. You abandoned me. It goes on and on and on, and I'm only starting to see a fraction of what comes at him all the time!"

"Ruh-roh! Sounds risky," she said.

"Yeah, no worries, I've seen pictures of her. I can take her." Elle gave me that look that only annoyed older sisters can give. I actually enjoyed making her look like that with some regularity. "I highly doubt she's ever encountered the likes of someone like me."

Elle laughed. She knows my escapades and my propensity to defend and protect the underdog. Probably why I'm a Seahawks fan.

Elle was the less precarious of the two of us, always doing what traditional society expected of her. Being the younger sister, I relished getting her into trouble any time I could. One of our more memorable moments happened a year earlier when Elle's boss had moved into a new home with his soon-to-be bride in an upscale Bellevue neighborhood. The new bride was unaware that the boss had closed on their new home, so Elle thought it would be sweet to help him out by decorating the interior with rose pedals, bubble bath, champagne and candles for their arrival. The boss gave Elle a brand-new key he cut at Home Depot that morning. "It fits the front door, but it may be a little sticky since it's new. I didn't get a chance to try it out," he told her. Elle wrote down the address and called me for assistance with her super-secret mission. Of course, I agreed.

Her boss was expected to arrive at the new home with his bride at 8:30 pm, giving us only a one-hour window to get in and get out. *No problem*. When we arrived, naturally the key didn't work. "I got this," I offered, "I'm good at glass sliders. There's got to be one around here somewhere." I may have heard Elle expressing some sort of discomfort as I snuck around the back of the house and found the sliding glass door off the kitchen. She reluctantly followed. I wasn't fibbing about being good at these: I had the door off the rails in under a minute. It was a stunningly beautiful home in a posh neighborhood, complete with high-end decor and modern technology. Despite the boxes everywhere, I was amazed at how the boss had already furnished the place having just closed on it. Elle was on the phone with her boss. "What do you mean there's no flag pole in the back yard? I'm standing under it right now," she told him. Only then did it dawn on us that the door key probably worked just fine. At the right house. Which was…elsewhere. I gently propped the glass door up against the side of the house, then we ran back to the car like a couple of teenagers pranking their friends before homecoming, rose petals and brut in hand. "GO GO GO GO GO," I whispered loudly. We flew out of the neighborhood before the alarm went off.

I've often wondered if there's a partial latent fingerprint or two somewhere in the archives of the Bellevue Police Department which closely resembles mine.

"I can't believe you're dating a cop," Elle said as we pulled into the stadium garage. "Especially one with a psycho ex-wife and kids."

"Yeah," I said. It was outside my normal risk zone. "So get this: imagine being a police officer-slash-FBI agent and having your spouse openly accuse you of abuse, drug running, abuse of power…imagine! She really did that! He is enduring investigation after investigation by agency after agency. And you know how it is, Elle, if you look long enough, you might just find something…but every time these things come back as unfounded. She's just a loon."

"You still need to be careful, especially since you have the "get behind me honey" mentality and go into protection mode for the underdog," Elle said thoughtfully. "If you make any kind of false step in her eyes, you could become the target."

Yeah-yeah, whatever, I thought.

"Wait," she squinted, "How many kids does he have?"

"Five."

"What! Are you *crazy*?!"

It was worth considering. Maybe later.

Watching the team warm up even for five minutes normally provided the necessary clues to determine what kind of game it would be, which was important since I like to know what to expect. Today didn't look very promising, especially given Aaron Rogers and company were looking mighty fine.

"Hey Elle, check out Kerney. He's not wearing a cup." Elle pretended not to care. But she did look.

"So about that ransom…did he pay up? What happened to that poor pen? Does Alex need to report you to Interpol for violations of the Geneva

Convention?"

"Oh, he paid all right!" I let her mind drift. "But I ran over the pen in my driveway after I got it back."

"Oh, the horror!"

Second loss this year. Dammit. Gonna be a long season.

# # #

October 12, 2008

7:46 pm

> **Holly**: Tell Justin congrats he's amazing. Please let your heart be open and willing to advocate for better communication with kiddos. Can I buy phones for Evelyn and Kevin?

> **Alex**: That's up to you. I'm not in favor of phones for Kevin or Evelyn at their age. They can use the house phone or the sibling's cells to call any time.

> **Holly**: One of the attorneys that is co-counsel for me advised it due to the lack of support you are giving to have them call. It is a normal way to settle your deficit.

> **Holly**: You must not be sitting down each day and making sure they make contact. One of my two attorneys will require it from a judge if you are not willing by my kind request.

7:58 pm

> **Holly**: So is there a good reason you did not have the children call today?

8:33 pm

> **Holly**: So is there a good reason you did not have the children call today?

> **Alex**: Please, enough. I told the older boys to call earlier; they will still do it. I just finished reading to Evelyn; she's asleep this time, so will call in the am.

Holly: No, NOT ENOUGH, a wife and a mother should never be considered a bother. She is created by the Lord as the perfect partner. Only sin and hatred keep husbands from honoring the treasure God gave him. If you become consistent it will be easy for the kiddos.

Holly: I was told by three professionals to not take a full psych exam unless you are also required to take one. In the spirit of justice, I demand equality.

Holly: Btw. I forward all texts with concerns for kiddos to Ron Taylor. It is best for him to understand your attitudes and actions.

October 13, 2008

To: Holly
From: Ron Taylor, GAL
CC: Alex
Subject: mother/child time

Holly, Alex,

Over the past few weeks Holly has suggested several times that Evelyn wants and needs more time with her mother and that the children are not calling her. She also has requested the right to resume driving. This letter will briefly respond to these requests.

Driving –
There is some indication that Holly has been involved in another fender bender. I would appreciate a response from you about this, Holly, and the insurance documentation from you, Alex. The children are unanimous that they would be uncomfortable if their mother resumed driving them. They explain that their mother has difficulty paying attention to her driving when they are with her in the car. I am pleased, however, with Martin's reassurances that he occasionally does drive the family to an activity and that he is not pressured by his mother to do this—he has the ability to offer to drive and can decline when he needs to. I am not supportive of Holly resuming her driving privileges with the children at this point.

Evelyn's time –
Evelyn describes enjoying her time with her mother and talked of a

willingness to do an overnight with Holly on one of the weekends each month. However, as the discussion progressed, she allowed that she would be doing this to please her mother and that she is doing fine with daytime only residential time herself. One of the issues I seek to understand better about Holly—perhaps through the psychological evaluation process—is how much she might be depending on the children to meet her own emotional needs vs. how well she meets theirs. At this juncture I am not supportive of providing for overnights for any of the children, including Evelyn.

Residential time in general –
The residential schedule that is currently in place is aimed almost totally at providing the children enough time with their mother to sustain their bond with her pending a final determination of how their time will be apportioned between two separate households. This is why the residential schedule is important. In the meantime, all of the children have busy schedules and have added responsibilities at home and at school. The family is no longer intact with a stay-at-home mother—rather there are two households with single parents in each. I sympathize with how difficult it is for especially the older boys to meet the residential schedule with school, sports and jobs pressing them. I have told all the children they need to comply with the residential schedule, but have given Martin and Justin the option of rescheduling time with Holly if their responsibilities call for it, encouraging them to make up missed time.

The children also describe a dearth of time with their father, stating that he has to work a lot and is generally not very available to them. They need some regular focused father/child time. It also might be good to do a family outing (dad and kids) to remind them you, Alex, enjoy them and can prioritize time for them.

Telephone contact –
The children describe often attempting to call their mother and getting no answer. I have encouraged them to keep trying and often. I am opposed, however, to mandating phone contact. I feel there is much to learn for all of us by watching the choices that these youngsters make. Rather than force contact, it would be much healthier to see what Holly can do to instill a desire in her children to be in regular contact with her.

I also do not support the idea of providing personal cell phones to the younger two children.

Psychological evaluation –

At this juncture, I am asking Rachel Townsend to set a hearing to request a court order that Holly receive a full psychological evaluation with Ed Chow. I have read Holly's text regarding no evaluation if Alex does not undergo one also. I see no basis for requiring an evaluation of Alex and am not going to press for this.

Attorneys –

By way of clarification: Alex has an attorney—Rachel Townsend—who has entered a Notice of Appearance and has been in direct communications with me. Holly has referred to several attorneys (though not by name) and continues to do so. Since the outset of this case when her first attorney withdrew in the first month, I have had one phone call from one attorney—no others; I have seen no Notice of Appearance from any attorney to represent Holly. I would very much appreciate it if Holly were able to engage an attorney, but want to be clear that without a Notice of Appearance and without some direct contact from an attorney I am operating on the basis that Holly is representing herself.

Regards,

Ron Taylor

# # #

October 17, 2008

It was Friday night, which meant Alex and I could go out for a date and not worry about getting up early. We settled on a walk around Green Lake in Seattle, a popular and sometimes overused location which still held its own pleasantness. Alex told the kids he was going for a walk at Green Lake tonight and wouldn't be home until later on. Evelyn stayed the night with her friend Chloe while the other siblings were home for the night watching movies together. Since separating from Holly, Alex had allowed the kids to see some movies beyond *The Princess Bride* and *Veggie Tales*. A 16-year-old son and his brothers watching *Batman*? Risky.

We met at my house and took my convertible to the lake. It was the closest thing to my own version of a mid-life crisis which I purchased brand new a year ago. I had the cash on hand at the time, which satisfied my own rule of never financing anything without a bathroom. Such a fun little car!

October evenings are simply stunning in Seattle when the leaves start finding their final colors. Green Lake is among Seattle's more popular walks despite the fact you can't actually use the lake itself. That would give us something to talk about, but I was hoping Alex would peel the onion a little more on his situation. I had started to get it about Holly, or at least I thought I did. She was a bit nuttier than most ex's I hear about, but maybe with the right balance of meds and therapy, along with some realization that we don't all get what we want, perhaps she could be reasonable again.

Alex took my right hand as we began our walk.

"So do the kids know where you are?" I asked.

He grinned. "Yep. I decided to tell them the truth."

"What? You actually told them about me?"

He laughed, "God, no! But they do know where I'm walking tonight. Don't worry, Nikki. All in good time."

Despite the technical fact of his marriage still existing on paper, Alex's separation and pending divorce was more certain than typical. Before we began dating, Alex sought and obtained official recognition of the end of his marriage from his church, something called an ecclesiastical divorce. Again, this was all new to me, but I understood there was no going back for him.

As we curved around the south end of the lake, I began to probe a little deeper. Alex was more open than I had expected as he talked about some of the major benchmark events which led to the breakdown of his marriage and the needed rescue of the children from their mother.

I learned how Holly didn't display any obvious signs of mental illness for the first several years into the marriage. However, some of the couples who befriended Alex and Holly became uncomfortable with the relationship as Holly would distance herself from the friends, then complain how people never sought her out. Alex encouraged functions at their home, but Holly was quick to cancel them.

I learned how Holly began to believe the entire family suffered from food allergies when their fourth child, Kevin, was born. Holly insisted on allergy testing with a naturopathic doctor who, naturally, found all sorts of minor intolerances among the kids. Since Alex was sensitive to wheat as an infant, Holly concluded the whole family was allergic to it, which resulted in the institution of a gluten free diet before it was en vogue. It didn't stop there: within two years, Holly had required all soy, gluten, corn, dairy, peanuts, strawberries, and non-cane sugar be removed from the family diet. Alex made gluten-free breads from rice and xanthan flower and helped cook chicken and rice almost every day. Cake and ice cream became code words for something that tasted nothing like cake or ice cream. The children would break down occasionally, angry that they couldn't eat with their friends anymore at birthday parties. This lasted over a year until Holly announced that rice had become toxic to her and probably to the children, too. At that point, Alex put his foot down and said they would no longer chase the food allergy ghost and would start eating normally again. Holly complained about being rejected and placed the blame of future illness at Alex's feet. Not surprisingly, nobody ended up dead or even needing an epinephrine injection.

I learned how as far back as 1998, Holly had required Alex to attend marriage counseling with a variety of counsellors from church or faith-based organizations. The reason? Holly believed Alex wasn't providing enough for his family, he didn't put Holly's interests above his own, and he didn't handle the money right. However, whenever the counsellor would begin to pin Holly down to her part in the problems, it suddenly was time for a new counsellor.

I learned Holly's first suicide attempt was in 2005 after three days of sleeplessness and three months of fighting the recommended anti-anxiety drugs. She had taken a large kitchen knife and held it to her stomach in the middle of the night, standing next to Alex while he slept. At least that's how she explained it later. Alex woke up and saw Holly mumbling to herself with both hands holding the knife ready to plunge. He scrambled out of bed and disarmed Holly, who claimed she believed Alex wanted her to die anyway, so she might as well take care of his problem. Alex remained awake the remainder of the night to monitor Holly before taking her to the doctor the next morning, where they found additional cut marks on her wrists. Holly spent the next ten days in the psych ward.

I learned Holly drove her car off the road into a deep ravine in 2006, where she remained trapped until a passerby noticed the car tracks indicating a problem. She was rescued from the car and spent the rest of the weekend in a retreat facility a family friend had arranged for her on Camano Island.

I learned how Alex had become a single father caring for someone who was either mentally disabled or who had chosen to sabotage her marriage by means of manipulation, deception, and abandonment. Holly completely isolated herself in her bedroom, demanding the children come visit her in her bed but never making effort to clean herself, engage with the family, or even come out to wish her youngest daughter a happy birthday. Family members and friends from their church made attempts to intervene with Holly, offering everything from personal care help to housekeeping to schooling the children. Two women who knew Holly for more than fifteen years came to the house one day and began to actually dump her out of bed, literally by lifting the mattress. Holly got up, threatened the women she'd call police if they didn't leave, then hid elsewhere in the house until they left. Then she went back to bed.

I learned how the children were embarrassed, hurt, sad, angry, disappointed, and often believed they were the reason Holly had abandoned them, despite all sorts of encouragement to the contrary.

And finally, I learned how in 2007, near the end of the nine straight months in bed, Holly ran out of the bedroom upon overhearing Katherine crying about mom being in bed all the time. Holly yelled at Alex, telling him if he knew how to be a good husband she might feel welcome in her own home. Katherine objected, then all hell broke loose with the kids defending each other from their mom's sudden rage. Alex got between Holly and one of the kids, which Holly used to make it look like she had been shoved into her room. She yelled something about ending it all while Alex heard her stomp to the side of the bedroom where his dresser was located. Alex ran into the room to see Holly removing his unloaded handgun from the dresser. As he closed the distance between them, Holly spun around with the gun pointed toward Alex's direction. Alex's defensive tactics training kicked in, which he used to quickly disarm Holly and put her down on the bed without harm. He held Holly there as she yelled, bit, squirmed, pinched, and made every effort to get away while telling him to shoot her. Alex held her there on the bed until help arrived. Alex later reflected on this moment as the day he knew the risks outweighed the benefits of staying at home, but even then it took several more months until he believed he had done all he could to save his marriage.

During the walk, I heard Alex's phone buzz again. It seemed he was trying to ignore it.

"Is it her?"

He reluctantly looked at his phone. "Yep."

"Let me respond!" I figured it may be time for someone to tell her off, and that was something I was pretty qualified at doing. Alex wasn't quite ready for it.

> **Holly**: You have become an amazing terrorist to my heart. This woman will continue to hope in God even though you persecute me. If you slay me yet I will live in Jesus, my light and my salvation.

"I gotta ask," I started. "What are the actual chances of you getting back together with her?"

"Between zero and none," he replied.

That was all I needed to hear.

# # #

October 20, 2008

Ding. At 4:01 am, I reached over to comprehend the noise and decide if it's an emergency callout to work early or something else. Prying my eyes open, I see the notification. Texts from Holly. Back to sleep for another 45 minutes of bliss.

Ding. 4:12 am. Not sure I really heard this one. Must be part of a dream.

Waking to my alarm at 4:50 am, I reached to my phone to turn it off. Oh, surprise: Holly apparently received the renewed orders over the weekend and read them overnight, all after I was manipulated into taking Evelyn to her for extra time Sunday, only to be rewarded with texts about how I need to be a better father, how I need to pay bills and give her another dresser.

Well good morning to you too, Holly. Should I read your texts before hitting the shower, or after when I'm preoccupied with the day? Since I was already holding the damn thing, I opened the messages.

4:01 am

> **Holly**: What are you trying to prove from a psych evaluation? I refuse to undergo one unless you agree to one also. I believe in equality rather than male dominion. They could simply release the results from your hiring process in Edmonds. That way you can be

frugal.

4:12 am

> **Holly**: You are a liar. I spoke to the superior to the detectives that did the investigation at county level. What he said is that he believed everything I wrote but that it did not fall within the statute of limitation. The only incident that did was when you hurt me by grabbing the FBI phone from me when I took it from you. The internal affairs investigation is not complete and Assistant Chief Rapp gave no indication it would be done this week. I can fwd the communications with an employee at Seattle Midwifery Institute about being a possible surrogate. I was not fired from The Y.M.C.A. It was a probationary period that ended because my residential time with the children conflicted with the work schedule as well as a woman mistreated my friend. I did not wreck the minivan. Another woman hit me while talking on the phone.

She had gone from regular crazy to the advanced type. I'd better jump in the shower.

4:51 am:

> **Holly**: You and Bob Jackson did prevent me from taking the children with me be intimidating them and me. And Billy Evanston jumped on the male dominion band wagon with the two of you. You have not provided funds for a legal defense for your mate of 20 years. You also have a signed document stating that you would pay for the transmission repairs.

4:54 am:

> **Holly**: I never entered your home over the past four months. I have been no closer to your front door than you have been to mine. Remember you put a check on my car and also under my front door mat, as well as a mixer on a table one foot from my front door. You approached me on the 5th Ave. corner when I asked you to leave the Suburban title documents and my check at Petosa's Grocery. You drove up and handed them to me. You broke your restraining orders more often than I did. I will not agree to withdraw mine. They will remain in effect as long as I am able to keep them there. You must discontinue to approach me in public until after there is a settlement in court. Attend to our children not your selfish ambitions. I know you are losing your position with the FBI in January.

What the hell? Can I just dry off? Doesn't estranged have some meaning?

5:02 am

> **Holly**: You are only winning your selfish motives just like your father did. He powered your mom down by hating what was beautiful about her. I will fight your abuse of power by prayer and advocacy that only Jesus knows best how to do. I will not trust any alcoholic and abusive men like your mom has.

5:05 am

> **Holly**: The church has always been a family to me with the exception of the one you are attending at present. I will continue to run to loving people who love my Jesus and are born again and walk in newness of life. I did not take this to the courts. You chose to step outside your promised vows.

I wonder what it will be like after the actual divorce...

5:07 am

> **Holly**: Remember what your commander in Moscow told you...no one on earth can truly vindicate or provide true justice. Only the Lord who tests the hearts of men can do this.

I caught Justin in the hallway headed for his shower. "Hey Dad, Mom starts a new job on Tuesday at a new diner opening in downtown Edmonds."

Just nod and smile. "Oh," I replied plainly. *That's gonna go well.*

October 31, 2008

Halloween was that weird holiday that put many American Christians in a tailspin. The thinking went something like this: If I love God, I cannot love evil. Halloween celebrates ghosts, scary imaginary creatures, and gory evilness. Churches responded to the angst by offering alternative cute dress up opportunities with face painting and a micro-carnival. The more orthodox churches insisted on having a superior celebration on All Saint's Day (November 1st), including the customary face paint and homemade costumes of Martin Luther, Jean Calvin, or John Knox, complete with skits. October 31st was to be avoided lest you be seen as uninformed, unwise, or worse: under the influence of the modern world. Insert maniacal laugh here.

When Holly began to allow the children a fragment of identification with their peers, she would allow them to go trick-or-treating in the immediate neighborhood, and only with us doing the escort. She wouldn't risk sending them with "those other parents who let their kids dress up as ghouls or scary things." This meant creating costumes since we had no extra money to spend. On our first such outing, Martin was four years old. He was dressed up in a large plastic bag filled with smaller balloons of various color. Yes, he was a walking bag of jelly beans. The major clue was the large black writing on the bag: "JELLY BEANS." Justin lucked out and went as a light bulb…his plastic bag was white. The clue he was a light bulb was…yeah, the marker. Katherine was the baby in a stroller who needed no help as the "baby in a stroller."

It took the kids a couple years to get the hang of taking candy from strangers. As Holly became more withdrawn from the family, the kids got permission from me to do Halloween with the Bauers or Joyners—those safe families from church who had made their way past the weirdness of the holiday to enjoy it for what it was meant to be: a whole lot of fun! In the modern world! With candy! Holly saw that happening around her and tried to embrace it, but she was internally conflicted. Now that the kids were between eight and sixteen years old and in that so-called ungodly, nasty, secular public-school system, I wondered how this would flesh out.

1:55 pm

> **Holly**: I'd like to take the kids trick or treating tonight. I have costumes for them to wear. I'll meet them at Evelyn's school carnival, you can pick them up there.

She better not bring a marker.

When I met the kids at the school, Evelyn was already embarrassed about her costume: ladybug wings with no actual costume to define them. I encouraged her and quickly rounded up some additional pieces to round it out. Kevin was a cowboy, which meant he wore jeans and a t-shirt and talked southern drawl slang with a straw hanging from his mouth to define his persona. Katherine was a fortune teller, giving her that one chance to cake on the makeup. Martin was a pirate because he had a bandana and was making the most of it. Justin was the smart one again and created his own costume: he dressed up as a cardboard box. No marker needed.

4. JUST THE FACTS

November 3, 2008

At 9:00 am I left the FBI office in Everett and headed to the courthouse for the next scheduled hearing. The GAL was reporting his findings and conclusions to the court regarding the ongoing care of the children and a requirement for Holly to obtain a full psychological evaluation from a court appointed psychologist, Dr. Ed Chow. By 9:35 am, it was clear Holly was not going to make it to the 9:00 hearing. Ron Taylor's concerns and recommendations were accepted by the court with no objection from me, requiring Holly undergo an evaluation to help identify her underlying disorder. Rachel Townsend sent the documents to Holly via email, prompting her response a short time later.

> **From: Holly**
> **To: Alex, Rachel, Ron**
>
> To all,
> I do not understand any of this. I did not understand that I could have responded to all past motions within 14 days. Each time we appeared in court Rachel Townsend had other obligations and we were never up first. I texted Alex this morning to make sure he knew I would be there. I was very frightened and have been counseled that I should not appear alone. I waited to find out if someone could come with me.
>
> I really do think this is all very unjust and unfair. I have been in contact with 20+ attorneys. It has been such a strong offense that no one wishes to take the case. I am not in a position to afford an attorney. I do not understand how Alex is affording all that he gains in his offense. I know it was wrong for Ron to tell Alex who my counselor referred me to for the evaluation. It is a power play that has been very uncomfortable for many years and many reasons.
>
> I do not believe Alex when he says Rachel Townsend is being fair.

Most husbands do not leave their wives homeless and defenseless and destroy her dignity and alienate them from their children. I am told that it has been very calculated and manipulative. I do not know how to defend myself in like kind to Alex's strengths gained from the career he has. He is a fabulous report writer. Nothing that I have said is a lie. Timing and statutes of limitation were the reason charges did not go forward.

I am praying the Lord will uphold me through the onslaught of his persecution. I am hoping in things unseen to be advocating for my cause. I am afraid in a situation I am untrained to proceed in a beneficial way. It has been a full-time job trying to manage this storm. I trust the Lord will send help soon.

I do not understand about the auto insurance. When does it end and how will I be able to work without a car? I do not understand why unpaid bills were not paid with $1,500.00 it will cost for evaluation. This is all very confusing and discouraging.

I did call Dr. Chow's office as demanded today. That is all that was clear to me. Could any of you help me understand the rest of the documents since you have not let me get help from Women's agencies and I do not have legal defense?

Please be kind.
Sincerely,

Holly

Four days later, Ron Taylor handled the response:

From: Ron Taylor
To: Holly Hill, Rachel Townsend
Cc: Alex

Holly,
I finally have a few minutes to get a brief response back to you about this e-mail. I am willing to provide some clarification of how/why things happen at this point because you do not have an attorney and if you can hear what I say, you might have less frustration than you have now.

Timing of hearings --
I understand your explanation of why you were not at the hearing at 9 am when it was set. What you need to understand is that at least I had mixed messages from you about whether or not you would be there and did not expect you to be there. Further, though it is often possible to "foot" a case to the end of the morning, this is not always a certainty, would not be asked for if there was doubt about whether or not you would be there and is ultimately up to the commissioner. Waiting for a "footed" hearing is also expensive as an attorney and a GAL were already there and would have waited up to another two hours for the actual hearing to take place. All in all, I have found it best to just be there at 9 am—the time the hearing is scheduled.

Attorney availability for you --
I truly wish you were represented by an attorney. Your lack of funds probably has to do with why an attorney has not taken your case, but I am helpless to affect this issue.

Mention of possible evaluator --
I did not and do not feel any obligation to keep possible providers confidential. The best way to proceed with data gathering is to openly identify and negotiate who will do evaluations—with awareness and input from all sides. This is not wrong.

Alex's actions --
It is my observation that Alex has and continues to take great care in how he deals with you. Your descriptions of being homeless, defenseless, w/o dignity and alienated from your children is more a product of your own choices than any "calculated or manipulative" actions on the part of others. Please try to look at this clearly. Alex probably does have skills that help him communicate, but it is not evident that he is using them in a manipulative manner. It may be the case that you have not lied about anything—but I am certain that you have said several things from your own perspective that are not very well reflected in what other people see and describe around you. I believe there is a possibility you may have a mental/emotional problem that is behind this. This is a big reason why I am so insistent you get a current evaluation.

Charges --
I assume you are referring to the internal investigation issues you instigated re: Alex. I have not yet received the final outcomes of this investigation so cannot respond to your comments about "timing

and statutes of limitation."

Auto insurance --
From what I understand, your driving habits have led to accidents and claims on the family insurance policy. If it were up to me, you would stop driving until we see what is behind your current state of being and what can be done about it. I am not surprised that Alex might be taking himself out of the liability loop re: your driving. Whatever is going on with you may not be something you invited to happen or have much control over, but it is clearly affecting many things in your life and you are going to have to get to the place where you assume responsibility for dealing with it nonetheless.

Women's agencies --
I am not preventing you from seeking help from "women's agencies." What I have done is point out to you that I respect these agencies, but that what you have described of their involvement with you (most likely based on your story as opposed to a full picture), they have given you advice that has harmed your standing in this case and with your family—and you have followed it and suffered for it. Have you considered the possibility that your struggles might be the result of abuse by someone other than Alex and from a different era of your life? Or that your focus might find more affirmation if it were towards your mental health status vs emotional victimization at the hand of your husband? This is a question yet to be sorted out— but your personal stance does not reflect a concern with both possibilities. I am pushing this "sorting out" process, not just because you and Alex deserve some peace in your lives, but mostly because your children are wonderful and really do deserve that peace.

I respect your faith and trust and expect healthier outcomes are possible for you and your family because of it. Thank you for contacting Dr. Chow.

Ron Taylor
GAL

November 8, 2008

Holly: Am I still covered on your car insurance?

Alex: Yes. I'll let you know when it will stop; I may just sign the

Suburban over to you.

Holly: There is a problem that does not permit me to continue driving it without further damaging engine. It is your truck. I will send the bill to you. Due to sexual assault I had to take Suburban to Biddle Chev. in Bothell. I trust you care about me getting a job and home. Please advise.

Alex: You cannot obligate me to repairs like this. You took it there, you pay for it. I want you to have job/home, but that is up to you.

Holly: Actually I am still your wife of 19 years. You are responsible for more than you are aware of. I will have the bill sent to you.

Oh. My. God. I pay her $1,000 a month, I have full responsibility and care of our five children, I have no money of my own to use, and I'm borrowing my parent's Buick....and now she expects me to pay for repairs to her car? Hell, no. In seconds, I located the phone number for Biddle Chevrolet.

"It's a great day at Biddle Chevrolet! How can I direct your call?"

I was not in the mood, but that didn't seem to matter. "Can I talk to your manager of crazy people asking for the accomplishment of the impossible?"

"New or used?"

"Used and abused."

"Transferring you to the used service department!" This guy was way, way too happy. Apparently he wasn't alone.

"Hey there, it's a great day at Biddle Chevrolet, this is Bill in service!"

"Uh, hi, Bill...this is Alex Hill calling about a Suburban my ex..."

"Oh yeah, the lady with the five kids and the abusive husb.... oh wait, uh..."

Bill wasn't exactly ready to be in the middle. I explained quickly how I was not in a position to pay for repairs for the vehicle and could not authorize the work if it was going to be up to me. I was clear that Holly was welcome to make arrangements to pay for the vehicle to be repaired as she thought necessary, but I could not be put in a position to be forced to pay for repairs.

Bill was glad for the call, said Holly had already gotten a rental car from Enterprise through the dealership, and promised someone other than her was going to pay for the repairs, but Holly did not name who it was. Bill's voice became more realistic as he opted to stop work before they started, saying he would take the matter up with Holly. I thanked Bill for his willingness to hear me out.

"Oh, believe me, we see a lot of crazy around here," he said. "No trouble at all, glad to help. Good luck with all that!"

It only took twenty minutes for the storm to resume with a mad series of texts.

> **Holly**: A friend is paying. Just another example of your harshness. Many witnesses this time. I paid for the repairs for you but you will not do the same for me. Praying for your soul. Love you more than anyone could love a sinner. Gr8 idea to sign Suburban over to me. Why don't you go take care of that at the dealership in Bothell that you just denied me help? Then I can trade it for something I can manage better.

> **Holly**: I do not need you anymore Alex. I wanted to give you an opportunity to show me the honor and kindness I deserve.

> **Holly**: My new attorney, Raymond Snyder, will be ordering you to free up the retirement funds to pay housing costs to get me into an equitable situation. It has not been fair for you to treat me the way you have. This all will be very expensive and hurtful to the kiddos. Remember that it was your choice to cause so much pain. I will pay for rental car and diagnosis. Suburban needs $700.00 of work. I would like it signed over to me while it is in a neutral spot. I let Bill in Service know that you will go there to get title from vehicle. Please make it happen so I can move forward.

I doubted Raymond Snyder even existed. After I delivered the title to the shop releasing interest in the vehicle, Holly traded it in for a used Hyundai. Little did I know: that car would soon become her primary residence.

# # #

November 10, 2008

Sally Wilson, my willing counterpart in Supply Chain Management at Rove Aerospace, listened with interest as I unfolded some of the things Alex had shared with me. Our lunches were becoming more frequent as she became my confidante regarding all things crazy.

"I just can't believe it," I explained. "Someone finally confronts her directly with compassion and understanding, and she manipulates it into some kind of attack on her. By the time she's done you are asking yourself, 'what did I do wrong?'"

Sally's eyes showed she was appropriately mortified while she quickly downed her bite of lettuce wedge. "Holy Jesus. Has Alex ever gone off on her?"

"Pretty sure he hasn't, and even if he has it probably wouldn't work. When Alex read the GAL's letter to me last night over the phone, he got choked up as if it were the first time in a long time someone stood up for him. I get it now, he's under a microscope with the court, his job, all these investigations about stupidly wild allegations from Psycho, so he has to be careful. I think that's what I'm gonna call her. Psycho. I get the sense it's always been this way."

"Wow." Sally shook her head. "It's like she's totally separated herself from reality. If I ever start to talk like this, just shoot me, okay?"

"Me first," I said.

"How's it going with the kids? Do they know about you yet?"

"Oh Hell no. And I like it that way! Don't get me wrong, I want to meet them someday, but with the divorce looming, I'm not sure if my fight or flight will win."

"Pretty sure it'd be the fight, knowing you."

I snickered. "You know me too well. Two nights ago we went on one of our secret walks. While we were just leaving the froyo place, Martin comes strolling in with some girl on his arm. Alex was so busted! But Martin couldn't say anything because he was busted too! They just sorta nodded at each other and kept walking, but I figured it was time to break the ice and pulled Alex back to the shop. Alex introduced me as a friend of his, but Martin saw right through it. He was all like, "uh-huh, nice to meet you, *friend!*" So later that night, Alex had to explain himself to the kids."

"Did he stick with the whole 'friend' thing?"

"Yeah, but it's becoming more of a joke among the older kids. They get it, and they are loving the tease."

Sally laughed. "They probably just love seeing him happy."

She was spot on.

# # #

November 13, 2008

> **To: Rachel Townsend**
> **From: Alex**
> **Re: Suburban**
>
> I have signed the Suburban over to Holly. It will be up to her to register it now; I am reporting it as sold/transferred to the State. Insurance will stop on the Suburban on Monday, November 17, and Holly will no longer be on my policy with Progressive.
>
> IMPORTANT: Holly was in another accident yesterday...with a Washington State Patrol Car. No injuries; Holly was cited for improper backing and no proof of insurance. Holly told me of the accident today; she blamed the patrol car for being "dark" after she backed into it at the Fred Meyer parking lot in Lynnwood.
>
> Alex

I answered Nikki's call on the first ring. "Hello, sexy." My voice was only moderately seductive. Definitely out of practice.

"Hey. Elle says you're my boy-toy. Thought I'd let you know."

"I'm you're *what?*"

"My boy-toy. She asked how things were going with my boy-toy. At first I thought she meant my purple one, but then I remembered she doesn't know about George."

I had a lot to process right then. The last time I saw a sex toy was behind the head board of a bed in Onalaska, Washington. The middle-aged wife of a kidnapping suspect, who was totally clueless about her husband's extra-curricular activities, had wondered why his last "job" had taken him so many extra days away from home. She kept herself pretty busy in the meantime; she had the largest assortment of sex toys I'd ever found during the execution of a search warrant. Or ever, for that matter. Other than finding porn or toys when serving warrants, nobody in my Presbyterian circle was into that sort of thing or willing to talk about it at church, so I was utterly clueless. Nikki, however, bragged about attending a "passion party" once where she joined a dozen other thirty-somethings who each walked away with their favorite color. She kept hers in her drawer, well tucked away even though she didn't have a bunch of curious kids in her house.

"I thought you got rid of that thing now that you have me."

"Oh no," she replied. "George stays. And I told Elle things were really good, but that's not why I called. Something hit my car on the way home today. I think it was an animal, maybe a raccoon."

"In the convertible?" Alex sounded alarmed. "Are you all right?"

"I'm totally fine, but I'm pretty sure my alignment is out of whack. I'm taking it in tomorrow for repairs. I'll pick up a rental at the same time. What do you think…do I take the Audi or the Range Rover?"

That little car represented all kinds of things for me. "Take the Rover."

"Yeah, I was thinking that. I already know I like the Audi. Hey…now I'll have a car Psycho won't know about. I could follow her around, see what she's up to during the day!"

"Eh, I'm not sure that's a good idea right now. You'd probably see what we already know. She's crazy. She does some crazy things. And if by chance you get spotted or found out, we'd all have hell to pay."

"Fine. But I'm still taking the Rover."

I was pretty sure Nikki had not entirely given up on the surveillance idea. Quite the opposite.

# # #

November 24, 2008

From: Alex
To: Rachel Townsend

Hi Rachel. I heard from Holly's sister that Holly is being evicted at the end of this month. The kids also said Mom "has to move" by then.

Holly requested I split my extra holiday pay with her. Given that I'm behind on many bills and scrambling to catch up, not to mention lack of payments to you, am I under any obligation to share extra money with Holly?

While I'm at it, Thanksgiving has been the time of year Holly typically falls apart. Any progress with the mental health evaluation?

Thank you, Rachel.

Alex

5. COLLATERAL DAMAGE

November 28, 2008

Despite the regular difficulties of Thanksgiving, I agreed to drop off the kids at Holly's parents' house after spending the morning with them at my sister's place in Marysville for our annual breakfast. The kids would spend the night with the grandparents who would bring them back home in the afternoon the following day. This gave me an unexpected window of opportunity to spend some free time with Nikki. She was excited to have me help hang Christmas lights at her house, an annual feat she completed no later than the morning after Thanksgiving. What I didn't know was what this actually involved.

I pulled into the driveway and saw thousands of Christmas lights already hung in place around the windows, eves, gutters, fence line, and front door of her little rambler. *Dang it, she's already done,* I thought. I thought wrong. Nikki was attempting to retrieve the top box from a tall stack of them in her single-car garage. I jumped out to help, lowering the heavy box as she explained it was her Christmas lights. "Wait, it looks like you've already finished hanging them," I said innocently.

"Not quite," she said.

At Nikki's direction, I began to wrap each individual spindle of the wood porch frame hand rail. There were forty-two of them. Each was to be wrapped in a spiral fashion, up and down. Twice.

#

Alex was on his knees, dutifully spinning a strand of a hundred colored lights around the first spindles. "Do you usually do this by yourself?" he asked.

"Every year," I said. "I love Christmas lights!" Truth was, I used to have help

71

from my ex-husband, but he hated it and had his own special way of letting me know that. The last time he participated in the decoration of the home, it was all I could do not to take the ladder down and drive away, leaving his sorry whiny ass stranded on the roof of our Bellevue house. It might have qualified as abusive had I actually done it. Alex, on the other hand, appeared to be enjoying himself. "Hey, we have all night to get the porch done," I said. "Let's go inside and have a drink!"

"Deal," he replied. Alex left the wad of lights and the staple gun on the porch.

"I had a Sex In The City martini party here last month with my girlfriends," I said. "Do you like martinis?"

"Never had one, except maybe a lemon drop my boss forced down my throat during the summer," he said. I saw this as an opportunity.

"Seriously? You've *never* had a cosmo?" I was going to rub this in.

Over the next three hours, I concocted every variety of martini I could remember from the previous party. Cherry-lime, caramel appletini, cosmo, chocolate espresso, and a shaken version of a White Russian. When Alex suggested we add a regular lemon drop to the mix, I had already run out of regular vodka. "I only have vanilla vodka," I said.

"Ooh, now that sounds like a winner!" he said.

As our laughter grew out of control, we both somehow had the presence of mind to turn off our cell phones to prevent any inadvertent social media postings. Probably best for the kids. At one point, Alex started telling a story involving the use of his hands while I sat on the tall table chair in my dining room. He swung to his left to emphasize what seemed to be an important point, knocking me squarely off the chair and onto my ass. I felt a sharp burning sensation on my elbow as I lay on the floor laughing hysterically and barely able to catch my breath. Alex was momentarily mortified, helping me up and asking several times if I was okay between his own fits of laughter. It didn't even slow us down.

Alex referred to alcohol as "the great revealer," and by 6 pm we were well on our way to those deep, important, meaningless conversations only experienced with the aid of adult beverages. I had consumed no less than two vanilla lemon drops and at least one of each of the above-mentioned drinks. Alex had kept up with me admirably, and we weren't quite done. Turns out both of us are "happy drunks" who take full advantage of that alcohol-induced sense of freedom of speech. We later figured out we likely passed out sometime between 7:30 and 8 pm after our second run at the cherry lime.

What would have been a normal evening for me of preparing everything for the next day's meal and festivities instead became one of the most delightful evenings I'd ever had. I left dirty dishes in the sink and didn't care. My countertops were littered with the evidence of a serious drunk fest. I had a ton of things to do before my family arrived the next day, and nothing about that bothered me at all. It felt so good.

# # #

I've never had to pee so bad in my entire life. I sat up and realized two things very quickly. First, I was on the floor wedged between a bed and a wall. Second, this was not my house. The pounding in my head got in the way of my visual analysis of my surroundings as I tried to figure out what the hell had happened. Driven by the call of nature, I managed to stand up, when I noticed a third thing. I had no clothes on. I held the mattress to prevent gravity from ruining my progress and noticed Nikki lying sideways in the bed twisted up in the top sheet. *Oh, right…I'm at Nikki's house.*

I stumbled into the bathroom across the hall just in the nick of time. 90 seconds later, I made my way out of the bathroom and into the kitchen. It was like a bomb had gone off. I walked to the sink to get some water but was assaulted by the smell from the half-full glass of cherry-lime martini. It sent a wave of cold sweat down my back. I should have puked, but I held steady for a few minutes until the sensation passed. I swallowed some water and returned to the bedroom, where I promptly passed out again on the bed.

I woke again to sunlight coming in through the bedroom window. Nikki woke next to me, both of us sideways on the bed. "What time is it?" she asked.

"Seven thirty," I said. "I gotta get home and feed the dog."

"Come back at noon. I should have things ready by then. My family is excited to meet you," she said groggily.

This was going to be a significant step for both of us. I was still amazed that I had met someone who liked me, a guy with about as much baggage as one can gather. As I headed out to the car, I saw the wad of Christmas lights still on the porch. Maybe I'll come back a little early.

#

I wanted to barf, but that would have ruined the vegetables I was cutting for fondue. I hadn't felt this queasy since I downed a bottle of gin with Mountain Dew after the laser light show at the Rush concert when I was 15. The scattered dishes, empty bottles, and various ingredients on the countertop were clues of what had been an epic night of fun. But I was definitely paying for it. *Getting old sucks*, I thought. Stirring the thick cheese fondue didn't help either, but somehow despite the pounding in my head and the strange bruise on my elbow, I made it through. Elle arrived an hour early to help out before the rest of my family showed up. "Morning, sunshine. You look like shit!"

She was right. "Stir this," I said, walking out of the kitchen without explanation. The bathroom mirror told the truth. Fifteen minutes later, I'd managed to hold in my guts and get myself a little more presentable. I still couldn't figure out why my elbow hurt. "Look Elle, Alex got drunk and hurt me!"

"You better have that looked at," she said, clearly not believing my version of the events. She handed me a cup of coffee. "Bottoms up, buttercup."

I giggled a little, starting to recall the events that led to my hangover. "I have a splitting headache and I've had the shakes all morning, but man it was worth it. Alex and I drank our Thanksgiving last night. Pretty sure I just slept for about 14 hours."

"Not quite enough, I gather," she said with a grin.

"Just keep stirring," I said.

Alex walked in. "Yo yo, how's the head?" he started. "Hey, you're not Nikki…what have you done with her?"

Elle set down the wooden spoon and extended a hand. "Hi Alex, I'm Elle. I've heard all about you."

"Yeah, but I *know* all about you," he said. "Nice to meet you, Elle. Hey Nikki, how can I help?"

I shot him an angry glance. "What did you do to me last night?" I asked accusingly. "I can hardly bend my elbow!" I had sorta remembered toppling off the chair and laughing on the floor while Alex helped me up, meaning I could easily leverage some blame on him for fun.

"I'm so sorry about that—did you get hurt?" His compassion was interrupted by our combined laughter as we hugged.

Elle was confused. "You guys are weird," she said, returning to her spoon.

# # #

6. MISREPRESENTATION

I met my choice counterparts, Detective Jim Richardson from Everett PD and Special Agent Shaun Perkins of the Naval Criminal Investigative Service, at 10:30 pm Saturday night in the parking lot of Kamiak High School. There were only three of us for this brief recon mission, something Supervisory Special Agent Nigel Marks asked as a favor. The other agents in the Everett FBI office already had a full weekend on another surveillance. Our assignment was to obtain street-level photographs of the target's residence and surrounding area. The tactical team would serve an arrest warrant the following morning. "It's not a terrorism subject, just some lawyer who's about to be disbarred," Nigel told me. After dividing up some responsibilities, Shaun hopped into my Bureau-funded car, a new Nissan Pathfinder, while Jim crept away in his Maxima. It dawned on me then how the FBI had never given task-force agents anything but foreign-made vehicles to blend in. It worked in Mukilteo. There wasn't a pickup of any kind in this upscale neighborhood.

I saw the upstairs lights go out in quick succession on our first pass by the 3,800 square foot house on Harbor Point Drive. The place was immaculate. "Some lawyer," Shaun said.

"Yeah, must be a corporate guy," I replied.

I parked down the street and watched for 15 minutes to ensure the occupants had gone to bed. "How are things with the ex?" Shaun asked.

"Typical," I said. "Although I don't expect she'll be showing up tonight. I made sure I didn't have a tail just to be sure."

Shaun had the unfortunate pleasure of meeting Holly on a similar outing a year earlier when she showed up at our rally point before tailing a terrorism subject on a late-night run to the airport. Holly suspected I was fooling around instead of actually stopping bad guys, so she followed me to the meet, leaving the kids without letting them know she was out. When she approached our team as we were gearing up, she acted like she was just passing through the neighborhood with cookies in the middle of the night. I was extremely embarrassed and worried that I would be questioned for telling someone, *anyone*, about our classified activity. At a minimum it altered my standing on the team as a distracted local with issues. Ever since that incident, Shaun would often ask if my "other partner" was going to tag along for the op.

Shaun and I made our way on foot to the residence while Jim kept overwatch down the street. We checked the gates for locks and the eves for signs of surveillance, took adequate photographs, then identified a good staging area out of view of the target house. Mission accomplished, we met back at the school where I uploaded the photos to a secure server and sent the brief report to the supervisor via encrypted email. He texted me back almost immediately.

> **Nigel**: Good work. Please come for the takedown at 0630. We'll stage at the location you identified.

"You guys gonna be here in the morning? I asked.

"If you're bringing the coffee," Jim replied.

While driving away, my phone rang. It was Evelyn. "Hi, Daddy!"

"Evelyn, it's like midnight, what on earth are you doing up?"

"I just wanted to talk to you," she said. She sounded happy and very, very awake. I could tell it was going to be a late night.

"I'll be home in ten minutes, Evelyn. I'll come to your room when I get home to make sure you're completely asleep, little one."

"Okay, Daddy. See you soon!"

I got home and found Evelyn passed out in my bed. *You little turkey!* I carried her to her room and deposited her into her bed among a hundred stuffed animals. It was like a twisted scene from *The Lion King*. Always creeped me out a little.

I returned to my room only to hear my phone buzzing. Text after text flooded in. I could see the notifications as Holly was berating me for leaving the children home alone. Shaking my head, I set the phone aside knowing I could go over it tomorrow. *Right now I need to get some sleep.* I silenced my phone, checked the alarm, and crawled into bed.

When my alarm went off at 5:30 am, it felt as though I had just shut my eyes. The screen showed 17 text messages from Holly. *Oh great, what a way to start the day.* I push the thoughts and the texts to the back burner in order to focus on the task at hand: get ready and go arrest a bad guy.

I showed up two minutes early with a box of coffee for the team. Overtime gigs like this on the weekend paid well, making the added $15 expense well worth the return. Nigel began handing out briefing packets.

"Okay you guys, here's the info on our target. This is your chance to finally arrest a lawyer." Muffled cheers went up from the team. "This asshole is now wanted for three counts of wire fraud, bank fraud, and money laundering. He's known to have defended some pretty bad actors in the past, mostly organized crime and biker gang types, all while living the suburban lifestyle none of you can have. You'll see his picture on page 2."

I opened up the packet and dropped my coffee when I read the name. *Raymond Snyder.* I approached Nigel at the side of his car where he was pouring his coffee. "Uh, Nigel?"

"What's up, Alex?"

"I can't be here. This is Holly's fucking attorney! Oh man, talk about a conflict of interest. Dammit! Any guidance here would be greatly appreciated."

"You're kidding, right?" I stared back at him with the not-kidding look.

Nigel sighed and turned toward the group, then said in a loud voice for all to hear, "Alex, thanks for dropping off the coffee. Now get out of here and catch up with your target before he flies the coop." He nodded to me with an understanding look. I peeled out of the parking lot and headed straight to Nikki's house.

#

Answering Alex's call on the first ring, I said, "You're up early. You bored? Lonely?" I loved turning his own phrases on him.

"Neither. Just come open the damn door before your coffee gets cold."

"But I haven't even made my…" *Oh, sweet! He's at my door.* I took the opportunity for some fun. "Be right there," I said.

I answered the door in my robe and quickly grabbed the coffee from his hand, then drug Alex in by the collar.

# # #

Church was different now. It took me some time to even accept the notion that I had a girlfriend while still legally married. It took longer to be comfortable in church knowing I had gotten naked with said girlfriend while drunk off my ass and had forgotten most of Thanksgiving. We had consumed a wide variety of martinis, the last of which involved cherry and lime. Both of us had to face swirling hangovers the next morning. By Sunday morning, my body had recovered, but my soul was still a little twisted up.

Holly's antics led me to look for another church to attend after her membership had been erased by the church leaders. I truly appreciated the people at Faith Presbyterian Church, but my continued presence at the congregation put all of them in the target zone. Holly had already threatened lawsuits against the church elders and staff, not to mention the disruptions she gave repeatedly during the worship service. One morning she came into the sanctuary yelling at the pastor, interrupting the sermon, then carrying on about how he had never given his wife the sexual attention she needed, or how one of the elders abandoned their role as a father with their wayward daughter. I knew that by keeping her attention on me, my departure would take her wrath away from that congregation.

This week, I went to Faith for what I expected was one of my final visits. I shared my thoughts with Terri, who had struggled herself with a bi-polar daughter. I had known Terri longer than anyone else in the church and had trusted her friendship and wisdom above all others. She was like a life-coach. Genuinely honest and generous, she was willing to accept people and their circumstance as just a part of history rather than being judgmental or arrogant. She loved God with all her heart and somehow never allowed that to contradict her love for her neighbors, whatever kind of people they were.

After singing hymns, quietly confessing all my recent sins, and praying about my own confusion in my newfound pseudo-single state, I felt some peace knowing what I had to do. I spoke privately with Terri in the foyer.

"I met someone," I started.

Terri sucked in a massive gasp of air. "Really! Oh, Alex, I'm so glad for you! Do tell!"

After the service was over, I jammed some guitar with Terri's son for a bit, then found her in the sanctuary where we talked. "She's amazing," I said. "She likes to say she believes in God, but doesn't pretend to know all the nuts and bolts about religion. She just loves life and appreciates its maker."

"Wow," she pondered. "So does she have kids?"

"Nope, no kids."

Terri sighed. "Alex, I'm just so happy for you. You deserve to be loved. Especially by someone who isn't crazy. She's not crazy, is she?"

"Not yet," I said. "But give me some time, I'll see what I can do."

December 1, 2008

I woke at 5:30 am to my alarm going off. I aimlessly reached toward the night stand, causing the laptop on my chest to fall to the floor. *Oh, shit.* I looked at the phone and saw several texts from Nikki which I apparently missed by falling asleep during our conversation. After getting ready for the day in the typical flurry of events, I spent a few minutes trying to finish up the letter to the GAL to let him know about Holly's escalating craziness over the weekend. When I was almost done, I dared to shoot a note to Nikki.

> **Alex**: OMG, sorry I fell asleep last night!

> **Nikki**: Whatev. Lol.

> **Alex**: Wanna walk tonight?

> **Nikki**: Sure, if you can stay awake…

Snarky. I headed out the door at 7 am on a perfectly damp Monday morning, hoping to make it to the pink building in under thirty minutes. My phone rang. "Hello, this is Alex."

"Alex, this is Gene Rapp. Are you able to come by the station this morning?"

Shit. It's first thing Monday morning and the Assistant Chief is calling me into his office. Several possibilities ran through my brain. Either I was getting put on admin leave for an internal investigation spawned by some wild-ass accusation from Holly, or the impact of the downed economy was going to affect my ability to stay working off campus at the FBI, or maybe, just maybe, someone figured out I had a hand in getting Holly's attorney arrested for some federal crimes. "Sure," I said. "What's up, boss?"

Assistant Chief Rapp handed me a piece of paper. "I figured you'd want to see this before it gets run in the newspaper," he said. "Not that it will, but you never know. Hey, you look a little tired."

"It was a different kind of Thanksgiving for me," I said, then turned to read the letter.

To: Rafael, editor at The Everett Herald, Assistant Chief Rapp, Mayor Troy Pope
From: Holly

Dear Rafael,

As a concerned wife of Edmonds Police Detective Alex Hill, I have recently been exploring the night-life here in Edmonds. I had three threatening and sorrowful events occur with three establishments: Engel's Pub, Daphne's Café, and The Loft.

Two weeks ago, both of the female bartenders at Engel's told me I deserved a recent sexual assault. They both said that I should have been ready for the assault and that I was foolish to have been so trusting. To defend myself, the following day I approached one of the two bartenders and told her what she had said was wrong and very unkind. No woman deserves to be raped and no good woman would be so lacking in compassion. She told me I had to leave or she would call the police. I took her threat and sat down on the outside bench and read a book for two hours. After the hours passed, I walked inside. A male bartender shouted profanities at me in front of other customers. The female bartender called the police. After the police gave me a trespass notice, I went home.

This week, I ventured out to The Loft to experience the night-life there. I was promised by the owner and the bartenders that they were a better establishment and would never 86 me there. Two days ago, after Theo, the owner of The Loft, shouted at me for trying to encourage him and defend a young female bartender, and listening to lies that another businessman had passed on to him in regards to me, I left his fine establishment. Yesterday I called to ask Theo for another meeting to redeem himself. When I arrived I was told I was no longer welcome. Mayor Pope and I said a few words to each other, then a phone was handed to me. It was Polly, Theo's wife, she began shouting at me calling me "a fucking little bitch and told me to get the hell out of her husband's establishment." I walked out without calling her names or shouting at anyone. I sat at a table outside. Assistant Chief Gene Rapp came in to the establishment while I waited for another officer to arrive. When asked to leave by an officer, I left and went home. Upon entering my home, I called 911 and two officers responded and took my report of the incident.

Later that same evening, I called Daphne's and spoke to Ezra, the bartender. He informed me that Jeff, the manager had left a note that afternoon telling the staff that I was not welcome and could no longer be served. A week prior to this I was having a non-alcoholic beverage at Daphne's while Jeff, the manager berated the owner and his wife and boasted that he was going to make the bar such a better place than it had been so far. I called Jeff when I returned home that night and cautioned him to be respectful to his boss and his wife. Jeff then shared his misgiving about me with Theo so that they created this filthy opinion of me and it was also a plate of untruths.

All three of these establishments have chosen not to serve me because they are protecting themselves from their own poor business practices. Sorrowfully, there are many men in high position here in Edmonds that have chosen to protect their positions rather than defend the honor of the women they serve. Men who will not make sacrifices for the women they are partners with are not very honorable themselves.

Seven years ago, Assistant Chief Gene Rapp and Mayor Troy Pope swore to protect and serve our family. My husband, Alex Hill, swore a vow to protect and serve the Edmonds Community. I, as the wife of an Edmonds Detective, I am grieved by the treatment I have received here over the past several months. The "It's An Edmonds Kind of Day" motto works during the day. The Edmonds Bowl night-life establishments have quite a reputation to restore for this particular local.

Sincerely,

Holly Hill
An Advocate for Women and Children

"The Mayor?" I said. "Oh, God. This is crazy!"

"I don't disagree," Gene said. "There's more. It looks like she sent this out yesterday afternoon, then last night she went down to Daphne's again and got herself trespassed from there after making another scene. When the officers gave her the trespass letter, they also issued her a criminal citation for telephone harassment against the owner of The Loft."

"So has she technically been arrested and released on a citation?"

"Yes. I'm not sure if they'll prosecute, but the officers had probable cause at the time, so I advised them to treat it like any other case. Nobody wants to deal with her because they then become the next target of her antics. So they let her walk on a citation rather than taking her to jail. Still, she wasn't too happy about it." Gene seemed conflicted, both annoyed that Holly's unnecessary behavior continued to involve the police, but also a level of empathy for her seemingly deteriorating state.

"I have a feeling this isn't the end of it," I said.

"She did have her regular rant about you," Gene said. "She's telling anyone who will listen that you are a dirty cop who used your badge to make her look bad and take the children from her. She calls 911 several times a day now complaining about something, then complaining about the officers who respond and try to help her." He looked squarely at me. "How are you holding up?"

"Honestly," I said, "her maligning of me in public is getting a little old. She's going to wind up getting herself in jail if this keeps up. Did you hear what she did last night?"

"Her charge that your three teenaged babysitters aren't enough? Yeah. It's best right now that you're assigned to the FBI, it will keep you from having a conflict on the street with her on duty. Can you imagine? You go to the disturbance call and have to taze your wife?"

I had considered this a thousand ways already and couldn't decide if it were a fantasy or a nightmare. I simply had to keep my distance and hope her continued public accusations against me would fall on deaf ears.

She's going to get me fired, I thought. I looked at my email before heading for the FBI office in Everett. Good thing I did.

> **To: Alex**
> **From: Rachel Townsend**
>
> I just got a call from an attorney named Laura Mattson who says she will be entering a Notice of Appearance on Holly's behalf. [I have never heard of her.] She requested a continuance of the trial date to allow her to prepare. I advised that I would speak with you about it. As I am closing my practice after your case, and you and I both want to get this case over with, likely we will not agree to the continuance. She may move forward with filing a motion.
>
> I'm in another trial starting tomorrow; as I get information I'll send it along to you. But I don't think I will have much time to attend to this case during this week.
>
> Rachel

Holy shit, she changes attorneys like underwear. Or addresses for that matter. I was having a hard time keeping track of them all. And every time she changes something else, my bill continued to mount, with no clue whatsoever as to how I would pay it off.

But I knew it was worth it. Time to document the weekend's events.

> **To: Ron Taylor**
> **From: Alex**
>
> Ron,
>
> On Friday night, we had our first attempt at an overnight with Evelyn and Holly. It went well for the most part; Evelyn was very glad and had a good time. Holly kept Evelyn later than her residential time on Saturday (12:30 pm), which is not a problem except that she asked Katherine and Kevin if she could have Evelyn stay with her until I got home; they said it was probably fine with Dad, so she took Evelyn home with her. Holly did not ask/confirm with me before just taking Evelyn for more time.

Here is the text stream. Note: I am not including several other harassing notes sent by Holly around the visit, just focusing on two issues.

---------- Forwarded texts ----------

Holly 12:37 pm: Can Evelyn stay with me until you pick her up?

Alex 1:16 pm: I just got this. Evelyn needed to come home with the others as planned unless cleared ahead of time. I will pick her up in 5 min. Will text when there.

Holly 1:17 pm: Kiddos all said you said it was okay. She did not wish to be there without an adult.

Alex 1:19 pm: Its NOT up to the kids Holly. You know this.

Holly 1:22 pm: Then tell the kiddos NOT TO LIE. I took her to your home and Kevin and Katherine told me you said it was fine. I texted you while I was there. Sue me and accuse me of crime. 7 more visits will cost pro-tem judge and city a fortune.

Alex 1:26 pm: Please send her out.

Holly 1:33 pm: Just do not send her out of your heart like you have done to me. Please advocate for her sweetness and her fears. She has night terrors because she is anxious you will take her away from me.

(NOTES: 1. Holly's restraining order violation criminal case resulted in the assignment of a pro-tem judge and several resets and a series of disturbing courtroom incidents at the Edmonds courthouse. 2. I asked Evelyn later if she was worried I might take her home during her overnight with Mom. Evelyn said no.)

Saturday: After putting the kids to bed at the regular time, I had some work to do in Mukilteo during the night. I left the house just before 10 pm with instructions to all three older kids that I would be out for a couple of hours for work. It is our routine that if I need to go out at night (which is not often), I get the younger kids to bed first before I leave so they don't worry and so the older kids don't have to handle that part.

At around 11:30, Evelyn called me, having woken up. She asked where I was; I let her know I was only 10 minutes away and had just finished up and was heading home from a bit of work I had to go do. She sounded happy and said she would wait in my room for me to get home.

When I got home, I got a text message from Holly:

Holly 12:08 am: Evelyn just called. She should not be at home without you. Stop making her scared and nervous. Get home where supposedly you are the better parent.

After I spoke with Evelyn on the phone, she called Holly. Evelyn later said she thought I wasn't supposed to be on the phone with her since I was driving, and she wanted to talk to someone, so she called Mom.

After Evelyn finished talking with Holly about the drum machine I found for the kids, Evelyn hung up and told me she tried to change the subject with Mom. I asked what she meant by that; she said Mom kept talking about how Dad wasn't there and how she was scared. Evelyn said she wasn't scared, just wanted to talk, but Mom kept talking about the scared part. Evelyn seemed proud that she changed the subject and annoyed that Holly kept on with it. I told Evelyn it was okay to call Mom any time if she really needed to, but if it was after bedtime it is best to ask first. I asked Evelyn if she was scared or worried; she said she was not scared, just wanted to talk. This was consistent with her demeanor when I spoke to her on the phone. Evelyn also said, "Oh yeah, Mommy wanted me to tell you some things for her.... she is glad you are still playing guitar in church, and she loves you." Evelyn said it was funny how Mom wanted her to tell me these messages, but Mom doesn't want the kids doing that sort of thing.

Holly 12:16 am: I am calling Ron Taylor right now. You having her worried like this is wrong. Her being left with Kevin is also wrong. Act like a police officer and defend your children and abide by city ordinances.

Holly 12:33 am: An on-duty officer will be checking in on you. It better be true that you were at work. Darn it Alex, stop scaring all of us!

At 12:34 pm, I called dispatch to see if I was needed. Holly had called 911 to report the children were left home alone; Sgt. David Arancio advised he would handle the call. I asked the dispatcher to have Sgt. Arancio call me directly on my cell phone. He did so a minute later. Sgt. Arancio knew I had a sixteen-year-old and a fifteen-year-old at home; I confirmed that they and the thirteen-year-old were all home, all aware that I was going to be out for a short time while I did some work. Sgt. Arancio said he did not intend on contacting Holly since there was no crime or violation of the parenting plan, which Edmonds Police has on file due to the restraining order currently in effect.

Over an hour later, I got more messages that woke me:

Holly 1:33 am: What is less threatening? The message sent before this one or the one when Evelyn called after midnight to tell me she was scared due to your absence?

Alex 1:34 am: Stop sending me messages in the middle of the night.

Holly 1:57 am: Stop waking me up with scared children who trust their mom to do anything to help them!

Ron, Holly seems to be projecting fear into Evelyn that is not there. There have been several instances of this, but I have only noted them lately. Evelyn may not be telling me everything about her feelings when I inquire, but the totality of her demeanor and her answers to me indicate Holly is stretching the reality of the situation to fit her own perception, which is not an accurate one. Holly is further taking this stretched perception and contacting the police (my employer) to report it. While Evelyn may not be excited that I occasionally have to do work at night, none of the children are afraid, having "night terrors," or are in any kind of danger or harm.

I continue to receive questions from people in the community asking if Holly is bi-polar and mentioning her ongoing problems at numerous businesses downtown.

I welcome any inquiries into this matter. Also, the results of the final internal investigation should be in this week from Chief Baker; will advise.

Alex

December 3, 2008

To: Rachel Townsend, Ron Taylor
From: Alex

All-

I learned today that Holly is being charged with a couple of counts of telephone harassment in Edmonds (misdemeanor), including to some business owners and the 911 center itself. She may not have received the citations in the mail yet, but I am told it will likely be today. I will be obtaining these police reports through Freedom of Information Act process and will get them to you as soon as they are available, which may be early next week.

This morning, the Edmonds Mayor's first e-mail was from Holly complaining about my so-called abuse of authority, detailing how she keeps getting kicked out of businesses because they favor me over her. The city is being bombarded with this type of activity. I believe it is reflective of her emotional and mental state. Either that, or I'm way more powerful than I thought. But I digress.

Alex

# # #

December 4, 2008

Thursdays were becoming the dedicated mid-week alone time for Alex and me. We took turns planning what to cook at my place for dinner after work, which usually meant I decided what we'd eat. After our early dinner, Alex would scoot back to Edmonds to pick up the kids from their weekly so-called Hamburger Date with their mom. Thursdays were a chance for me to show off some of my mom's old recipes and not have to cook a solo meal. This week was Chicken Kiev.

Just as I pulled the dish out of the oven, Alex got a call from Justin. He spoke in hushed, encouraging tones for a minute, then hung up. "Everything okay,"

I asked.

"Not exactly," he said. "Justin reports Holly lost it when they tried to take the kids into a restaurant for dinner but were turned away by a manager. Something about how she wasn't supposed to be there, but she was arguing that it was okay since she had the kids with her."

"What does having the kids with her have to do with it?" I asked. *Is she actually using the kids as leverage to overcome her trespassed status?*

"Nothing, clearly," he said. "But she kept insisting until the police were called. Then she called 911 herself demanding the sergeant show up and hear her out."

"Oh, I'll bet that went well," I quipped.

"It ended up with three officers there escorting Holly out of the building. Of course they didn't arrest her in front of the kids, but I'd imagine she may get something in the mail after this."

"You'd better get there," I said. I put some chicken into a plastic container and handed it to him. "They need you right now."

Alex took the container and hugged me tight. "Sorry about this," he said.

"Don't worry, just go. Go!" I exclaimed. I wiggled out of his embrace and pushed him out the door. I knew this wouldn't be the last time our plans were interrupted.

# # #

December 10, 2008

Sgt. Jensen had warned me to avoid the station today since Holly was scheduled to appear for her most recent telephone harassment and trespassing charges. Just as well, since I knew the office was in a twitter over some suits from headquarters showing up unexpectedly. I had just arrived at the FBI parking garage and was making my way through the *Get Smart* maze of controls when the first texts arrived.

Holly: 8th appearance in court today for pre-trial. Trial next week. Dismissal of your evil charges against me for loving Evelyn.

Holly: I did not know you had hoped I would become a defense attorney. Thank you for the experience.

It boggled the mind. Holly would eventually rack up seven different criminal charges over six months, with only one of them sticking, putting her on probation with the local court for two years. It never made a hint of difference, which proved the point: there wasn't a court in the land capable of managing her current state, that awful space between crazy and criminal.

I finished the trek into the office and walked into the bullpen where I was surprised by a full room of FBI, CIA, and other three-letter agents, along with analysts, private industry leadership staff, and cops, all offering back-pats, thanks and congratulations. I was dumbfounded. Nigel Marks took the lead to straighten me out.

"Alex, we all know you're headed back to patrol at your home agency in a couple weeks, and this is the last day several of us will be in the office together. So we wanted to present you with some tokens of appreciation while we could all be here."

My brain had left Holly's texts in the dust as Nigel escorted me to the front of the room. Representatives from the Coast Guard, NCIS, and Microsoft each presented certificates of appreciation. Nigel then retrieved a box from his office and started acting oddly official. At the same time, I saw the tall man in the dark suit who followed him out of his office. I recognized him immediately.

"Today we have a special guest from headquarters who stopped by to be briefed on one of our ongoing investigations, a case initiated by Detective Alex Hill and run out of this office for the last two years. During that time, operations in Washington DC, New York, Los Angeles, Miami, Cairo, and Paris have all worked under the direction of the headquarters Terrorism Financing Operations Section. Here to present our token of appreciation from the Federal Bureau of Investigation is the Director of the FBI himself, Robert Mueller.

As the room applauded, Nigel pulled a clear glass plaque out of the box and handed it to the Director, who smiled and handed it to me, shaking my hand. "This case is a perfect example of the partnerships needed between federal, state, and local law enforcement organizations to address the most pressing threat to our country. Alex, our nation is safer because of your dedication and hard work. On behalf of the FBI, thank you for your service."

Someone snapped a few photographs as I shook Mueller's hand in what felt like a very staged moment. Before I could even try to formulate an intelligent response, Nigel took the floor. "Thank you, Director. If I'm not mistaken, Detective James Richardson from Everett PD has something to add. Jim? Has anybody seen Jim?"

"Right here," Jim called out, un-burying himself from his cubicle. Jim was really only classy on the inside. He approached the front. "Alex, as a reminder of your mission here, the fellas all pooled together and got you this." He reached into a brown paper bag and pulled out a brand-new Osama Bin Laden doll, dressed in fatigues and a turban with a pull-string in his back. Jim handed me the bag and the doll.

Without hesitation, I pulled the string. "Stop bombing us, I was only kidding," the doll said.

It was pretty awkward, to be honest. Fortunately, Mueller was lightly amused, which gave us all permission to laugh. At least my mind told me so. Jim shook my hand. "It's been a tremendous privilege to share the most important work of our careers together, Alex. You are one of the best detectives in the state—."

"You're the other one," I interjected.

After some kind speeches and shared memories, I thanked the group for allowing me to participate with such an amazing team of professionals in the most challenging work of our lives.

So many things were coming to an end. My assignment. My hope of being that one police officer who stuck it through thick and thin despite all the hardships. My late night trash runs and surveillance operations. My super cool government-issued vehicle.

My marriage of nearly 20 years.

December 15, 2008

    To: Ron Taylor
    From: Alex

Ron,

I heard from Chief Baker today; he is still working on going through the internal investigation (it is more than 6 inches thick). I don't yet have a sense of when to expect it being done, though I am confused why it has taken this long. I think it has gone beyond the allowable time frame already per our policy, mostly due to scheduling problems.

Also, I heard from Michelle Stark, the principal at Edmonds Elementary. She does not want Holly to come to the school at this point, mostly due to her lashing out during their earlier communications. Holly called the school numerous times on several days in a pattern that Mrs. Stark described as harassing phone calls. As you are aware, Holly has been charged and arraigned with another misdemeanor for similar behavior at a downtown Edmonds bar.

Alex

December 16, 2008

To: Rachel Townsend
From: Alex
Subject: Fwd: The previous e-mail you lost

Rachel, somehow this is the type of communication I hope to curtail. Also, I need to somehow limit the massive amount of extra time Holly keeps demanding.

---------- Forwarded message ----------
From: Holly
To: Alex, Ron

Alex,

I have been making copies of pertinent e-mails and your responses. I delete them shortly after so that kiddos cannot read them while they are here. I also know from you that you could trace them. I am trying to defend my position and guard myself from your evil offense. Therefore, I do not have the e-mail you requested I re-send.

Again, I will seek counsel from my attorney.

Look forward to you following through with your promises.

Joyfully,
Your Beloved Bride

To: Ron Taylor
From: Alex

I spoke with Martin two nights ago about the upcoming trial in Edmonds regarding Holly's violation of the restraining order. Holly was speaking with her friend in Martin's presence about plans for the week. The friend mentioned Friday the 19th; Holly said she was busy that day going to court. She then turned to Martin and said, "And Martin is the star witness since he is being forced to testify against his own mother!"

This was very upsetting to Martin. He told me that he has told Holly that he was not forced to testify at all; rather, he chose to.

I spoke with Martin about the trial and reminded him that his answers to the police that night, his statement that he wrote, and anything he may be asked to say in court by the attorney should be viewed as speaking the truth of a matter, and with the hope that it will be ultimately helpful for Mom in the long run. I reminded him first that he was not required to say anything. Martin said he just doesn't want to have to explain the entire event; he is glad to answer specific questions...he hopes his written statement is sufficient for most of it.

I will be taking Martin to the courthouse tomorrow at 3:30 or 4 pm so he is familiar with the surroundings. He will also meet the prosecutor, Mr. Everett.

This is a delicate matter and I would appreciate your input both to Martin and myself. I'm hating the fact this trial has been extended 8 times now until the Friday before Christmas. It was completely unnecessary.

Alex

To: Alex
From: Ron Taylor

The best way to understand Holly's behavior is that she is ill. Her decisions are part logical and part the result of serious thinking errors that she at this point is unable to control. Holly will reject this idea, but everything I have seen in this case point to that understanding. This concept may help Martin. He should have legitimate feelings of loss regarding his mother (loss or her ability to be rational), but not entertain any guilt or anger towards himself out of her verbal expressions to him or around him. Holly is NOT thinking clearly at all. I don't have a problem with the children gaining this perspective about her -- but it would probably be healthier and safer for their counselor to tell them -- perhaps with you present.

Hope this helps.

Ron

To: Alex
From: Holly

Alex,

You are the wedge between the kiddos and myself. You do not comprehend the gift of a mother. You did not grow up with yours because your mean father kept you from her. Kevin hugged me and was cheerful through all of our visit Saturday. All the kiddos were happy to plan individual time. Your attitude and power-control issues are the mountain between true communion in our family. I faithfully attend two counseling appointment every week. My degree program was specifically chosen to deal with this chaos. Hearts of the fathers in our nation have become self-absorbed and defend their own purposes rather than desires of their wives and children. The Titanic motto..."WOMEN AND CHILDREN FIRST" is God's own purpose.

Jesus sees the pain you are causing our family. He is the SEED AND ROOT of all I do. I will prosper without your help and so will our children. We desire for you to water us all to beautiful growth. In your lack, Jesus will be the power we need for all we do.

I am waiting for you to make the connection you promised at Edmonds Elementary. It will be fun to help with the Christmas Happenings. Remember, Evelyn asked for you to participate also. Advocate for your wife and children. We are all very deserving. You are always blessed when you humbly give.

Joyfully,
Your Beloved Bride

12:48 pm

    Holly: Will Justin be coming to Harbor Square?

1:06 pm

    Holly: Will Justin be coming to Harbor Square?

1:37 pm

    Holly: Will Justin be coming to Harbor Square?

1:40 pm

    Alex: Please stop the repeated texts. I have not heard back from Justin yet so I don't know if he's coming to the gym or not.

1:42 pm

    Holly: I repeat because I deserve to be responded to. A quick text of "I will let you know" is not 2 difficult. Freedom of speech is my right.

1:45 pm

    Alex: You don't have the right to harass. I will do my best to respond in a timely manner; I have lots of other obligations besides responding to your requests.

1:47 pm

    Holly: Ditto! you harass me also. Harassment is ur forte! I am at work also. This is about the kiddos not about you. Stop taking center stage. It is so embarrassing for all of your family.

# # #

7. BEYOND REASONABLE DOUBT

December 17, 2008

In the Seattle metro area, we experience snow maybe two or three times each winter, sometimes skipping a year. 2008 was different. On December 17, it began to snow after the morning commute was complete. By the time people were ready to go home for work, the roads had achieved a solid layer of ice at least an inch thick, with another layer of snow on top of the ice. Articulated buses were seen jackknifed all over the region. People abandoned their vehicles on the freeway after running out of fuel in hours of gridlock. I've seen two feet of snow in Seattle before, but this came as a total surprise and brought the region to its knees for days.

Nikki had a hair appointment that morning in Bellevue. She called from her car on her way back.

"Hey, Nik! How's the mane?"

"I love my hairdresser," she said. "But today I really wish she lived closer to home. Have you been out on the roads?"

"Oh yeah," I said. "It's getting worse by the minute. How does the Sky do in the snow?"

"I guess we'll find out!"

Nikki made it past Kirkland toward the Woodinville cutoff when she called back.

"Alex, this is crazy out here. There's another four inches of snow on top of the frozen road now and people have no clue how to drive in it. If I stop, I won't be able to get going again."

I imagined her front bumper, only four inches off the ground, acting as a cattle guard blasting snow out of her way. Nikki's Saturn Sky looked like a cross between a Corvette and a Batmobile. The image in my mind was undoubtedly cooler than the reality.

"You'd better focus. Call me if you get stuck, I'll find a way to rescue you."

# # #

Oh, joy. A rear-wheel-drive sports car in five inches of Seattle snow. *Yee-haw!* Commuters started to abandon their cars. Semi-trucks were stopped everywhere with drivers chaining up. Not me. The driving lessons my dad gave me at Spokane's Joe Albi football stadium parking lot were about to pay off. I plowed up and down the hills of I-405 and slalomed through the losers until I somehow arrived at my home. I pulled into the driveway and paused for the garage door to open—just enough time to become completely stuck in the driveway. *Are you kidding me?* No amount of rocking the manual transmission would move the car.

I entered the house in time to see headlights point straight into the living room. I rushed to the front window to watch a Ford F-150 plow into the three-foot ditch on the side of my yard. Shaking my head, muttering to myself about "invincible" 4X4s, I walked outside to see the twenty-something neo-lumberjack climbing out of his truck. I helped him figure out he needed to drive to the end of the ditch, then pop out at the driveway. Five minutes later he was on his way.

To the delight of children everywhere, the King 5 weather-man said the surprise storm was going to linger for a few days. *Dammit! I left my laptop at work.* Guess I won't be working for a few days. Maybe Elle would pick me up for the game this weekend.

I texted Alex to let him know I'd made it home in one piece.

# # #

December 19, 2008

To: Alex
From: Holly

Alex,

Katherine has requested dinner at Sandy B's and then seeing the movie Australia afterwards. The movie is showing downtown. Can you please speak with her and pin down the day she would like to do this.

We had fun yesterday. I missed your presence. Sledding with the girls was fun but it would have been sweeter with you alongside us. You will always be my favorite musician that I wanted to have a beautiful family to love you and be your back-up. It is the cheerleader in me.

I received notice that Court has been cancelled. Have you decided not to prosecute me? Has God reentered your life to bring us back together as a family? These are my hopes and dreams.

Love always,

Holly

#

Day Two of confinement. Fourteen inches of beautiful snow lay on the ground. My car was frozen shut, and inside was a pound of coffee that I had picked up before visiting my hair stylist. Now even I know it's not a good idea to pour hot water on frozen car. But COME ON! I was having caffeine withdrawals! My car had a clamshell trunk and hood opening system. Using a ten-quart pot of hot water, I scooped out 2 cups at a time, gently pouring it right at the seams of the trunk. Viola! I did a happy dance in the driveway that almost landed me on my ass. *COFFEE!* As I slid into the house, my phone was ringing.

"Hey! I got the coffee out of the trunk!" I proclaimed. "Hold on. I need to grind." *Oh man, that smells good.* "Ok. Operation Caffeine Infusion is underway. You may now speak."

"Did you use hot water?" he asked in his best dad-voice.

"Maybe," I giggled while also changing the subject. "I've convinced Christie, our Environment, Health, and Safety manager at work, to come get me and Sally for a lunch date at the Blazing Onion." I was secretly hoping he'd be able to come over today. Alex had been busy at work…throw in the snow and having to cart five kids around town, there was little time for himself.

"Busy tonight?" I asked.

"Yes, but I'm pretty sure you need some groceries. I'd love to take you shopping."

"Thank you, I'll be ready at 5:30."

With two cups of liquid love onboard, I shoveled my car out of the driveway and realized it would be funny to make it look like I did it with a garden tool. I staged the scene before Christie arrived at 11:30. She hopped out of her 4x4 ready and willing to brave the Seattle Hill area to pick up Sally. She handed me my laptop and asked, "Did you shovel this all by yourself?"

I nodded toward the snowbank and the little green handled garden shovel. "It took me a while," I said, grinning ear to ear.

She shook her head and got back in the truck.

# # #

After hanging up with Nikki, the texts from Holly-who-loves-me were nonstop. Clearly, she'd been reading the renewed orders like only she can.

> **Holly**: I do not understand why you can approach me when I am not allowed to contact you. You broke my restraining order against you 4 times. How do you get away with it?

> **Holly**: I DO NOT WANT YOU TO BAIT ME AGAIN. YOU SHOOT ME IN THE FOOT WHILE I AM TRYING TO DANCE. Then...YOU HAVE THE KIDDOS APPLAUD MY FAILURES ON THE SIDELINES. Enough! Have someone else get my things to me. I love you. I cannot tolerate your abuse anymore.

> **Holly**: I did it because I believed you to be the man I married. You are not right now. I am still hopeful for the veil of injustice and hate will be lifted from your heart. We are all suffering from your sinful choice to break a vow before God.

> **Holly**: Yesterday was hard for me too. Knowing you want me to look all bad and you all good is painful. Using our children against me is also horrid to me. It is difficult to manage the terrorism to my

hopes and heart.

Holly: Loving you through this takes all my strength. Singing as I go. Trusting harder that I have ever had to for love to the husband who became my enemy and uses our children to bolster his cause.

Holly: Did you put photo ornaments on ur tree?

One would think these text messages are all it would take to convince the courts that she indeed is mentally unstable. But no, I get to pay for psych evaluations, a GAL, an attorney, and a therapist to prove it.

Responding to these communications was a chore. Selecting which ones to respond to would lay the foundation for the court's direction on what was deemed appropriate communications. This process required a Zen-like mindset, complete with the deep-breathing exercises, sitting cross-legged with my middle fingers touching my thumbs. I purposely set aside two times a day to address her flood of texts, emails, phone calls and subsequent voicemails. It was the only way I was going to remain sane.

To: Holly
From: Alex

If Katherine requested it, that's fine with me...she can pin down a time with you and just keep me informed. I will check with her tonight.

Alex

12:56 pm

Holly: Is it too much trouble to find knitting supplies? I purchased items to knit Santa hats. The white yarn came in a box. The red is still with you. Martin said he would wear a different hat if I made it. The board for the dresser is needed.

Holly: Little Boo gave me 1 of 2 school picture packs. She said you ordered 1 for me. Thank you. She wants a new baby sibling for Christmas. The board will keep baby from falling off changing top of dresser. Please send back Evie's snow clothes.

4:27 pm

Holly: Evelyn just told me that you have told her that all the judges think you are safer to live with. Stop scaring her! Do you have some special IN with the judges? Evelyn says you told her you have said the judges like you. This is not just or right.

What?! Okay, this deserves a response.

4:40 pm

Alex: Holly, I have said nothing of the sort. I have only spoken in answer to Evelyn about "adults" deciding things, meaning you, me, Ron, etc. never judges. Please, we both have been advised not to discuss this topic with the children.

Wait for it…wait for it…. Putting my phone on silent, my mind wandered to Nikki. I couldn't wait to share what was coming in.

4:41 pm

Holly: Unsafe = leaving kiddos alone when you tell them they can only call you, leaving Evelyn by herself with no one home, letting her stay with a thief and a liar with STD, leaving Evelyn with Camille while she is blitzed, leaving Evelyn with Chloe while a stalker who beat Camille is at her apt. TRUTH.

Holly: Our family was not meant to take this unkindness from you. How do you sleep at night knowing your actions and words are painful and unmerciful? You were not created for this. Run from Satan's grip. Pray for what it might mean to sacrifice the sake of the 6 others in your family. Then you will be FREE!

Holly: I would never leave you homeless. I would have run to help you if someone raped you. I would earn enough to help you get started in a new career. I would leave you food on your doorstep. I would give you my car. I would give you children to love you. I would never divorce you. I would shop for your clothes. GIVE. LOVE. SACRIFICE.

# # #

I opened the door to howling laughter. Alex was doubled over slapping his knees and couldn't talk. He pointed to the little garden shovel still sticking out of the snowbank. After finally composing himself, Alex stomped the snow off his boots with tears of laughter still running down his face before entering.

"You are incredible. I needed that laugh."

I responded with a quick kiss, not letting him take his coat off. "Let's go! I need you to take me to the store."

"Deal."

Alex led the way out the door and walked toward his car, only to get bombarded with the stockpile of snowballs I had staged earlier for the ambush. The ensuing battle was epic.

"Those who strategically plan for the battle will win," I yelled as I scrambled into his car. He managed to smash a handful of snow on my hat before I shut the door, spraying snow inside the car.

I still won. Heh, heh.

# # #

Shopping with Nikki was not what I considered normal. With the holidays right around the corner, she was on deck to make twice-baked potatoes for her family gathering at Elle's house. She quickly moved through the aisles picking up item after item, not stopping to look at the price. When we arrived at the cheese aisle, I stopped her when she went for the pre-grated Tillamook Sharp Cheddar. *$7.99?*

"Why not get this one?" I said innocently, pointing the store-brand brick of half-priced cheddar. She looked at me like I was part-alien.

"Hmm…so many reasons, where do I start? For starters, it's not *sharp*. My mom drilled in to me: quality over price. I was raised to buy local to support local farmers, and to use trusted and tried products. Plus, I don't want to have to grate it!" She looked at me like this was normal for her, then continued. "Growing up, we didn't have money issues. Bargain shopping is something we didn't have to do. Second-hand stores were for Halloween costumes," she said while examining the overpriced packages of bacon.

Wow, not worrying about money. That was a concept so foreign to me I couldn't respond without sounding like a penny-pinching miser. Because I am a penny-pinching miser. I was raised by a frugal, resourceful man who supported local farmers by picking their apples at night.

For years, Holly ran up bills at the local thrift stores for things we didn't need. I can't remember the last time I paid full price for anything. Certainly not cheese, for crying out loud.

Nikki appeared clueless to my angst and continued down the aisles at a pace I'd never before experienced. Here was a woman who knew exactly who she was and what she wanted and needed. To top it off, she was funny, pretty, and intelligent. I started to wonder how long before she decided my life was too chaotic.

# # #

The full depth of his internal financial struggle was reflective in his eyes as I shopped. While I'm not rich, my mindset has always been, *it's just money. I'll make more.* For me, it was only me. For him, it was six people relying on his ability to stretch one dollar into four.

After checking out, I showed Alex the receipt and was so proud to claim I'd saved 5.8%. He gave me a golf clap.

"Next time, you're going shopping with me. I'll show you how to save money."

"Deal!" I said.

# # #

December 20, 2008

7:04 pm

> **Holly:** Your mom divorced your dad. My mom divorced my dad. I WILL NEVER SIGN PAPERS FOR A DIVORCE. I can not knowingly disobey my Lord. If you can dishonor God by breaking a marriage vow; your signature will be the only one on the documents.

Based on that text I was certain I would have several emails from Holly. Checking email, I noticed Terri was online. I pinged her on Google Messenger.

Alex: Hey!

Terri: Are your ears burning? I just got a text from Holly which I planned to ignore again. It was weirdly nice.

Alex: I've gotten a blast today.

Terri: Ah, the calm before the storm?

Alex: More like the calm in the eye of the storm. We were supposed to go to trial yesterday on the restraining order violation, but it was cancelled due to this crazy weather. Martin has to testify…ugh. He is up to it and met with the prosecutor already, but it's not fun for any of us. Holly is "trying to avoid being evicted," which means she hasn't been paying rent.

Terri: Oh man. We all feared this would happen.

Alex: Yeah. She's been blasting me today with a bunch of 'how evil you are to me' texts, explaining how she would have never done what I did to her, etc. She has worn out her welcome with a bunch of folks who tried to help her.

Terri: She is perfect; we are all evil.

Alex: Yep.

Terri: Can she move in with that lady, the mom of Evelyn's friend?

Alex: Nope, that lady, Camille, is already tired of Holly coming over and staying far past the natural point of welcome. She had to tell her to stop coming over unannounced. When Evelyn plays with Camille's daughter, Holly tries to come over for any excuse. Camille shut that down pretty well.

Terri: Wow. How's Evie holding up?

Alex: She's is in the shower right now singing Rudolph! Cute. She's got the Miley Cyrus twang and slide thing going.

Terri: Haha twang and slide! So, Holly…Wow.

Alex: Yeah. She keeps throwing the blame on me. Usually I can let it just bounce off, but sometimes it digs.

Terri: Of course.

Alex: Minutes ago she was telling me today again how she would never sign any divorce papers. I almost replied and told her to stop sending these things to me. I erased it before sending.

Terri: Good for you. It's hard not to engage.

Alex: Yep.

Terri: I want to respond with the truth but she only wants to believe her own lie. It's like she enjoys the conflict, then feels vindicated or something when she proclaims her stance. My daughter does the same thing. Maybe the best way to torture them is to not respond....lol.

Alex: !! Yeah. I gotta go help the little squirt get her hair dry before we put up Christmas stuff.

Terri: Hang in there. Hug the twanger for me.

Alex: Thank you. Have a great night, see ya 'morrow if we have church. So much snow!

It was nice having Terri to bounce things off of, considering she had been the victim of Holly's harassment on numerous occasions after trying to be her friend.

I suddenly remembered I was supposed to be checking my email.

To: Alex
From: Holly

Alex,

All kiddos are not uncomfortable with me. It is you that is uncomfortable. Your attitude reflected in your deeds have been the reason for negativity for our family. You began choosing against my hopes while we were engaged and then continued to strip me of all I held dear. You hoped that your lies would eventually become my hopes. I am too hopeful and too strong to let you take my identity.

Mock me and take my babes with you. Takers never prosper. I am hopeful you become a giver again. You were created for so much more than the sorrowful life you have chosen for your family. Staying the night with my aunt one time in our marriage was NOT WORTH YOU BARRING ME FROM OUR HOME AND OUR CHILDREN.

God promises to help the righteous. I do not love you or the kiddos any less. My losses are making me stronger and more sure that God redeems the sorrows that evildoers bring upon the innocent. Your lies will find you out. Just like we taught our children. Lying is the most defiant sin. It challenges man to believe that God does not know all things.

Lovingly honest,

Holly

I'm beginning to see how Holly has now rendered her dramatic departure from the family as a simple one-time overnight at her Aunt's house. Unbelievable. New texts interrupted my analysis.

Holly: Katherine should call to make a plan so that I can plan around her.

Holly: Please ask Kevin to call. He called four times last week. He went somewhere alone with me last weekend. If he is hesitant it is because your attitude AND ACTIONS ARE NOT TEACHING HIM TO LOVE A WIFE AND HIS MOM.

December 21, 2008:

8:53 am

Holly: It is a beautiful morning! Please tell kiddos "Happy Lord's Day" from mom. There are Santa pictures being taken at The Walnut Café today. I know it is your day. If there is an opportunity between 1 and 4, I would love to do it.

3:16 pm

Holly: After speaking with many counselors this week, an answer to why kiddos were more tender and kind to weeks ago was found. You are nervous because I have a defense. Please remember to play act. HOW YOU FEEL CANNOT INFLUENCE THE KIDDOS. You require this of me. In mutuality, apply the same rule to yourself.

5:21 pm

Holly: I do not understand why you would be so unkind to me. I do know I love you despite your reason. I do know I would die for you. I do know I love the kiddos. I would die for them. Please ask the kiddos to call their mom. It would mean a great deal to me.

Holly: When I was given the Fred Meyer Gift Card I bought shoes and clothes for the kiddos. I have not seen Evelyn, Katherine, or Justin wear the shoes. Could you let me return them if they do not want them? Justin's black athletic shoes could be stretched, possibly. I cannot afford to waste the gift.

Holly: Did you get Katherine a microphone for Christmas?

Holly: Please give the kiddos a hug and tell them I love them.

Holly: We each have a week during Christmas break. The Parenting Plan stands. I have this week. You have next. Kiddos spend Christmas Eve with you.

December 22, 2008

To: Ron, Rachel
From: Alex

I need to address a couple of issues. 1) communicating vs. harassment, 2) Christmas break, 3) frequent and regular interruption during my days off with the kids.

1) I am finding it harder to swallow Holly's pointed anger toward me through her texts and e-mails. I'll send you some of her typical communications with me; it's similar to what you've seen already but is escalating. I want to keep communication avenues open with

Holly; I just don't know if there is a way to curb this manner of it. I have literally hundreds of messages from Holly that I am not recording or forwarding; it is too much to attend to.

The Restraining Order violation trial has been postponed due to weather, likely until Jan 7. Edmonds PD sent Holly a letter this week instructing her in the proper ways of using the police department and asking her not to use the PD to deal with her civil or divorce issues. I expect this is a precursor to the Internal Affairs findings which are expected any time.

2) I have twice asked Holly if she wanted to spend Christmas morning with the children, then they would have 3 pm on with me. This is a reverse of Thanksgiving, which worked out well. On 12/20 Holly responded, "Our original Parenting Plan stands for the holiday break. This was confirmed by Ron yesterday." Then tonight, 12/21, Holly wrote "We each have a week during Christmas break. The Parenting Plan stands. I have this week. You have next. Kiddos spend Christmas Eve with you."

Ron, please advise regarding the schedule during the kids' break, if there are to be any changes other than sharing the day on the holidays, 12/25 and 01/01. I am encouraging the kids to spend a good chunk of Christmas Eve with mom.

3) Ron, your last counsel to me about not responding to Holly's texts after the answer has been very helpful to me. However, the texts keep coming, and especially on the weekends while I am spending time with the children. This weekend, I received 28 texts on Saturday and 11 texts on Sunday, plus e-mails. This is typical. Holly continues to ask for different items of property and blame me for her entire situation, then she sneaks by the house to deposit bags of old food from the food bank on my porch. I understand that Holly's condition means I'll be managing awkward communications on a fairly regular basis, but I think at some point the "disturbing the peace" clause has some meaning. I will continue to avoid reporting this as a restraining order violation...I would rather the GAL or the court direct her to cease these kind of communications if that is even possible. This weekend, in addition to the messages, Holly made several requests for property to be delivered to her (Christmas decorations, photographs, etc.). I was able to work it out through a third party (whom Holly later condemned as a liar, thief, etc.), but it again was a distraction when I

was with the kids. Some of the kids became aware I was taking more ornaments to Holly and they complained, saying she already had more than we did....the result here is that the kids develop a further negative opinion of mom, something I am trying to protect against every day.

I know these things are tedious and may seem insignificant to a degree, but I am very concerned at this time (pending criminal trial, IA outcome likely unfavorable to Holly, pending eviction, holiday season) about Holly's sudden rise in confrontational and victim-syndrome behavior. I am still very much of the opinion that changing the schedule to afford more time for Holly to be with the kids will have an adverse effect on the children and their relationship with their mother. The children are doing increasingly well at home and at school.

My thanks,

Alex

9:49 pm

Holly: I always tell the kiddos that only God knows. I do not want them thinking that you, myself, or Ron Taylor will decide. No matter what men decide...God alone is the True Judge. You were taught this by one of your first commanders in Idaho.

December 23, 2008

The annual Holiday Threat Intelligence brief was typical: *We currently have no credible information of a particular threat to the United States*. It boggled my mind how the same useless phrase was used ad nauseam, especially only a month after the Mumbai attacks. The well-coordinated terrorist attack in Mumbai was still being dissected by every intelligence agency on the planet, only to conclude what was already readily apparent: It ain't over. Intelligence analysts and counterterrorism agents saw this as a complete game-changer, a model for future incidents. 300 injured, 174 dead, a burning Marriott Hotel, and world-wide coverage as it happened. The kind of stuff that made me want to keep doing this work.

Today, I would have to put international events into a local context for some regional mucky-mucks. These were the sponsors, the chiefs and supervisors of the local cops who had been assigned to the unit, each of whom had obtained a secret clearance in order to keep tabs on their off-campus troops. We found more commanders would attend the watered-down briefing of classified intel if we added a barbecue lunch. My boss, Sergeant Chuck Jensen, wasn't one to miss it.

Chuck waltzed his six-foot-three frame into the pink building like a kid in a candy store. I think he always wanted to get a little mixed up with some international espionage or something super cool. Supervising me let him live his fantasy vicariously. "Hey boss," I said. "I'm manning the grill so make yourself at home. Your briefing packet is on the conference table." He gave me the nod and made a bee-line for the unit supervisor, Nigel Marks.

"Nigel! Great to see ya." The glad-handing had begun.

"Looking good, Chuck," Nigel replied, taking charge of the handshake. "Get over here and get some of this grub. Alex is just bringing in his famous Infidel Ribs from the porch."

Country style pork, to be specific. It was cheap, but when boiled in beer and rubbed with some brown sugar, cayenne pepper, and salt, they really came to life on the grill.

"We're sure gonna miss this guy," Nigel said, walking Chuck toward his office. "This will be his last briefing before going back to real police work."

"He's not going to know what to do with himself," Chuck replied. "Although with his home situation, it may be a good thing for him to be closer to the kids right about now."

"What's with his wife?" Nigel asked, trying not to let me hear. It wasn't working but I managed to fane deafness.

"His *ex-wife* in about a month, hopefully," Chuck said. "She's nuts, man. I don't know how he juggled raising five kids on his own this year while getting constantly harassed by her. If it'd been me, I'm pretty sure I would have lost it already, or done something pretty stupid."

Nigel shook his head. "I don't know how he kept it together while keeping us all on our toes with our cases. This guy dug up more shit on local bad guys than we ever thought could exist. From the whole ferry thing to jihadi recruiters and terrorist financiers...yeah, we're gonna miss him."

"I have a feeling he'll be around, ready for that call," Chuck said.

"Soup's on!" I announced as my phone started blaring.

Nikki. I retreated to the break room. "This is Alex."

"You don't say? I was hoping so, since this is Alex's number." Nikki had the perfect amount of smart-ass in her voice. "Busy? You sound all official-like."

"Sorry," I said, realizing I had gotten into that mode. "I just delivered the ribs to the masses. Last briefing today, then I have a couple Guardian leads to run down followed by an interview of some guy in Shoreline who has Headquarters all spun up."

"What for?"

"You know I can't tell you that."

"Or you'd have to kill me, right?"

"You're a learner," I said.

"Can you come over tonight? I have a little Christmas present for you since I probably won't see you until after the holidays."

"Love to," I said. "I have a little somethin-somthin for you, too." At least I would by the time I arrived, probably involving chocolate. "Is your driveway clear yet?"

"Mostly," she said. "Logan Road is still a little dicey but nothing your car can't handle. Bed time is ten."

This dating thing had gone from super cool to freaking amazing. "Hmm. Oh crap, I gotta take a call." It was the station. "See you tonight!"

I clicked over. "Alex, I have the city prosecutor on hold for you. Can I put her through?"

I was simultaneously hopeful and horrified. *What now?*

"Do it."

# # #

Dating Alex was certainly an adventure. I wondered if the finalization of his divorce would make matters harder or easier. I still held out a fragment of hope that Holly would eventually settle down and become a little more reasonable, despite evidence to the contrary. Either way, like my sister, I was surprised I hadn't just cut and run. I usually have no problem at all putting things in my rear-view mirror.

I knew the holidays were about to bring a different level of challenge to Alex and the kids. I decided it would be prudent to give him a little extra space over the next week or two while he got through it. Part of me knew it was important for him to get through this one on his own.

# # #

3:11 pm

Alex: Terri! The prosecutor just called: Holly just pled guilty to the restraining order violation. Probation for 12 months. Martin won't have to testify now. It's over.

Terri: Good news!

Alex: Yep. Serious relief.

Terri: Is she mad? What does probation mean anyway?

Alex: Well...don't know if she is mad or not. Katherine is going to a movie with her so I will likely hear something pretty soon.

Terri: Hmmm...Katherine said "I am so done with her" on her Facebook status—was she talking about her mom?

Alex: Probably wasn't about the movie. Probation means she has to comply with all Superior court orders (family stuff) and have no other violations of law for 12 months. She got The Loft charges dismissed and has some community service hours to work. Overall it's a good thing. The prosecutor said her time in the courtroom was pretty, well, lively.

Terri: Wowzers. So does Katherine know about it?

Alex: No. And, sadly, last night Katherine was crying after a phone call with Holly where Holly was telling Katherine the kids were all supposed to be just with Mom during the first week of Christmas break, and only have Christmas eve with Dad, etc. The GAL got involved earlier in the day to clarify this was not the case. It seems Holly is not doing very well just understanding basic things. Yet she can still carry on a whopper conversation.

Terri: Wow. Just…wow. Hey, how's the lady friend? Are you guys still seeing each other?

Alex: Yeah, though the kids are still in the dark. She's a Godsend, Terri.

Terri: I'm so glad you guys found each other. Is it getting serious?

Alex: I don't know. We enjoy each other, that's for sure. I wonder sometimes why someone like her would choose to enter this crazy life I lead, or even if she'll stick around.

Terri: It's okay to be glad for some good, Alex.

Alex: Glad for that.

I didn't need Terri's approval, but it was definitely welcome.

December 24, 2008

To: Ron Taylor
From: Alex

Ron,

Yesterday, Holly entered a guilty plea at Edmonds Municipal court for the Restraining order Violation (DV). Both her 365-day jail sentence and most of the $5,000 fine were deferred for 12 months on certain conditions: No criminal violations of law or alcohol/drug related infractions, probation for 12 months, do not go upon the property and have <u>no contact</u> with Alex Hill or the children except as provided by the parenting plan or any restraining order, and continue with counseling as needed.

The Prosecutor told me the judge made it clear that Holly was to comply with all Superior Court orders and the parenting plan. I do not think the issue of a mental evaluation was specified. Holly's signature is on the document.

Alex

December 25, 2008

The kids had drawn names from a hat to decide who their 'person' was for gifting just as we had done since Kevin, number four, was born. A $20 limit meant I funded the whole exchange for $100, allowing each of them to find something they could give to their sibling. I had made my way out to Fred Meyer the night before to buy what I could for each of them with my remaining money, stretching each dollar as far as it would go. Fortunately, we would spend Christmas morning with my mom and sister in Marysville, both of whom loved to provide plenty of gifts for them to unwrap.

After the kids endured the afternoon with Holly, they returned home exhausted and with an inordinate amount of used clothing, trinkets, and general crap from their mom. Still, they made the best of it. I was proud of them.

The evening was more melancholy than I wanted, with a number of quiet, private moments as each of us realized our family had changed forever. When I tucked each of the kids in that night, their hugs had a deeper meaning than ever before. I had been warned about relying on the children for strength or comfort. But there was no denying the love they had for me.

December 30, 2008

To: Ron Taylor
From: Alex

Ron,

Evelyn has a friend from school named Chloe. Her mom, Camille, is the woman Holly wanted to live with a while ago. In the last few weeks, Holly has overstepped many boundaries with Camille, resulting in several interventions by Holly's church and now another call to the police, this time by Camille. Holly will likely be charged again with harassment.

This will directly effect Evelyn since Holly now sees Camille as an evil liar, etc. Holly has already threatened to turn Camille in to CPS over wild accusations and has demanded Evelyn not spend time with her friend. While I see Camille has a few human misgivings, she is not any danger to her child or ours. Chloe is a dear friend to Evelyn.

I am advising you of this so you are aware of Holly's continuing pattern of destroying relationships with people who try to help her, and of her rising agitation generally. Lots of yelling at Camille's apartment from Holly; Chloe is now afraid of Holly.

I will forward the report and citation (if issued) once it becomes available.

Sad.

Alex

December 31, 2008

12:39 pm

Holly: Will you please ask Justin if I can go with him to Harbor Square today, if he has not already gone?

Holly: Do you know true peace? Have you experienced the consolation of God's love to you through six beautiful family members loving you despite yourself? That is my prayer for you. I love you now as much as ever before.

Holly: You have the family home, financial security, a secure job, 5 children by 1 woman, parents that support you, beer to put you to sleep, our friends siding with you, continued fellowship with a church that sides with you against your wife, and control in the court system. You had a successful year. I hope you are truly content with your life.

Holly: From now on, every time I have the kiddos here I will review each text sent to you. It will help them know the number of requests and sweet comments towards them are made. It will also hold you accountable to truthfully pass on every kindness I endeavor to bring to fruition. There seems to be a gap in communication. Hopeful you are not the reason for the gap. I believe in what is best in you, Alex. Wish everyone at the Joyner's A Very Blessed New Year. I will check to see that you do this.

We spent New Year's Eve in the usual way, at Joyner's with a boat load of Presbyterians. The kids were slated to spend the night there after an evening of radical board games and skits. After we rang in the new year in with sparkling cider and a large box of illegal fireworks in the cul-de-sac, I said good-bye to the kids and headed to Nikki's house, calling her on the way.

"You up, sexy?"

"Just waiting for you."

Screw you, sparkling cider, I thought as I raced to Lynnwood. She was waiting, all right. At the door. We welcomed the new year in together in a very adult fashion.

And I still made it home before dawn.

8. DELAYS, DELAYS

January 1, 2009

A new year brought hope of a fresh start, a new beginning. And maybe a new-used vacuum, apparently, from a mystery donor on my front porch. Oh goodie. This thing was only about 40 years old, was bag-less, had a frayed cord, smelled like death, and was caked in other people's dirt. *I wonder who was so thoughtful to bring me a present so I'd find it this morning?* I let the dog out and ignored the lifeless device. *What on earth will she bring next?* For a split second I wondered what the neighbors thought. Too late for that, I suppose.

A new year also brought the reality of my re-assignment from counterterrorism to the patrol division. I was a wee bit concerned for my ability to fit into those nifty wool uniforms from 7 years and 25 pounds ago. 2008 took a significant toll on my body while I focused on anything but that. And though I still enjoyed police work, I was pensive being re-assigned from the most incredible work I'd ever done to juggling calls for service which could very well involve some of Edmonds PD's crazy customers. Some well known, crazy customers. Like my soon-to-be ex.

While it was frustrating watching my co-workers wind up in her target zone, it was probably best not having to face the Taser vs. pepper spray decision when arresting Holly in downtown Edmonds for refusing to leave a grocery store. Awkward is that understatement which comes to mind.

Time to face the music. Time to go back to work with the good people who have been dealing with Holly on the front lines. Terrorism? Eh, it can wait. Time to write some parking tickets. But first, two weeks of vacation to start the new year right. Gotta ease into these things, you know.

The trial for the divorce was scheduled to happen January 9, my actual reason for taking time off. This was crunch time. Would it ever end? Would I finally be able to openly introduce Nikki to my world? Why was I even waiting? Would Holly be able to convince the court she needs more than $1,000/month from me? Or that the kids should be obligated to spend additional time with her? Holly believed she was going to get primary custody of the children and have me finance her fantasy life with the kids, despite the amazingly crazy things she had done and the harm she had induced to them and to her own family. But would a judge be able to see through her rhetoric in the course of courtroom testimony? Being a police officer comes with a rising amount of skepticism and disbelief from many these days. *Am I the man she paints to the world? Am I the crazy one?*

Better have some cereal. Choices: Raisin Bran, Raisin Bran Crunch, Generic Raisin Bran, Fruit Loops, Honey Nut Cheerios. *Why are four of these seven boxes empty?* By compiling the ground remains of several boxes I came up with an adequate bowl of filler and sat down to eat, but my thoughts plagued me and keep me from resting. I took my bowl onto the back deck overlooking Shell Creek. The shallow stream running through the backyard had become a dear friend to me, reminding me that life continues to flow and move forward through all matter of scenery. As I breathed in the crisp, damp January air, I remembered today was a holiday, guaranteeing one thing: Extra text messages from Holly.

8:31 am

>**Holly**: Happy New Beginnings in 2009! Mercy is new each morning! Rejoice in the promise that faith to do God's will take you beyond anything your heart imagines. Imagination is a gift greater than knowledge. It is the truest form of intelligence. I stood in the tide with my pink boots at midnight and imagined you loving the children and I like "the best Fisherman" would. I believe God is going to open the eyes of your heart.

9:21 am

>**Holly**: hat time, would the kiddos like to come?

Did she mean "what time" or "hat time"? What the hell is hat time?

>**Holly**: Will you ask Katherine to call? I will miss our beautiful girl today.

10:06 am

>**Alex**: I will remind her. Kids have friends over, not available for hat time.

I couldn't resist.

10:55 am

>**Holly**: Will you do a Polar Bear Plunge with me at 1 pm? A group

called Edmonds Uplift does it together. Please. Please. Please. Maybe Martin or Justin would if you will not.

Are you out of your freaking mind, woman? Oh wait....

2:55 pm

Holly: are kiddos coming at 3?

Well, I was considering breaking the parenting plan for the first time ever....

2:56 pm

Alex: Yep. Boys are walking; I'm headed there with Evie now, will drop her off on Bell Street.

January 2, 2009

9:21 am

Holly: Good Morning—I am leaving myself available for the kiddos the next three days before they return to school. Their wishes are my commands for now. Please forward this on to them.

9:31 am

Alex: I don't forward texts to them but will be glad to remind them of this.

9:47 am

Holly: I will forward it to Ron. I will tell the kiddos That I sent it next time I am with them. Remember that Ron texted that I could spend extra time with them over the break. I did ask them if you had passed on texts from last week. They said no. Accountability is good for everyone.

Um...Ignoring that. Pot and kettle thing here.

10:12 am

Holly: I am going for a beach walk in the sunshine. Will you please call the kiddos and ask if anyone would like to go?

3:37 pm

Holly: So did you ask Evelyn if she wanted to go for a walk?

Alex: She is not home.

Holly: Okay. Is Katherine home yet? We only spent 2 hours together Tuesday.

Alex: No

January 3, 2009

9:12 am

Holly: There is an Awana Dinner tonight at church. Will you let the girls go with me? There are a lot of teens that are leaders in training. All family members are welcome. Of course, I would love it if you all came. Boys are welcome. Lots of cute servants there. ;-P

10:33 am

Holly: Will you ask Justin if we can work out together today? Then I can get the charger to him. Thank you (did you know these are Pooh's favorite 2 words? His favorite 1 is...BABY) Love you muchly.

11:47 am

Holly: Rsvp re: the Awana dinner tonight. Please and thank you with banana cream pie on top.

11:51 am

Alex: Evie, Katherine, and Kev are at friends tonight. I passed message to Justin re: gym/charger.

11:51 am

Holly: Okay. Thank you. Do I have to not be in Edmonds once you return to patrol? How will I know where you are going to be so that I do not break R.O.?

Oh, if only.

12:14 pm

Holly: The boys are welcome to join the Awana group for dinner at church. It is a free meal, as Joseph Joyner would say. ;-P

12:51 pm

Holly: Why do you have to take off two weeks between your FBI job and patrol? How will you be able to pay monthly bills on reduced salary? How are kiddos and I going to make it financially?

So much backspacing, so little time. The restraining order was clear that communications between the parties was to be about the children and only for the sake of coordinating the parenting plan. It was not open space to joust, belittle, entice, harass, reflect, proclaim undying love, plead for extra time, or anything else. I decided to ignore the messages which did not qualify as legitimate, hoping to reward only the reasonable.

After arranging activities for the kids for the day and dropping them off with friends for the night, I drove to Nikki's house to get ready for an evening at her sister's house. Elle was hosting a winter party and was apparently eager to bring me into the fold of the family. I was excited to do something together and to get to know her family. When I arrived, I filled Nikki in on the ongoing messages from Holly. Nikki had her own take on the uptick in unnecessary communications.

"Alex, you know she believes you will come back to her, right? It's as if nothing ever happened and she is planning to force you back from your wandering ways by leveraging money and kids. At some point you're going to have to fire off another warning note or something."

She was right, although I couldn't wrap my brain around the idea that Holly wanted me back. It seemed more likely she wanted me to lose my job or meet an untimely death.

"All in good time, hon." Wait, did I just...

"Did you just call me hon? As in honey? Honey sweetie-pie? Kicking it up a notch, eh, schmookums?"

After a nap which was more pleasant than restful, we took a look at the recent influx.

2:16 pm

    Holly: will the boys be coming to church for dinner?

2:45 pm

    Holly: will the boys be coming to church for dinner?

3:02 pm

    Holly: I want the Alex back that cherished the person Holly is. What are you willing to surrender to make that happen? I have surrendered my home, my children, my career goals, my position as a wife and mother, my status as a citizen treated equally with others, and my friends and family. What seems fair to you?

3:08 pm

Holly: Spoke to Officer Mike Lane today at The Walnut Cafe. He did not know you were divorcing me and that you stole the children away from their mom. ARE YOU embarrassed to tell ur partners at EPD WHAT YOU ARE ARE DOING?   Very commonplace for law enforcement officers to divorce their spouses. Join the 60% and hold your chin up.

3:16 pm

Holly: Justin left his Facebook login page on my desktop. I cannot get past his open page to my own Facebook. Can you have him call to help me?

4:05 pm

Holly: Your persistent lack of response to issues regarding the children is wrong. Please try hard to honor me.

"I'm starting to think she's not well," Nikki said.

# # #

January 4, 2009

Ok, I told myself, *it's official. I like this guy.*

Which means I'm probably crazy.

If tonight's party at my sister's was going to be anything like the last one, I'd be helping people out of the Hostas conspicuously planted next to the front porch and giving unsuspecting husbands garbage bags for the ride home.

Elle and I got our love of gatherings from our parent's ability to throw one hell of a party a few times a year. At the age of 12, I was a pretty good bartender and knew just when to disappear before the antics got too adult. I'd typically walk away with $100 cash in tip money. I learned: the heavier the pour the better the tips. I also learned to sense that moment when it was prudent to leave and not become the victim of a witnessing to something involving naked old people. Honestly, I learned that just a moment too late one summer at Lake Pend Oreille.

We arrived to find a dozen guests already inside. Most of them were somewhat familiar to me, however, the last time they saw me I was married to a really tall guy. This became an interesting conversation throughout the night. Several times, I introduced Alex as my lover and later switched it up to my bodyguard, all without Alex knowing.

While I was perfectly comfortable in this social environment, Alex was unfamiliar with this level of adulting fun. It only took a couple glasses of Makers Mark to loosen him up. At one point, I saw him pick up some devil horns and place them on his head, grinning ear to ear.

Around eleven o'clock, we called it a night. I poured Alex into the passenger seat and attempted to convince him how driving with the top down in January wasn't the best idea. He laughed all the way home at his own efforts to convince me otherwise, occasionally inserting comment about how cool my sister and her friends were. As we pulled up to his house a half hour later, there were a few lights on inside suggesting at least some of the kids were awake. He leaned over, gave me a kiss and giggled. He'd never come home drunk before. We laughed and kissed one more time. He quietly got out of the car, carefully squeezed the door shut, and crept up to the front door. Just as he was turning the handle, I tapped the horn twice. I could see him laughing in my headlights while he stood on the porch shaking his head, followed by additional house lights starting to flicker on inside.

I couldn't wait to hear how he managed to explain his condition to his kids!

# # #

I vaguely remembered getting out of bed to let the dog out, then fending off the finger pointing, commentary, and stares from the kids as they tried to interpret their father's first known hangover. I was not very capable of helping this process and quickly returned to bed, hoping the anvil on my brain would subside.

Consciousness returned to me in its usual way, my phone buzzing on the night stand. Of course, it refused to wait for the headache to pass. I drew the strength of my unidentified ancestors to lift my troubled frame away from the pillow and grab the buzzing phone.

10:27 am

> **Holly**: Remind Martin and Justin that there is dinner before Youth group at 6 pm tonight at church.

Well that was worth it, I thought. A hot shower, a cup of coffee, and some warmed up leftovers from sometime earlier this week were sufficient to bring me back to the land of the living. I called Nikki. "You did this to me."

"Oh no, you did this to yourself, big fella," she replied. "I only provided the environment and a tiny bit of encouragement. Feeling perky?"

"Rmph."

Nikki laughed. "Well, you were a lot of fun, that's for sure. Can't wait to show you the pictures."

"The *what*? Oh, Lord, you have evidence?"

"And video," Nikki said. "You were amazing leading the rendition of Sweet Caroline with your horns. Hey, I gotta run. Call ya tonight?"

"At your own risk."

I hung up the phone trying to play the tape back in my head of the previous evening. There were a few gaps, but I did recall singing that song with everyone. I did not recall leading the charge.

At around 6:45 pm, I discovered two bags of random food in plastic bags on the front porch of my home when I let the dog out. The footprints crossing the driveway in the light dusting of snow looked to be about a size 8. *Did she just come to my house again? And leave food?*

7:00 pm

> **Holly**: Mr. Spy, please tell the kiddos I love them and would do anything to help them. Let me know if there is anything you want delivered to your home again. Come rain, sun, sleet, or snow I will do it for any of you. I would love to hear from the kiddos.

7:31 pm

> **Holly**: I volunteer at the Edmonds Food Bank on MONDAYS AND TUESDAYS. If school is cancelled the kiddos can come and serve. It is a beautiful testimony of giving to the poor from the

abundance of others.

8:13 pm

> **Holly**: I love you. Pass it on to our children. Good-night to you all.

I didn't miss the fact that her "volunteering" at the food bank was actually her court-ordered community service. The irony was also not missed that she had placed the exact product of her community service onto the very porch which landed her in community service in the first place. But since she didn't step inside, and I didn't have actual proof it was her, and perhaps because it was yet another example of how crazy she is and how I could potentially use this microcosm as an apt example of who she really is in some future novel, I let it go.

At least she loves me. *Oh, GOD!*

January 5, 2009

6:11 am

> **Holly**: Standing Sentinel. A man stands expecting the worst from me. He stands between what is dear to my heart. He wields a power that protects his fortress and puts enmity between myself and my destined allies. He once was my comrade and now is my earthly judge. He anticipates my pending doom.

6:17 am

> **Holly**: He is the chosen husband of my youth. He is the man I longed to please. He is the reason for the sacrifices of my own desires. He is the shared life-source of the offspring of my inner sanctuary. He is now my separated companion. I love him.

6:37 am

> **Holly**: Good Morning! Please tell the kiddos I love them and am praying for their start to a new season in school again. Tell them that their mom treasures them.

2:22 pm

> **Holly**: Will you please see if Evelyn will meet me for dinner tonight for Mexican pizza downtown?

I had to do something about this or Holly would succeed in running my cell phone battery dry. Not to mention my will to live.

4:30 pm

To: Rachel Townsend
From: Alex
Subject: Phone call

Rachel,

I drafted this, then thought better to send it to you. Please take a look and let me know if I should just suck it up and wait another two weeks until the divorce trial. I'm concerned that her coming onto my porch yesterday and today's phone call are demonstrating her increasing refusal to observe boundaries.

> *Holly,*
>
> *I received your text message request to have Evelyn for dinner this afternoon, followed by a telephone call from you and subsequent voice mail message repeating your request. The court orders are clear on this matter: communication between us is restricted to e-mail and text messaging, the texting being intended for brief, necessary communications about the children and logistics of scheduled visits. I do not want you to call me.*
>
> *Regarding the text messages, please reduce the volume of texts you have been sending by simply limiting the communication to what the court order directs. Keeping communications available between us for the kid's sake is important to both of us, but it does not mean you can ask me to pass messages to the kids every day, nor does it give you the right to harass me with pointed jabs about how you think I stole the children from you, how I am blind to the truth, or have ruined your life. You are of course welcome to think what you believe, and I don't mean to criticize that; just please do not continue to confront me with it. I understand your position and do not need to hear about it every day.*
>
> *Thank you,*
> *Alex*

Thanks again for all your help here, Rachel.

Alex

5:01 pm

To: Alex
From: Rachel Townsend

Sounds fine and I was thinking that someone should send such a note.

I am also glad you have remembered to get yourself into the For Kids Sake seminar. I plan to sit down and prepare a list of things for you to do to get ready for the trial, such as collecting various docs re assets and debts, etc. Without the results of the internal investigations from your Chief and the delay in the GAL report, Holly may be successful getting the trial continued.

Rachel

January 9, 2009

12:08 pm

To: Ron, Rachel
From: Alex

It's painful to continue to have to document these things, but I think you will see why.

Yesterday, right after the kids' visit with Holly, I took Katherine to a 4-H meeting. Katherine said Holly wanted to come to her choir class. Katherine told Holly she didn't want her to come, but Holly persisted. Katherine is concerned that Holly will come anyway. Katherine also mentioned that mom's new boyfriend and boss is no longer around since he tried to have sex with her. I re-directed the conversation to how it's good that Mom wants to be involved with her and how great 4-H is.

Holly then sent the following at 7:03 pm: "**Remember I had asked if I could do gingerbread houses with Evelyn's class? Now you are going instead. Why shun me this way?**"

Ron, you will recall the Principal decided not to have Holly come to the school for this event due to her behavior at the school and in many subsequent phone calls in the Fall. Mrs. Stark has not changed her position on this. I have been volunteering time at the school on my off days, including today for the gingerbread event. Still, I'd support Holly going to special events after school when cleared by the school administrator.

At 7:08 pm, she sent the next one: **"Did Ron speak to you about Camille? Be sure the girls do not get left alone and that Camille does not call me a fucking bitch in front of Evelyn. It is hurtful that your companions are hateful to the children's mom."**

Ron, you've already clarified there was no need at this point for any prohibition about Evelyn's time with Chloe or her mom, Camille. I believe you are aware that Holly has been cited by Edmonds PD for harassment of Camille.

This morning, January 9, Holly sent this at 8:08 am: **"Have fun at Evelyn's school doing what you said I would get to do with her. I am sure the other moms will enjoy your presence. Why do you enjoy being my enemy? <u>Maybe you would like to try to kill me again like 2 years ago</u>."**

Ron, there are so many crossed lines in Holly's messages to me, but this one is alarming to me. Holly starting to talk about killing again; this was something she did several times prior to taking a bottle of pills...projecting that I wanted her to be dead or similar statements.

On the other hand, the kids' visit appeared to go well Thursday night.

Alex

8:43 pm

To: Rachel, Alex, Ron
From: Holly

To all involved,

Last night Evelyn became frustrated again at not being understood. No one could comfort her. She went into the bathroom and hid under a towel and started hitting herself in the face. She is so desperate to be truly loved for who she is.

It is not uncommon for a child that was unwanted to be ignored and unheard. Obviously, the gap of age tells you all that there was hesitation about the last two Hill children. Alex did not want Evelyn. I fought to be true to my conscience. I had told Alex in marriage counseling before we wed that I hoped to have a large family and would not do anything unnatural to prevent the offspring. After Evelyn, Alex agreed with my doctor that I should stop the process. I saw a doctor today that confirms what my OB-GYN has advocated for. I am still fertile and should never have had the tubal ligation. It disconnected and disturbed the core of my being.

Please release Evelyn from the bond of Alex's control and misguided thinking. She deserves to be loved for who she is created to be. Her time with Camille Zuber is not best. Camille has lied many times to me. She is a very heavy drinker. She was abused by a man last year who is stalking her. He came by one evening while Evelyn and Chloe (both 8 years old) were left alone by Camille. I am having Carrie Menzel, Domestic Violence Coordinator for Edmonds, help me research Camille's situation. Alex should be fully aware of her ex-husband's abuse. He was the officer that responded in Shoreline after Camille had been beaten to a pulp.

Please stand up for our daughter's safety. She does not deserve to be in any threatening situation right now. Guard her sense of security. She wakes up at night frightened and seeking comfort. Please advocate for what is best for our children.

Sincerely Hopeful,

Holly Hill, Alex's Wife and Evelyn's Mom

# # #

9. FINALLY FINAL

January 21, 2009

> **Alex**: Trial postponed two weeks while new attorney gets up to speed for Holly. I've cancelled my day off and am headed in to work.

I had long since lost any concern that Alex would not go through with the divorce; Holly was clearly crazy and hell-bent on his destruction. But the last-minute delay emphasized yet again the unpredictable nature of Alex's world. I'm not gonna lie: this gave me some pause. I had already been anxious about the prospect of moving this relationship to the next level by meeting Alex's kids. The two-week delay gave me time to ponder if this is really the direction I wanted to go. He's a real neat guy and all…but this thing is laden with drama and risk, two things I'm not normally accustomed to voluntarily inherit. Still, among all the instability was this unexplainable level of strength and calm that I craved.

Maybe I'm the crazy one.

# # #

February 4, 2009

After Holly used the two-week delay to retain her 4th attorney, I sat in the waiting room of Rachel Townsend's office before the proceedings, wondering how I got there. I was alone, at the brink of the official end of my marriage with the actual safety and welfare of the kids hanging in the balance. In my mind, I still wrestled with thoughts of doubt, wondering if I had truly done everything I could to save the marriage, wondering if I had made the right decision to file for divorce, wondering if the impact of this path I'd chosen would be best for the kids, or be best for anything.

"Come on in, Alex," Rachel said from her open door. I hadn't noticed. "We've got about ten minutes before we head over to the court.

# # #

Nikki: Hey. Hang in there.

There was no answer. I didn't expect one, I just wanted him to know I was pulling for him. I wanted him to be reminded that in spite of how hard this must be for him, there was life after divorce.

I had complete confidence he would prevail, but the judges in Snohomish County weren't exactly predictable. Nobody in their right mind would let that woman have primary or any sort of real custody of her kids. But if some man-hating, bleeding heart freak who didn't bother to read the entire file wound up on the bench that morning, all Alex's efforts could be for naught. If this didn't go well, I was worried my master prankster status may morph into something a little darker. That is, if I elected to keep this whole thing going.

I caught myself wondering again if I should even be in this relationship. After several months experiencing Alex's grief and the disintegration of his model family, it was clear to me that a relationship with him was going to be complicated, at a minimum. His job wasn't going to get any easier. The needs of the children were not going to get simpler. He had at least another 8 years dealing with his ex, who might not welcome the fact that I was becoming a mother-figure to her kids. The simple life with a clean house, predictable work schedule, and healthy finances could very well become a thing of the past if I continued down this road. I could wind up being a *stepmom*. Of *five* kids!

They clearly needed one, that was for sure. And this man, this good man, needed someone to be there for him. Alex was the last person on his own list of people to care for. That would catch up with him pretty quickly.

But it may catch up with me even quicker.

# # #

Day two of the proceedings involved the finishing of my testimony along with the presentation of witnesses. The judge said he would take all things into consideration before rendering his decision on February 19th, two weeks later.

February 5, 2009

To: Rachel, Ron
From: Alex

1. I have received the Chief's final memo regarding my internal investigation. The complaint has been found "not sustained" on 6 counts and "exonerated" on the 7th. This means all accusations against me either have no merit or are without evidence to support them.

2. Holly texted me yesterday saying she has found a new room for rent, but I have no other details. The last three places she said she would be staying at have all fallen through. I believe she thought she had a place but the homeowner thought differently. I have requested information for her plan for the kids' visit this Thursday and the weekend, but have not heard back. She is upset that I don't pass every one of her communications to the kids (tell the kids good morning, tell them goodnight, etc.).

3. This text just in: **Holly**: Still sleeping in Suburban. Trying hard to secure something by tomorrow.

That's about it. Oh, Kevin sprained his other wrist at lacrosse practice today. We're starting a collection on the wall of braces and splints...sort of a collage....

Alex

# # #

February 19, 2009

It was the long-awaited day when a Snohomish County commissioner would render his decision about Alex's divorce. I pride myself on not being a home wrecker, or at least that's how I always considered myself. I don't date married men. Well, at least I *didn't* date married men. I didn't really consider Alex married; they had been separated for a year and the separation was more severe than just a couple people in an argument. But technically he was still legally bound to that woman until sometime around 9:30 am today. I never wanted to be "the other woman" who was being comforted by her boyfriend that it would all be over soon, and we could be free to live our dreams in the light of the sun. And here I was craving this day to be over so that there would be no hesitation for either of us moving forward.

Oh, shit. That means I'd actually have to meet the kids. While I was super excited to know them personally, I was simultaneously terrified to meet them. I just don't know how to manage the expectations, or lack thereof, from *five* of them.

While getting dressed and mapping out my day, it dawned on me that this significant day was also a Thursday. Odds are, the regular Thursday visit had a strong chance of drama or being fully disrupted. I wondered if Alex had a backup plan. It was after 6 am, so I knew he was up for the day. I gave him a call. "Whachya wearing?"

"I made it past my socks. Now I'm between the white shirt and the blue shirt."

"Go with the white. You don't want to be a power broker."

"Good call."

"And a red tie. I'm sure you got plenty of those, you freaking *Republican*."

"It's more of a maroon," he said. "I have a bunch of blue ties, I'll have you know."

"Okay, go with a blue one. By the way, I was thinking about the kids and their pending visit today after the oral decision. If this doesn't go the way Holly's fantasy demands, she may blow a gasket and totally lose it. Are the kids still planning on going over to her place today? Isn't it that massive house off Talbot Road now?"

"They are, and that is the place she's living, at least for now. I got a call from her landlord yesterday; he was asking all kinds of questions having come to the conclusion that she is a wee bit cray-cray."

"People seem to be figuring it out a lot quicker these days," I said.

"Very true," he said. "It used to take two or three weeks interacting with her. Now by week two, even the people with big hearts for her start to get it. She's really starting to deteriorate."

Alex had long accepted the fact that Holly's behaviors and risky lifestyle increased her overall risk of survival, but it still tapped into his heart of compassion. Several times between Thanksgiving and January, Holly's parents and siblings had reached out to Alex all concerned that she was getting suicidal again. Every time she got kicked out of a business or evicted by a landlord, Holly made her desperation known by leaving messages on her family's phones either sobbing uncontrollably or yelling at them for 'siding' with Alex. The reality was nobody trusted her anymore, which only added to her despair. Her sisters had warned her that she could lose all rights of being a parent, but that never seemed to have its intended effect.

I knew that this would be an emotional day for Alex, regardless of how ready he was to move on. There was no way in hell Holly would win custody of the kids, which meant Holly was on the edge of losing the very thing that she lived for. As crazy as she really was, there was no doubt Holly very much loved her kids, to the degree she was able. When today's hearing was finished, the judge will have read his decision and likely granted Alex's version of the parenting plan with severe restraints on Holly. She would wind up more alone than she's ever been. It would be the right thing for the kids, for Alex, and honestly even for Holly.

"Maybe this will be the thing that forces her to get the mental health help she needs," I suggested.

"I hope so," Alex replied. "It would be good for all of us."

#

The hearing didn't start on time as Holly was late. Her attorney stood at the front of the courtroom looking like she was as confused as any of us. Thoughts rushed through my mind as I sat in the long oak pew on the right side of the aisle. Had she given up? Did she wreck another car? Did she jump in front of a train? Did she just run away? Was she even alive? The bench seats in the courtroom were identical to the ones in the church Holly and I had attended for eight years, the church where I had been a deacon. *Same seats, different day,* I thought. A very different day.

After about 20 minutes, the judge entered the room as the clerk announced, "All rise. The honorable Judge Kevin Stevens presiding." Judge Stevens took roll like a professor in a master's class. Holly's attorney sheepishly told the judge she didn't know where her client was.

"I've called, texted, and emailed her several times over the last hour, your honor. I'm not getting any response. She was supposed to meet with me 45 minutes ago and she didn't show. I'm honestly a little worried."

The judge didn't seem to be stunned. "Given the number of delays in this matter and the dynamics of the parties involved, I'm going to move forward and give my decision now. Counsellor, you are welcome to follow up with your client at a later date to ensure she is aware of the outcome."

"I'll take care of that, your honor," the attorney said.

The judge then read a prepared statement over the course of the next 15 minutes. He waxed eloquently starting with quotes from famous authors about the nature of marriage and love, and the fragility of both in our modern world. He pointed out the victims of failed marriages are always the children first, even in extreme circumstances where divorce is a good and necessary thing. By the time he was finished, it was clear that my parenting plan was being enacted without any variation imposed by the court. Holly would be restrained to communicating with me only for the purpose of fulfilling the parenting plan, and only by email or text message. She was not to initiate any communication with the children until she underwent a full mental health evaluation and complied with any treatment deemed appropriate by an approved care provider. If she complied with this and showed significant progress in her ability to be emotionally and physically stable, she could then re-visit the residential schedule. Until then, the children would live with me and visit Holly on Thursdays after school to 7 pm, and every other Saturday from noon to 7 pm. The children could request additional time with their mom on Saturday evenings overnight to Sundays pending approval by me. The judge gave me considerable latitude to make alterations in the best interests of the children, having commented on my ability to make good choices for the kids over the past year and more.

I felt a swarm of relief and vindication come over me while I listened to the judge. Memories of good times together as a family were overlaid with memories of Holly's anger, yelling, pulling the girls' hair, blame, and demands. I had been willing to stay in this marriage until Holly finally left. Now it was officially over. In spite of the massive relief, I also felt a huge weight of grief creeping in. I never planned on this kind of ending.

But one question remained for all of us. *Where was Holly?*

# # #

Alex walked in the wide-open front door of my rambler in what had become his typical style. I liked keeping the house cold for some reason. "Knock-knock, c'mon in," he announced. I met him in the front room in a fantastic embrace with a lasting kiss. I gripped his shoulders the way I had at our first meeting, noticing his muscles had become even more tight. I took his hand and led him to the kitchen. "So, she didn't even show?"

"Nope. And nobody knows where she is." Alex sounded both worried and giddy. "At least there was no blow-ups in the courtroom!"

"Yeah, there's that," I said. I pulled out a bubbling tray of chicken cordon blue from the oven. "Dinner's ready. Would you pour the wine for us?"

Alex devoured the meal and told me the gritty details of the judge rendering his decision. "So where are the kids?"

"I told them that mom wasn't available for the visit today but didn't explain why. Terri and the Kirkland clans invited everyone over to their place tonight since school is out tomorrow. I told Martin to go ahead and take the gang over after school. They landed about an hour ago and are already in Xbox heaven and eating gluten-filled white bread. Sort of a surreptitious celebration, I suppose."

I topped off Alex's glass. "Sounds good to me," I said, looking slyly at him. "Did I ever tell you about the 15-second stare?"

"No. Is this one of your Yoda tricks?"

"Maybe. Actually, yeah…" I let my voice linger a bit and stared at Alex's eyes for a solid fifteen seconds. He looked down, then looked up again to see me still at it. "It's one of my go-to techniques when I want to let a man know that I'd like to take off his pants." I looked down toward his fly, then raised my eyebrow and tipped my head slightly backwards with my lips barely apart. I could see him beginning to swell.

The dishes never even made it to the sink that night.

# # #

Sgt. Chuck Jensen's voice was loud enough in the stillness of the morning that I was sure Nikki could hear it over my phone, even above the fan in her bedroom making the winter morning unreasonably cold. I would never understand why a 62-degree room needed further cooling. "So Alex, did you hear what happened?"

"No, Sarge," I said, trying to sound alert at 6:30 am, my head pulsating from whatever fluid I had consumed the night before. "What's up?"

"Holly was arrested Wednesday night for trespassing at the grocery store."

"QFC? But those people are total pacifists! What did she do?"

"You're never going to believe this," he started, which only led my mind to the darkest of places. Fortunately, he started laughing.

"Get control of yourself, man!"

"Sorry," he said, taking deep breaths. "It's just so..." He needed few more internal yoga poses to submerge the humor. "Okay. Holly went there and started yelling about one of the managers, accusing him of raping her in front of a bunch of customers. We had trespassed her last week from the store when she kept coming back to the store trying to get the manager to let her live with him. Alex, I'm not sure if you knew this, and I'm sorry if it's disturbing...but apparently Holly and the manager got romantically involved at some point. On Sunday, the manager called 911 to have her trespassed from the business after she refused to stop contacting him there. He had tried to cut off their short relationship after figuring out she was crazy, but as you can imagine, that didn't stop her—she kept badgering him at work until this episode when her version of their events had a dramatic change in the facts." I could see Nikki's wide eyes in the dark room as she had propped herself up on her elbow. This was better than daytime television.

Sgt. Jensen continued. "So when Sgt. Wudarki told her to leave or be arrested on Wednesday night, she refused to budge until he told her she was under arrest. Holly started yelling when Wudarki took her arm to put her in handcuffs, then shoved him and started running across the parking lot. Wudarki chased her through the parking lot, Holly screaming nonsense all the way about being assaulted by the police and abuse of authority. And you know Wudarki, Alex...Woody's not exactly the sprinter he used to be, if you know what I mean."

I visualized Wudarki, only two years away from retirement, reluctantly running through the parking lot chasing Holly, trying to convince her to stop before using any force. That is, if she didn't just outrun him. "So did he catch her?"

"That's the funny part," Jensen said. "He didn't stand a chance until Officer Lane showed up and cut her off when she tried to cross the road in traffic. She ran into the stopped police car and started yelling about how everyone was trying to run her down. Wudarki finally caught up and got her in handcuffs after catching his own breath while she kept screaming. It was quite a scene, right there in the middle of the road, especially with Lane laughing his ass off."

These were my co-workers and friends. As hysterical as it was to think of Wudarki chasing Holly, I felt horrible that they were roped in to dealing with the craziness of my life again. "Well," I said, "that explains why she didn't show up to our final court date for the divorce."

"Seriously?" he said.

"Yeah. Chuck, I'm so sorry our department has to deal with this."

"Don't worry about it, Alex. We're all together when it comes to shit like this, and you aren't the first one to deal with a crazy ex. Okay, maybe yours is a little crazier than the average, but still, we deal with nut-jobs every day. It's just our role."

He was right. The police had become the front line on dealing with mental illness, regardless of how well-equipped we were to handle the task.

I hung up with Chuck as Nikki flipped on the light. "Oh. My. God," she said. "You just can't make this shit up! You need to write a book."

Later that day, Rachel copied me in on her note to the new attorney.

From: Rachel Townsend
To: Laura Mattson

Hi Laura:

In case you are unaware, Alex learned the reason that Holly wasn't present at the oral decision was because she was in jail. She was arrested the prior night for trespass at the food store where a friend

138

of hers worked—evidently someone with whom she had a personal relationship. Alex didn't know where she was exactly or when she would be released.

Alex also advised me that to the best of his knowledge, Holly is no longer at the Talbot Road address. He understands she had started to move her things out the day she was arrested.

Rachel

While I realized Holly's incarceration was temporary and not any sort of real solution, I still held out hope it would start the ball rolling on getting her the help she needed. Maybe going to jail would be that "rock bottom" so many of our friends kept saying she'd have to hit before turning a corner.

Holly: I forgive you. Forgiveness is king over the laws of men.

Holly: I'll never forget how you used your position to deny me the right to love our children. Due to your selfish abuse of authority, I expect to see the children this weekend.

Holly: My redeemer lives, even in the darkest of places. I found two new friends who also were maligned by convincing men. We are finding ways to help each other.

Seems like rock bottom keeps getting re-defined.

# # #

10. BIRTHDAY SEASON

And with that, shit just got real. Now that Alex was legally divorced, he would be eager to introduce me to the kids. All of them. Should I meet the kids one by one? Or just rip the Band-Aid off and do it all at once? Alex invited me over for breakfast this morning, so I have a feeling the decision is going to be made for me. I'm not real accustomed to sharing control in my world.

I made my way to the new, swanky Frost Donuts shop in Mill Creek to pick up a box of the latest craze: the bacon maple bar. I was early enough to score a dozen of the new fangled bad boys. I selected another dozen to include lemon filled, raspberry filled, huckleberry cake, apple fritter, old fashioned glazed, chocolate Bismarck, Homer, powdered sugar, glazed buttermilk, and plain maple bar. As the clerk was boxing them up, it dawned on me that I was participating in an age-old stereotype. I was buying donuts for a cop's family. With bacon.

Rude? Heh, heh.

A half hour later, I took several deep breaths before pulling into Alex's driveway. I thought I was ready. I thought I was prepared.

I was very, very wrong.

#

Nikki pulled into the driveway in her beautiful black convertable, prompting ten eyeballs to gawk out the front window. They all yelled in unison. "Dad! Your GIRLFRIEND is here!"

"And she has donuts!" Kevin yelled. All five of them scrambled for the door, which in itself was a sight to behold. It was like combining an Irish version of the Three Stooges with the running of the bulls at Pamplona. Someone was bound to get hurt, and none of them cared.

Justin beat his way to the front door where he flung it open, the other four cramming the doorway around him to see Nikki walking up the stairs. Nikki exuded confidence, causing the children to stare in awe as she stopped in front of them. Evelyn broke the silence, looking up at Nikki with her head tilted. "Are those for us?"

"It would be rude for me to keep them to myself, don't you think?"

Evelyn squinted, then nodded. The siblings all followed suit, looking like a door full of bobble heads until Nikki handed the box to Justin with instructions. "Take them to the kitchen. We'll share them in a bit."

And with that, they were gone (kids and donuts), leaving me with Nikki alone at the front door. "Won't you come in?" I asked, taking her hand.

Nikki caked on her airy, seductive tone. "I just want...a bacon maple bar."

"A what? You couldn't just bring donuts, you had to add bacon? What kind of cop do you think I am?"

She leaned in. "Gonna go out on a limb here...one who likes..." She put my hand on her chest. "...donuts. And bacon." She blinked a couple extra times and pulled my hand to her mouth, putting her teeth around my pinkie.

Kevin's voice rose above the dull roar of the others. "Rmphf mar gaahd! Deesh ah sho guud!" I looked up to see him with two half-eaten bacon maple bars occupying his hands, only because he had already crammed another whole one in his mouth. I glanced back at Nikki and shook my head with the look of, "I have no idea how he happened." I accidentally said it out loud.

"Pfritty shuur ahma-doptid," Kevin coughed out in response. Nikki stayed in character and addressed the 12-year old redhead.

"Kevin, swallow."

"That's what he said!" Justin exclaimed from the kitchen, quite proud of himself.

Katherine chimed in. "Ew, Justin!"

"Watch this," Martin said, as he tipped up a glass of milk and filled the rest of his own donut-packed mouth with the white liquid. Unable to entirely contain himself, he turned toward Kevin and blasted the milk out his nose.

# # #

The scene I had just witnessed was difficult to explain in chronological order; perhaps it's just easier to describe the result. All five kids were sent to the showers after spending ten minutes trying to mop the kitchen like only a group of five kids of a single dad could do it. It wasn't pretty, but it more or less got the job done while Alex and I hung out in the front room pretending not to care. Miraculously, the second box of donuts and a single bacon maple bar remained unscathed.

"Want me to come back later?" I asked.

"Nah, we're good," Alex said. "It's just another Saturday. Let me show you around while the gang finishes getting cleaned up."

We walked down the hall past the main bathroom where Katherine and Evelyn were draining the hot water tank. "Save the whales," Alex yelled as we passed by. Opposite the bathroom was an open bedroom door. I could see a thick bunk bed made of heavy pine. More importantly, I could smell the unmistakable odor of boy. Athlete boy, to be precise. The next room was for Katherine and Evelyn, who clearly struggled deciding how many stuffed animals constituted too many stuffed animals. Their twin beds were capable of bunking, but instead had been set parallel to each other with a dresser between them at the heads. Two dressers capped off the other end of the room, with a standard sized closet. The doors to the closet leaned out at the bottom, causing me to deduce they had crammed stuff in the closet while "cleaning."

Across the hall, Alex's master bedroom had its own sliding door to the long deck overlooking the creek in the back yard. The room was stark with little or no decoration. A queen-size bed straight out of the 70's filled the better part of the room, with a white Martha Washington style blanket on top. Complete with tassels. Clearly a holdover from Holly's homemaking. At the end of the bed was a laundry basked full of, how shall I say....mail. Junk mail. In the laundry basket. On the dresser was a bankers box with manila folders and papers overflowing the edges. In one corner I saw a walk-in closet with very few clothes hanging in it. Most of the clothes were in a pair of laundry baskets on the closet floor. The attached bathroom was the narrowest one I'd ever seen, complete with black and white checkered tile flooring and some gaudy bright brass fixtures.

Alex took me downstairs revealing the daylight basement. The stairs emptied out into a pink carpeted transition area with two adjacent rooms on the back side of the house: a bathroom heavily involved with shower activity by three boys doing the round-robin thing, and a laundry room. Or at least I assumed it was a laundry room, since there was a wall of laundry baskets stacked shoulder-high with clothing spilling out between the layers, creating the slopes and glaciers to the entire structure. I could see a utility sink inside the door and was pretty sure I saw a washer/dryer against the far wall. I knew better than to look into the sink. There was something odd about the laundry machines but I couldn't put my finger on it. Plus, I was quickly distracted again by the sheer volume of laundry.

"It's getting a little behind, but I'll crash through a good chunk of it tomorrow, probably when I'm on the phone with you," Alex said. "And this over here is Martin's room." I couldn't tell if Alex was ignoring the 5,000 moving boxes loosely stacked in the open area between the laundry room and Martin's room, but he failed to address the elephant in the room, so to speak. I could see evidence of past attempts to find things among the stacks of boxes. Two or three narrow trails remained visible despite the overflowing stacks and the refusal of their contents to stay inside the boxes. I thought the smell of the boys room was going to be my nemesis, the one thing that caught my stomach off guard. I was wrong.

Alex nonchalantly continued the tour. "And this is the rec room." The floor was still pink, mostly. The navy colored couch showed signs of extreme wear involving food and sibling rivalry. I must have been staring at the 20-year old television and its armoire-looking cabinet. "Those were commandeered from a fire sale at the Everett Red Lion by my parents before it was torn down." *How resourceful*, I thought. I then noticed the lower outer window pane closest to the front porch was smashed, which Alex explained was due to an errant lacrosse ball hurled by an unnamed suspect.

I could see some lines in the carpet, proof that Alex had spent his morning "cleaning" before my arrival. I started to realize how I was cataloguing ways to fix things in my mind. Then, right then, for a split second, I hit my limit. My entire life flashed before my eyes. This was that bright light moment they all talk about, when those who suddenly are faced with the loss of their own life are wonderfully drawn into the great beyond, that place where peace, joy, and bliss await. My life, at that very moment, was changing forever, and the heavens were letting me know. The old life of simplicity was fading to black. The new life of family-style love and joy was taking over.

Nobody said anything about laundry.

Somehow, I snapped out of it as Alex led me outside through a sliding glass door next to Martin's room. The west side of the yard was shaded mostly by a large tree with a swing Alex had made and hung from a low branch. Shell Creek flowed behind the house, generating a perfectly beautiful sound as water flowing over small rocks toward Puget Sound. The creek was about a foot and a half deep and five feet wide. Behind the creek was a place Alex referred to as "the back forty" where the family dog would take care of his business. He even washed his feet on the way back.

The peaceful sounds of the cool flowing water quickly comforted me. I realized how important that creek had become to this family. It had been a source of comfort to each of them countless times. Not to mention it separated them from the immediate responsibility of countless piles of poop.

We made our way back to the front of the house and into the kitchen where the children had re-emerged. This time, I somehow smelled fresh-cooked bacon. I was trying not to say anything this time, but Alex sensed I was trying to determine the source of that old familiar smell.

"I put it in just as you were getting here," Alex explained.

"In? In *what*, exactly?" *Please God, don't let him do microwave bacon.*

"In the oven." Alex opened the oven door, releasing a wave of steam and light smoke from the oven. He pulled out a large aluminum cookie sheet covered in…bacon.

"You…baked it?"

"Every time," he said as he scraped the bacon from the pan onto a plate. "It's a whole lot easier than trying to flip it, especially with kids trying to become chefs. Twenty-two minutes and cleanup's a breeze."

I'd seen a lot of things, but I'd never seen this. Or most of what I had experienced in the last 22 minutes.

Alex turned his attention to a griddle where he had begun cooking pancakes. He flipped eight pancakes that maximized the available space on the griddle, then grabbed a stack of presumably clean plates from the dishwasher and set them near the end of the counter. "Here we go!" he announced to the house. Without any further direction, all five children came out of nowhere, grabbed a plate, and stood in the kitchen at random intervals. I soon figured out why the taller ones were in the back as Alex started hurling pancakes over his shoulder from the grill one at a time. Each launch was accompanied by the phrase, "Eeeee-YUP!" I still don't know why, though Alex said it had something to do with Monty Python's *Holy Grail*. Only two pancakes hit the ground, confirming the five-second rule was alive and well in the Hill House.

Each kid wound up with a couple pancakes and three strips of unusually flat bacon. All of it was then subjected to an enormous amount of Mrs. Butterworth's syrup.

Now, I like syrup. Even the cheap shit. But I'm pretty sure they should have eaten with spoons for their version of a balanced breakfast.

I grabbed a piece of bacon and nervously sat to eat. Alex flipped me a pancake, landing it half way on the remaining plates on the counter. "There's butter in the cupboard," he said with a nod. I found the butter dish, which was actually just the top plate in the stack with a half-used cube of butter on it. "Oh," he added, "there's margarine in the fridge if you prefer."

"I don't *do* margarine," I replied plainly. "But thanks. Do you know what's *in* that shit?" Alex shrugged as he poured another round of cakes.

It was a lot to take in. Much to my surprise, I didn't really have to do anything, including come up with questions to ask the children so I could learn about them. Once they swallowed, these kids were actually pleasant to be around. All of them talked to me, but mostly just went on with life, harassing and teasing each other, as well as their dad. I figured there was a level of showing off going on, but even with that I never heard anyone being unhappy. At a very base level, they were all quite happy.

As strange as it was, and while the OCD side of myself was in complete agony, I felt it. I felt love. They all loved each other. I saw it in the way they talked, how they interacted, how they relied on each other.

# # #

The end of February marked the beginning of Birthday Season. Katherine started it, barely missing March by a few hours. Martin followed two weeks later, then Kevin three days after that. Evelyn's birthday was three weeks after Kevin, marking the end of the season. Justin, poor Justin, would have to wait until the end of summer.

I relied on my tax return every year to fund the season, that sole financial benefit of fathering a basketball team. That meant I had an extra $500 or so to purchase birthday presents and sponsor creative parties. Having spent pretty much everything I had on the trial and the GAL, it would be slim pickings this year. I still had a massive balance owed to my attorney hanging over my head.

"I got the cake, the food, and the decor," Nikki said. "You get the invite list for Katherine's party." She had inserted herself into the fray without any noticeable hesitation. It was actually quite a surprise; I still wondered why this successful, professionally-minded woman had embraced this freaky family. I mean, I'm pretty cool and all…but I have a serious amount of baggage to consider. I'd been careful not to dump everything on the table at once, but at the same time I didn't try to conceal the realities of life with five kids and a crazy ex-wife. I was confident Nikki had considered the risks and made her decision to stick around in spite of them.

She did more than stick around: Nikki had explained to me how her niece was like her only child. She routinely spent a massive amount of money on her niece every year for her birthday and Christmas. Massive to me, at least. The niece was off at college now, so Nikki warned me she was turning her love of special occasions to the kids. My feelings of awkwardness were overcome by feelings of gratitude as we all were overcome with thankfulness for Nikki's thoughtful care toward this family. It seemed natural, almost easy for her to fit in with us. More than that, we all were eager to fit in with her. Nikki was edgy and fun, gorgeous and smart, friendly and kind.

> *If this is what they call love*
> *I can't believe I'm in it*
> *Thanking heaven every minute*
> *I'm the luckiest boy in this town.*

#

Standing in line at Starbucks prompted me to make my to-do list once again for the day. Seems to be my thing.

Costco: Pick up cake, tube of hamburgers, ketchup, mayo, ice cream, paper plates, plastic wear, napkins, Coke, and pickles. Oh, and mustard. And ranch dressing, potato chips, grapes, and milk for all that cereal in the cupboard. I wonder if he needs laundry detergent? Yeah, I'll get one of those. For breakfast after the sleepover: Eggs, pancake mix, bacon, and orange juice. Better get two. That should do for eight girls, plus Alex's six and me...I'm going to be feeding 15 people. That is, if nobody else came.

Then it occurred to me. Every one of these kids had a friend. Or two. I wasn't just cooking for five kids. I'd be cooking for 20 people. Multiple times during Birthday Season. Good God...I probably should have thought that through a bit more.

It also became clear that Alex either benefited from or was subjected to duty-sex sometime around his and Holly's birthdays, resulting in four of the five children being born within a six-week span. Justin was the Thanksgiving sex baby, perhaps the only love-child of the group.

Coffee in hand, I drove to Costco and parked the Sky in my usual quadrant far from the front entrance. As I locked the door and looked back to see the lights flash in agreement, I realized my grocery list might be bigger than the car itself. I would need all my Tetris skills to make this work. Challenge accepted.

Several hundred dollars later, I squeezed the final grapes into the trunk above the gas tank and headed to Alex's house. I even managed to stop at the Party Store to pick up balloons and a small helium tank. By the time I pulled back into Alex's driveway, I was my own micro-version of the Griswolds, minus grandma strapped to the top.

Alex was overwhelmed with gratitude when we unloaded the Sky. "I don't know what to say," he said.

"It's totally my pleasure," I said. "By the way, I'm taking Katherine shopping for her birthday. And you're coming with us."

A certain look of fear flashed in Alex's eyes. "Okay..."

"The boys can blow up the balloons while we are gone." I went inside and found Justin and Kevin in the basement tossing a lacrosse ball back and forth to each other in some sort of challenge to see who could catch the fastest. Funny, I thought lacrosse was an outdoor sport. "Hey guys, sorry to interrupt—"

Kevin had taken advantage of my distraction and nailed Justin in the gut with a quick stick. "Oh, ho-ho! You lose, Justin!" Justin smacked Kevin in the ribs with his stick. Kevin laughed harder, taunting his win. Something then exploded from inside me. "BOYS!"

They froze instantly, staring at me full of mischief and respect, waiting to see what happened next. "Do you know how to use a helium tank?"

"I do," Kevin quickly replied.

"You do not, you dork," Justin interjected. "I know how, Nikki. How many balloons do you want blown up?"

"All of them," I said, tossing a hundred neon balloons to them both. "Fill them up and tie a six-foot piece of ribbon to each one. Your dad and I are taking Katherine shopping and will drop her off at a friends before she comes back tonight for the party. Cool?"

"Cool," they said in unison.

"Kevin?"

"Yeah?"

"There's only enough helium for the balloons, so don't even think about trying to get high on it or making chipmunk videos."

"Crap," said Kevin, disappointed.

"See you in a few hours."

# # #

Nikki led Katherine away from the shoes department into the junior's area at Macy's, which was like trying to convince a Labrador to ignore a squeaky child holding a steak. Katherine was growing up, and I was little help to her in the fashion department. After years of collecting hand-me-downs from my sister and her daughters, it had become clear that clothes manufactured in the nineties weren't exactly desirable in 2009. Katherine did the best she could with our annual treks to Old Navy and Walmart, which was where our family budget had led us for years. Today was different, especially with someone who majored in fashion merchandising in college leading the way.

Katherine tried on no less than 40 items in the first 90 minutes. For most any single dad, this was somehow tied to purgatory. Sometime, somewhere in my past, I had done something to deserve being forced against my will and better judgment into a world of fabric, hangers, and hidden price tags. And no matter where we went, there was never a place to sit, which was all I wanted to do after the first 30 minutes were over. Okay, I may have wanted a drink by then. A really, really stiff drink.

By the time we checked out, Nikki had convinced Katherine to collect nearly ten different garments. I did the math and knew this was well beyond my $150 limit. Nikki was giddy as she checked out and swiped her card. Katherine kept looking at me with huge eyes, checking for assurance that this was all okay. I smiled at her and nodded, then nearly lost it as I saw her eyes welling up with tears.

"I've never had so many pretty—" Katherine mauled Nikki with a hug, burying her face into her shoulder. "Thank you so much!" she said repeatedly.

Nikki wasn't quite sure how to handle the rush of emotion from Katherine, who until that moment had remained restrained, cordial, and quiet, mostly watching Nikki from a distance. "You deserve it, Katherine. You're a beautiful 14-year old girl. These things will look great on you!"

Katherine turned to me and hugged me tight. "Are you sure it's okay, Dad?"

"Of course, Katherine. She's right: you deserve it all."

We dropped Katherine off at her friend's house for the afternoon, then headed back to my place to see how the boys were coming along. We found them giggling like mice in a sea of balloons in the basement. They both were sucking helium out of a balloon. Yes, out of it.

"I suppose it was inevitable," Nikki said.

All I could do was shake my head. At least they had completed most of the task. Only 50 balloons to go.

We hung paper streamers on the porch, in the kitchen, and from the corners of the front room. Balloons were tied to every chair in the house and on the front porch handrails. When Katherine returned home for dinner, she couldn't hold back the tears.

Neither could I.

# # #

With Part I successfully accomplished, Birthday Season Part II was only two weeks away. Birthdays were always very important to me, perhaps more than I had even understood until I saw Katherine's reaction to what I considered a reasonable approach to the annual event. Alex had planned to combine Martin and Kevin's birthdays into one event since they were only a few days apart. Martin was turning 17, Kevin was turning 12.

"Hey, I was thinking," I said. Maybe for the boys we skip the streamers and just take everyone out to dinner. Do they have a favorite place?" I was thinking maybe Red Robin, the Spaghetti Factory (*barf-noodles!*), or perhaps Macaroni Grill. Something nice. I wasn't ready for his answer.

Alex lit up. "They love the Golden Corral!"

It was like he said it on purpose. Without any hesitation or reservation. I swallowed hard, shoving the reflux back down my throat.

"Sounds great." Blink. Blink. Smile.

"Then it's settled. And I'm picking up the tab—"

"I got the tab, you get the gifts," I interrupted. "I would have just made dinner for all y'all anyway, so we're good. Golden Corral it is."

Alex didn't object. I wish he had; I would have upped the ante and relocated our celebration to another food source. The last time I ate at a buffet, I think I was twelve. Wait, that wasn't me...I've never eaten at one. Nor had I ever shopped at a Walmart on purpose. Or been in want of anything I couldn't have. My parents had a big house on the hill outside of Spokane with a pool, a pool table, and everything to go with it all. We had to earn our allowance and freedom with work and responsibility, but my folks never shirked on quality of anything. Dad was a navy veteran and a successful service manager with Xerox; Mom was a marketing guru with an advertising company. Both of them knew how to throw a party and keep high standards for their associations. And while I know, I'm not supposed to fix the man I'm dating, I felt like he was welcoming my kind of change.

A week later, there I was holding a warm plate in front of the rump roast guy with the paper chef's hat, hoping the food I was about to eat would not kill me dead right there. DRT, Alex called it. I was literally sick, probably from spring allergies, which turned out to be a blessing since I couldn't smell or taste anything that day. I couldn't believe how much chocolate milk, fish sticks, and mac-and-cheese these kids could consume in a sitting. All for under $75 with the coupons Alex brought, making the friends' meals free. I've never actually held a coupon, let alone used one. Wait, that's not true: I used a coupon for an oil change once. But I digress. After I sawed my way through the day-old meat, I sought refuge in the sight of some pumpkin pie. My favorite. I carried my small little plate piled high with whipped cream, grabbed a fresh fork from the dispenser, and sat back at my seat. When I pressed the fork into the alleged pie, something went terribly wrong. It was as if someone had poured baby shit into a crust, then set it under a heat lamp so they could add whipped cream to a taught surface. Didn't work for me. "Want some pie, Justin?"

"Sure!" I couldn't watch, so I ventured off to the soft serve machine. *Sprinkles on top will make everything all better*, I thought. I found the designated dish, aimed the downspout, and pulled the handle. The machine barfed out a quart of ice cream diarrhea. The sprinkles didn't have a chance.

Birthday Season Part II was a success. Part III would be in three weeks.

# # #

Nikki let me drive the Sky top-down into Seattle for a Sunday downtown. When we passed by the University District and approached the Ship Canal Bridge, I was suddenly overcome with an unusual feeling of happiness. I threw my hands in the air near the crest of the bridge overlooking downtown Seattle and let out a vocal burst of joy. I felt no need to explain myself or worry about the kids or think I should be doing something else. It was that moment when I literally and figuratively crossed a bridge into a whole new sense of freedom.

The weather was perfect for a Space Needle tour, allowing us to take in the spectacular view from what was once the tallest building west of the Mississippi. We held gloved hands as we walked the grounds of the Seattle Center and wound up in the Center House for a late afternoon lunch. We sat in a quiet corner and bantered with each other about our respective phones. Nikki had the latest iPhone with a bright pink case. I pretended to be an airhead version of her talking on her phone. She used mine to take my picture doing it, then made that photo my profile pic for years to come. I was just happy in the moment, not realizing this was all the foundational building of an entire life which lay ahead.

I couldn't believe I was there. I couldn't believe she hadn't run away. Or that I hadn't run away for that matter.

When we arrived back at my house, Nikki came in to say hello to the kids. Evelyn was the first to run up to her with a big hug. Evelyn held onto Nikki's jacket and looked up at her. "Nikki?"

"Yes, Evelyn?" I honestly had an instant flush of fear wave over me. Evelyn was not known for her ability to tailor her questions to appropriate audiences. I held back my wince and readied myself for whatever came next.

Evelyn paused. "Never mind," she said.

"Evelyn," I said in that *hey-that-was-weird* kind of way.

Evelyn looked at me, then back at Nikki, still holding her jacket. "Are you coming to my birthday?"

Whew.

"Yes, I am," Nikki said. "This Saturday, the 18th, so your friends can stay the night. And yes, Evelyn. There will be balloons."

Evelyn's face beamed with her cheeky grin.

April 14, 2009

> **Holly**: Despite ur rejection of me, I LOVE YOU more than anyone in world. A baby was born today that you & your mom did not believe we should have had.

Nothing like waking up on your daughter's birthday to have your ex-wife remind you that your mother inquired about the wisdom of having more than four kids after your obstetrician warned you of certain major health risks. Or that you communicated those inquiries in the spirit of open dialogue and care, only to have it used against you for the next several years as some sort of proof that you hate children. Specifically, the fifth child. And women. And anything that conflicts with work. Or reason. The next text would probably involve something about how not knowing my birth mother led to my destructive attitude about family.

At least she still loves me more than anyone in the world.

April 18, 2009

Evelyn's birthday brought unique challenges for my little situation. Evelyn's closest friends were daughters of our former church's leadership. This meant their parents would be doing the drop-offs, which meant they'd want to catch up on my life, which meant they'd be there long enough to require a formal introduction to Nikki. Meeting the church ladies should be a welcome event, but I knew Nikki had felt judged for not being Presbyterian enough or something like that, despite her attendance with me to the church down the street from my house on a few occasions. Nikki's willingness to come to church was less important to me than her faith in God, however she chose to express it. I could not jive with a dedicated atheist or agnostic, but I didn't have any trouble being with someone whose religious expression varied greatly from my own. Hell, I was in the process of re-evaluating the whole expression anyway.

Terri was first on scene and wasted no time running up the stairs to hug Nikki. It was beautiful to see my two worlds collide. When the others arrived en masse, they all simultaneously got out of their respective minivans and Suburbans with dolled up girls in tow holding small pretty gift bags. These women had all been a complete Godsend for years while our family searched for welcome friendship, but each of them had come to their own limit with Holly some point along the way. Some tried counseling her, others just tried to be nice. But either way, by the time she left our family she made sure to include all of them in the dreaded category of Alex's Supporters. These people hated divorce but were willing to put pen to paper and call out Holly when they learned she had sought sole or even shared custody of the kids. They got it.

Evelyn greeted each girl upon arrival in the driveway. She was quite the sight in contrast with the others: she wore a pink dress with her hair in a high, self-imposed pony tail, and oversized cowboy boots.

It was interesting to me watching Nikki engage them all, one by one. They all had heard of Nikki from me or Terri, the only church lady I had confided in. Nikki's easy demeanor and self-control was perfection in motion. After brief conversations, each of the ladies left, leaving their precious cargo in our hands for the night.

Nikki handled preparing the hamburgers on the grill while I tried to entertain eight 10-year-old girls. I got the short end of that stick, for sure. Dinner was announced, and Evelyn sat down to her absolute favorite meal.

Cheeseburgers.

A year earlier, I had taken Evelyn to a Burger King drive-through for a quick after-school snack. "How 'bout a junior Whopper, kid?"

"I want a real one. A Whooper, not a junior one."

I looked in the rear-view mirror with a raised eyebrow. "Yeah? All right, suit yourself." I collected the order from the second window and headed for the house, which was less than seven minutes away. Evelyn had wolfed down the entire Whopper before we hit 9th Avenue with three minutes to spare.

"Oh my God, kid. Are you okay?! What happened to that thing?"

Evelyn grinned at me in the mirror, sucking on a Coke. "I ate it," she said plainly. There is no way the massive subsequent belch should have emerged from a healthy 88-pound, 9-year old girl. It made me check my right shoulder for Whopper fragmentation.

So it was easy deciding what to serve at Evelyn's 10th birthday party. Nikki's burgers were simply outstanding, complete with toasted buns, double-cheese, avocado (much to the boys' disgust), lettuce, tomato, and all manner of condiments. The brothers helped clean up, then got a little pissy when they figured out the girls would all be sleeping on the basement floor, preventing their use of the Xbox. They got over it when I sent them away with 20 bucks for the yogurt shop.

Nikki and I retired to the back porch and let the creek do its work on us. "Thank you for everything, Nikki," I said.

"My pleasure," she replied.

"So what do you think of the church ladies?"

Nikki paused. "Terri is amazing, Becky is suspicious, Jackie is a bubbly love-ball, Marianne is a little tense but super kind, and Gretchen is fun but a little uncertain if it's okay to like me. All in all, I can see how they've been good for the kids."

"But?"

"Well, I just feel like they aren't going to take me for who I am. Like I need to be fixed or something."

She was right. Aside from Terri, the other women's good intentions would always include making sure Nikki became part of their fold. It was a culture I had long since decided to push against, hoping to help these people relax and focus on the good things everyone brings to life rather than getting stuck in eschatology or their own particular corner of theology. I'd gained zero ground in this effort for years and knew this church was not really my home, but I kept the family there a long time for the benefit of stability and accountability.

"I know what you mean. They can't really help it; this is how they're programmed. Good intentions, but only according to the system." Nikki knew where I stood and accepted my faith. I was so glad to accept hers.

Pickup was at 9 am the next morning, at which time only one of the church ladies arrived in a Suburban for the 11-mile carpool back to Bothell. Birthday Season was officially over.

11. Scan for Content

May 7, 2009

In one of Holly's more open acts in the ongoing desperate quest for relevance, she arranged with Kevin and Evelyn's school to "help out" in preparation for the annual school musical. A rather artsy-fartsy member of the community had a 6th grade daughter in school, giving her license to produce and direct an elementary school musical of whimsical proportions. Holly saw this as a perfect opportunity to display not only her own amazing drama skills, but also her expertise as a child educator, a mentor for tweeners, an advocate for the downtrodden, and a loud voice for the shy. Which all added up to a complete disaster in the making.

On day two of the scheduled after-school rehearsals, Holly had wandered into a conflict with the capricious director. Holly didn't exactly win. I heard about it the following morning when I got a call from the school principal, Mrs. Donovan.

"Alex, are you able to swing by this morning before school starts? We had a little run-in with your ex-wife after school yesterday and I'm concerned she may try to further her point today. We need to talk."

"Of course, I'll be there by 7:30." This was going to be yet another Thursday my pals back at the JTTF would have used for comparison purposes.

When I arrived at the school, I went to the front office where I talked to the receptionist, a woman who could have easily doubled as The Black Knight in any Monty Python skit. "Mr. Hill, please take a seat. Mrs. Donovan will be with you momentarily."

I said nothing and obediently sat down. I had literally been summoned to the Principal's Office and began to have mixed feelings about being there. I shook out of it. "Sure is warming up for summer," I said. "Did you guys get that air conditioning in the budget you were shooting for?"

Ms. Humidity herself turned only her eyes toward me, glancing at me persistently for a full two-seconds before silently returning to the meaningless task at her desk. Something must have happened to her as a small child on the farm, something that made her face look that way, all hard and crusty.

"Alex? C'mon in, thanks for coming in so early." Mrs. Donovan was the penultimate antithesis to the receptionist. They had figured out how to get along, but it was clearly an effort.

After pulling a chair, I learned how Holly had scheduled a classroom visit for both Evelyn and Kevin's classrooms on the previous day. Shockingly, it didn't go so well. Holly left the front office after yelling and screaming, threatening to have all of them removed from their positions by the Superintendent himself.

"And, she did go to the District office demanding to talk with the Superintendent."

"Oh, God," I said.

"She didn't get her wish as he was out of town. The Assistant Superintendent drew the short straw. Holly complained that we had prevented her access to her children. It didn't seem to matter when I showed Holly her own parenting plan showing she didn't have custody during school time. Do I have that right? I have your guys' order right here."

"That's basically correct," I agreed. "The only real enforceable rule here is if she disturbs the children's peace. Outside of that, you can treat it the same as any other person who comes into the school without official business. She's welcome to all the records at any time, but she is restricted from the children outside of her scheduled time, except when I agree for additional time."

"I can see why," the Principal said. "I can't have her coming in here threatening my staff. Her little blowup had a pretty big impact, even on you-know-who." She tilted her head toward the door where the receptionist was casting annoyance to her next victim. Maybe she just needed a good, solid hug.

I expressed my empathy and ensured Mrs. Donovan the office staff would have my support for them going forward.

"The main reason I wanted you to come in early was for this." She held up a sealed envelope with Holly's name on the front. "I'll be delivering a letter this morning when she shows up. The District has signed off on it already; it restricts her from coming on campus without prior written authorization from me or the office staff directly. If she can engage in a reasonable conversation with me over the phone, I'm happy to have her here, as I'm sure you are if she can hold it together."

"Definitely," I said. "And if she doesn't?"

"Don't worry, Alex. We've dealt with all manner of crazy, weird, and awkward around here before. Our focus is to ensure the safety and well-being of the kids. And you have some pretty cool ones—although I hear Kevin likes to jump off tall things."

"Yeah, there's that," I admitted. "Do what you gotta do if he tries anything stupid."

We shook hands and I left, glad for the support. Less than an hour later, Holly sounded off.

> **Holly**: You love your power play. You give me weekends out of town. You terrorize me here at the school. This proves your offensive tactics. CLASSIC P.A.S.
>
> **Alex**: You are still welcome to meet with teachers in classroom after school if scheduled and ok with school admin. That has been my position. Your behavior has been the basis for the school's own decision about your involvement there.
>
> **Holly**: Truth: What happened today was further evidence incriminating you. My attorney knew that if we gave you a little rope you would hang yourself.
>
> **Alex**: You are off the mark and using texts to harass. Please stop. I hope your time with the kids today is sweet; they are looking forward to it.

Okay, that wasn't entirely true but I wanted to change the subject. The kids were doing their best to try and make these court-ordered visits something good. But they were kids, and their mom's antics were becoming more visible to them. After dropping them off at Holly's latest apartment, it was the kids' turn to sound off.

Martin: Mom is yelling at the girls saying you ruined her day at school.

Alex: I am so sorry. Please stay if at all possible. You may come home if you can't stay, but that means everyone; please don't leave Evelyn there.

Katherine: Why? Mom is yelling at us and telling us to go home because you don't want us here. She is forcing us out!

Martin: Aaannnd now the only way it works is if we act like everyone is happy and nothing ever happened.

Martin: Actually, it's always the best thing. Never bring it up, never talk about it. Or else it happens again.

Somehow they made it home in one piece, but nobody was in the visiting mood that night. I made sure to make my evening rounds to each of them, complete with actual hugs and letting them know how much I loved them. These kids were going through hell and I didn't know how to make it better. So I did what every parent does when they see their kids suffer.

I prayed.

May 9, 2009

Martin: Hey I asked mom what she wanted for mother's day she said the angel perfume its at Macy's ok cool thanks. Later.

I bit the bullet again and decided to buy the gift for the kids to give to their mom as I knew it was necessary to make their day with her have a chance of success. When I was in the process of swiping my credit card to make my ex-wife believe the children had pooled their resources to bless her with something pretty, I think that's the moment it hit me of how absurd this was. I'm paying $1,000 a month to sponsor her ability to harass me, then I pay $75 to make it smell better.

Wow.

#

May 10, 2009

With Edmonds in the rear-view mirror, we hauled ass in the Sky to meet my parents for Mother's day. The kids were all accounted for at their friends' homes, freeing Alex up for the weekend. We first stopped at Pike Place Market in Seattle and spent way too much money on three whole steamed Dungeness crabs. My parents went nuts over fresh crab. With the treasure in the trunk, we headed over Snoqualmie Pass. As we passed over the Columbia River at Vantage, I told Alex it should take us about 3 1/2 hours to get there, start to finish.

"More like 3 1/2 hours from here," he said.

"Start to finish," I repeated.

"Are you crazy?" he said. "It's a 300-mile drive...how do you expect us to get there in under five hours?"

"I always do," I said coyly. I typically managed to get there in under 4 hours anyway. I put on my dork voice. "Oh, dat's right...you're an officuh ov duh law."

"Your car," he said, dropping it into 4th gear.

It's a weird thing when cops speed. It takes some of the fun out of it and replaces it with a bunch of expectation. It's all...safe, even at 110 mph. Alex was an expert driver and it showed. And I-90 in Eastern Washington was the perfect highway for making our carbon footprint a little more visible.

With Alex driving, I got to control the music and Alex's phone. As expected, Holly had attempted to come with us.

> **Holly**: Please know that I will always love you best. If that irritates you, take your irritation out on God. It was He who set us up.

"Does she realize you two are divorced?"

"I'm starting to wonder."

We made it to my parent's house overlooking Liberty Lake just east of Spokane. They built the house 20 years ago as their retirement home and final investment, one of their only investments that made it through the recession and financial market crash of 2008. It was a beautiful home nestled in the pine trees a quarter mile from the lake shore.

For their first meeting, I had arranged with my Dad to take Alex to a shooting range, something my dad had been wanting to do since I was married to my previous husband. Dad was a former military veteran who served in both the Army and the Navy before embarking on his 35-year career with Xerox.

"Alex, this is my dad, Rich Myers."

"Mr. Myers," Alex said, extending his hand.

"So you're the guitar-playing cop, eh?" Dad's 6'3" frame towered above Alex, who was just a hair under 5'11".

"All lies," Alex said with a smile. "Well, maybe not the cop part. Nice home you have here."

Dad nodded with approval. "Let me show you around," he said, leading us to the back deck overlooking Liberty Lake through a spread of pine trees. "It's been a good home for us, except for all these goddam trees." He looked back at me. "They do block the wind, I guess." He had that twinkle in his eye, the one that showed up when he thought he was being clever. I definitely took after my dad more than my mom.

After the quick tour, all four of us piled into my parent's Lexus and went to the gun range. It surprised me a little when my mom got into the car. She was not all that interested in firearms; I chalked it up to her want to be a good hostess. What surprised me more was the shaking in my dad's hands; it had gotten considerably more advanced from the last time I saw him. Not that big of a deal, except that he was holding a loaded .40 caliber Glock.

Alex was on high alert, looking like a salesman trying to keep a potential client happy while telling them their baby was ugly. "You got this, Rich?"

"Oh yeah." Sing-song. Nonchalant.

I have no idea how Dad put 80% of his rounds in the ten ring. Maybe he was timing the shakes or something in a sort of *Matrix* kind of way.

We went back to the house, had a gourmet dinner with crab prepared by my very capable mom, then enjoyed some light conversation and wine from the winery where my parents volunteered their time. This was the last year I would trek to Spokane for Mother's Day since my parents had announced they were moving to the west side to be closer to Elle and me. My parents quickly fell in love with Alex. I was certain they had questions about what life would look like for me in his family.

We returned the next morning to Washington's west side, clearing the mountains by mid-afternoon. Alex said he didn't want to risk explaining a speeding ticket to his boss. Whatever. Most of the way back, I kept thinking about Mother's Day. It had always meant doing something for my mom, but those days were numbered and here I was in a relationship with a man who had five kids. If this went all the way, I potentially could wind up on the receiving end of Mother's Day.

That was supposed to scare the shit out of me. Maybe it did, but not enough to run. Would the kids call me mom? Stepmom? Wicked stepmother? I giggled to myself.

"What's so funny?" Alex asked. Apparently my giggle was a little out loud.

"Oh, I was just thinking how weird it is that I won't be going back to Spokane again for Mother's Day. It may change quite a bit; I'm not sure what that will look like."

Alex looked at me while I stared at the wind turbines of the Wild Horse Wind Farm outside of Ellensburg. "Maybe the change will be good," he said.

Likely so, but I was still processing whether I wanted to become a mother myself after I had given up on the idea so long ago.

# # #

May 20, 2009

Waiting for it, I held my breath. It was already 9:30 am and nothing. No mystery sacks of bread on my porch, no requests to take the kids to the nail salon, no indications of undying love in the midst of tragedy, no divorce advice or accusations of parental alienation or references to dating in college. Nothing. Surely on what would have been our 20th anniversary, Holly would unleash a string of texts and emails like I'd never seen. *It's the calm before the storm*, I thought. I was on my second cup of Arabica from my favorite Columbian pal when it finally hit.

9:40 am

>**Holly**: please speak to kids about honoring my privacy. One of them deleted all my email messages. I hope and pray you had nothing to do with it.

>**Holly**: Supposedly it was Katherine, she deleted 210 of my messages. They were dear and important memories, letters and pictures that were irreplaceable. It was very wrong. Almost as wrong as you trying to replace me with that woman.

I may have actually liked her thinking I had something to do with her cyber intrusion. Truth was I had no reach there whatsoever, despite the work I did on a daily basis with the FBI. Most of the world perceived counter-terror agents with the FBI having a massive ability to monitor everyone's phones, emails, and texts at the same time, scrubbing them daily for clues of terror or criminal activity. We in the biz actually loved the perception, it made the job a hell of a lot easier most of the time. All I had to do was merely suggest I knew what was really going on and they'd cave. I had one guy totally convinced I was fluent in Arabic during an interview about the Hummer he bought in Washington with an Oregon identification to avoid the sales tax. When I looked at him cross-eyed at his lame explanation of the jihadist magazines I found in his apartment during the 'fraud investigation,' he dropped his head and started coughing up all kinds of names. I never meant for this kind of leverage to spill over into my marriage. My kids maybe, but not my marriage. Oh, well, it wasn't like I had a ton of success altering her perspectives.

The better part of today's news is that Nikki had made it into the classification of "that woman." She'd get a kick out of that.

A few minutes later, Holly sent a single group text to me and all the kids:

>**Holly**: I am so glad I was married to the man of my dreams 20 years ago. I have a beautiful friend and 5 amazing kiddos. Seize the day, family! I love you all.

And that was it. No more. It was weirdly anti-climactic.

# # #

May 21, 2009

Thursdays became our weekly time to have dinner together while the kids made their way after school to Holly's place, wherever that might be that week. It was Alex's turn to cook; he had asked me to come by after work with a bottle of wine. Knowing his modus operandi of cooking usually involved a Crock Pot and a serious lack of anything green, I also brought a bag of salad along. Just in case.

I arrived at the house and found Alex in the laundry room downstairs. "Hey there, handsome!"

"Enter at your own risk." Alex was digging through an unimaginable mound of laundry. He came up with a single sock. "There you are, you little freak!"

"Hey, now!"

"I was referring to the sock," he said.

"You're talking to a sock?"

"Don't tell the neighbors. Or any of Holly's many attorneys. Check it out." Alex handed me his phone.

> **Holly**: FYI. I want to let you know that I will be getting a circle of attorneys to advocate for modifications that are more mutual.

The little red guy on my left shoulder took over. I started to draft a reply on his phone.

"Try this on for size," I said with a grin.

Alex looked at the message I had entered. He sighed. "I don't know," he said. "Not really my style."

"How's that been working for ya?"

"You have a point." Alex took a deep breath, closed his eyes, and made a giant sweeping motion with his index finger landing on the Send button. I

Never Been This Close To Crazy

heard the click. I couldn't believe I heard the click. He actually did it.

> **Alex**: Also FYI...Kids and I will be gone from June 22 through about July 5 on vacation to Idaho per the parenting plan.

"See, I knew you had some balls," I laughed. "You want a sandwich or something? Maybe a beer or a cigarette?"

"I'll show you some balls," he said, throwing a random sock at me, chasing me up the stairs. He caught me at the front door, spun me around, and pressed his lips against mine. I gave in for a second, then pressed my tongue to his lips, then up to his nose, causing the appropriate disgusted retreat. I ducked under his arm and ran up the rest of the stairs into the kitchen laughing the whole way.

"Keep your balls to yourself, ya perv!" He stood at the front entry just shaking his head.

I was right. There wasn't a fresh vegetable within the boundaries of the house. Good thing I brought a salad.

Burgers finished to perfection, we sat to eat at the table. "So yesterday was your anniversary?"

#

May 22, 2009

After almost two days not receiving any texts from Holly, I concluded either her many attorneys had successfully warned her against the regular barrage of unnecessary communications, she got arrested, or her phone busted. Turns out it was the latter.

> **Holly**: G'morn. I will not shame you through fair process for better involvement with kids. Love others as you would like to be loved really matters to me.

> **Holly**: You are my forever friend. Betrayal is not my card to play. Truth always wins. I do pray you will be able to be mutual to bless the kiddos.

Holly: Women and children first. I would like to take Evelyn to breakfast and bring treats to her class. I would also like to end the day with her siblings.

Holly: It would increase donations if a cute swimmer from a younger generation joined the volunteers to save Yost Pool.

Martin called just as school let out. "Hey kid, what's up?"

"Dad, I'm going to go meet with Mom since I'm not gonna see her at the Thursday thing this week. Cool?"

"Of course. Home by dinner? Nikki is making pasties."

"What's that? Sounds inappropriate."

Martin was one of those kids who seemed really pleasant and naive, but had a fairly well developed juvenile male mind. "Not the kind that cover nipples, you dork. It's pronounced Pass-tees. It's some kind of Cornish meat pie thing; goes all the way back to Chaucer."

"Who?"

So much for that Classical Christian education. To be fair, it only went through the 8th grade and was hit-and-miss at that. "Never mind. Have fun with mom. And Martin?"

"Yeah?"

"I'm glad you're doing this. She loves all you guys a lot, even if she has a hard time showing it. Taking your own time with her is really good. It's how things will be for all of you, ultimately."

"I know, Dad. See you tonight."

I was really proud of Martin for putting aside his own massive frustration with his mother. Martin was the only other licensed driver in the family after Holly left home, leaving him with the responsibility to help transport the kids around, including to the mom visits. He didn't mind at all, but Holly tried to make an issue of it, saying it was part of my hyper-control model of parenting and avoiding my own responsibilities, making the children do my bidding. Whatever. I had made a deal with him: I would supply a vehicle, fuel, registration and insurance if he would do the needed carting around of the siblings when I was not available. Outside of that, he was welcome to use the car for his own outings as well, provided he always kept me in the loop and was able to tell me the end game before he left for anywhere. It worked out well with Martin, so I continued the arrangement as each child became the oldest licensed driver in the home.

After I hung up with Martin, I decided to clear off the stack of messages which had come in over the last hour or two from Holly. I applied my usual method: scan, correlate themes, figure out which items self-resolved, and find the one or two things I might be able to actually answer, if any. Holly had been living out of her car for a couple weeks but apparently had just found another woman who offered her space in her South-Edmonds condo. I was relieved knowing the kids would likely have a place for their 'residential time'. I also knew it would likely follow the all-too-familiar path of destruction at some point. People who helped Holly through her troubles all ended up not allowing her to live with them. Maybe this time she could turn a corner and become more stable.

Holly's residential time with the kids was Thursday for dinner and Saturdays from noon to 7 pm, with an option for an overnight if she had a place to be and if the kids wanted to do it. None of the kids wanted overnights with her, with the exception of Evelyn on rare occasions, especially if she could bring a friend with her. The trouble was each of her friends developed a fear of Holly due to her emotional outbursts, putting Evelyn in an increasingly awkward position and impacted her ability to keep friends.

Holly: Can I meet Evelyn at the bus?

Holly: Please may I do something with Evelyn, today?

Holly: Do you have time to trade bed frames, today?

Holly: Laura needs a copy of our 2008 tax return. The refund needs to be shared equally.

Holly: Two questions. Tax return and refund. Fax these to my attorney. When? When is Katherine's talent show?

Holly: I want to work together with you. I hate court. It is your weapon. My attorney and I are hoping and praying you will be kind without going back to court.

Holly: Can I take Evie and Katherine to get our nails done downtown?

There it is. "Hey, Katherine?" She was in her bedroom.

"Yeah?"

"Mom is wondering if you and Evelyn might want to go downtown for some nails. Interested?"

After a pause, "Yeah. When?"

"Probably now. Give her a shout on your phone. I'll let her know you'll call her."

Alex: The girls will meet you downtown if you are there.

Holly: Groovy! Thank you for responding. Can we work out a direct deposit so that I do not have to drive to courthouse to get check.

Ignoring that.

Holly: Don't understand your desire to control everything. Knowing what is best for OUR kiddos should be a shared mission. Have to bow to you. Court ruled.

Holly: Court is 20 miles away. You will not meet deadline. It is held 6 days. If you wish to look as if you follow order, you should deposit per request.

Uh, you're the one who wanted it handled through the court…

Holly: You have been overly controlling. Your position ruined our family. What have I done today that you do not forgive? Bitterness and unloving ruling are not befitting a man who claims JESUS as LORD.

Holly: Home is with you for our children. You want to be their mom. Stop your abuse of authority.

Holly: Taking the shame and accusations and guilt to the cross all day everyday. I could not love you and forgive you without mercy and grace God provides.

Holly: Something for you to ponder. You, having an estranged mom, lack high regard for femininity. I, having an estranged dad, lack high regard for masculinity.

Well, that explains everything!

Holly: Alex—run to JESUS today. Confess that you have a crack in your armor. You hurt the woman who believes you are so deserving of your own family. Start today to cherish our children more than your power to stonewall love.

Holly: Do you understand the hurt you have caused your family? Bend your knees and receive a transformation. JESUS IS READY TO HELP YOU. You are so loved.

Holly: Tired of the fight. Please honor me. I do not want more family court. Please stop stoning me. I desire mutuality. Kiddos need to see it.

Holly: You gave me nothing but debt and loneliness in the divorce content that I had a shower while homeless.

I simply lost the strength, interest, and will to respond, even to myself. Delete all? Click.

12. MONEY LAUNDRY

June 1, 2009

The days approaching my 41st birthday were giving Holly some focused energy as she poured on the pressure. She began using email from the local public library as a primary means to tell me what to think.

> **To: Alex**
> **From: Holly**
>
> Alex,
>
> I would like you to modify the parenting plan and release your hold on Evelyn. If I were in a different position, I would love to have them all. My God-given calling is motherhood. You can never take that away. This divorce left me no worldly wealth. I am rich in love for you and for our kiddos. I will not plow forward professionally while the hearts of our children need an advocate for their souls. Evelyn does not want to hurt you. She just needs her mommy.
>
> I know you to be kind-hearted. I trust that you understand that God did not create you to be female or have the heart of a mother. I love you, Alex. Please loosen your power. It is hard to admit a crack in your shield.
>
> Bend your knees and ask God to use His Spirit to wash mercy over you. Then rise and do good to the baby of the family and the bride of your youth. I offer you nothing but forgiveness.
>
> Please Alex, free yourself from the bondage of control and trust Jesus to help you AND I bless our children as He intended.
>
> In the shadow of His wings,
>
> Holly

June 8, 2009

Holly: I paid for a season pass for Yost. Kiddos may enter with up to 6 swimmers at a time. A blessing for the friendly tribe.

Holly: As International Chief Executive of Production Management, I have solved your crisis. I am depositing $1,000.00 into your checking account to help you with the Idaho trip. Spoil the kiddos.

Holly: Tomorrow is your birthday. I wish you knew your real mom. I think you did not know what to do with a woman who would die to have you live.

The night before my birthday, I received the weirdest one yet. The content was pretty familiar, but the note was addressed to me and what appeared to be five other men. I could only conclude these were men with whom she had some level of romantic interlude.

To: Alex (and five other men)
From: Holly

Heavenly Father,

I praise you for the family you gave me. Please watch over and bless Martin, Justin, Katherine, Kevin, and Evelyn with a lively faith, a fervent charity, and a courageous hope of reaching many for your Kingdom.

I pray for my children to lead a life rich in the teachings of the Bible. I pray that my children grow into adulthood with a strong sense of spirituality and grace.

I pray that my children will always call on you, the Father, in the name of Jesus, with their prayers of thanks, and prayers for peace. I pray that my children strive to enrich the lives of the people they meet, and that they never leave anyone sad. Please let forgiveness be the last thought to close each day.

I confess that I am an imperfect parent, in need of your grace. Please help me to guide them to You. Let me never put complete trust in any created thing to save them.

Please bless my children with enjoyment in all You have created. Let them delight in each drop of grace they experience. Breathe your Spirit into their daily thoughts and actions so that they bless You for the bliss in this life. As they long for great things, please let them not go after idols, rather have You, alone, as the fulfillment of their every desire.

Let praise to You, their King, be the keynote of their songs. Be the music in their souls that forces their feet to dance. Please turn their minds to rejoicing in every sorrow that they must endure. As they raise their hands, put the banner of glory and honor to You, in them.

Bless them with the faith to move mountains. Give them over to a sweet surrender to Your Son, as the only true Lover of their souls. Pour Christ's Spirit over them and give them all they need to serve You.

Thank You for bringing Heaven to earth, in the form of Your Son. Keep my family close to You, by the embrace of your Spirit. Let us walk in the light of Your love, in hope that others may be drawn to You and behold Your glory.

In Jesus' powerful name,

AMEN

When I showed the note to Nikki, she utilized the power of social media and her speedy research skills to find three of the five men on Facebook.

All three were attorneys.

"I have my doubts these guys got past the first paragraph," I said.

Nikki was annoyed. "She sure knows how to waste people's time."

June 9, 2009

Holly: Happy Birthday to YOU. Will you let me give you a gift, in person?

#

It had become easier for Alex to ignore Holly's irrelevant messaging, but the volume kept coming at a crazy rate. I had one goal for Alex's birthday: I wanted his family and his friends to be free to celebrate the man he was, apart from any nonsense or distraction. *Is that too much to hope?* I wondered.

Don't answer that.

Alex was under the impression that the kids wanted to celebrate his birthday in a similar way to how they had done it in the past, with a picnic at Marina Beach. This spot was certainly a good one for a party, but had always been chosen for the ease of handling little kids. The park had a great playground climbing structure and a beach on Puget Sound next to the Port of Edmonds Marina. Beside it was one of the few off-leash dog parks in the Seattle area. We arrived and parked next to the dog park, then walked out to the barbecue pits. A crowd had already gathered there of Alex's friends from work, lacrosse and church. Two of Alex's more interesting friends were there, Alonso and Julio, who had appointed themselves Alex's favorite Colombian and Mexican, respectively. I was delighted with Alex's surprised expression. He quickly realized he didn't have to cook, or set up, or feel responsible for the kids. He could just enjoy the people while we took care of the rest. That was something he'd never experienced as an adult.

As the hamburgers and hot dogs began to run out, people started to hover around for the obligatory singing of Happy Birthday. That's when it happened.

Martin and Katherine speed-walked up to Alex like a couple of suspicious Olympic hopefuls. Martin took the lead. "Dad! Mom just sent us a text saying she was coming to bring you a present or something. We told her not to come, but I think I see her now!"

It was like one of those moments when someone in a crowd turns sideways and looks up at the sky, causing every other person in the crowd to do the same. One by one, all forty of us stopped what we were doing and craned our necks to watch Holly's approach. She was carrying a plastic grocery bag with something about the size of a book inside. Alex reluctantly stepped forward to meet her apart from the crowd, like Daniel going to meet Goliath, only this time the monster Philistine was caged up inside the frail frame of a very unwelcome person.

I glanced around and realized every person there had somehow been negatively affected by Holly, some severely, over the past year. Terri's nervous and hyped-up voice whispered over my shoulder. "Hide me, Nikki!"

"*What?*" I said.

"Hide me!" she whispered intensely. "She can't know I'm here! If she sees me she'll try to grab on to me and think I'll help her or something and Alex's party will be over. Don't let her see me!"

I looked over at Julio, who had positioned himself between Alex and the group. Julio's Navy SeaBees frame was absolutely huge to start with, and now he looked like a pissed off Mexican Dwayne Johnson, only thicker. Julio's thin lips frowned to divide the hemispheres of his face as he looked down his nose toward the imposer. Pretty sure Holly noticed.

Holly finished her encroachment to Alex and held out the sack. "I brought you this for your birthday," she said sheepishly.

Alex took the bag. "Okay, see you later," he said flatly.

She turned to walk away, then spun around and snarled back, "You can't tell me what to do. I can be here if I want, it's a public place!"

Forty heads simultaneously tipped a little to the left with the look of, "Really?" Except mine, which had somehow made its way next to Alex where I seized the advantage.

"You're disturbing my peace, Holly, and the peace of your children. Leave." I felt it coming.

Holly pushed her face forward. "I don't have to do anything you say—"

At that moment, our favorite Mexican, the inconvenient peacemaker, the mountain of a man himself boomed his amazing voice over the crowd. "Everybody! Happy birth-day to you! Happy birth-day, to you!"

It was the greatest shunning known to humanity. The crowd all turned their backs on Holly toward Alex who had retreated from the delivery. We roared out the song, holding out the "dear Alex" part until Holly finally turned around and fled. Sadly, nobody took a video.

Rejuvenated, we cut the Costco cake and fed everyone until they were blue in the face with that scary balloon frosting they load on top. I found Julio and gave him a hug. "You're my hero, man."

"I just knew it was time to sing," he said. "Especially when I saw your fists ball up! That might have been tough to explain to Alex's kids."

I thought about it. "Yeah, I suppose."

Terri chimed in. "You guys! Can you believe she showed up? That was so crazy!" She turned to Julio. "You have a beautiful voice, young man!"

Holly's gift never made it home. I snuck it into the circular file at the beach. I'm not really even sure what it was. Alex never asked.

# # #

June 10, 2009

As if nothing happened, Holly continued with her flurry of strange notes after her disruption at my birthday party.

> **Holly**: Only highly intelligent people can be wordsmiths. My new business is named BEYOND CONCEPTION. I'm studying to become a doula.

> **Holly**: Can we plan and throw an 'end of school-graduation' party for our kiddos, together? Does this Saturday work?

Scratching my head.

June 19, 2009

Holly arranged to come to Edmonds Elementary for an end-of-year barbecue. She took the opportunity to approach me at the event and press me for information about my financial situation. I avoided the conversation but attempted to be cordial in the social setting.

"I have some money, Alex, and I know you only have your parent's station wagon, which isn't all that great. I'll send over some money so you can rent a van for your vacation trip to Idaho with the kids. That way they'll be more comfortable.

I told her I would figure out something but thanked her for the offer, then found something to qualify as a reason for me to turn my attention elsewhere. Or I just ducked into the bathroom, but either way I ended the conversation.

When I came out, I found Evelyn who told me Holly had left. "Daddy, I'm gonna paint your face now."

"Oh are you?" I asked. I knew this would be a losing battle. "Okay, let's do this." The woman at the face-painting station doctored my mug with a purple and green goatee until I looked like a Jester in a medieval jousting tournament. Evelyn was very pleased. She had red hearts on her cheeks.

I took the kids home after the event, then headed to the Play It Again used sporting goods store to try and score some cheap lacrosse balls. The Buick crapped out in the middle of the intersection of Highway 99 and 196th Street Southwest at 5:30 pm on a Friday. I got out to try and push the beast myself with little success when a pair of hefty guys from the nearby LA Fitness saw an opportunity. "Need a hand?"

"Sure," I beamed. "Thanks!" Both men hesitated when they saw my face, which I had completely forgotten was any different than usual. Their hesitation made my mind race through the card catalogue of every felon I'd arrested in the last ten years, including the terrorist variety who were supposed to be somewhere other than state-side. One of the men started laughing, covering his own face. My 22 years of training and experience as a law enforcement professional thought of this as a clue, which then reminded me of my own painted up mug.

"School party for the kids," I explained. But by then both men had lost it. The three of us stood in the middle of the highway bent over howling until we could re-compose and start pushing the woody off the road.

When Holly left the event she apparently went to a car rental company, then to Wells Fargo bank where she deposited $500 into my checking account. She sent a text.

> **Holly**: Try to find something cheaper than the $520, that's the quote I got from Enterprise car rental. Also, I sent your June maintenance payment back to you so you don't have to struggle on the trip. I know how tight you keep the money.

I was shocked, both that she had money to throw around and that she had my banking information after I had changed it a year ago.

I wasn't about to look a gift horse in the mouth, so I counted my blessings for the timing of being able to rent a van with my money returned from my ex the same day my parent's station wagon broke down. Things were looking up. However, by the time I made it to the rental car company, all vehicles capable of transporting the six of us with gear had been rented out. Nikki picked me up at the rental office.

The following day, a friend from church, Ralph O'Brien, called and offered for me to use their 15-passenger van for the trip to Idaho at no cost. Grateful, Nikki and I went to Woodinville to pick up the vehicle, an actual answer to prayer.

# # #

The mandatory noon to 7 pm visit was wrapping up for the kids as Alex and I arrived at the home in tandem with the O'Brien's van. A surprise afternoon rain shower left a sweet, fresh smell in the air. I smuggled ingredients in from my car to make a salad to supplement Alex's burgers he was making for us that night. The prep work was complete when the kids began to trickle in. Justin and Kevin went straight for the food, which was not uncommon after one of their Saturday visits with Holly. Evelyn disappeared downstairs with Martin, followed by Katherine and a friend she had with her. The friend, Reagan, was a loud little 8th grader with a knack for voicing her opinion about things.

Katherine and Reagan came up the stairs and like a pair of constipated kids about to blow a secret. Katherine did the honors.

"Dad, Mom is out front and she wants to talk to you."

It was like they felt guilty for saying it. Alex didn't jump to the topic but instead told Katherine that it was dinner time, and he would take care of Mom later. "You girls go ahead and have a seat, I'll get the others."

Alex called for Evelyn and Martin at the top of the stairs. Katherine decided to let the rest of the message out. "Mom says she wants the money back."

"What?" he said, looking back.

Katherine continued, "Mom said she gave you money for a rental car and she wants it back since you didn't rent anything. She said she gave you $500."

"Katherine, I want you to let it go; this is something I will work out with Mom."

Katherine remained visibly upset. "She said she gave you $1,000 for our trip, too. Is that true Dad?"

"Katherine, that's enough—this is between your mother and me. Let it go." Martin and Evelyn uncomfortably made their way to the table and sat with the others.

Dinner was more tense than usual as the kids were distracted with concern for what was going to happen next. "Mom was crying making a scene all the way here when she walked us home from our visit downtown," Katherine explained. "Now she's sitting out there sobbing."

Reagan started to say something then stopped herself. "What was that, Reagan?" I asked.

"Nevermind."

I prodded her a bit until she spoke. "Holly was talking about you, Nikki. She's crazy you know. No offense, Katherine." Reagan continued, "I told her that you are the nicest person I've ever met. Holly said you probably make huge payments on your car."

I laughed. Justin shook his head and remained silent. "First," I said, "not that it matters nor is it anyone's business, but I do not have a car payment. Second, if you are ever thinking about owning a car as impractical as mine, you'd better not make payments on it either. And third, let's be aware that your mom is going through a tough time. She's lost a lot and you all are leaving for ten days on vacation tomorrow."

"I feel sorry for her sometimes," Katherine admitted. "And now she's acting all mental and weird, right in front of my friend!"

Alex slipped his phone to me under the table. I stole a look at the text which had come in.

Holly: Pls step out with a 500.00 check. Thank the Lord for Ralph and Nikki. I should not have trusted you to rent a van.

Alex: Leave please. There are no vans available until next week. The O'Brien's offered today—of course I would return the money. My checkbook is not here; will mail it. Very inappropriate to involve kids in $ discussion. I appreciated your offer as you know. I will certainly return the money.

Holly: Transfer the $1,500.00 back to my account. I checked and you did not save the money for the kiddos.

As we finished up and Alex headed out the front door to deal with Holly, I decided it was time to interject a little frivolity.

"Hey, Evie, will you go out and grab the tongs from the barbecue?"

She dutifully went out the slider but couldn't locate the tongs—because they weren't there. Confused, she turned around to ask. Just as she looked toward me through the adjacent kitchen window, I pulled out the sink sprayer, pointed it at her, and let it fly. She got a face full of water.

"Ha-ha! Got you!" I yelled, still soaking her with the spray. Martin joined in the fun, grabbing a squirt gun from the bathroom and going after me while Evie grabbed the garden hose from the deck. I locked the back door, which didn't stop her from spraying me with copious amounts of water through the window. Everyone joined in with squeals and laughter which could be heard by all throughout the neighborhood. Which, as it turns out, included Holly. Mission accomplished.

Alex came up the stairs in total disbelief at the mayhem. I unlocked the back door and joined forces with Evie, targeting Alex.

We spent the next hour mopping up the kitchen, loving every minute of it.

# # #

As we finished cleaning up, I could tell Nikki's efforts to be understanding were dwindling fast.

"This is really hard on the kids, Alex."

I nodded. "You're right. The problem is she didn't break the order by coming onto the property. She was just being crazy in view of everyone. No law against that."

"Doesn't disturbing the peace mean something? For fuck's sakes, my peace was certainly disturbed! I can't imagine your peace not being disturbed."

"I've already run that one up the chain," Alex explained. "The police will take a report for the incident, but they won't take action on the disturbance since it's subjective. That would take a clearer violation, like coming inside or breaking the distance clause. I'll file the report later tonight."

Unbelievable. "What did you say to her when you went outside?"

"I told her it was time for her to go. She fired back with, 'I don't have to do anything you say—I am more than 300 feet from your door, I already measured it!' She had a few choice words for me as I walked back to the extremely happy household full of giggles and laughter."

"She needs to move on," Nikki said.

"I couldn't agree more."

# # #

Alex told me the vacation was essentially ordered by the children's psychologist so they'd have some time to forget the daily problems of the divorce and focus on enjoying each other. Every one of the kids felt bad for their mom, and she routinely made the most of that. It was all I could do not to go outside and tell her off.

The remainder of the evening was filled with text messages from Holly to Alex that noticeably upset him. It was as if the restraining order prohibiting Holly from disturbing this family's peace had little value at all.

After the kids finished packing their bags for the trip, Alex saw them off to bed while I waited in the front room on the God-awful couch. Copper looked at me with his old, tired eyes as he lay next to the piano. "You lookin' at me, boy?"

He was. With suspicion. Alex returned to the front room and handed me his phone. "Here's the rest of the story," he said. I looked through the messages from Holly.

> **Holly**: When I went to pay ahead for your car the rental location had several options suitable for the kiddos. Where did you try? The bank accidentally revealed your balance. Stop involving Martin in your secrets. Stop complaining to kiddos about paying my maintenance. I will e-mail Ralph to keep you honest.

> **Holly**: Learning about the past many year's lies. License plate exposes Nikki's address in Bellevue. Truth will win.

I laughed. "She thinks I live in Bellevue!"

I squeezed the pressure from Alex's shoulders until he begged for mercy. I meant for it to be relaxing, but the fun part of me took over again. At least it broke the spell of negative pressure on him.

"I'm gonna head out, you'll need your sleep tonight. Copper will be fine, I'll come by each day a couple times to make sure."

"Thank you," he said. "You're the best, Nikki."

"I know." Blink.

I zipped home and ran a load of laundry before going to bed. Scanning Facebook for the next hour led me to finally reach for the light just after midnight. I set my alarm out of pure habit as my phone suddenly buzzed back at me. Alex had forwarded me the other messages that came in from Holly after I left, the last one a few minutes after midnight.

> **Holly**: I am keeping track of the number of nights you leave kiddos alone after 9 pm. You are over 20 for the year, a fabulous judge in King County is helping.

> **Holly**: I have lists of license plates of cars at your home. I kept records all year. Truth will win. Our kiddos deserve honest parents. Get home tonight.

> **Holly**: Many friends are helping me. For the kids sake.

I called Alex. "Are you still up?"

"Yeah," he said. "I'm filing a police report for today's events. That was ridiculous; if ever 'disturbing the peace' meant something, it was tonight. I know the prosecutor will likely duck it, but I have to get it documented. It's wrong, what she did, no matter how despondent, wronged, and messed up she feels. She knows better. I've called patrol, they will be by in about 20 minutes to pick up my statement."

"Good," I said. "Maybe that will be some closure so you can leave it behind tomorrow."

"Maybe," he said. "The worse part is that the whole drama interrupted my intent to celebrate *your* birthday. I'm really glad to be going on this trip with the kids, but I wish we could be here for your birthday this week. You've done so much for all of us, Nikki."

He was fishing for a word to express his adoration. I interrupted his thoughts to make sure he didn't find it. "All my pleasure, Alex. You've got a great family and you all deserve a little support. Plus I had a blast."

"Well," he finished, "have a great birthday."

"Have a great trip," I said. Traveling across the state in a van full of goofy teenagers sleeping on air mattresses seemed like more of a recipe for chaotic stress to me than a pleasure trip. I'm more of the pool and palm tree type when it comes to relaxing.

#

June 21, 2009

4:53 am

> **Holly**: Happy father's day. ENJOY THE KIDDOS. You are loved very much. Tell the kiddos I love them. Be safe.

4:58 am

> **Holly**: Choice of vacation spots were poor. Tender for children. First two years should be neutral locations. Parental Alienation Syndrome is ruling. Pray.

5:02 am

> **Holly**: My first priority is to the children. New lawyer is a psychologist. National law enforcement agency now involved. No

fear only love and hope for kiddos. A circle of professionals who specialize in PAS will be advocating for our children. Pray for humility.

8:02 am

Alex: Holly, please stop contacting me while we are on vacation.

8:03 am

Holly: No. You have no authority to make me stop on issues involving children. Text reveals abuse of power and will be forwarded.

8:44 am

Holly: Are you and Martin insured to drive the O'Brien's van? I will be checking to make sure. For the Kids Sake.

1:15 pm

Holly: Police will be investigating the abuse at Faith while you are gone. Katherine's text revealed the morbid abuse you chose there. Sin finds you out.

4:52 pm

Holly: The kids' texts are being forwarded. You may call Sergeant Stringfield at Bothell P.D. to inquire. Now YOU have to answer to attorneys and police.

10:46 pm

Holly: Redeem the kids' memories. Both sides. Mom and Dad matter. You should have visited your own dad on Sunday. You chose selfishness. Your example teaches.

June 22, 2009

The day was full of horseback riding, bucking hay, squealing girls, hollering boys, and the smell of horse poop and gunfire. We had a ball on the Parker's ranch in Deary, Idaho. It was also Nikki's 42nd birthday. I snuck away to the guest room to call her.

"Happy birthday to youuuu," I sang, replicating her most awful voice possible. I figured she'd appreciate that.

"How lovely," she said.

We chatted for a few minutes, leaving me feeling a little awkward as I wanted to finish the call with something like, "Hey, love ya." But it was still too soon; something like that may actually tip the scales and cause her to run. And that would be bad since she was in charge of the dog while we were away. Yeah, no go. I finished with the tamer, "Can't wait to see you when we get back next week! We have tons of pictures."

"Looking forward to it," she said.

She sounded tired. "You keeping busy?" I asked.

"Eh, just getting some laundry done."

I had no idea.

# # #

June 24, 2009

I must be crazy. I thought maybe while Alex and the kids were gone and I had uninterrupted access to their home, I could tackle the laundry stack and bring some order to the chaos of Boxville in the basement.

It took all day Sunday after they left and every evening after work that week to come even close. When the following Sunday rolled around, I'd finished washing, drying, folding, and putting away every single stitch of laundry I could find. I whittled down the sock basket to less than 20 rogue socks, which I then threw away.

Fifty-two loads of laundry.

And not just regular laundry. I finally figured out why the washer and dryer looked odd to me. Both were on a five-inch platform, which made my five-two stature just short of successful in reaching the contents of the washer to move them to the dryer. Each time I had to get a chair and climb up to reach the spun laundry, risking falling in each time. I honestly could have died doing Alex's laundry.

On the good hand, I did find $11.80 in small change by Sunday morning with time to make a dent in the maze of boxes. I suspected most of the stuff in there was either useless, irrelevant, or old. What I found in that pile was about

50% homeschool texts and supplies, 30% photographs of Holly and the kids, 10% sporting equipment, and 9% clothes. *Shit! I just did the laundry!* I soon realized the clothes were destined for donations. I worked up a sweat stacking the homeschool supplies in one corner and the photographs in another, then found some space for the sports gear and donations in the garage.

The photographs were the most revealing. As I looked through each box, I started to see a pattern. Most of the photographs were in envelopes with a loose attempt at organization. The rest were scattered. As time went on for this family, Holly's appearance became more pinched, more disturbed. Alex may not have noticed, but looking at it from an outsider's perspective, it was clear as day. The trend began around the birth of their child, Katherine. Alex told me that was an emergency C-section birth due to the baby's breech position during labor. Maybe the birth itself, the surgery, or even postpartum depression did the damage. But something changed, something that turned Holly from an ultra-kindhearted Christian woman into a person who despised her life and everyone in it…except her children. The pictures also showed she would do anything she could for them. At least until she checked out in 2005.

Alex was in less than about 5% of the pictures, probably because he was the one who remembered to photograph the occasions.

As their entire lives lay before me, I was faced with that nagging choice. *Am I ready for this? Am I that crazy to think I could be part of all this, this thing? Plus the psycho ex-wife?*

I suppose I wouldn't have done 52 loads of laundry if the answer was no.

#

13. SUMMERTIME

Discovering Nikki's little secret operation when we returned blew us all away. I honestly couldn't believe how many actual pairs of socks we owned. If she hadn't been scared away from the laundry or the labyrinth in the basement, she just might actually stick around.

It really made me think. I couldn't wait to see her the following night to thank her. Properly.

# # #

July 1, 2009

> **Alex**: Holly, please understand: it really hurts when you keep saying I didn't have a mom. I know you mean well, but it has nothing to do with logistics for our kids.

> **Holly**: You should really stop telling me what to think and say. Your mom was smart to leave your dad who didn't validate her gifts or yours. She sacrificed to adopt you then the man she trusted took you. She was reduced to a weekend visitor. Give special love to Evelyn. You were also an unwanted baby. Her memories center around the woman you abandoned because you have no mommy memories.

I gave the phone back to Alex. "It's not working," I said. "She's still a bitch." Alex hadn't read past the first sentence of Holly's response to his latest request for her to stop harassing him, this time trying the extra humble approach.

My anger towards Holly was growing. In spite of being evicted several times, living in a car, getting fired from a so-called job at the food bank, and ostracizing her own sisters and parents, she seemed to have no external consequences for her erratic, harassing behavior. Alex labored at making sure he didn't say bad things about Holly around the kids, while they regularly reported her negative insinuations after the mandated visits. Any time she "moved" to a new residence, Alex had to make the adjustment for transportation to the new location. If she made good on her wild dream of moving to Arizona or North Carolina, I'm pretty certain she'd try to require Alex deliver the kids there every Thursday for dinner.

"You're right—" Alex started. I interrupted.

"What was that? Say it again."

"You're right?"

"Yeah, that." I basked in the sunshine of vindication for a moment with my face to the summer sky through the open top of the convertible. "Feels good." It actually did feel good, feeling the warmth of the afternoon sun on the Sunset Avenue overlook of Puget Sound. It was nice having Alex back from his vacation with the kids. This might be a really long lunch break.

Alex gave me a strange look. "You aren't wrong much, are you," he poked.

"You're a learner," I replied.

"You're right," he said with a grin. He leaned in for a kiss; I met it with a last second tongue lashing, licking his nose and startling him back in his seat. "Bleh, what the—" I quickly grabbed his neck and interrupted his objection with an actual kiss. I could feel him drifting in the bliss of the moment.

Alex regained his composure. "And you were right about Holly's continued fixation on me. She 'happened by' the bank yesterday when I was there. While she was at the cashier window next to mine, she told me she would always be my wife and never re-marry."

"You're divorced...doesn't she get that?" My God, she was really getting crazy.

"It's weird," Alex said. "It's like she's regressing back into her previous existence. She called me last night after we got back but I didn't answer. I think she left a message but I'm just so tired of her antics that I ignored it."

I took the phone back. "Better check it, just in case," I said. With Alex's nod, I opened the voice mail message and put it on speaker.

"Hi this is Momma, I called for Martin, Justin, Kevin, Katherine and Evelyn

and I want you to know that I love you. I miss you. I miss your smiles. Your daddy wins. Mommy is done. I cannot fight your daddy this way. I'm not able. I'll be praying for you. I love you."

"Uh oh," I started.

"Yeah." Alex looked worried. After all she had done to make life miserable for him, he still had a strong base of compassion for her.

"Hey, Nik?"

"Yeah?"

"Thank you. I can't believe you did all that."

I smiled. "Eh, I was bored."

#

July 9, 2009

Holly: Gene Rapp happens to be the only officer who isn't divorced. Get a clue.

Holly: My hope is that over the coming days the desires of my heart will be rewarded. My perfect husband, Jesus, loves to see me smile.

July 11, 2009

Holly: Good morning, your plans with my mom did not include me, I wanted my mom and Grandma to join me at North Sound Church. My small group I sing with, the Sawhorse Swingers, perform on Sundays from 1 to 3 and Mondays 9:30 to noon. There is dancing on Sundays. We do the Hokey Pokey. My heart matters, too. I want you to tell Katherine to honor the parenting plan. Need you to take responsibility for the divorce you wanted.

Katherine called me on the edge of hyperventilating. "Dad, Evelyn and I are late coming back from Grandview with Grandma. Mom got really mad at me but it was not my fault; we tried calling Mom this morning but she wouldn't answer her phone. I finally got through to her and tried to let her know what was going on, but she just kept yelling and not listening."

"I'm sorry, Katherine. You didn't do anything wrong. Mom will be happy to see you guys when you arrive."

"She's so mad, Dad." Katherine was dreading this visit. I could hear Holly's mom trying to console the girls, apologizing for the slow traffic over Snoqualmie Pass.

"Katherine, you know how she is; she'll calm down and try to make the best of it. Where are you guys now?"

"We just passed Issaquah, I think."

They'd be back within the hour, putting them almost 2 hours behind schedule. Holly's mom had arranged with me to take the girls to *Rent* on Friday night in Yakima, then stay over night in a hotel in her home town of Grandview before heading home with her 86-year old mother in the morning. As long as they hit the road by 9:30 am, the girls would get back in time for the scheduled noon visit with Holly. Holly wasn't invited on the trip or involved in the planning, which totally pissed her off. When Great Grandma naturally missed the departure deadline on account of getting up late, Holly went from pissed-off to regular angry with a twist of Conspiracy Theory.

I tried to bring Katherine back to stability. "Katherine, hang in. I'll see you tonight. Love you, sweetheart. Stay close with Evelyn."

"I will, Dad. She's kinda being a little, well, you know."

I knew. Within seconds of hanging up, Holly sounded off, right on cue.

> **Holly**: 2 hours late today, 2 of the kids with other plans. I am not your punching bag, this hurts. I deserve my time. Going to Rent and Grandview were not emergent. You are funny. Sometimes your driveway is fine, other times you tell on me to police. LOL. Paper plans are fallible. We are imperfect PEOPLE. Smile and choose giggles over guilt. Hope you had a nice day. Could you put together one box of things from the household items you think I would cherish?

Oh, God, I thought. *Just wait until she finds out her parents want to bring Katherine to Equador in January for a holiday visit.* I called Nikki to fill her in.

"Please tell me you didn't give her another box of…whatever." Nikki sounded annoyed.

"Nope, I'm done with that," I assured her.

"I would have taken a crap in a box and handed it to her," she said.

I laughed. "Somehow I think that may have backfired. If she doesn't yet know where you live, she'd make it her mission to find out!"

Timing is everything. *Ding.*

> **Holly**: Your lady's license came back as a blue Saturn Sky. Maybe police made a mistake. She's worked with you for years. Late nights? Blow jobs? Under-covers? Btw, the only man in Edmonds I was intimate with was John Jones—4 months after you filed a dissolution. Best sex ever, by the way. I was faithful with you. He had me jailed.

"Uh, Nikki?"

"Another random text?"

"Maybe less random and more freakish." I explained how Holly had apparently paid someone to give her license plate information on Nikki's car. And still got it wrong. Maybe I'm not the only one at risk here. I read the text to Nikki verbatim.

"Best sex ever?! Really? Oh I can only hope she comes my way. Bring it on, babe! I gotta tell you, Alex, if she does, I'm probably not gonna hold back. There could be some jail time involved."

I spent years conducting threat assessments from all manner of actors, from the Ted Kaczynski groupies to the friends of Major Nidal Hasan, the Shoe-Bomber Richard Reid, or Anwar Al-Awlaki, the man who inspired most western jihadi wannabes. Holly didn't fit the mold. Nikki, on the other hand…now she was something I'd call Actionable Intelligence. I had to quickly decide between detection and disruption. I went with neither.

"I know nothing," I said, borrowing my worst German accent.

# # #

I knew Alex needed some level of plausible deniability from the imaginary fellow on my left shoulder. I admit it, my mind went to all manner of methods and results. Part of being the younger sister, I think. I kept coming back to a scenario involving six feet of chain link and cinder blocks. No go…we'd need a boat.

"Hey, ever thought about getting a boat?"

"I have my parent's boat," he replied.

"Not a car, you dork. An actual boat. Didn't you grow up on a river or something?"

"Oh that. Yeah, but with the whole single dad thing on a policeman's salary, I refined my future boat goals to the inflatable kind with plastic oars. I did have one for a while."

Alex told me about a 19-foot Glasspar he picked up in Idaho with a 1950's style 55-horse Johnson outboard. "It even had a steering wheel! But I ended up using it as a trade-in for a minivan," he said.

Oh my God. I suppose it shouldn't have surprised me that he had a minivan. "So you're a real life soccer mom, it seems."

"Oh I got that shit nailed," he said. "We went from the Ford Windstar to the Dodge Grand Caravan, then upgraded to the Ford Econoline 15-passenger behemoth. Fire-engine red. I could cram a lot of gear back there."

I just left it alone and switched gears back to the point. "I've always wanted a boat."

"And you usually get your way," he said.

"Yep." Forget the boat, I gotta do something about his car situation. Maybe Sally is ready to get rid of that old Mitsubishi she has at her house. It'd be perfect: Sally had complained about a transmission problem but mentioned it still ran. That was more than could be said for the station wagon…it was starting to really wear thin.

"What do you think about a small SUV? I might know someone who has an option."

"That'd be awesome," he said. "But I only have about $1,000 from the tax return knowing I'd have to get a car at some point."

"I'll see what I can do." I knew he would not accept any financial help from me, but if I could score a low price on a car, that would be just as good.

A week later, the 1999 Mitsubishi Montero Sport was registered to Alex for $750. Shiny, green, and in all its glorious four-wheel-drive, Alex was as happy as I'd seen him. "You know, it's only gonna take a couple Happy Meals to ruin this thing. Sally took excellent care of this car."

"I'm on it," he said. "This one's gotta last us a while. The Buick is up and running again, but it likely won't last for long."

Kevin and Martin affectionately named the vehicle Ludicrous. The rest of us just called it The Mitz. And while it did suffer a fair amount of French Fries, four of the kids learned to drive in that car.

# # #

July 12, 2009

> **Holly**: Hi daddy its Evelyn I'm going to ask mom if I can come home early.

Answering this was a catch-22, so I just let it go. Evelyn usually just played games on Holly's phone. I wondered if she'd seen any pictures or call history. Snapping out of it, I forced myself to remember she's only 9 years old and probably had no interest in the intelligence available at her fingertips, nor should I even be thinking about that. Evelyn was already growing tired of her mother's doting over her as if she was still a toddler.

> **Holly**: There is an awesome jazz band at Taki tonite. I think the sax is a classic Selmer. Please forgive me for falsifying Nikki. Several people told me you have worked with her for years. I do wish you would not entertain her in place of kiddos. Not healthy for them so soon. For the Kid's Sake having a female stepping in as a partner- even a friend-depicts that your desire is to alienate mom-memories. Try alone for awhile.

As if Holly had been trying to be alone for awhile. She already had two date-rape claims under her belt.

July 13, 2009

> **Holly**: Will you pass me books, instruments, music stand, pictures, a bicycle that is not being used, and a large dose of compassion. Thank you. I am going to be very blunt and honest—you are lying to me with kiddos witnessing. Martin knew you were sharing the tax refund, but then you kept it all for yourself. SELFISH.

Let's see: I work every overtime opportunity to pay $1,000 a month in spousal maintenance for the next three years, have custody of all five children and no child support or reliability from the mom who left in January 2008 and does nothing but go around spreading horrible rumors about her police officer ex-husband, all for the privilege of being called selfish since I kept the withholding I already earned when part of it was returned to me for raising the kids. Yeah, no.

> **Holly**: Are you getting items to give to me? The best example to our children is the faithfulness to your word. I play rhythm instruments-the red sticks and a tambourine would be greatly appreciated.

> **Holly**: Is there a reason you are not responding?

July 16, 2009

> **Holly**: Good morning. I will always be near to help what you love most go forward in strength. Please have the kids bring instruments when they come.

> **Holly**: Kiddos arrived with no money for the bus. You have to transport them or pay for it. I do not transport, you do. Sad you taught my precious daughter to call me a stupid liar. You ruined years of our lives by loving power and being deluded. Humble yourself. I drove here cause my purse was stolen. I carry only what I need. I was at a tennis lesson. Do you trust my tennis teacher to drive them?

> **Alex**: I will ensure kids get to you. You are responsible for any mid-time transportation.

This was getting ridiculous, especially for the kids.

> **Katherine**: Ugh Dad, I don't want to be here. Mom's all pissed off again and going off about you. Why do we have to go visit her when she doesn't even have her own place for us to go? Isn't it called Residential Time?

She had a point.

July 17, 2009

I fired up Facebook while waiting in the front office of the orthodontist. Evelyn was the last one to embark on the metal-mouth journey. Time to share.

> *Praying for my little girl about to get braces and a double-helix designed by Jack Bauer himself. If the Senate Intelligence committee is looking for some new techniques post-water boarding, just go with the local orthodontist. Those guys get all the tools!*

It was like an invitation for another note from Holly. T-minus five...four...three...

> **Holly**: No matter how much pain came from this divorce, I love you, The Top Man! Life's gift of 5 jewels were from you. I am honored.

I just don't get it.

July 23, 2009

> **Holly**: My best years so far were being your wife. You are not easy to let go of. Every joy and trial were worth loving you.

I was getting better at analyzing the incoming missiles from Holly and filter out the useful information from the regular waves of nonsense. But they still came through in a fairly steady stream. Working patrol allowed me to ignore the phone for a couple hours at a time, providing a little relief.

I stopped at the office to check email. A handwritten note from one of the clerks in the Records Department caught my eye.

Hello Alex,

I put some paperwork in your box from Holly. I had Assistant Chief Rapp look at the order and it didn't appear to have anything that would be violated by leaving them for you.

Let me know if there is anything we need to know up here.

Thanks,
Nancy

I went upstairs to the mail slots and retrieved the packet of papers. Inside were a couple of hand-written notes with hearts drawn on them in crayon, some copies of articles on Parental Alienation Syndrome, and some fragments of one of Evelyn's torn drawings she made while on a visit. I couldn't tell what it was intended to resemble. All of it was at least unnecessary, more like a jab. Now she had my admin people dancing around trying to "do the right thing" and not get in trouble with her. Amazing.

It took several months for the department to seriously tire of Holly's antics. In the end, she was issued a warning letter from the police department's attorney, advising her she would be charged with trespassing if she came to the station without a legitimate emergency to report. Wiggle room: define "emergency" for a crazy person.

July 29, 2009

Holly: Parental Alienation Syndrome has a powerful hold on your heart and actions. I can never change you. Your choice to rule our family as you do is unloving. Out of love grace I will cover your sin against me 6 years ago. I lost a godly lover. You'll not be able to cherish in a Christ-like way without repentance. I'm choosing not build a case against you. Our children are too important to me. You will stand in God's court. I had your full mental and psych. test done. Your claims were refuted. I will never treat you dishonestly.

# # #

August 8, 2009

A day after their Thursday visit with Holly, several of the kids met up with her in downtown Edmonds for frozen yogurt or time at the beach. The kids initiated the contact, surprising me a little but certainly leaving me happy they were reaching out. On Saturday morning, Evelyn told me she wanted to go hang out with her friend Chloe for the day instead of going to Holly's. I hadn't heard any official change of plan, so I told Evelyn I'd check with her mom. Katherine had already arranged to miss the Saturday visit and the boys all seemed to be trying to put some sort of unstoppable mandatory activity in place so they could skip out.

I thought I'd better keep it simple, hoping to minimize any confusion.

> **Alex**: Hi... I told Evelyn to expect to be with you 12-7 today. She was asking if the last couple days sub'd for the visit. Is this correct?

> **Holly**: I expect that you have encouraged ALL our kiddos that this is my long-awaited time for family togetherness.

> **Holly**: The boys and Katherine choose outside of family. They don't honor me even when they are not working. You taught them by your example.

> **Holly**: I believed you when you promised me a large loving and forever connected family. Now I trust no one. I'm hoping your power doesn't hurt kids.

> **Holly**: I'm home happy to bless children all weekend and every moment in the future. I made a vow that meant. I knew God would enable me to keep it.

> **Holly**: Evelyn told me that you said I don't love you. Stop lying. Forgiveness for the horrid way you forsook me comes from a deep love for the man you are.

Holly: Your mask of power does not fool me. I know the beautiful man hiding beneath a uniform and court documents.

Alex: Holly, please stop this. I never said that to Evelyn…I always speak favorably about you to the kids. I'll cancel plans to ensure all kids are at your residence at noon.

Holly: Let Katherine stick to her plan. I do not want her to be disappointed. Be a man who helps them CHOOSE honor. Forced love and honor are imposters.

Holly: Do not include kiddos this way. It makes me out to be the bad parent. STOP THE MADNESS.

Holly: I asked you out of true honor. You didn't field their questions/plans well. Don't make changes now. Let them stick with plans. Try again next time.

Holly: Stop blaming me. They told me their plans. I texted you. You amended plans. I want you to be better prepared. Divorce is your choice—manage it well.

Holly: I need to clean/run some errands. I shared my heart. You did not need to include kids. Stick with plans. We'll work towards better tomorrows.

Holly: You do not need to do anything for me. I want you to bring Evelyn here at noon.

I made sure Evelyn made it to Holly's by noon and did an overt override on the boys' afternoon plans, requiring them to make the visit in as positive a way as I could muster. Nikki came along for the ride and made copious efforts to encourage Evelyn to enjoy her visit. Before she got out of the car, I gave her a big hug over the center console. "I love you, Evelyn."

"I love you, Daddy."

Watching her walk up to the corner of the apartment complex, my insides were tearing apart. I hated this. I never wanted a broken family; I had done an unusually absurd amount of things trying to prevent it from becoming a reality.

Nikki read right through me and changed the subject for everyone by rolling down the passenger window. "Bye, Evelyn!" She waved violently with a massive smile. Evelyn turned her head and hollered back, "Bye, Nikki!"

Holly's face was as pinched as ever as we drove away. "Did you do that on purpose?" I asked.

"Maybe," Nikki replied.

We spent a pleasant afternoon in downtown Seattle and had an early dinner at The Pike Place Brewery. When we returned at seven o'clock for the pickup, I turned the car around before stopping to wait for the kids to emerge, putting my side of the car closest to Holly's apartment. Nikki noticed. "What, you don't trust me?"

"Oh I trust you. I fully trust you'll do something to innocently spin her up if given the opportunity." I immediately felt bad for saying it, but it didn't matter as the kids spilled out of the apartment. Holly stayed in the safety of the indoors, having apparently learned her lesson, rendering any of Nikki's secret plans foiled.

"You could learn a thing or two from me," she said with that killer grin. "Say it. Saaaay it…"

"You're right."

Satisfied, Nikki turned her attention to the kids. "How'd it go, guys?"

"Fine," they all said in drone-like unison.

Kevin took over from the rear-facing back seat. "Dad, I'm gonna hang out with Mike & Ike when we get home, okay?" It wasn't their actual names, but we all knew the ones he meant. Mike & Ike were the kids of an investment banker who lived two doors down from us. They seemed like cub scout cherubs but I pegged the younger one for an Eddie Haskell type.

"Just be in by dark," I said.

Nikki left the house around 9 pm after an otherwise non-eventful evening, leaving me for some alone time on the piano. I fumbled my way through the circle of fifths, sustaining major 7th chords over the span of the keyboard before each transition. For 20 minutes I was lost in my own music, soaking in the harmonics of the stand-up full board Yamaha piano until my breath was unnoticeable. The exercise gave way to some Billy Joel's She's Always A Woman To Me as I pondered Nikki's manner and ways. I was enamored with this woman.

At 10:15 pm, I snapped out of it, realizing it had been dark for a good while and Kevin was not yet home. I told the others I was going out to drag Kevin in, threw on a hoodie, and walked toward the neighbor's house. As I turned north on 8th Avenue, two girls came walking by. They were about the same age as Kevin.

"Excuse me," I said. "Have you seen a group of boys?"

"You're Kevin's dad, right?" one of them said.

"Do you know where he is?"

She tried to sound vague. "I think he's over there by the church. The one past the school."

"Ah, thank you," I said. The girls quickly skedaddled away. Probably knew I was a cop.

I walked past Holy Rosary school on a thin trail made by local ruffians until it emptied out by the Edmonds Free Methodist Church. This was the church that operated the Edmonds Food Bank, the source of some of my front porch mystery gifts. As I approached the large flat-roofed building from the south, I could see some kids in the side entryway. Two of them were climbing up a maple tree next to the roof, while a third one was trying to jump up and grab a branch. I pulled my hood over my head to make myself entirely dark and quietly walked to the scene to get a better look. I stopped next to a parking sign just in time to see Kevin scramble from the maple to the rooftop. The others egged him on until Kevin suddenly leapt to the tree, caught a branch, swung like Batman and landed awkwardly on the ground. Hushed giggles and commentary followed, including "You're crazy, man!" and "I can't believe you did that!" The monkeys descended from the tree and joined the others on the ground as they walked away. Straight to me.

At the last possible second, I stepped into the light from the church sign, directly in the path of the delinquents. Mike & Ike's pace immediately cut in half as Kevin broke the silence. "Hey, Dad! How's it going?"

I looked at his beaming face, full of his own pride and pleasure, all part of his coping mechanism for dealing with stress. "I'm well, Kevin. Boys," I turned to the others, "Time for you to go home."

They split.

"Kevin, you didn't keep your word. Do you realize what can happen if you get caught or wind up doing some damage here? Not to mention what happens to me if my kids have trouble with the law?"

"I'm sorry," Kevin said, bowing his head. "I didn't mean to be late."

"You didn't mean not to be late, son. Live on purpose." He was fully receiving the message. "You have five minutes to get home. Run."

Kevin split. I turned and followed him at a comfortable walk, certain his run would do its work. I was feeling pretty good about my parenting methodology as he disappeared into the darkness, when I heard a noise behind me. I turned my hooded head just enough to be blinded by a spotlight.

"Sir, police, stop! Show me your hands! Do it now!"

Sergeant Arancio's commanding voice over the PA was interrupted by a second police car conspicuously screaming to a halt with an agitated German Shepherd barking his brains out. I put my hands out wide and slowly turned around with an awkward shit-eating grin under my hoodie.

"Hill?"

I did the math. They thought I was breaking in to the church. "Just out for an evening stroll. Can you put the land shark away please?"

They did. I quickly debriefed the responding officers explaining how I had found my son and his friends climbing on the tree and roof of the church.

"We got a call from a neighbor about a rooftop burglary in progress at the church," Arancio explained. "Then when I get here, there you are all blacked out walking away from the scene of the crime. You're lucky the K9 didn't get here first!"

"I'll make sure there's no damage, but in the meantime, I just sent Kevin running back home for his little stunt. If you hustle, you can intercept him and do a dad a favor."

Arancio clicked his tongue and pointed his finger at me with his million-dollar smile. He was sort of a cross between Tom Cruise and Matt Damon: clever, handsome, and a complete dick when necessary. Between his adequate encounters with the post-married Holly and his own affinity for the dramatic, Arancio had become an understanding sort for my 'situation' as it were and was eager to help out. As he sped off in his slick-top cruiser, I went back to the scene with the K9 officer and his four-legged loudmouth, finding no evidence of any damage.

Arancio intercepted Kevin in front of the house and gave him the full meal deal, explaining in great detail how he not only put himself and his friends at risk, he almost got his dad torn apart by a police dog who hadn't played with his toy in a while. After an adequate education, Arancio switched gears to the compassionate side and ensured Kevin knew he had a friend. Kevin gave me a hug when I walked up and headed into the house. "Thank you, Sarge."

"Totally my pleasure to serve. How you holding up?"

"It's a challenge," I said. "But honestly, these are pretty amazing kids. And, I've met someone."

He smiled wryly. "The gal in the black sports car?"

Figures. He'd likely been keeping an eye on the place during graveyard shift after reports of Holly's stalking my house had circulated the ranks. "Yeah, she's a good lady. Keeps me in check, that's for sure."

"Somebody's got to," he said.

That's the Edmonds kind of police.

August 10, 2009

I inefficiently answered my cell on the second ring. *Dammit.* "Hello, this is Alex."

The annoyed voice on the other end carried low pitch, high decibels, and a thick Ukrainian accent. "Alex, this is Gustav Gruzinsky. You gotta get some control on that crazy wife of yours, man."

Gustav was a local real estate broker who decided he could do big business if he put his larger-than-life happy face on all the local Community Transit buses. To some degree, it seemed to be working, but that didn't stop a local competitor from calling the FBI complaining about his business practices with certain foreign customers, implying his national loyalties may not be all that American. Naturally, this brought him across my desk in my last year at the JTTF in the form of a lead. For that reason, I knew him better than he knew me. The investigation revealed the guy may have some irregular investment methods, but none of it was illegal and he was as American as apple pie. This was particularly refreshing since our kids went to school together.

"Gustav, I have been divorced for six months and separated a year before that. What happened?"

"Your kid was hanging out with Sergei on Saturday morning as you know and apparently they got into some fun involving lacquer spray cans and a bonfire. I came home to find Kevin proudly showing off his singed arm hair to some other kid while my kid was trying to build some kind of flame thrower. They were being dumbasses, but they're fine—then later on your, uh, your ex calls me freaking out and all hell bent on turning me in to Child Protection Services. What the hell is wrong with her?"

Where to start. "Goose, you and I have been through a lot, but you don't know the half of it when it comes to my ex."

"Nor do I want to. I can't afford a problem like that, Alex!"

"Don't worry, Gustav. She's nuts, but you're a good dad and both our boys get to be boys and take risks sometimes. I'm just glad they didn't burn your house down. I got your back."

Gustav actually liked the fact that his persona attracted the attention of the authorities. He was that kind of extrovert. He also liked having a local cop tied to the FBI in his back pocket. "Thanks, brother. If she keeps it up, believe me I'll slap a restraining order on her faster than she can blink in a snowstorm! She got no idea who she's dealing with."

"Get in line," I said. "But definitely let me know if she keeps coming your way or actually files a complaint with CPS. We can probably help each other out here as long as the boys don't keep playing with fire."

"I told her not to fuck with me when she called and kept yelling at me, then I hung up on her. She's a crazy bitch, that woman!"

I suddenly felt envious. In the space of a few seconds, Gustav had accomplished several things I never had the courage to do: Call Holly names, use threats to keep her at bay, tell her to fuck off, and hang up on her during a rant.

I called Kevin. "You okay, Kev?"

"Oh yeah. Did Sergei's dad call you?"

"Yep."

"Dad, it's nothing. We were fooling around on the treadmill and I fell down, so I have a scrape on my arm. I've had worse falling on my bike. And the burn, well that was stupid, but it's just a little red on my hand. I'm fine."

"Okay good. Learn anything?"

"Every time, haha!"

Good enough. I returned my focus to crushing crime on the mean streets of this beautiful retirement community. I should have known the texts would start rolling in. I ignored them until I got off work, a necessary strategy I had developed to keep my own sanity while carrying a gun.

Holly: Please take Kevin to the doctor to have the burns he got while staying with Sergei evaluated. I am calling Edmonds Family Medicine to make the pediatrician aware.

Holly: Gustav responded with 'listen Holly do not fuck with me.' Once he saw the boys lighting things on fire, he took the lighter. Did Kevin get burned?

Holly: He told the burn story to others. CPS has the report. I am his guardian. Stop the abuse.

Holly: How did the injuries from the treadmill occur? Feet usually run on a treadmill, how did he get sores on his forearm and hand?

Holly: How did he fall? He was also burned. The burn was from playing with lighter and something flammable, not A TREADMILL.

Holly: Maybe your parents ignored this type of incident. I will not. I hope you stop lying to yourself and others.

Holly: Katherine has my phone charger. I need it back. Please bring it to me.

Holly: Please take Kevin to the doctor to evaluate the burns he got while staying with Sergei. I am calling the doctor to make him aware. Please do take him even if you believe there is no reason. Then he will be assured you are concerned. I will make sure you follow through. I will call the walk-in clinic to check that Kevin gets seen today.

I closed the phone and left the station for my 7-minute walk home. *Prepare to be disappointed, Holly.*

I made it home by 6:30 pm to find the Crock Pot I had filled that morning had boiled over, leaving a pool of beef and potato juice on the tile countertop. At least it didn't hit the floor. I pulled the plug and lifted the lid, unleashing a billow of beautiful aroma. "Dinner's ready!"

Katherine slowly rounded the corner. "Dad, can we have a vegetable tonight?" Maybe she was adopted or something, but this want of greens all the time was getting old.

"Sure, there's some cucumbers in the fridge. Slice 'em up." She looked proud to have introduced balance to our meal. Katherine had taken on the role of house mom after Holly left, putting her in that weird position with her brothers of having some sort of maternal authority over them. And since I was not a very good mother, I welcomed the effort while trying to also keep her in the kid zone. It was futile. Katherine was now 14 and starting to figure out she could get good grades and hold her own in the school choir. Her attempts to keep the siblings on a laundry schedule weren't very well received, resulting in complaints of her being bossy and mean…two words I would have never anticipated for this ultra-sweet girly-girl.

After gorging on cheap boiled meat and reconstituting the kitchen, Nikki arrived for an evening walk. No doubt she'd be interested in the latest episode of Edmonds Reality TV.

# # #

I parked in the driveway, swapped out my pumps for some tennis shoes, and opened Alex's front door with a knock, a grin, and a complete lack of hesitation. "Hey!"

"Hey, you! C'mon up. Want some meat?"

I looked at the remaining slab of leftovers as he lifted it out of the slow cooker. "Please tell me you had a salad or something with that."

"I made sure," Katherine interjected. "Dad skipped that part again."

Alex looked at me over his shoulder from the kitchen sink and gave a boyish shrug. "What can I say? Not a good mom."

"Good job," I told Katherine.

The kids headed for evening routines: the boys went to the basement for their allowed hour of video games while the girls recorded themselves singing pop karaoke on the computer. Alex and I started our walk as the sun began casting long shadows from the west. We made our way to the waterfront and found our favorite bench unoccupied at the end of Sunset Avenue overlooking the ferry terminal to our left and Whidbey Island to the right. I loved this place, a place we had taken in our share of sunsets with hopefully many more to come. "So," I began. "What's the latest?"

"Take a look," he said, handing me his phone while concealing a sigh. I scrolled through the messages of the day from Holly.

"Is she fucking cra—wait, why am I saying that again? For fuck's sakes! He's a BOY. He's supposed to be adventurous and risky. I saw the road rash on his arm, it's barely even a thing. Can you imagine what she'd do if she found out he'd jumped off the roof of the church?"

"That one skirted the radar," he said. "She went ham on this one, as if she was waiting for something like this to happen. The problem is that she's barking up a pretty rough tree. Gustav Gruzinsky is a good guy, but his threshold for patience with loonies isn't exactly very high. His family knows people who know people…if Holly keeps this up, I could see him resorting to extra-legal means."

"More than that," I said, "she's looking for every opportunity to say you are unfit as a father. At some point, the kids need to realize this." Alex pondered the thought. "And even more, if she keeps complaining to people about you, she's gonna meet some ignorant bastard who wants to prove his devotion to her and try to take you out."

I had worried about this possibility for some time, but didn't want to be alarmist about it. Holly had already thrown her affections to several less-than-reputable types and was in the habit of expanding her false narrative about how evil Alex was to have stolen the kids from her and left her destitute despite her ultra perfection as a mother. She had already been arrested a couple times, kicked out of bars and businesses, and been ditched by a few attorneys. Somewhere along the line she was going to meet someone dangerous. Someone who would either beat the shit out of her for talking back, or who would believe her nonsense and go for some street justice on a dirty cop.

Alex's phone rang, showing a call from the station. I handed it to him.

"Hello, this is Alex. Yeah. No, he's fine. Seriously? Yeah, no problem, I'll meet you there in fifteen minutes." He hung up and took my hand. "Time to head home. She called 911. Arancio has to do a welfare check on Kevin."

# # #

"Kevin, come here, you have a visitor!" I grinned at Arancio, implying I was about to screw with my kid and needed his participation. He nodded. Kevin came out to the front porch a little surprised to see the sergeant again so soon. "I've been home all night, for real!"

"Which means you haven't been doing any fire-dancing, right?"

"Is that why you're here? Oh God, Dad!"

"Kevin, your dad isn't the one who called us. Your mom called saying you needed immediate medical attention and to possibly be taken into custody for your own protection. Do you feel like your dad is neglecting you?"

Kevin pointed at me. "Him? Are you kidding?"

"Does this face look like the kidding type?" Arancio circled his finger around his face. I couldn't help it—I just started laughing. Hard. We all did.

"Glad you're fine, Kevin. I'll note it and try to set your mom at ease."

"Good luck with that, Sarge," Kevin replied and turned up the stairs. Arancio called after him.

"No more flame throwers!"

"Got it!"

I shook Arancio's hand. "Thanks, Dick. Sorry you keep getting drug into this thing."

"Oh dude, it's pure entertainment for me. Holly called and was insisting on the one hand that I immediately take Kevin to a hospital, then refused to identify a clear reason why that should happen. I told her she can't just talk out of her butt and expect people to do things because she just thinks it out loud. She made no sense at all, but I knew if I didn't just do the welfare check, she'd file another complaint on us."

"Another complaint?"

"Oh you probably don't know. There are seven of us now who have had formal complaints filed against us for everything from abuse of power, dereliction of duty, excessive force, conduct violations...you name it. Everyone's been cleared, but you know how that goes."

I did. But I had no idea how widespread her antics had gone. My mere presence in the department had become a liability. Promotion was becoming out of the question.

August 11, 2009

4:59 am

> **Holly**: You NEED to read about PAS. You have made our children like traitors if they love their mom.
>
> **Holly**: KIDDOS are who I'm fighting for. Sgt. Arancio is absolutely wrong. I talk from my heart not my butt. Kevin WAS injured and deserves to be protected.
>
> **Holly**: How are you coming along with my phone charger and school glass project for our girls?

8:39 am

> **Holly**: Can you be trusted for anything other than a check a month? When shall I tell the woman at the ceramic store Evelyn will finish? When can I retrieve my charger?

> **Holly**: I would like to see you help Katherine follow through with charger. When is a good time to get it? Where would you like me to get it?

6:21 pm

> **Holly**: Gustav called you yesterday. How is Kevin? He was honorable to tell the truth. Did he get any burns from lighting something in a can?

August 13, 2009

> **Holly**: Have you noticed that when you shut me out our kids follow your example? I love you and I forgive you. I have great hope each day will be sweeter. So many people love you. We are hopeful you bow and experience healing that will bless many generations to come. You are loved.

> **Holly**: This is to help you. I am your chosen help mate. It was a forever vow. The only thing that truly breaks it is if you shun the promise by marrying another. Then I will pray for that marriage. Because...you are my covenant spouse.

> **Holly**: Good morning. Please remind all kiddos that Thursday is the special day with their precious mom that loves them dearly. I expect you to have Martin and Justin plan an alternative time with me.

> **Alex**: All kiddos will be at your apartment today at 3 unless obligated to job.

> **Holly**: You have to tell ALL kiddos that they put the time with me first and other activities second. That is honor to all of us. Thank you. Threats are not kind. I will keep you fully aware of what is coming. A motion should go through within the month.

> **Holly**: Going to bed sobbing. Why did you teach my sons to

disregard their mom? It is one day. You forgot me again. Is it so hard to remind them to call me?

I was beginning to realize that Holly's harassment of me would not stop. Unless, maybe, if she got married to someone else. Maybe then.

August 14, 2009

To: Alex
From: Holly

Alex,

By the grace of God, I wake every morning still loving you. I hope you know that it is not only about a covenant. Love for you had to do with the handsome, friendly, intelligent, and very talented man that God purposely put beside me as a friend. The friend became my lover, then he was my husband, then he was a hard-working career man, then he became the father to the five most beautiful children in this world, and now he is my friend again. Life is a delicate and lovely process. Our greatest sorrows are meant to create a sense of urgency to run to our Heavenly Father and find in Him what we can never find in a person. Learning not to trust you has been hard. I wanted you to be so much stronger and more compassionate than what I now see in you. Please forgive me. If any woman could have an excess of hope; I think it just might be Holly.

Please try to understand that I meant you no harm on Monday. The report to CPS was directed at Gustav, not at you. He should have been more aware of what the kids were doing. Even if, and Kevin still holds to there being a lighter and fire involved, there was no flame that burned my child, there was definitely negligence involved. I honor our son for knowing it was not right and having the courage to speak up. It tells me his character is sensitive to the truth and he loves himself enough to speak up and know he will be listened to. I trust that you would not have spoken to me the way Gustav or Sergeant Arancio did. I was not fucking with anyone, nor was I talking out my butt.

Above all other virtues, honesty reigns supreme in my book. I think fight for the truth of a heart is vital. Even when the truth I hope for is not there, at least if a person or myself am honest, the issue of the heart can be cherished and compassion can be administered according to the need or want. So I cannot discern the truths in your heart. I can only tell you mine. I am angry that you would take a one-night stay at my aunt's and use it against the children and I to gain so much for yourself. Leaders in your department all know that I was reaching out to you and tried to be back in the home with my family Sunday, March 2, 2008. Dr. Maleek knows that the week before, I was committed to helping our marriage survive, at any cost. There are still documented letters from professionals that state the same.

No matter how hard I may try to justify what you did, I cannot. There is not an ounce of divorce in my heart. I never believed in it. I still do not. There will always be a stronghold of covenant commitment ascribed to the desire of my soul in a marriage. I believe that is what love is about. So from March 3, 2008, and on into eternity, my desire will be to be married with no signature on any divorce paper. I am who I am, and I cannot lie. I believe the false arrest by your partners was God's way of keeping me from the temptation to sign and agree with your onslaught.

At this time, what remains is a mother and a father that dearly love our children, although very imperfectly. Please try to understand the email in regards to Parental Alienation. The website gives a list of things to avoid. It was intended to help both of us. The children's hearts and spirits come first. "Suffer not the children." Anyone that causes a child to stumble...I could have unloaded the whole verse at church that morning. The end (lest you be cast into the bottom of the sea) did not seem like an appropriate benediction. All the same, the weight of the whole verse should cause every parent to tread lightly and prayerfully in regards to their behavior and motives involving a child. Many of my friends and relatives are praying for you and the elders at Faith to see the gravity of the sorrows inflicted on our children as well as others...especially the young women. Even Sgt. Stringfield at Bothell Police is hopeful to see a sweet spirit arise form the unloving actions of the elders there. I did not lie about the bruise the elder caused when grabbing my arm. I do not think he intended the harm, but it happened all the same.

I am hopeful that you will stand up for justice in your church and your workplace and your family. I intend on becoming involved somehow with the Criminal Justice Training Panel at the state level. I think training and teaching to issues is the best way to see change. Divorce is sky-rocketing in Law Enforcement and Parental Alienation is more common in Officer families than most others. Fighting for the Family, has always been my "heart cause." In doing so, I will be fighting for you and our kiddos as well as other marriages and families. Family is the foundation of our society. I am hopeful to make a positive difference.

I love you this day more than yesterday. Please encourage our older sons to make up their lost time from yesterday.

With Sincere Love,

Holly

Oh the irony of it all. It wasn't that the letter didn't have an effect on me. This was one of the more cogent writings from Holly, most of which bounced between disconnected thoughts and fragments of reality. This was different, more calculated and consistent. Not that it was anywhere near accurate; her attempt to re-enter the home in March 2008 came with a host of nutty demands, starting with me vacating the house, going to in-patient treatment, and leaving the children with her. Unreal.

Her notion that the domestic violence coordinator and other leaders in the police department were somehow in support of her decisions and actions was completely ridiculous. For me, it all verified I had pulled the right trigger at the last possible second. Still, her pleadings about family, hating divorce, and some of the phrasings we used to repeat to each other out of commitment to the marriage struck a hard chord.

I still didn't hate her by any stretch, and I still wanted her to be well, if not for herself then at least for the kids. But the tone of this letter, so reflective of her posture in the past, finally helped me grasp the mastery of her manipulations.

August 15, 2009

Alex: Holly, please stop initiating contact with the children. I have and will keep encouraging all of them to have frequent contact with you.

Holly: You have allowed it for months. Now you are defending court orders like a commander because you are defensive knowing an attorney is backing.

Alex: That has nothing to do with it.

Holly: Yes it does. Read Parental Alienation article. Did you enforce the kiddos time with mom? Absolutely not! I have so much proof to defend myself. I am not letting you terrorize me or my children any longer. Back down and do what is honorable.

Alex: It is simple: do not initiate the contact. Copying me in does not negate the standard. Just follow the parenting plan.

Holly: The contact is directed to you to remind them what you said. It's what moms do. It is to honor you first and to help them honor equality in parenting.

Holly: This is all being documented from now on. Daily contact is essential for Evelyn. You not helping her is a shame.

Holly: You forced me to "fight like a man and an attorney and an officer." I won't give up until you treat me like an honored equal. No mom—no real family.

Holly: The kiddos know to respond out of fear when you are involved. It comes from your career position.

Holly: Come from the hearts, soon. Legalism from you hurt our whole family. We all need refreshing love and the Spirit's leading, not just ALEX.

Holly: I have learned to dance to your music. You have shot me down way too long. I'm rising up to fight for the family life you promised. God didn't forget.

14. DISORDERLY CONDUCT

September 6, 2009

The Saturday visit didn't go too well. I summed it up in a note to my attorney.

To: Rachel
From: Alex

Today, Holly had residential time with the children from 12-7. At 4:19 pm, Katherine sent a text: "Mom said there would be a lawsuit." At 5:18 pm, Justin sent, "Ok mom has been yelling at everyone for the past hour." At the same time, Katherine called crying hard, then tried to explain how she got kicked out of Mom's house. She asked to be picked up. I spoke with Justin, who said Holly had been yelling at people all afternoon: at the Verizon store, in the parking lot to various drivers (calling people bitches, etc.), and in her home. Holly told Evelyn to stop yelling or she would get kicked out of her apartment. Katherine and Justin said mom kept talking about "the lawsuit against your father for all the horrid things he did against me!" Several comments were made about lawsuits, divorce, etc.

Katherine said, again, that she never wanted to go back there because every time she gets yelled at and feels horrible. Justin said it's still their Mom, so they are going to have to see her no matter what. Justin and Katherine both said they had not explained these things to Dr. Maleek at the counseling sessions with him.

I picked them up an hour early. Holly stood in front of my car, blocking my exit and refusing to move. When I backed away she yelled, "Thanks—that's not what you would've done if the kids weren't here!" I was able to safely drive a different way out of the parking lot.

The kids were relieved to get out of there. I sent Holly a text message saying I was taking the kids home who had been told to leave or who were distraught at the ongoing inappropriate behavior. I later learned

Holly's phone has been disconnected.

Alex

Later that night, I received an email from Holly—addressed not just to me, but also to the Chief of Police and a half dozen attorneys.

> **To: Alex, et al**
> **From: Holly**
>
> Alex: I will not tolerate you ignoring Evelyn any longer. Justin has got to stop saying we are retarded and stupid and silly. Katherine, Evelyn, and I are not your son's verbal punching bag. He may not pick her up and carry her outside and lock the door behind her. You taught him this. Stop saying you are a good dad and realize the results of your choices.
>
> Kevin laughed when a car almost backed into me. Justin told me how retarded I was to work so hard to connect Kevin's phone. Kevin needs to see a doctor about not gaining enough weight.
>
> Justin and Kevin mocked Katherine for trying to be helpful. Katherine, Kevin, and Justin left without telling me where they were going or when they were returning. Evelyn said she feels better when she is not with them because they call her names and ignore her. They all called her a spoiled brat and said they wished they could just spank her. None of the children are allowed to lock me out of the rooms of my apartment any longer. You locked me out of cars, out of homes, and out of places of comfort. Stop passing on your abuse to our children.
>
> Holly

September 10, 2009

Justin stormed into the house after school in disgust. "Jesus!"

"Whoa," I said. "What's up?"

"Mom says she's getting married this Saturday to a man who owns a boat.

She figured the visits would be more fun that way."

This one surprised even me. "Who?"

"That Phil guy, she introduced us during the last visit saying he was a friend of hers who has a boat. Supposedly he is a fisherman or something. She's out of her mind, Dad."

Smart kid, I thought. "Well," I started, "we'll see how this goes I suppose." I purposefully modeled disinterest, hoping he'd catch on. He was already out the door with his lacrosse stick in hand. I heard the whip of the stick repeatedly in the front yard as Justin tore up the remaining grass that survived the summer. The return of fall meant the lawn would soon yield to rain, cleats, and ground-ball practice until it was nothing more than a mud pit. And somehow it would spring back next year as if nothing happened. Renting has its benefits.

I stepped to the back deck and called Nikki. "What do we know about Holly's new boyfriend, this Paul guy?"

Nikki's computer keyboard started clicking madly. "Not much…he has a boat at the marina at the moment, he probably doesn't live here, and he probably doesn't have a job or a car. This is the guy Holly tried to introduce us to during our walk down there, right?"

"I'm guessing so. Anyway, apparently they're slated to get hitched this weekend."

"What?" Nikki's disbelief was pretty clear.

"That's what she's telling the kids anyway. I have my doubts."

"Alex, this is one of those guys. If he's entertaining her, he may believe her lies about you, and that could be bad for you, let alone the kids."

"I'll look into it. I don't care who she dates, even who she wants to bring around the kids. But if he's a known risk, that crosses a line."

"Be careful…"

"I will. I won't use any police info, that's the quickest way for me to lose my job. Open source all the way."

Without a last name, a vehicle, the specific boat, or any other fragment of data, I came up empty. I called a buddy at the port and told him the situation; he said he'd let me know if he figured it out.

That night when I went to bed, my phone buzzed. I hoped it was Nikki. No dice.

> **Holly**: Hi. I still believe in the beauty underneath ugly choices. I will free kiddos from deceit. My mom taught me to live in truth. Our kiddos will be taught the same.

> **Holly**: Please give hugs and love to the kiddos from mom. Honor what is honorable. I love them more than life itself. You know that is true.

> **Holly**: Cunning cops that love power abuse do not compare to wives and moms who love you and your children enough to let you have your glory.

At least we have a date night tomorrow. The anniversary of 9-11 had been a date of high alert for the last seven years. This year I could let it go.

# # #

Alex arrived in the station wagon in a nice pair of jeans and a new short sleeve button-up. "Old Navy?" I asked.

"School shopping," he said. "It was buy-one-get-one, so I lucked out."

We jumped in the Sky and headed for Mill Creek. I wanted some Mexican food more than ever, so we landed at La Palmera, the most happening joint in the village. Alex reminisced about his night there with his boss, Chuck Jensen, when he introduced him to Patron Silver, or what he remembered of it anyway. We laughed our way through the evening, both of us eager to get back to my place and forego the Old Navy attire.

Two grande margaritas and a couple quesadillas later, that's exactly what we did. We barely made it into my front room before the passion took over. An hour later, we lay next to each other on my bed cooling off, pillows everywhere, both of us staring at the ceiling in full afterglow mode. I brought us back to reality. "So, anything new from psycho?"

"I haven't even checked since I left the house," he said. The boys have babysitting duty tonight so the kids know we're on a date. I told them I'd be home by midnight."

"I'll check!" I grabbed his phone and saw the notification of multiple texts from Holly. "This will be fun," I giggled. Not sure really what had come over me, maybe the tequila.

> **Holly**: Another night when Evelyn wonders if she is safe. Daddy loves himself and Nikki more than her. Your choices make her anxious.

> **Holly**: If any other kiddos want to tour the boat, Mom loves their company. I choose to be home every night when kiddos are with me.

"Oh, that little bitch!" I hated her posturing as the ethical one when she's the one that has done so much damage to these kids.

"Looks like she's taking note of my absence from home," Alex said. "She likes to do that."

> **Holly**: The boat would be cool for kids to see. Who cares about family? Alex wants kids in bed anxious while he gives he and Nikki their desires.

> **Holly**: Our kids have remained faithful. Read texts. Sons follow wisdom of mom.

Man, she's weird. "I'm sorry, Alex...she's a freak," I said.

Alex just shook his head.

> **Holly**: Do you understand that I am a survivor of abuse? I am beautiful. I overcame so much.

> **Holly**: Do you understand that you were a child abandoned and abused? You are beautiful. You overcame so much.

"She's not gonna let go, Alex."

"She doesn't have a choice."

But I knew otherwise. Women hell-bent on keeping their men within their span of control will go to great lengths to ensure it happens. Either that, or they'll risk everything trying. Add that to the mama bear thing and her perception that Alex was simultaneously abusive and wonderful, and you sum up to a risky hot mess.

Alex wasn't the only one at risk.

# # #

September 20, 2009

Maybe Holly was seeing a new midnight therapist or something. I couldn't figure it out, but my ability to understand didn't slow down her effort to inform. Even at 6:42 am.

> **Holly**: I see your true colors, that is why I love you. Your badge, your lies, your church, your role as a father, or coach will never hide the man I know and love.

> **Holly**: A godly man sees his wife as helper, even in discernment. I honored your wishes and bore much pain in surrender.

> **Holly**: Why would you take advantage of such strong love? Why guard your interests and not mine? Is that love or a lie to God?

> **Holly**: I could never hate you. Childbearing and nurturing our kiddos healed my childhood abuse. To abandon me re-kindled deep pain.

> **Holly**: Leaving me to strangers and abusers was what my parents did. I witnessed more than I knew how to manage.

> **Holly**: When you are not able to be home with the kiddos, I am available to lovingly care for them. This was what you promised. Please will you set aside the power of bitterness and pride. Please love your children and I enough to surrender. BLESS and BE BLESSED.

Holly: I love your weaknesses. I know your nightmares. I have not laughed when you cried. I believe in you. I love you-my friend/husband/friend again. FORGIVENESS RULES!

Holly: I know it is asking so much…I wanted to be your lover not only your friend and a mom. Why was that too hard for you?

Holly: Please tell Katherine that she has taught me so much about GOD's beautiful holiness. Tell her I LOVE HER…so much. She has a sweet spot that nothing will ever replace, in my heart.

Holly: Hi. Please tell the kiddos I love them.

I rolled out of bed and let the dog out. Evelyn was already up making some toast a full hour before she had to be ready. "Daddy? If I take a shower three days in a row, does that mean I can skip the next three days?"

I just stared at her, considering the possibility that this was all a dream. She handed me a piece of toast, then lifted her arm and sniffed her armpit. "See, I'm good!"

"What day are we on here, Evelyn?"

"Day three." She said it all serious-like, apparently having convinced herself that she wasn't completely offensive to public health.

"Thanks for the toast, kid. Hit the shower."

Frown. Squint. Scowl. Hard sigh. "Fine."

How do they turn into that? I wondered. *And so young!*

# # #

September 26, 2009

Fall lacrosse season was fully under way, giving me the opportunity to skip becoming the typical soccer mom and go straight to lacrosse mom, aka lax-mom. Didn't matter if they were your kids: if you were an adult woman and helped out the lacrosse team, the players called you Mama. Alex helped coach the Chiefs for the last however many years, so it was easy for me to step in. I knew nothing about lacrosse, but I knew how to slice up oranges for halftime.

Alex was proud being with a woman who was decidedly sane.

Holly came to the game in her usual way, a little late, unkempt, and with her arm in a sling. She had been evicted yet again from her last housing venture and apparently the vehicle she had used was no longer an option, leaving her now both homeless and carless. As I sat in my fold-up camping chair behind the home team trying unsuccessfully to mind my own business, I overheard Holly explaining to a group of parents how she managed to figure out which bus to take to get there, even with a broken arm. Her effort to gain sympathy was non-stop.

I checked myself: here's a woman who has lost virtually everything important to her, albeit by her own doing, and I was finding some sort of disgust at her attempts to drain other people of their generosity. I supposed it bothered me because it was all so unnecessary. She did these things to herself, ruining her relationship with a supremely giving man, abandoning her own family, refusing to cooperate with anyone who tried to help her, and refusing to take responsibility for her own actions. This didn't seem like mental illness to me, though I quickly told myself that I was far from an expert on the subject. If she could just take that massive amount of determination to get people to do things for her and blame them, then put that energy into something marginally productive, she'd not only have a quickly improved situation but would also have grounds to increase her time with her kids. It seemed pretty simple to me, but I didn't know if it would ever happen.

Having obtained a little sympathy from the group, she turned her attention to the field. "Go, Kevin, go Justin, all right you guys way to go! Woo-hoo!" Awkward.

As Holly passed me, she locked her menacing eyes on mine and glared. I cracked a smile in return unaware of what was about to take place. She continued to pace back and forth mostly behind me, fists balled up, arms stiff, face pinched, shoulders raised, and jaw clenched. I tried to ignore it but my Spidey-senses were on full tilt.

At halftime, I grabbed the bag of oranges and took them to Alex for distribution. The sweaty kids all sounded off with a big, "Thank you, Mama Nik!" Alex gave me a loving glance. I collected the dirty, empty rinds in the bag from the team, then approached Alex as he talked to Kevin.

"Remember to use your team. Pop out for the feed when Schleisman clears midfield, then drive for an iso. That's what they expect. When the defense slides, dump it straight back to Gumdrop. He's gonna be open for the shot right over your shoulder."

"Got it," Kevin said. "Hey thanks for the goodies, Nikki!" He gave me a muddy, sweaty hug.

Ew. "Any time," I said.

Alex was pleased. "I think they're getting used to you," he said.

"I think I like it," I replied. "I'll just go throw these away."

I started the walk to the far corner of the field where the only garbage can had been placed to keep the bees away from the crowd. Half way there, I sensed it. She approached at an unusually high speed from the side, turning at the last second to match my pace beside me. I prepared myself to be punched but continued my path, confident I could return the favor in spades.

"Your being here gives off negative energy," Holly started. "I love you dearly but I don't want you around *my* children."

I have never had a conversation with this woman prior to this day and was baffled by her statement. I'm certain my expression was one of confusion. "That's unfortunate you feel that way," I said.

"I'm warning you, stay away from my children." Her verbal intensity was beginning to match her pinched face.

I calmly tossed the bag of orange remains into the garbage, then turned to face her. "Is that as a threat?"

"Keep it up and you'll find out!"

My mouth curled itself into a well rehearsed sarcastic smile as I leaned toward her. "Okay!" I stood there as Holly spun around and started to walk away. I may have been a tad disappointed not getting to deck her. Holly's departure didn't last—she paced me again on the way back to the parent section.

"There are lawsuits pending against Alex and it's going to get really ugly," she announced. I ignored her entirely and continued my walk back to Alex as halftime was just getting over.

Holly hovered from distance as I got Alex's attention. "Call me."

"You okay?" he asked, clearly able to see I was not able to entirely ignore Holly's little show.

"I'm great," I stated. "That was an interesting little exchange! I need to leave now, just call me later." I didn't want to risk affording Holly the chance to completely disrupt the event. My lax-mom thing would have to wait.

I walked to the parking lot, stopping briefly to talk with another understanding parent who saw Holly doing her thing. It was clear most of the parents had endured something like this before with her. I fired up the Sky and started to back out of my parking space where I could then see Alex and Justin walking toward me. It appeared they didn't know Holly was following them. "Hey, do you need to talk?"

Before I could answer, Holly yelled at me. "Keep your mouth shut, Nikki!"

"I'll take that as another threat," I replied.

Holly yelled back, "It's not a threat!" as she ran out of the parking lot and across the street.

Alex was dumbfounded. "Just call me," I said, then pulled out of the parking lot, spinning my tires just a bit in the gravel. It was hard to keep that little turbo under control, after all.

She had crossed the line. I felt threatened by her. This crazy bitch was going to be more of an issue than Alex gave her credit for.

I knew just what I had to do. I drove straight to the Lynnwood Police Department and filed an incident report. The following Monday, I obtained a temporary protection order against Holly. I had no idea how much fun it would be getting her served.

# # #

It killed me. I had never seen Nikki that kind of hot. It was simultaneously impressive and frightening. Mostly, I feared she had reached her internal final straw and put this whole relationship in her rear-view mirror.

Oddly, that didn't happen. She called to reassure me that she left for our sakes and was headed to Lynnwood PD to file a report. For someone who never had kids, she sure had a solid "Get Behind Me, Honey" instinct.

Holly didn't waste any time sounding off.

> **Holly**: For you to nurture a relationship with NIKKI visibly so often in the face of our children...is a hellish scheme. Play with her privately.

> **Alex**: Absolutely none of your business.

September 27, 2009

The following day, another unfortunate incident occurred, this time in front of my home. I had finally reached my limit. I drafted the following statement and delivered it to the police department, demanding an investigation of Cyberstalking and Court Order Violation:

Sworn Statement of Alex Hill:

On September 27, 2009, I was on duty with the Edmonds Police Department. While at home on a break, one of my children came to me and said, "Dad, mom is outside and wants you to come out and talk to her." At that same time, Lynnwood Police requested priority assistance from Edmonds Police with an emergency call in Lynnwood. I responded on my hand-held radio that I would be en route with other units.

I quickly walked outside my house and toward my assigned, marked patrol vehicle, which was parked in my driveway facing out toward the street. Holly Hill, my ex-wife, was standing in front of the house in the yard and started saying something to me; I told her I had to leave right away for an emergency in Lynnwood. Holly ignored this and walked toward me, insisting that Martin (17) had told her I wanted to talk to her. This was untrue: 30 minutes prior, Martin had heard Holly say she wanted to take the girls (Evelyn-9 and Katherine-14) to lunch, so Martin told Holly she had to clear it with Dad since it was outside of her residential time. Holly took this to mean I wanted to talk to her, which was baseless. The kids all walked home on their own and arrived home about 10 minutes before Holly arrived at my home.

As Holly was approaching me, she was still in the grass of my front lawn. I told Holly I had to leave for an emergency right now, and that she needed to get out of the yard. Holly paused, then walked hard to the very edge of the roadway next to the grass and glared at me. I started my patrol car. Holly started yelling at me about something unintelligible, still in front of my house where the kids were. I rolled up my open window and got on my police radio asking for Assistant Chief Rapp to contact me by cell phone. As I was asking for this on the radio, Holly walked in front of the police car, stopped, and yelled, "You're going to have to run me over!" I couldn't believe it; this was reminiscent of another recent incident where Holly stood in front of my personal vehicle when I was picking up children from a visit in Shoreline two weeks ago; she then refused to move until I backed away against the regular flow of traffic.

Holly stood in front of my patrol car for about 5 to 10 seconds, then yelled "I thought you had to go to an emergency!" while walking away, west on Dayton street. I paused a minute to breathe and jotted down the last thing I had heard her say on my mobile computer (something about how she loves me more than I loved her). This notation posted at 12:19 pm. I did not want to leave until Holly was away from my house, out of concern for my children and the likely possibility that she would continue or escalate her interference with my egress.

When Holly was a few feet past the front of the house, I began to drive my patrol car from my driveway toward 7th Avenue. Holly was walking westbound on the north side of Daley street near the bridge at Shell Creek as I pulled out of my driveway. As I began to head westbound, Holly turned to see me, looked away, and immediately walked to the exact middle of the roadway, preventing me from driving past her. Holly continued walking this way for about 10 seconds, causing me to slow down and wait to see what she would do next. Eventually, Holly began to edge toward the left side of the road, still in the roadway. When she was far enough out of the middle, I passed her. As I drove past, Holly again turned and walked toward the driver's side of my patrol car, yelling at me. I got past her before she could touch the car.

As I was passing Holly, I received the return call from Assistant Chief Rapp. I told him Holly had gotten in front of the patrol car and had been in my yard. He asked if another patrol car was needed at the scene; I said both Holly and I had left the residence and that I would go to the station and write a statement after the emergency was over in Lynnwood.

I ended the call with the Assistant Chief and headed north on 7th Avenue, still only a block from my residence. At that point, I attempted to find out details of the emergency in Lynnwood. I found that during Holly's interruption, the Lynnwood situation had resolved and Edmonds' assistance was no longer required.

When I got to the station, I began to receive text messages from Holly. They are as follows, unedited, with my reply in italics:

12:23 pm: Evelyn leaned into the crook of my neck and whispered that NIKKI is your lover. You asked the kiddos to lie. TRUTH.

12:35 pm: Evelyn knew I deserved the truth. She said you asked other kiddos to hide the truth. You fought with deceit.

12:37 pm: *Stop texting me. Not only is it untrue, it is harassment. E-mail only from now on.*

12:59 pm: Our daughter did not tell me the most painful truth of my whole life to distance you. It was to free me.

1:03 pm: Stick to court orders. I will text. I do not pay for internet. Would have been so sweet to just tell ME I was not what you wanted anymore.

1:07 pm: The legal arena made you a powerful deceiver. Kiddos are so needful of honesty and consistency. You are better than your schemes.

My son Justin (16) called at 12:46 pm and told me he heard Holly yelling at me in front of the house. He did not know she was in the yard. Martin spoke to me as well and said he saw Holly in the yard of the house.

Holly has been clearly advised on numerous occasions to stay off the property of my residence, including a restraining order under threat of arrest for this very offense. Holly's violations of this order are recurrent and her intensity of confrontational behavior is escalating. Two days ago, Holly disturbed my peace again at Kevin's (12) lacrosse game in Lynnwood, resulting in one person there calling police and filing for an anti-harassment order and embarrassing both Justin and Kevin at the game.

End of statement.

September 28, 2009

Holly: I beg forgiveness. It hurts so bad that I was not good enough for you. You hate my beautiful spirit. I'm not getting past the abandonment.

Holly: I wanted you to pursue dreams with me, not leave me to the nightmare of aloneness and pain. Forsaking me hurts like hell.

I received a voice mail from the children's psychologist later that day, validating the decision I had made. My boss had told me to hide behind the professionals.

Hello Alex, Jamil Maleek here, sorry I did not get back to you earlier. I read your statement. It is very distressing and concerning, in terms of behavioral reinforcement and enforcement. The likelihood is that it will get worse, so I encourage you to follow through with whatever legal support you can and, in terms of the police and filing your own reports, and making sure she follows all the others so that there is an external structure set with other law enforcement with her because it…by just thinking you can handle it yourself, that's probably only going to enable it to make it worse.

15. Public Service

It had been a few days since Nikki obtained a protection order from the court, but with Holly being homeless and carless, it wasn't all that simple locating her outside of her residential time with the kids. Neither Nikki nor I was willing to utilize that time to serve documents while she was agitated, which would assure a rotten time for the kids. Nikki decided she would find someone to help track Holly down and get her served with the order. Nikki was very determined to make this happen, maybe even more than I was.

Holly's escalation continued over the week and for weeks to follow. She had other fronts in her battle with reality, not just with me.

October 1, 2009

> **Holly**: I need you to help me. I think I love another man as much as you. I want you to tell me it's ok.

The fact crossed my mind: if Holly gets married, I no longer have to pay $1,000 a month to fuel her insanity. So of course I'd bless it! But that obviously wasn't my role. Obvious to me, anyway.

October 3, 2009

> **Holly**: I have not met him. My realtor friend is his business partner. He lives in AZ. He is coming to see me tomorrow.

> **Holly**: Papers did not free my heart from you. I still love you as husband. Your love blessed me so much. Hurts to feel like I am not honest. SOS! Can you save me?

> **Holly**: Kevin did not call yesterday. Really want to hear his voice and know he is ok. Please ask him to call. Pass on a hug and mom loves him.

Holly: Rick will not come to meet kiddos and I without a free yes from you. It is the certainty of the gift wrapped in your love that I hoped for. Thank you for what you could give. I would like to guard my heart and the kiddos by keeping away from events where your partner is.

Holly: Rick will honor me by only meeting kiddos. Parenting and events that we did together I will do singly until I am sure kiddos are healed.

Again, the ability for her to self-assess is out the window. *Who the hell is Rick?*

October 9, 2009

Holly: I want to buy you a Home. I know finances have been hard. Love you all.

October 10, 2009

Holly: Hi. I need to figure out how to live on your maintenance.

Nikki and her friend Christie Waters finally had some success locating Holly and getting her served. Of course, Holly didn't think so.

Snohomish County District Court
Statement of Christie Waters

In response to petitioner Nikki Myers' request to serve documents to the respondent (Holly Hill), I was walking West on Main St, at approximately 4:08 pm. I spotted respondent walking East on the same street. Respondent passed by and I followed said respondent into 'A Very Taki Tiki Bar & Grill'. I lost sight of the respondent, figuring she had gone into the restroom, and stood by a table for a moment looking at the baseball game playing on TV while waiting for the her to exit the restroom. The respondent walked out of the restroom and immediately exited the building. I proceeded to follow the respondent West on Main St. walking towards the Edmonds Ferry Dock.

I caught up with said respondent at the stop light crosswalk on the corner of Sunset at approximately 4:21 pm. I then said, "Hi Holly" as I held out the service documents to the respondent. The respondent turned towards me brushing the service document envelope with her forearm as she turned. The respondent proceeded to tell me "I don't have to take that. I don't know you." Then the respondent turned back toward the crosswalk proceeded to cross and then turned back as she continued to walk yelling to me, "Don't touch me! I don't know you! What is your name? I don't have to take anything from you." I simply stated, "I didn't touch you" as she was briskly walking away. I promptly turned around and walked back West up Main St to my parked vehicle. I then conversed with the petitioner who asked me to attempt another personal service on the respondent, noting that she didn't have to take the documents, just to be served with them.

I entered my vehicle and proceeded to circle around to Railroad St via Dayton to try to spot the respondent again. I saw her as she was talking on the phone and crossing in the crosswalk at the intersection of Railroad St continuing to walk East up Main St. I drove up Main St past the respondent and parked on 2nd Avenue next to the United States Post Office in Edmonds, WA. I walked to the Main Street intersection and the respondent was no where to be seen. I then proceeded to walk down to Sunset but did not see the respondent. I returned to my vehicle and drove back over to Dayton Street, then West to the railroad, and North to Main Street again to see if I could relocate the respondent's position. There I spotted her again walking East up Main Street.

I drove East past the respondent and parked on 6th Street. At 4:57 pm, I observed the respondent again walking East up Main St into 'A Very Taki Tiki Bar & Grill'. I proceeded into the Tiki and stood near the restrooms until I spotted the respondent who was seated at a table in the back of the establishment. At 5:03pm I approached the respondent and as the respondent recognized me from my previous personal service attempt, said respondent proceeded to spin out of her chair while yelling at me "You have got to stop following me!" I immediately answered "You're served" and dropped the envelope containing the service documents onto the respondent's phone and purse left on the table as the respondent continued to run out the back door of the establishment into the alley. I turned and walked out the front door of the establishment, returned to my vehicle and left the area.

End of statement. Christie Waters.

Martin: Hey, fill me in! I walked in the Tiki and I saw mom out of the corner of my eye run out the back. Her stuff is still here with a big envelope.

I called Martin. "Hey, so you were at the Tiki?"

"Yeah, mom wanted me to come to some meeting she was having with a guy. Something about Amway. She was pretty freaked-out! Should I pick up this envelope?"

"Nope. Martin, I'm pretty sure your mom has some things going on other than our family stuff."

Dr. Maleek, had cautioned me at one point to stop preventing the kids from seeing their mom in her actual condition. This was one of those times I just needed to let the evidence speak for itself. At 17 years old, Martin wasn't afraid to face it, either.

"So did you sign up?"

"With that crap? Dad, you always said multi-level marketing ruins your relationships with family and friends by exploiting them. Not interested."

Smart kid.

October 11, 2009

Holly: Hi. Please stop chasing me. The woman came next into the Tiki. I was meeting a man for business. I left. Docs are at Tiki. Police Officers responded.

Holly: Never saw envelope from stalker woman. Does Nikki have priority over me at lacrosse games?

October 16, 2009

Since Holly failed to show up for her hearing on Nikki's petition for a restraining order, the court issued the temporary order. The newly signed document would also need to be served, showing Holly that it was now a permanent order, not just a temporary one. Here we go again. Nikki would need someone different than Christie to accomplish the task, someone Holly would not run from. Someone she might be attracted to…

October 20, 2009

Holly: If your friend NIKKI used the woman stalker to follow me in order to try to serve me, IT FAILED. Martin was present. I did not touch envelope. The manager threw the envelope away. From now on your girlfriend is part of the lawsuit.

Holly: Stop the terrorism. Your power play in presence of kiddos is wrong. If having a partner that does not love GOD or family is your choice, be careful how it effects kiddos.

Holly: Someone will accompany me to every event that kiddos are involved in. You and associates can't continue this alienation abuse to my family.

Holly: Incident was an assault and will be processed as such. Like I said privately, your choice does not help kiddos heal.

October 21, 2009

Holly: Good morning. There is a pumpkin patch party today, at my apt. complex. May Evelyn and a friend come? She wants to.

Holly: I will get pumpkins to carve. I want to take kiddos to WHERE THE WILD THINGS ARE. It is a book my mom gave us.

Holly: Please. Do not deny me.

Alex: No…we have plans.

Holly: Of course, All About Alex. Nice mantra for a Godly family.

Holly: All new legal documents from my attorneys will be served to you at work by an official process server. IT WILL NOT BE WHEN KIDS PRESENT.

Holly: I have learned much letting you go first in court. Our kiddos deserve truth, justice, and REAL MERCY. This is FOR THE KIDS SAKE.

Holly: 967vrp black Saturn Sky. Peels out with top down after speaking angrily to ALEX.

Holly: Justin and Kevin were 2 feet away in wagon.

Holly: Standing by the ferry. I get to chose the next baby's name.

Holly: An organization that legally advocates for children. I am contacting them with attorney's support. Please stop abuse to kiddos.

Holly: Sgt. McAllister is talking to the SECRETARY OF STATE. He then will have an informed response to what you tried to do using Nikki against kiddo's mom.

October 24, 2009

Holly: Sgt. ARANCIO called as Sgt. McAllister asked him to. Someone falsely read contents of envelope intended for me OR he said you may have ... filled in missing info.

Holly: Somehow he found out that the woman tried to serve me papers that have to do with a lacrosse team. Does this have restraints on me that gives preference to NIKKI MYERS at our son's games?

October 28, 2009

Evelyn: Dad, I don't like what Mom says about Nikki. Mom says she hangs around too much. But we all like her a lot.

# # #

October 31, 2009

It wasn't hard to convince our favorite Mexican that it was his civic duty to help serve my protection order on Holly. Julio was all over it.

Julio and I waited in his red Jeep Liberty watching the lacrosse game from a distance. I was able to see Holly finally get into a black Toyota Rav-4 rental car after the game. We followed her from the game, figuring she would actually go somewhere on purpose. She did not. After jumping onto 196th Street from 64th Avenue West, we headed toward Highway 99, then to downtown Lynnwood. At 44th Avenue, Holly busted a yellow light and headed north. So did we. She hauled ass up 44th all the way to 168th Street, wound around uphill to 164th Street until she got to I-5. I could see her violently talking on her phone the whole time. She then turned onto southbound I-5 and took the exit to 405 toward Bellevue.

I started to fret a little. "Julio, how much gas do you have?"

"I'm good, darlin. We Tex-Mex fellas are well prepared." That he was.

Holly careened off the freeway at Canyon Park, heading south on the Bothell-Everett Highway. She then took a quick right on 228th Street, passed the FEMA complex, and took the back roads through Brier to Logan Park, not far from my house. Still hollering on the phone, she turned left and headed west on Larch Way, then north on Cypress Way back up to Filbert where it dumps out on 196th. She finally landed at a trashy used car dealership across the street from the Old Spaghetti Factory. That place apparently rents cars, for a price.

Holly's Alderwood tour racked up about 12 miles for no apparent reason. She changed lanes frequently, sped through town, cut drivers off, and drove in what Alex would have described as counter-surveillance techniques, except they were ridiculously bad.

Julio pulled into a parking space at the gas station next to the car lot, ready for a quick exit. Once Holly was well engaged with a salesman in the lot, Julio got out with the envelope and walked up to Holly and the salesman. I watched Julio hold out the envelope. Holly reached for the envelope, but then retracted her hand as Julio let go, allowing the envelope to drop at her feet. Julio turned and started walking back to the Jeep with Holly in tow, causing me to duck down in the back seat hoping not to be noticed. As Julio got in the car, I could hear Holly yelling, "Who are you? You must tell me your name!" Julio ignored her, starting the engine while Holly walked in front of the car and stood there, blocking his path and screaming at him. She looked like she was pretending to be memorizing the license plate number. Julio yelled out the window, "Holly, do not block my car!" He started to inch forward until Holly finally got out of the way. I crawled up to the passenger seat, allowing Holly to see me watching her as we drove away.

I could see Holly in total overload, completely unsure of what she was supposed to do next. Julio and I laughed our way back to my place. I called Alex and told him the story.

"Sounds like a textbook process service to me," he said. I'll meet you guys at the house, I'm not far away now."

When Alex arrived, he held out his phone. "This just in!" I snatched it from him.

> **Holly**: Red Jeep, 366YPK. A man with Nikki in the car followed me to friend's business. Again. Did not touch document. Owner shredded papers. Failure #2. STOP.

Amazing. She just proved she received the documents. Couldn't be better. The phone started ringing. "Alex, it appears you have a call from a…Holly Hill?"

"Voice mail," he replied.

We all stared at the phone until the voice mail indicator lit up. Alex put it on speaker.

> *"I have changed cars seventeen times because that woman has people following me! I'm at the dealership now with some helpful people who are advocating for my safety! I'm having attorneys document all of this!"*

The phone call wasn't enough.

> **Holly**: Good day to you. Did not receive docs from man that followed me. Owner saved me. Attorneys documented foulness towards kiddos.

#

16. CRAZY VS MAD

November 6, 2009

> **Holly**: You are very angry, bitter, and hurtful. Why won't I read the court orders? Because it will not help me focus on loving kiddos. You chose to love your job, your parents, your church, and another woman more than your wife. I choose to love God, you, your children, my friends, and myself. Anything that distracts me from those focal points are a waste of my time. Please let me run my race with freedom. Tell the kiddos good morning and I love them.

#

All the kids except Evelyn had found things to do with friends after the Saturday visit at their mom's. Evelyn was staying over with Holly, leaving Alex and I alone for the night. Alex was nervous about the overnight, which usually ended with Evelyn upset or confused. But Alex continued to encourage Evelyn to stay the extra time with Holly, saying he wanted to do whatever he could to help maintain each of the kids' relationship with their mom.

We drove to Holly's latest apartment in south Edmonds to pick up Evelyn at noon, the pre-arranged time. She ran out to the car shortly after we arrived while Holly waited in the parking lot of the apartment complex. As Evelyn got in with a pouty face, Holly stood at the bottom of the stairs looking on. When she saw me in the front passenger seat of the Mitz, Holly's face became pinched. I may have enjoyed that look just a little, knowing that my very presence was an affront to the woman who nobody wished to confront. I might have even scratched my forehead with my middle finger.

It didn't take long after we got home for Holly to sound off on Alex's phone.

> **Holly**: Hi! Evelyn said you will not let her go places alone with mommy because of the divorce. She said she thinks you are jealous

...and do not want her to have more time with me. My landlord will let her live here half time. I would not take her from you. We are equals. You can back down to dad and not mom when you choose GOD.

Holly: Parental alienation is a morbid sin. Keeping Evelyn from me will not benefit you. Her cry to live with me was returned with your selfish side. I promised God I would love and honor you. FOR LIFE. Kiddos all heard her cries. Dads that love Jesus with all their heart put wives and kiddos first. I will keep days free for her. It is my promise to you. I will not have a regular job. I remain free for our children...and grandchildren. God called me, I follow. God bless you sweet man. Watched Seattle Officer Brenton's memorial service today. I am thankful for you, keep yourself unscathed. GUARD JUSTICE AND TRUTH.

"What is she talking about?" I asked.

Alex shook his head. "I don't have the foggiest idea. Evelyn just spent the night with her and has gone to each one of the visits. It seems like she is twisting Evelyn's compassion for her into a desire to live with her. Evelyn has never given any indication that she wanted to do that; I usually have to push her out the door to just go see her mom. And I always encourage her to stay overnight with her last night despite the damage it seems to do to her."

I had noticed it before. Every Sunday afternoon after staying the night with Holly, including this one, Evelyn was particularly moody. Alex concluded Evelyn was feeling bad for her mom, who usually wound up crying in front of the kids over some current calamity she had gotten herself into, or in tears about missing the way the kids were when they were younger. It would take until dinner time for Evelyn to snap out of it, when she would ask those bizarre questions that only children think of.

Tonight was no exception. Evelyn walked into the front room where Alex and I had been watching the Seahawks on television. She climbed up onto Alex's legs and plopped herself between us. She had not showered since yesterday, and while she was cute, she was grossing me out a little.

"Nikki?"

"Yes?" I held my breath.

"Why don't you have any children?"

Here we go. "Well," I started, "why don't you have any children, Evelyn?"

"I don't even have a boyfriend," she said. "Plus, I'm not sure I want any."

I knew I needed to tread lightly here. My last husband had never wanted kids, but he didn't let that little secret out until years into the marriage. By the time he did, I had pretty much passed on the idea as well, knowing that if I did have children, I'd likely wind up a single mother, something I didn't want to become. "I thought you liked Spencer," I teased, avoiding the question.

"He smells," Evelyn said, scrunching up her nose.

"Uh, Houston," Alex said in his police radio voice, "we have a pot and kettle situation here."

"Speaking of smelling Evelyn, I think it may be time to take your shower for the week," I said.

Evelyn looked up at me, then tucked her face into her shirt and quickly came up for air with her nose scrunched up again. "You're right," she said. Evelyn elbowed her way over Alex's lap, leaving him buckled over slightly with his eyes bulging and his mouth gaping with a silent scream.

"How ya doing, there?" I asked. "Need any help?"

Alex let out a tiny squeak. "Eh…"

I slid my fingers into his waistband, grabbing his belt buckle and pulling it away from his skin, then looked into his face. "Better?"

He let out a long sigh. "Yeah. That kid has some reckless elbows."

I took advantage of our moment alone and reached my fingers down further, causing the immediate intended reaction. I felt Alex's phone buzz again and quickly grabbed it from his pocket with my other hand. I figured he could use the extra room.

> **Holly**: Because you cherish yourself and the friends that support your misdeeds more than the woman who loves and forgives you. God will repay my deeds as well as yours.

Talk about a mood killer.

#

November 19, 2009

The Chief Operating Officer for Rove Aerospace, the tightly wound Will McGuire, had become complacent. Will and the other two C-suite leaders always parked in the three unmarked spots in front of the building, strategically located next to the marked disabled parking stalls. This had become one of Will's own little statements of privilege, and for some reason nobody ever challenged it. Will was one of those legend leaders who was one part entitled and one part unproductive. Not that I was being particularly productive these days, which is probably what led me to conjure up my little plan.

I had arrived early that morning and noticed Will's parking spot was empty. Taking advantage of my own early arrival, I parked in Will's spot simply to annoy him. The rest of the employee parking was in the rear of the facility, a large parking lot which required most employees a five-minute walk just to make it to the door. Since Will didn't know what kind of car I drove, the occupation of "his" spot wouldn't likely be pinned on me.

I watched as Will arrived ten minutes later in his gold BMW sedan from my office window. He turned wide from the roadway as he usually did, a behavior I had watched out my window on any number of early mornings. He abruptly stopped behind my car, clearly annoyed that someone had taken his spot. The grin crept over my face. Will backed up, then pulled into one of the six clearly-marked visitor parking spots which lined the roadway side of the parking lot, opposite the disabled spots. Before he walked in the front door, Will walked over to my car trying to figure out who it belonged to. He quickly gave up and came inside.

I printed out a notice mimicking a warning notice from the facility security office. The notice read, "This parking spot is designated for visitors only: please use the employee parking lot." I put it under his windshield and waited for the morning to pass. At lunch time, I saw Will go out to his car, retrieve the note from his windshield, and promptly tear it up in disgust. He got in his car and drove away. I called Sally.

"Hey, can you bring your car to the front lot?" I said innocently.

"Sure, what's up?"

"Trust me."

"Just this once," Sally replied. I scurried out to the lot and moved my car to the fire lane. Sally pulled up a few minutes later.

"Does Will know your car?" I asked.

Sally's eyes got big, which was close to normal anyway. "Are you messing with him again? Didn't he learn his lesson when you filled his office with Styrofoam peanuts?"

"He still thinks one of the engineers did that. I'm in HR, you know," I said, tipping my head from side to side. "I'd know if he wanted to file a complaint."

"You're dangerous," she said with a grin. Sally parked her car in the spot while I took mine to the rear lot. When I got back to my office, she was there waiting. "Mind if I join you?"

"At your own risk," I said. We shut the door, pulled the blinds to minimum visibility, and waited. A few minutes later, Will returned, making the same sweeping turn into the front lot, where he was met with another vehicle in his spot. This time he got out and looked around.

"Do you think he can see us?" Sally whispered.

"Through those Coke-bottom lenses? I doubt it," I replied. "Plus, I turned the light off in here to make sure we weren't backlit."

"You're good!"

Will gave up in a huff and sped to the rear lot. I could hear him grousing when he entered the building, loudly trying to identify his imposter. No luck.

I printed and delivered a second warning notice undetected. "Please park in the executives parking spots. These spots are for employees only."

Two weeks later, I may or may not have changed Will's desk phone system to Mandarin and linked all his paper clips together.

"It's true," Sally said. "You do get dangerous when you're bored. How's the love life?"

"It's weird. Alex is great, the kids are getting used to me, and we had a total blast on Halloween. Psycho, on the other hand, is continuing to lose it."

"Uh-oh," Sally replied. "Was she always loony, or do you think it was some sort of postpartum depression? She can't have always been like that if they kept having children, right?"

"I don't know," I said. "I get the sense she always loved being a mom, and to some degree she was a really good one, at least in the beginning. She clearly loves her children and will do anything for them. Unless it involves taking responsibility for her actions and not blaming everyone else."

"Sounds difficult," Sally said.

"It's just weird. She'll go for weeks without flying off the handle too much, then she'll completely go off on Alex in the middle of them trying to figure out who's coming to a visit with her and who has lacrosse practice or whatever. She sends hundreds of emails and texts every week to him, sometimes saying she loves him forever, sometimes telling him to stop being a terrorist. It doesn't seem to be getting any better. Take a look at the latest one—Alex forwarded it to me this morning.

> **TO**: Alex
> **FROM**: Holly
> **SUBJECT**: Hope
>
> My love language is time. You forsook me by loving your career. You promised me a partner to share daily life with. Getting me into a window out of the cold was not my heart cry. It was for you to understand that I need to have comfortable time with our children to bless their heart desires. I can go without material comforts and clean houses if I have a hand to hold and a heart to care about my desires. Where did that Alex go?
>
> Sadly, you have followed after your career position, your extended family and friend's praise, rather than your covenant family in the Lord. I am so grieved that your mom and sister come first in your plans. It hurts to know that our sons have this as an example of how to love their wives.

The Lord is waiting to heal your broken path. And I am extending you the grace and time you need. The kiddo's pain is my concern because you think I do not care about yours. You are not the ALEX I chose to marry right now. I trust you will return to humility and mercy.

I will not demand my own way. I want as much time with the kiddos as I can get. I will not get a regular job because it will not allow me time to heal and bless the kiddos with their desires. It will not be too long before I am a grandma like my sister. I am content with little excess. God loves and has never forsaken me. I have hope and a song in my heart. Your $1,000 a month for me is barely sufficient for me to survive and bless the children, but I will always put them first. Give them cinnamon bread, not stones, Alex.

Holly

"Yeah, that's weird," Sally said.

"The whole thing sometimes gets to Alex. He fluctuates between worry about her committing suicide and worry about her putting the kids in her car and driving them far away. And she frequently uses her religion to leverage guilt on him. He tries to not let it affect him, but I can tell it still hits home once in a while."

"He probably really appreciates you, Nikki."

Both of us had pretty much forgotten about Will McGuire by that point. I wondered how Alex was doing.

# # #

17. HOLIDAY EXPOSURE

People in Seattle take more Prozac and Zoloft than most places on the planet. The early sailors to the Pacific Northwest certainly needed it; they were a bunch of grumpy, irritable, melancholic criminals hell-bent on blaming their woes on the environment or each other. The names of nautical landmarks around the Salish Sea say it all. Cape Disappointment. Mutiny Bay. Point No Point. Deception Pass. Lynch Cove. False Bay. Point Defiance. Foulweather Bluff. Swindler's Cove. Destruction Island. Shipwreck Point. It shouldn't come as a surprise that people around here need overpowered lights on their mirrors in order to prevent clinical depression. And coffee. Lots of coffee.

Yet somehow, the predominantly gray days, the hope of a foggy morning burn-off, the steady rain-shower mix of winter and the perpetual soggy grass seemed to fit me well. It made me all…misty. The winter jet stream did not, however, make me want to engage the motoring public for minor traffic violations. Or what I considered minor, anyway, which, on this damp afternoon, was pretty much everything.

I stood under the eves of the downtown businesses with my steaming drip coffee in hand during a mid-afternoon patrol break and watched people fail to fully stop for the stop signs at the main intersection of downtown Edmonds. It was that blessed mix of entertainment and frustration, perfect for my dark mood. Finally one particularly clueless dork blew the stop sign and turned the wrong way against the offset fountain in the middle of the intersection. It's not the first time this has happened since I stood there in plain view trying to ingest enough caffeine to stay alive, it just pushed me over the edge *that* time.

"Whoa! Whoa! Whoa!" I yelled as I stepped into the wet roadway with my hand held up. The thirty year-old Lexus driver looked up at me through the wet windshield with a sheepish, clueless half-smile and mouthed the word "sorry" as he continued his left turn past me without stopping. I mumbled his license plate to myself out loud and wrote it down on my notepad. *Maybe a nice note in the mail would help him figure it out*, I thought. But I knew better. In 28 years of policing, I'd only sent a ticket in the mail to an un-stopped violator once; this guy didn't even compare. I let it go and returned to my perch, only then noticing I had lost a third of my coffee in my haste to get the driver's attention.

Figures.

The street lights were already coming on signaling the fast approach of night. Thanks to the brilliancy of Daylight Savings Time, evening in the Seattle area started at 4:30 pm. But we sure enjoyed that extra hour of morning light from 6:30 to 7:30 am before most of us are even conscious. Idiots. I can't stand the idea of Arizona heat, but how did those guys opt out of this national rule? No biggie, at least I can pretend to be a night shift officer and carry my flashlight with a purpose.

With Nikki out of town on another business trip to sunny Burbank, I had extra time to think. I treasured that time more than I normally accounted. And on this particular afternoon with the small town of Edmonds being almost entirely asleep, it seemed I had plenty of time to ponder. It reminded me of when I was young and would get stuck half-way through the process of putting on my socks. My dad would come into my room to see me sitting aimlessly on my bed with one sock partially on my right foot. "Whadaya doin?" he'd ask, obviously frustrated why I wasn't doing something productive.

"Thinking," I'd reply. Truth was, I wasn't really sure most of the time. Sometimes I was thinking about people; friends, my infatuation with a pretty 8th grader, maybe a teacher's mannerisms. Sometimes I was thinking about my dad and his unpleasant ways, or my stepmother's regular demand of constant activity. Other times it was about sounds, spaceships, or humor. *Mork & Mindy* was a favorite escape; here's a guy from outer space who was funnier than shit, had a beautiful girl helping him navigate his new surroundings, and wore rainbow suspenders. Steve Martin, Bill Cosby, and Jonathan Winters were all right up my alley, but Robin Williams was my guy. If I could help people be happy like him, I thought, then I'd be happy too.

I chugged the last gulp of cold coffee and stuffed the paper cup into the mostly full trash can next to the Starbucks, got into the Crown Victoria with 95,000 miles, and drove toward the waterfront. I watched the Edmonds Ferry from Sunset Avenue as it pulled away from the dock with a light load of vehicles. The massive boat had a 212-car capacity but during the winter months only held regular commuters and commercial traffic. The 4:40 run was on time as usual, starting out with the *long, short-short* blow of the horn. The lights on the vessel made it stand out on the water in the surrounding darkness as it slowly churned toward the Olympic Peninsula. A sense of pride crept up inside me as I recalled the JTTF operation 6 years prior which neutralized a threat to this iconic part of the Seattle culture without anyone in the public any wiser. Because of the work of a dozen people, life as we knew it continued its very regular, boring, normal way.

My mood was interrupted by a phone call from an unknown number. "Hello?"

Holly was hysterical. "Alex! I'm locked out of my apartment. Can you please come let me in? The kids will be here any minute and I don't have a place for them to go!"

"I'm at work, Holly! You'll need to figure this out on your—"

"You always cared more about your work than you did about your wife!"

"Neither of those are the case, but either way I cannot help you at the moment. You're going to figure this out, and you're going to be okay. Holly?" The phone had gone dead, which was probably best.

That night when the kids somehow made it home, Martin showed me notes he had taken on his phone. "I just couldn't believe it, Dad. She was so mean about Nikki."

I looked at the note, which essentially was a run-on sentence full of disparaging remarks about Nikki, how she could never be a real mother, how she and her fancy car could never compare to a mother's love, and how I was a fool to chose her over the mother of the children. "I'm so sorry about this, Martin."

"Dad, I told her to knock it off, but she just kept going. We finally left the visit early because she wouldn't shut up."

I had debated for years trying to figure out why Holly had become so angry, so willing to speak horribly about other people, or of me. It didn't make sense to me. We had years of being the model family, happy, with respectful kids and a stable home, even on a single income. I still don't know when it really started, or even when I knew it had completely caved in. Given her months secluded to her bed, her bizarre handling of relationships, or her inability to accept her own responsibility for a problem, I had concluded at least there was some aspect of mental illness. But without any sure diagnosis, it was never clarified, leaving me to wonder if she was mentally ill or she just hated her life. Or me.

# # #

November 28, 2009

Evelyn, Katherine and Kevin helped put up my tree this year, keeping with my tradition of finishing the Christmas decorations by the first weekend after Thanksgiving. They were thrilled at how everything matched and was so sparkly. I convinced them that they needed a fresh-cut 12-foot tree in their front room with brand new lights and ornaments. Kevin was onboard with cutting anything down and Evelyn and Katherine couldn't contain themselves at the thought of getting new ornaments for their Christmas tree.

Alex arrived just as the Angel was being placed on the top of the tree by Kevin. "Knock knock," Alex announced as he entered. Evelyn ran to embrace him, talking so fast Alex couldn't keep up with her. He sat down on the couch, pulled her onto his lap and made her start over. She relayed her excitement about getting a BIG tree how Kevin was going to cut down.

"Are we, now?" Alex asked, tilting his head my way with the silent little "Are you nuts?" in his eyes.

"Absolutely!" I said. "We just need to see if Justin and Martin can come along. It'll be fun! Got a full tank?"

An hour later, we all piled into the Buick and headed to Snohomish singing Grandma Got Run Over By A Reindeer. The Reade Christmas Tree Farm boasted the largest selection of U-cut trees in the region, and size didn't matter. Everything was $35. The boys armed themselves with crosscut hand saws and tromped through the selection as the girls pointed out their votes for the perfect tree. Evelyn hugged a 14-foot Nordman Fir and would not let go. Natural selection, I suppose.

A half hour later we were on our way home with a gigantic tree strapped to the top of the wood-paneled station wagon. I never in a million years thought I would be part of this scene.

I loved it.

# # #

Nikki promised she wouldn't spend "too much" as she headed out with Evie and Katherine in tow. Not sure what to expect with that, I turned my attention to the boys who were fighting over who got to cut the twine off the Buick. Fortunately, no blood came of it.

After chopping off the bottom inch and trimming the lower boughs, we squeezed the giant fir through the front door and up the stairs, into the kitchen, back into the hallway, ahead to the fireplace, opposite end into the kitchen, shimmy past the piano, and into the front room. Easy-peasy. With the red bucket and new-fangled tree stand in place, the only thing left was to stand it up.

That's when we discovered how impractical it is to put a 14-foot tree into a room with a 13.5-foot ceiling. Back down she goes. We clipped the top and sawed our way through the trunk yet again with my dad's plywood saw. An hour later, the tree stood tall in a bucket of water, barely touching the ceiling. Nikki and the girls waltzed in just in time.

"Need some help out here!"

Justin and Kevin scrambled out to the car and helped Nikki and the girls haul in a dozen bags and boxes. I was speechless. I was overwhelmed when the task was fully completed. Nikki directed the spastic children like a maestro with a full orchestra. Ladders, chairs, couches, hooks, plugs, balls, and a deadly warning to the dog to stay the hell away all concluded with the most beautiful tree I'd ever seen.

Nikki gave me the honors of setting the star on top. I set the star as Katherine turned off the house lights. We all sat there in great anticipation as Martin plugged in the lights, illuminating the night with beauty and awe. For the next five minutes, nobody moved, but somehow we all ended up together, side by side in a moment of silent bliss.

Until the dog farted.

December 24, 2009

Since I had to work patrol on Christmas day, we celebrated the holiday on Christmas Eve. Nikki joined us for a dinner of roasted turkey and stuffing, as was the tradition in my family. Nikki had warned me she was bringing gifts for me and the children, but she didn't say anything about volume. She brought three packages per child, plus a few extra ones for the whole family and a couple for me. Every box was wrapped in precisely the same way, with perfect edges, real bows and ribbon. None of that curling-stuff.

Nikki handed out a box to each of us which was conspicuously the same size. This started a new tradition for all of us which would last for many years to come. Jammies. Cool jammies. Print flannel, even.

I was beyond grateful. The kids were beyond belief. And Nikki? Well...she was...Nikki. Her love for all of us was evident and supremely selfless. She expected nothing in return. She gave freely, according to our need, drawing out our own hopes which had been buried for years under piles of fear.

It was the first time I had ever seen the kids in a state of unhindered hope. Nikki was giving more than a positive image of motherhood. She was providing a lasting, beautiful impression of humanity.

December 31, 2009

After making it through Thanksgiving and Christmas surprisingly well, Alex decided it was time I started to meet the people in his life. I had met Terri at his house and spent time with her at his surprise birthday party. I found her to be surprisingly supportive. Terri held an annual gathering at her home in Kirkland for New Year's Eve where friends and families spent the evening playing games, making up skits, and playing a ruthless game of *Catch Phrase*. Terri convinced Alex to bring me along. I was a little uneasy agreeing to go to this event, figuring this group of hard-core Orthodox Presbyterians wouldn't have much in common with the likes of me. It wasn't just the Church Ladies this time. "Oh, it'll be fine," Alex assured me. Yeah, fine like a sarcastic wife when her husband asks how her day went. *Fine.*

We arrived at the modest tri-level home and walked in unannounced. Terri was already at the door trying to push a massive pile of shoes away from the landing. "Oh, those boys!", she said, barely looking up to see who was coming inside. I wasn't sure if taking shoes off in the house with the Mahalo sign by the door was the protocol, but it seemed the thing to do so I began to remove my pumps. This attracted Terri's attention. "Oh I *love* your shoes! Welcome to our home—I'm so glad you're here!" she said, giving me a big hug. "Because now," she said, cupping her hand for a whisper, "we can help each other deal with *crazy people*! Oh my God Alex, did you hear what she sent me today?"

"Not since the weekend. She sure seems to like you, Terri."

"Ha! She's so mean! I can't wait to show you, but come on in you guys. There's wine, cheese, some leftover rice over here, and Gretchen made some reformed eggs. Alex, where are the kids?"

"They're next door at your brother's house pretending to babysit. Martin drove them over earlier."

And just like that, Terri disappeared into the throng of people who had crammed into the kitchen. There were people everywhere, most of them still wearing their shoes. I wasn't going to last long.

"How bout some wine," Alex suggested.

I imagined chugging the entire bottle just to cope. "Uh, yeah…red if they got it." And just like that, Alex nodded, winked, and disappeared into the mass of people, leaving me solo.

I stood in the entry looking up at the vaulted ceilings of the living room where the words "I love Joseph" were painted into the upper wall. "*That's fucking awesome*," I thought as I remembered Sally's warning not to cuss. After ensuring I had a basic idea of where the exits were, I considered trying to follow Alex into the kitchen and looked down to see if there was a clear path without shoes or other obstructions. Three knee-high children zipped in front of me past my legs, dodging shoes and pinballing their way to the stairs while yelling something unintelligible. They looked like little Anime characters, ethnically Asian of some kind, wearing loose-fitting costumes and carrying toy swords. I hoped they were toys and further wondered when one of them, the red-haired Gringo of the bunch, turned and pointed his sword at me, then snarled and growled like the 4-year old he was before scampering down the stairs to the basement, slamming the door in triumph. I blinked on purpose and tried to start making my way to the kitchen but Alex had already returned with two glasses of wine in hand.

"Did ya miss me?" It was like this was all normal to him.

"Yeah, I was nearly warded off by the goon squad. How many people are here?"

"Oh, probably 60. Last year there were like 75," he said, as if it were just a number of insignificance. "Half of them leave by 10:30. Stick with me."

Alex began the process of introducing me to some of these people. I was introduced as Alex's "friend," which didn't bother me since I knew there may be one or two present who were sympathetic to Holly. As the night went on, it was clear that these people mostly were just glad to see Alex relaxed and happy, not having to worry or be distracted by his crazy wife, and in the presence of a "friend." At least 95% of the women present were stay-at-home moms, so by all definitions I was the outcast. It was at that moment when I considered how many of those women might wind up crazy, not having an identity of their own beyond motherhood.

We made it all the way to midnight, the dreaded moment when lovers kiss and disappointment sets in for the lonely. Alex surprised me with a kiss which was not very hidden from the crowd, most of whom were trying to avoid staring at us anyway. We said our goodbyes, found our shoes in the remaining pile, and walked out to the car. I tossed the keys to Alex due to my 4th glass of red.

"Top up? Top down?"

"It's Seattle for God's sake," I gaffed. "It's sure to rain."

"Yeah but if we just go fast enough, it'll never fall inside the cockpit." Alex was getting way too scientific.

"Top up. Period."

After strapping into the Sky, Alex looked at his phone and groaned. I snatched it from his hand.

> **Holly**: Hope you are enjoying the celebrating with friends and the kiddos. Please give the kiddos a hug at midnight from their mom. I am alone crying myself to sleep because you have chosen hatred over love this year. Hoping and praying your blind eyes choose sight and truth next year. You are a better man than you chose to be this year.

"You okay?" I asked.

"Better than ever," he said.

# # #

18. Does She Have An Off Button?

January 1, 2010

Having been originally married at 20 years old, I didn't spend a lot of time in the adult dating realm. It's not as if I never dated or had a girlfriend; my youth pastor once commented if I didn't have at least one girl on my arm, he wouldn't recognize me. It was embarrassingly true.

Introducing Nikki to the kids was one thing. As time went on, the question began to emerge of living together. I frankly didn't know how to navigate this course. My entire background had been steeped in fundamentalist and patriarchal ideals like preparing a home for your future spouse, marrying her, then moving her in.

Nikki wasn't exactly the Proverbial wife type, at least not according to her. Traditional standards were made to be challenged and tested. "Don't tell me what to do" was her mantra. And while she still believes in the division of blue and pink jobs, where you lay your head had nothing to do with what other people think. It was much more pragmatic.

As 2009 became 2010, Nikki and I spent more and more time together, which gave the kids more ammo to harass dad. Kevin usually started the morning fray on the weekends. "So dad…when's Nikki coming over?"

"Shut up." This was interpreted by Kevin to mean take it a few steps further.

"You guys gonna go topless somewhere?" He was so pleased with his own wit.

"Look kid, just because she has a convertible has nothing to do with it." What Kevin didn't know is that Nikki had snuck over late last night and stayed in my room. I had drafted the crafty plan in my head to tell the kids either she had shown up early this morning, in case any of them asked. It wasn't entirely untrue.

The front door suddenly flew open. "Hey Mr. Hill! How's the new girlfriend?" It was Jack. I'm not sure how we met Jack Schultz, but he sure had a way of entering people's lives and just staying right there. On a scale of goofiness, Jack had his own gears. Kevin liked him because he made Kevin seem tame and reasonable. Jack was that likable kid who wanted to hang around the cool sports kids but was never motivated enough to get on the team. Athletic enough, but no drive to compete. Eventually, Jack joined the Track team, running thousands of miles for no reason whatsoever.

"Don't know what you're talking about, Jack. Why are you here?"

"Ooh, yeah, you know what I'm talking about. That pretty blonde gal with the super cool sports car! It's Nikki, right? I saw you guys downtown at the coffee shop the other day and you were like trying to ignore me! Haha!"

"Jack," I said with a straight face, "I always try to ignore you."

"Haha! Such a kidder!"

Nikki had been in the bedroom listening to the episode and decided it was prime time to insert herself into the kitchen. "Jack, why are you here?"

Jack choked on a wad of freshly fried bacon he had stuffed into his mouth. I held my breath, knowing Kevin was already developing the onslaught of witty comments in his mind from Nikki's unexplained emergence. "Uh, I smelled bacon when I was just walking by. I love bacon! Did you make this? It's so good!"

"I made it, Jack," I said. "Just leave a little for the rest of us." I glanced at Kevin. He had gone to the front window looking for Nikki's car. "Hey Kevin, go grab some eggs from the fridge downstairs."

"Sure thing, daddy-o. *Morning*, Nikki!!"

"Morning, Kevin," she said with a knowing grin. Kevin was continuing to do the math. "It's not here, Kevin. Your dad picked me up early this morning." *Real* early.

"What? Oh…I was wondering where…I thought maybe you guys had…hey look, bacon!"

Kevin uncomfortably slid into the kitchen as Nikki confidently sat on the couch. She quickly stood up with a jolt, looking behind her and ultimately pulling out a lacrosse ball, a French fry wrapper, two pieces of candy and a fork. She stopped by the trash can before handing me the utensil. "You may want this," she said.

"Well *there* you are!", I exclaimed, taking the fork. Nikki was, well, friendly about it. The condition of that couch was starting to gross me out. Nikki bravely returned to it.

Evelyn had emerged and sat down next to Nikki with supremely stinky feet on the equally ugly couch. Unlike Nikki, Evelyn had no personal bubble. And at the moment, it mattered. "Hey Evelyn, how bout you go get a shower and I'll make some cookies after breakfast."

"I wanna make cookies with you!" Evelyn shot up and danced into the kitchen.

"Not until you take a shower!"

Evelyn paused and looked sideways at Nikki. The child remained thin-lipped and measured her up for a good 5-seconds. Jack and Kevin both paused to watch the showdown, chewing slowly on the bacon. Without a word, Evelyn loud-stepped her way down the hall into the bathroom, shutting the door with purpose.

I yelled after her. "Save the whales!" She had a way of turning a shower into a hot water drought for the rest of us.

"I KNOW!"

Nikki proudly sauntered into the kitchen and began pulling out ingredients she had stashed away during one of our shopping trips. She shot a sneaky glance my way with that grin that said, "*Heh heh...you had no idea I bought all this and hid it in your house right under your nose!*" Yoda strikes again.

"Dibs on the bowl," Kevin exclaimed.

Katherine called out from her room. "I get the beaters!"

"But I get the bowl!", Kevin announced.

"Wait for me!" Evelyn yelled through the bathroom door. The water was running but she was clearly not in it.

"Y'all will get nothing until your chores are done," I said, trying to instill a bit of give over the gets.

Justin came up the stairs surprised to hear Nikki's voice. "Hey, lady," he said.

"Morning, Justin. You'd better hurry up if you want some bacon."

Justin put Jack in a headlock. "C'mon you little pussy! Drop it!" Somehow Jack emerged unscathed, laughing loudly with a short piece of bacon in hand.

"Haha! Such a kidder!"

I looked at Nikki as she took it all in. *This has got to be overwhelming*, I thought. I watched Nikki walk to the table and saw the shocked look on her face when she saw the plate of bacon. The empty plate of bacon.

"JACK!!!"

"Haha," Jack nervously laughed as he slid toward the front door. "Welp, gotta go! Hey thanks for the bacon, Alex!"

"Jack, you'd better run!" Nikki went to the front window to see Jack slowly bouncing down the front stairs, cramming a piece of bacon in his mouth.

I never saw this one coming. When the kids were slightly younger, the boys were into the AirSoft craze, allowing perfectly mellow homeschooled suburban children to transform into raging lunatics without actually harming one another, provided they kept some sort of eye protection involved. In a moment of weakness coming home from a day trip to Stevens Pass, I stopped at a little store and was talked into an AirSoft gun. *It's for the kids*, I rationalized. But since Dad was the one who would use it in our urban land wars, I needed to maintain firepower advantage. Which meant I chose the AR-15 replica with the 300 round capacity. Oh yeah, baby. Dad gun-it.

Then I left it by the front window on account of a murder of evil crows who had found their entertainment by pooping on cars parked in front of my house. And since crows are born from Middle Earth and raised by the Devil himself, they were starting to mock to my occasional and ineffective barrage of flying rubber pellets as they stared at me from the power lines above. Actually, I'm pretty sure they aren't "born" at all…they simply appear, like ogres or trolls. Honestly, has anyone ever witnessed a crow egg? They simply don't exist.

Nikki raised the AirSoft GRF37 rifle to her shoulder, ported it through the open window, took careful aim, and blasted Jack in the back of the head on her first shot.

"OW!" Jack yelled, grabbing his head with his left palm, spinning back to see his beautiful blonde assailant in the window. "Hey!"

"Bob and weave, Jack!" She sprayed the ground around him with a rash of rubber. "Bob and weave!"

We didn't hear from Jack for some time. Or his parents, for that matter, causing me to wonder if the lawsuit had found a ready attorney. Thankfully, Jack sheepishly surfaced on a Saturday morning two weeks later, a little older, a little wiser.

Since the bacon was gone, Nikki turned her sights on the remaining cinnamon rolls she had also whipped up from a Pillsbury can. I'm probably not supposed to write that, either.

January 6, 2010

To: Holly
From: Alex

Holly, I need to answer some of your recent phone messages and a couple of other issues.

1. Please use email for our basic communications. If you have requests for alterations to the parenting plan, send them in writing. This will ensure clarity of your requests and also follows the court order for communications. Texting is ok for issues that are time-sensitive when your phone service is restored.

2. I have provided Kevin with a cell phone. You don't need to keep his Sprint line available for him.

3. I will be transporting Katherine home from Vancouver when she returns from Equador. I am glad to encourage extra time for you with her when she gets back. I'm sure she will be eager to see you.

4. Last weekend, Jan 2-3, the kids spent time with you on both days. Friday was the holiday to share, which I ensured the kids would be available to attend with you. You chose to spend it with the girls only. Part way through, Katherine asked if I would come pick up Evelyn from the theater due to her behavior. I did not hear from you, so I told Katherine no.

The following day, the boys and Evelyn were compelled to spend time with you. I received your request to spend time with Evelyn while I took Katherine to Vancouver. I did not answer this request, but heard from Kevin in the early afternoon that all 4 kids were with you at the gym. I was, at that time, making arrangements for Evelyn to be picked up by a friend for a playdate. I cancelled those plans.

In essence, you took a day with the kids without my consent or knowledge. Please follow the parenting plan. We can agree to make adjustments, but not without the knowledge and consent of the other parent.

As a result of this past weekend, the kids think next weekend is Dad's. Not sure how you want to handle that. You did suggest (I think) at one point that we swap weekends... I'm fine with that. Let me know if that's a problem.

5. I don't plan on altering the parenting plan while Katherine is in Equador per your request for more time with Evelyn.

Alex

January 7, 2010

Martin: Hey Dad, Evelyn used my phone last time to send this to Mom: "*it doesn't make sense that we saw you so much last weekend and its still your weekend.*" Then Mom wrote back: "*well does it make sense that sweet mommy sees you so little? No. Its okay Evelyn, we just had some sweet extra special time.*" Evelyn didn't want to stay with mom the last time she had an overnight and Mom basically told her she had to. Meant to tell you.

Alex: Wow. Wish I had known....sorry to hear it. The good thing about Evelyn is that she will eventually speak her own mind!

Martin: Well yeah but Mom won't have it…Evelyn is still under her little control thing.

In spite of the court's direction that phone calls were to be utilized only for emergencies, Holly left me the following voice mail:

Hi Alex, this is Holly. You know I just can't afford a phone and I don't have a computer, so what I got is what I got. I got my voice and you know I see a counselor every week that the City of Edmonds Police Department provided for me. The DV coordinator is writing in reports to the City of Edmonds Police and she told me yesterday she thinks it's really important that Evelyn gets extra time with Mommy while Katherine is gone. You're expecting a lot of her to be the only girl in a house with 3 brothers and one Daddy. So, I'd like to be able to have you call me. My roommate and I can make it possible for Evelyn to spend some extra time with me. Also, I think the time on Thursdays needs to be separated out by boys and girls while Katherine is gone. We need to try and increase a little bit of personal time with each of the kids so they don't end up having some physiological problems that will be detrimental for the rest of their lives. I know you love those kids, so I'm hoping you will bend a little bit without having to have litigation to make that happen. Like I said, these things are all being documented every single week by a counselor and there are 4 attorneys sitting ready. I'm not threatening you at all. I'm just telling you: I'm hoping that you'll mediate rather than litigate. But if litigation is the only thing that speaks to you, then this is not a threat—I'll have to go through with that. But Evelyn needs more time with mom. She's saying that she wants life to be taken away. That's not fair for her so please rise up for the sake of our kids and bend a little. OK, I know you love them, so I'm going to trust that. Please give me a call.

January 9, 2010

To: Alex
From: Holly
Cc: Laura

Hello,

There are several issues regarding our children that need to be addressed.

1.   You   must   give   permission   for   me   to   receive   school

information. You only included yourself as parent. So far, a man cannot bear children. I am the other parent. My parents have a local phone number and should be included as emergency contact, not just your parents.

2. Both Evelyn and Kevin are expressing themselves as "not worthy" in life. In charades this week, Evelyn acted out a dying child that became an angel. Christmas Eve, she said she to go back to before she was born, she said she was happy there with God. She wrote down that the thing she wanted to throw away and forget from 2009, was LIFE. Kevin calls himself stupid and says he wants to commit suicide. He is expressing many, never been used words, that are rude, very often. It is important that the children remain in counseling.

3. Due to your check having a hold placed on it, I would like to receive them, on or before the first, through D.S.H.S. I will send more details on this.

4. Please do not transfer envelopes of any kind, while dropping off the children.

5. Please begin to recognize the issues around Parental Alienation Syndrome. There are many great websites that explain what is happening due to your choices in the divorce you gave our family. Knowledge is power, if chosen to help souls grow.

6. I am only reachable by the landline where I live. I will stop at the library to send emails, as I am able. My resources are for myself and the children when they with me. This means I am limited on communication.

Sincerely,

Holly

January 12, 2010

To: Holly
From: Alex

Hi Holly. I received your message a few days ago and saw you were using a yahoo account. I didn't have this one, so I'm not sure if you received my previous emails I sent when you stopped using a cell phone. I will re-send those and try to answer some of the things you sent.

As a baseline, I will stick to the parenting plan unless we can make needed adjustments ahead of time and noted somehow in writing (text, email, etc.).

1. I will re-contact the schools to ensure they know you are Mom and have full access to their records. The only reason your parents are not named as emergency contacts is because they are living in Equador!

2. All the kids, especially the younger ones, have remained in counseling and will continue to as deemed beneficial by the counsellor.

3. Checks were given to you directly at your request, for your benefit, and outside the viewing of the kids. I don't know why your bank held the last deposit, but I ensured funds were there before I issued the check. In the future, to avoid confusion or potential awkwardness, I will follow the court order and provide the money to the court as originally directed by the first of each month. I agree to not pass envelopes during child exchanges and only request you will do the same.

4. I am very familiar with PAS and have several checks in place to ensure it does not occur on my side. I have and will continue to encourage the children's love, respect, communication, and affections toward you. The parenting plan is a judge's order, not mine.

5. I will use both of your email addresses for communication unless you have one that you prefer I use. When your cell phone is active again, send me a text if you would like to use that method again. With all communications, please let's avoid personal criticism and keep to the directives of the parenting plan. Of course, any emergencies can be communicated in any manner.

Alex

12:05 pm

To: Alex
From: Holly

Alex,

Because you remain unable to see the need for changes, I will be forwarding your emails to some trusted attorneys that will be helping work toward mutuality in parenting. I am choosing to receive counsel in how to respond to you.

Thank you,

Holly

12:17 pm

To: Alex
From: Holly

Alex,

Please do not be harsh with me in comments regarding the parenting plan. Remember that this divorce and all the litigation were your choice and not mine. I did not agree to them. I was not given a voice and had little attorney representation.

I will be forwarding your emails to several trusted attorneys that have reviewed the case and are willing to help bless the children and I with fairness and the best relationship as possible. All efforts will be for healing and positive action to help our family move forward in strength.

Thank you,

Holly

January 24, 2010

To: Alex
From: Holly

Alex,

I am very concerned about how the boys are treating Evelyn. They shut her down so often. Her little heart is broken over it. She is a star for forgiving them and continuing to try. When they tell her to SHUT UP or that SHE IS SO FRUSTRATING, it hurts her. Yesterday her mind was so troubled she felt like she could not do anything well. Please ask the boys to encourage her and build her up.

She needs her mom, not Nikki. Please consider getting her into different counseling. I am trusting that you do not want our children to struggle as you and I did. Estrangement and abandonment by a spouse are serious and really damaging.

Kevin is embarrassed by the acne on his forehead. Please take him to the doctor. My mom did it for me on a single income. Please do everything you can to negate his feeling stupid. He continues to say he is dumb. Try options available to him at school. I trust that you will reach outside yourself and find him appropriate tutors. He has very bright older brothers that he compares himself to. Because he has fair skin and red hair his scarring is harder to heal. Our doctor will help you. Do what you can to bolster his sense of self-worth.

Praying for Katherine to have much grace and mercy from her teachers. I know she missed a lot of work, due to the teachers not communicating with her.

Thank you for encouraging contact with Justin. As of yet I do not see a result. It will not be a benefit to have an estranged relationship. Counseling and accountability for you as the parent in charge is essential. Many witness the effects of your controlling spirit over the kiddos. Free them by getting the help you need.

Thank you,

Holly

To: Holly
From: Alex

Hi Holly, Katherine is safely home! We are going out for a bite, then I will bring her to your place and pick her up when she is ready. She tried to call you but the line was busy. She is excited to be back!

Alex

January 25, 2010

To: Alex
From: Holly

Hi Alex,

I can never stop being a mom. I am glad Katherine is home safe and had a great time. Thank you for the transportation help. It was great to see her and get some picture-looking and hugs in. I hope and pray all goes well with her catching up on sleep and school stuff.

Her esteem and fitness do matter. Maybe Nikki and I can add different aspects. I would love to see her have the confidence to try out for drill team. There is a girl's fitness class that just started a Harbor Square. She is always welcome to join me after school for a class.

Thanks again for all the running around,

Holly

Was it possible that Holly had turned a corner with her mental health? She seemed to be communicating more reasonably, not lashing out at every opportunity, and responding well to routine and minor change. She had kept her new apartment for more than a month. I saw her working at Costco serving samples, the first actual job she had since being fired from spinning signs for a furniture store on a street corner. While I knew better than to hold out a lot of hope that this was an indicator for the future, at least for now the pressure on the rest of the world was easing up.

Holly: Keep your mouth shut about this. Evelyn told me that you met Nikki at Starbucks two years ago. That would be while we were married. Your private life away from us, while you worked in secret, killed your family. I never left you in my heart. The men I have dated fear your position. I feared your position, but prayed you would prosper because you are my first choice. I never forsook you and would still give you more than I would take for myself.

Then again, maybe not.

> **Holly**: Evelyn said you tell the kiddos and friends that our divorce is my fault. I sweetly said that when Justin is frustrated because she is loud, that it is BOTH of their selfishness that causes conflict. She asked if I was mad at you. I told her I would kiss you on the nose and hug you and forgive you for treating me so unkindly. That is and was my promise to you. No one will ever replace you. People still tell me that I love you as if you are my husband. It is true. I may choose a lover, but You Are My Only Husband. That was a forever promise.

Okay, *definitely* not.

February 12, 2010

4:40 am

> **Holly**: Good morning. Please know that I think about the kiddos all day and every day. THEY are my first earthly priority. I am not in a relationship with a man. I am trying to understand whether or not that would benefit me and the kiddos. I hated the estrangement from my parent's divorce. My mom having partners present with us was hard because she did not value my dad or speak compassionately about him. I will not do that to you. I will not confuse my children. YOU are the man I want them to love and honor. There can never be a stepdad who is better than YOU. Divorce made me an adulteress by your doing. I did not choose singleness. I am a sensual woman that was very deprived by your lack of initiative to cherish my body. I was the mom and you treated me like a friend and not a lover. Being closed off to my desires was painful. You got your need to be head of our family met. You shut me down and abandoned me.

February 14, 2010

6:57 am

Holly: I called Evelyn's phone and sent her a test text. Will you please help her respond so I know her phone works? For the rest of the time, I know you only want the kiddos to talk to me if they first initiate. I am trying very hard to obey your orders. I am praying for your Dad. Enjoy the long weekend with the kiddos. Thank you for the time with Evelyn, yesterday. *****MOM (you gave me my 5 stars)

Holly: Any good reason why you love the kiddos being in communication with MOSTLY you? Do the kiddos fill your empty heart? Do you covet the praise of people thinking you are the better parent? Encouraging Evelyn to call is a gift to yourself. Loving the mommy is loving yourself. Go ahead try to put me first. I did it for 20 years. YOU MIGHT FIND IT BLESSES YOUR SOCKS OFF TO SACRIFICE WHAT YOU WANT FOR THE BRIDE YOU PROMISED TO BE SACRIFICIAL until death. I believe in the God you made these promises to. Its a simple step. Go for it!

9:47 am

Holly: Please hug our sweethearts for me. I LOVE THEM WITH A PART OF ME THAT NO PERSON CAN EVER REPLACE. Happy Valentine's Day. Love you all. I am praying for your dad. So thankful he never rose up against me or lied about me like your mom and sister. He needed you to help him soften. God has used you in his life I am still glad I pushed you to live near your parents. Kinda wish you would have loved me more than them. But I will not hold it against you. Step on your toes, give you a hug and kiss your nose, maybe.

# # #

February 19, 2010

I waited to call until I figured Alex was out of briefing and in need of his first cup of coffee. Sally and Julio had been chomping at me to get the four of us together. Since today was Alex's actual Friday, I figured it should work.

"Hey, what are ya doing tonight?"

"Something with you, hopefully!"

"Mind-reader! Azul's. Be outside the lamp post at 7. Come alone."

"But what abou—"

I hung up before he could finish. *That was fun*, I thought. I called Sally.

"We're on."

"Copy that." Click. We were getting in to this.

My phone started buzzing. "Can't you take a hint? I said 7, what more do you need?"

He laughed. "Azul's is that swanky place in Mill Creek, right?"

Swanky? "Uh, yeah, I...guess. It's not like The Met or anything. You can wear your jeans. Not the Costco ones, the *other* ones. You did your laundry, right?"

"Sure," he said. "Once a month whether I need to or not."

"Anything new from the ex?"

"Since yesterday or this morning?" he asked.

"Let's go with today." It was only 8 am; couldn't be too much.

"Oh yeah, Holly is all twisted up about her tax situation while enrolling in a displaced homemaker program."

"A what?" I had to repeat his words in my mind to get the gist.

"Displaced homemaker program. Some bleeding-heart Democrat thought it was a good idea and got a grant or something."

"Hey now! I resemble that remark!"

"You're more of an Eastern Washington Democrat. You love your liberal social freedoms but still want your guns."

Ignoring that. "Forward me the email. I get to perform at a boring C-level meeting in a few minutes. I could use some entertainment. Maybe I'll draft you a suitable reply. One that she'll understand."

And then Alex surprised me. "Okay," he said. "I'm in."

I got settled in the board room and opened Alex's email. It was unreal. Clearly she doesn't realize her maintenance money is taxable, as well as the distribution of retirement funds. I've seen many Qualified Domestic Relations Orders in my time in HR, and all of them—all—account for the tax that will be owed. Pretty sure she spent hers.

This was gonna be fun.

To: Alex
From: Nikki

Here you go, sweet-pea! ;)

I am applying for a Displaced Homemaker program, to go back to school. **Won't this interfere with your time with the children?** I need the kiddos social security numbers. **Homemaker lesson 101: Know your kids' SSNs.** Please email or text them to me. **On which of your dozen phones?** I will destroy transmission, once I transfer them to the forms. **Adding this to your list of destruction.** Thank you. **You're welcome.**

Also Alex, I really struggled getting Evelyn home to your place last night. **Who's the parent here?** My phone battery had died. **Maybe if you back off on the thousands of text messages it would last longer.** I got a small charge in the bathroom at the bookstore. **Bet THAT was fun.** You can trust me with her. **Uh, nope, nope. Not gonna do that.** DRUGS WERE THE ONLY TIME I COULD NOT FOCUS ON ISSUES OF MY TRUE HEART. **Could be a clue.** I was willing to give you the family and job you needed praise in. **WHAT? You gave me a job? This is just crazy.** I was broken when you forcefully told me how to think. **I think that's those other voices in your head.** The love of power stinks. The power of love brings light and life and hope. **You can have both if you stay on your meds.** I PRAY FOR YOU ALL THROUGH EACH DAY. I had to let go of everything I hoped and dreamed of because you forced me to be shut out. I love you all the same. **Uh, you walked out, remember?**

Don't be stubborn about sending me the SSN's for kiddos. **OK!** You would think that having the children as your sole possession would gain you the praise you desire. **I got nothin.** At least respond as to whether you will do it. YES OR NO is god's desire. **Yes or No.** I will go forward strong without you. **Thank God!** The kiddos will learn the truth of your deception and folly in trying to demean their mom. **Oh, won't that be an enlightening day!**

For the wife of your youth and the mother of your 5 beautiful children, rise up and act like a responsible man. **Check!** I owe over ten thousand dollars in taxes this year for paying off your debts. **Uhhhh wait, MY DEBTS?**

I have told you for as long as I have known you, I make my choices out of desire, not necessity. **How's that working for you?**

Holly

# # #

I was parked in the 23900 block of 84th Avenue West pretending to run radar while sorting through my email. It still worked; the good people of Edmonds checked their speed when passing by, tapping their brakes in sheer panic and fear of getting busted for accidentally going 5-over. I did the same thing whenever I passed a cop on the side of the road. Even in my patrol car.

Sgt. Jensen did too, only this time he came to a full stop in the road. "Alex, meet me over at the church parking lot on 236th."

"Copy that," I said in my best cop movie star voice.

We met at the Lutheran Church lot and parked opposite each other, windows down, our side-view mirrors microns from touching. "So are you distracted?" he asked.

"Yeah, sorta. Holly sent me another doozy. This time, Nikki sent me her version of a response. Her version is a little gutsier than mine."

"Dude! Let me see!"

"Oh boss, you don't wanna get mixed up in this."

Chuck looked at me as if that was ridiculous. "Alex, that's ridiculous—I already am. Pass it over."

I did. Within seconds he was laughing his ass off. "You gotta send this. It's awesome! God, don't ever get on Nikki's bad side, Alex."

"No shit!"

"You really like this gal, don't ya?" Jensen was on to me.

"Guilty as charged," I said. "Pretty sure it's more than 'like'."

He smiled. "I'll leave you to it, lover-boy. Just try to stop somebody out here before the day's over, will ya?"

"Copy that. Ten-four. Roger-dodger." Chuck rolled his eyes as he tore out of the parking lot.

I did my final edit and sent my version of the reply.

To: Holly
From: Alex

I sent you a secure email with the SSNs.

Alex

9:35 am

> **Holly**: I will not be ignored by you. If you feel pushed around, deal with it. Your perceptions are your own. I will not be blamed. Grow up and stop using people to bolster yourself.

> **Holly**: Maybe you should get Nikki there to pack lunches with thermos full of warm soup and homemade bread. Kiddos say she thinks they are too much to manage but she has a car and money. They want their food at school for hot lunch with their friends, not stuck in cupboards at your house. The kiddos go without lunch and are afraid of exposing you. I will not let fear stop me from blessing my children. Your words will never break my spirit again. Those children were ordained to have a fighter for their mother. I back down to no one.

> **Holly**: Just remember I am older and wiser. I saved every forsaken promise you wrote or spoke to myself and the children. Where is my half of last year's tax refund? Where did you flush your vows to

God? I LOVE YOU ENOUGH TO GIVE THE MERCY OF TRUTH THAT EXPOSES LIES. Our children will not be deceived by your delusion. This facade has come to reality. We will stand as equals here and in heaven. I will not shame you as you did me. I will fight for truth in our family. No limit to what a mother will do for her children. YOU chose a lioness and I will defend my pride. Just lay there and look good. I didn't harass you. Just the bold truth with no fear of the badge you are so proud of. "VENGEANCE BELONGS TO THE LORD."

9:48 am

Holly: Finding out I will have to pay a lot of taxes over the next ten years because you used me to get ahead financially did not make me happy. I am tired of being your servant. I want the kiddos to keep their metabolism stable by eating well. My life is now all about them. I do not need to go thru you. I CAN GO AROUND YOUR CONTROL. I just choose to keep you informed because you chose to be the responsible parent in school and court. I care about you and them. I am trying to be nice even though it hurts.

Holly: You spoil Katherine and deprive Evie. She reminds you of me. You are so afraid she will continue to want to be with her mom. These texts will be sent to my attorney. You are not creating happy family memories if you chose for Nikki to be there. The blow will end up hurting me, you, and Evelyn.

9:55 am

Holly: Being at the Nutcracker backstage for Katherine was such a sweet memory. This is Evelyn's first big performance. I WILL tell her how badly I wanted to be there. She WILL ask why I was not able to be. I WILL tell her that you would not allow it. YOUR CONTROL IS UGLY PRIDE. No truly loving dad acts like this. I grieve for your soul.

Gonna do my best to ignore this again. Getting better at it!

11:40 am

Holly: Do you know that Evelyn prays that you will marry me again? I am holding out for that. I believe a dad and grandpa and best friend are good enough...as long as you read a good book about good sex with a woman who has been abused...we would be okay. It was important to be lovers not just parents and best friends. I would do anything for you and the kiddos. just need to do the loving thing for

ME. It would have blessed YOU.

Okay, time to reply.

> **Alex**: Two things: 1) Please minimize text messages, limiting to the coordination of visits and implementation of the parenting plan; as the plan states. 2) My car will not be available for your transportation. Transportation during residential time is provided by the residential parent. I have sent an email to address other concerns we share.

> **Holly**: I will obey God before you. Love rules. I care about our family because they are my family. I do not fear you.

Hmm…well *that* went well.

# # #

March 8, 2010

> **Nikki**: You up for a walk after lacrosse practice?

> **Alex**: Sounds perfect. See you at my place around 8?

> **Nikki**: K

It was nice not having to wait for Alex at the lamp post down the street. The kids were getting a kick out of me pulling up in the driveway and usually used the occasion to jab their dad with some harassing commentary about his "girlfriend in the hot car" coming for him. Being aware of this made it all the more fun to make sure I revved the engine a little extra when landing in the driveway. I knocked and entered, announcing myself with Alex's own goofy phrasing, "Knock-knock, c'mon in!" Three voices called back with some sing-song form of *"Hi,* Nikki….hey Daaaad, *Nikki's* heeere!" We had now been dating for almost a year and a half and I was starting to accept the presence of these kids as part of my own new normal. Occasionally, I'd double-check myself wondering how I wound up here and if I actually had accounted for what it was doing to me.

Evelyn ran to the top of the stairs to greet me first. She was unusually clean in one of Alex's old white t-shirts; clearly Alex had somehow sweet-talked her into taking a bath that week. "Did you brush your teeth?" I asked her.

"Yeah." I said nothing but kept looking at her. "Well….I think so."

"*I* think," I said while rustling her hair, "that you may want to double-check."

Evelyn grinned sheepishly and ran back into the bathroom, beginning her brushing in earnest. Alex came out from his bedroom with a light raincoat on. "Impressive, huh?" he asked, pointing his thumb to the bathroom.

"Better be careful, she may make a habit of being clean," I quipped. He squeezed my shoulder while passing by me in the hallway, then addressed the children about our pending walk.

"Okay gang, we're headed out for a walk. Evelyn, hit the hay by 9 o'clock and I'll come give you a love when we get back."

"Ungphf-kgyay-baah-daah," she replied through her toothbrush.

We made our way hand-in-hand to the waterfront and found a dry bench overlooking the ferry dock and central Puget Sound. It had rained earlier but the clouds had peeled back revealing a warm, comfortable evening as winter was fading to spring. We sat close to each other, looking over the water and watching the lights from the dock and the half moon flickering on the subtle surface waves.

"So," he started, "I finished my shot across the bow to Holly."

"Yeah?" I said. "Can I take a look?"

"Have at it," he said, handing me his phone with the email on display. I read it completely.

To: Holly
From: Alex

There are some things I need to address.

1. **No further use of my car, including during your scheduled residential time**. When Martin is 18 and has his own car and insurance, he may choose to give you rides when you need them. In the meantime, please be responsible for yourself and

do not make Martin or me responsible for you. I am not going to provide transportation for you.

2. **Stop making decisions and plans for the children during their residential time with me**. When the kids are with me, please do not make arrangements for me to get them together with people or do things. I am responsible for them and will manage my time for them.

3. **Start following the parenting plan regarding our communications.** The parenting plan is clear: "Communications between the parents should be minimized and be by email or text message, and be about the children only for the purpose of planning and parenting plan facilitation." You can think and say what you like, but please do not communicate any more of the following:
    a. your hopes to marry, love, bless, follow, or reconcile with me
    b. how I need to feed, clothe, love, care for, communicate with or protect the children
    c. text messages outside of normal hours: 8 am to 8 pm, other than actual emergencies
    d. direct communications to the children without their initiation
    e. disparaging remarks about me and the divorce in front of or to the children.

I hear more frequently now of communications you send to the children via text message or phone call which were not initiated by the children. I'm not hunting for these; the kids tell me about it directly. This is clearly spelled out in the parenting plan and borders on violating the restraining order, as it sometimes is disturbing to the children.

I hear frequently now of talk in front of the children, even to complete strangers, about how your ex-husband left you in a terrible position, how the divorce is his fault, and countless other negative remarks about me. It's fine for you to have these opinions...You can say what you like to others, but you and I both must keep it away from the kids. We both get frustrated sometimes and may not be 100% gracious in spite of our efforts to speak well of each other to the kids. Just understand that the kids are upset about your negative speech about me.

I can no longer tolerate your continuing harassment over the telephone. When you are told "no" or not allowed some variance you request on the parenting plan, your usual response is a series of angry, critical, out of control text messages that appear to be designed to hurt me. Constantly accusing me of parental alienation, making terrible statements about my parents and family, threats to take me to court, and all of it at all hours of the day and night is nothing short of harassment. I do not want to hear how you feel like a hooker, how you think your mom can't connect emotionally, how you want to have other people's babies, how your relatives are expected to die within 24 hours again, how you are holding out to marry me again, how I'm your favorite friend, how you think I need to read a book about sex, how you miss the kids, etc. It's not that some of these things are meaningless; they are simply not appropriate to send to me on a telephone text message.

Understand that my lack of response to many of your text messages is for at least one of these reasons:
  a. the communication is mostly or entirely harassment
  b. the communication is during my work or busy time with children
  c. the request has already been answered

4. Do not require the children to visit dying relatives. If the children elect to visit anyone you care for who appears to be dying, that's fine. But if they say they do not want to go, please do not force them to do so.

5. Do not send food to my house. I know you mean well with this, but I do not want to continue receiving food from the food bank or Costco from you. If you wish to start providing child support for the children, we can discuss that separately via email.

6. Do not ask for "make up" time with children who cannot attend a visit. The parenting plan is clear about this. The older children can make arrangements with you to visit if their routine prevents it during residential time, and I do not get in the way of them meeting you for breakfast and the like. The younger children are not required to juggle this sort of thing.

I welcome a response to this message, but not if it is simply to further harass. If any of these requests go against the parenting plan, please let me know and I will reconsider.

Alex

"I'm proud of you, Alex. It's perfect; it's what needs to be said, but in a straightforward and non-vindictive way. I know this was hard to write." He was looking quietly off in the distance. "Did you send it yet?"

"Yep." I could tell he was worried about the potential fallout. I squared him up and kissed him firmly.

"Nikki?"

"Yes?"

He paused. "I love you."

"Well it's about damn time," I said. Blink. Blink.

"Well you could have said it too!"

"Yeah, but I didn't." I could see the gears grinding in his head.

"Hey, Alex?"

"Yes?"

"I love me too."

Fade to black.

# # #

March 13, 2010

> **Martin**: Dad, Mom blew up at me at my birthday breakfast. Katherine and Evelyn heard it all. Mom said that she is not getting married to her men friends because she wants the monthly maintenance and the revenge/punishment that comes with it for you. Pretty sure I'm just gonna give mom a nice little break from seeing me for a bit.

Alex: O wow. Ok.... Sorry.

March 18, 2010

> **Holly**: It is difficult to be without a mom at home. From experience and coursework, I know that exaggerated pain can be a heart crying out for unmet needs, wants, and desires. Be gentle with all of our kiddos. They have suffered much due to your choice to destroy our family unit.

The kids made it to downtown Edmonds for the Thursday visit with Holly, meeting her at Starbucks to get things started. It was uncomfortable at best since they had no home to go to for the visit, no place to land. I thought about the homeless families I worked with on Highway 99 and wondered how they did these visits. They just didn't; usually one of the parents was long gone when the other one tried to raise the children. It was hard to reconcile my head around the idea that Holly had become one of these people, a homeless single mother who was mad at the world because she couldn't have her children with her.

At around 5:30 pm, Justin sent me a note.

> **Justin**: Hey Dad, is it ok if I'm home? I'm really tired and sore and just don't feel like doing anything! Also I have no clean clothes at the moment!

I suspected there was more to Justin's request than clean clothes. A subsequent phone call from Katherine confirmed it.

"Dad, I wanna come home. Mom is freaking out again and going on about how awful you are. She's being super angry and negative about everything, complaining about being homeless and blaming you for everything."

This was extremely tough for them, but I remembered the time I spent frustrated that I had allowed the children to continue to be subjected to Holly's damaging emotional pressure when she was still at home with us. The court ordered residential time for each parent. Holly was couch-surfing, currently staying with a new-found friend, but didn't have a residence. So all of this time was actually in question anyway. This wasn't good. I knew what

I had to do.

"Wrap it up, Katherine. Do your best, then come home. Everyone."

"We will, Dad. I'm sorry, I know you're trying to make sure we—"

"Katherine, it's okay. There will be more opportunities for better days. Come on home. Call me back if you need a ride."

I knew there would be some hell to pay for stopping the visit early, but I was confident it was the right thing to do based on what I had heard. It didn't take long for Holly to sound off.

> **Holly**: Working around YOU and YOUR decisions. The girls will need to take the bus. I have a car. I will take Chloe and myself to my apartment. Evelyn would like to stay overnight with Chloe. Camille IS FINE WITH EVERYTHING.

March 22, 2010

> **To: Alex,**
> **From: Holly**
>
> Alex,
>
> I want to be fair to you and gracious. I will no longer be deciding how to respond to you without attorney representation. This is a case of parental alienation and abuse of power. I am sad to take it to the same level that you did, but have determined that it is the only way to defend myself and our children against the choices you have made.
>
> Sincerely,
>
> Holly

March 31, 2010

4:45 am came earlier than usual. My late-night rendezvous with the cereal aisle had me straining to decide between the Raisin Bran Clusters and the Honey Nut & Oats with Almonds in my cupboard. I'd left Nikki's house at around midnight after playing with her hair until my alarm woke me up. Time with Nikki included an alarm to be sure and get home at a "reasonable hour" in the event Homeless Holly was hanging out on 7th Avenue waiting to monitor my activity. The 4 hours of sleep I'd been getting on nights like these was starting to catch up with me.

I went with the Clusters. Because Dads matter, dammit.

I scrambled mindlessly through my daily routine and snuck out the door without waking the kids. The short jog to work in the misty morning darkness of spring made me strangely happy. The hint of salt in the air told me the prevailing winds were coming in from the West, adding even more moisture to the already saturated Pacific Northwest air. By the time I got to work, I had to dry out.

Briefing started at 6:10 sharp with Sergeant Jensen at the helm. He'd nicknamed our patrol squad The Jurassic Crew at my bequest. The average age on this squad was 49. I was the young guy by a long shot, keeping the average from an otherwise solid 53. All but two of the guys on the crew were already eligible to retire. This phenomenon is normally something to be avoided, resulting in a slew of old farts who don't give a single shit about anything but keeping their steady cash flow coming until they pay off their mortgage. But this crew was reasonably productive, with the exception of some routine bitching which happened every day at briefing.

The bitching over, we all departed to our respective patrol beats after slowly checking email and paying respects to the Traffic Unit and Detectives offices. Sgt. Jensen and I had worked together in Detectives for my JTTF years. Since he was my boss, he obtained a security clearance, allowing me to keep him well informed of the secret happenings in the world of counterterrorism and my involvement in it all. He understood the irony of my underwhelming assignment to the residential beat despite the ongoing threats and financing in the region, most of which was now going unchecked.

I swung by the house to ensure the kids were up and at 'em. Nothing like the cops barging in when you're eating your dad's cereal. Martin met me at the door, heading out to warm up the Mitz. "You guys about ready?" I asked.

"Kevin's still eating, I told him I was leaving in 5 minutes," Martin sneered.

"Kevin?!"

"Coming!" I heard his bowl hit the sink in a splash of water with no apparent thought of the existence of the dishwasher perfectly installed next to the sink. At least the bran wouldn't stick to the sides of the bowl.

The herd of kids hustled past me with one-armed hugs and salutations. They climbed into the car, which was somehow still running despite every opportunity to quit. That car was the very representation of our family: plenty of scratches, regularly leaking fluids, plenty of wonder if it would last long enough to make it to the next life phase. I was proud to watch them drive away, all five of them. Martin would stop at the elementary school first where Evelyn would be 20 minutes early, then the middle school to drop off Kevin, then to the high school where he was a senior, Justin was a junior, and Katherine was a freshman. We had sorta made an impact on the front office staff at the school.

I looked down at my dog who stood next to me on the front porch, noticing he was looking older than ever. The red and white Border Collie had been there through it all. "Good boy, Copper. Good boy." I led him to his crate, gave him his treat, and shut the door.

> **Holly**: Letting you pay maintenance outside of court, was to be gracious. The delinquencies would have hurt you. If you hurt, I hurt. Please let me know when the transfer is made.

> **Holly**: I AM YOUR FRIEND. Mom has a free night at the Holiday Inn Express, in Marysville. It is impossible for me to steal your children. You have top security clearance, and could find me. I AM NOT YOUR ENEMY, YOUR FEARS AND ANXIETY ARE.

> **Holly**: Please know that I do love you best. If that bothers you, take the irritation out on God, He set us up! Practically speaking, I need to know how and when you will be paying my maintenance on Thursday. Also, the quicker we know what you are willing to give us in time with the kiddos, the smoother plans and the sweet hopes build. I trust there is a beautiful man whose desire is to bless our children and their children...FOR MANY GENERATIONS...TO THE GLORY OF GOD. SING PRAISES. HE ROSE TO GIVE US LIFE ABUNDANTLY.

19. LAST STRAWS

April 1, 2010

One of the benefits I enjoyed for having full custody of the five children after the divorce was the freedom to fully finance their lives without also having to pay for the whims of a spouse who loved nothing more than to save hundreds of dollars at the thrift store. Which meant, of course, spending hundreds of dollars at the thrift store, $3.99 at a time. The guy who owns the thrift store actually owns hundreds of them across the country and has amassed a fortune for himself in the hundreds of millions of dollars, $3.99 at a time. It's a genius business model really: take over a dying retail store property pennies on the dollar, fill it with crap from donation bins and throwaway items from people needing a tax write-off, hire people off the street with all array of mental or criminal disorders, pay them minimum wage with subsidized labor dollars from government programs designed to put the homeless to work, use prisoners in community-custody working off their sentences to sort and fold the laundry, put all this cost-free merchandise on the shelves and open the doors to mentally challenged shoppers with an incessant appetite to find a great deal. "Look honey, I got this whole bag for 40% off!" 40% off of *what?*

But while my admiration of treasures from the thrift store journeys was gladly over, I still got to finance the phenomenon by means of a special little concept called Spousal Maintenance. It's a pretty accurate term, really. The spouse who supported the financial standard of the family is expected to continue that standard for the spouse who benefitted from that support for a period of time after the divorce, usually somewhere in the 4:1 ratio. Every 3-5 years of marriage equals one year of maintenance.

In my case, I had to pay $1,000/month to Holly. Considering it was all I could do to keep food on the table and fully care for the five kids, this was a serious challenge. On more than one occasion, friends at work leant cash to me just so I could make the deadline; maintenance was due on the 1st of the month and pay day was the 5th. I'd find ways to work overtime or off-duty gigs just to make ends meet and usually pay back those who helped out.

The maintenance requirement was ordered for three years, or until the receiving party re-married. *Like that would ever happen,* I thought. *I have plenty of risk factors, but her? She's…crazy!*

Holly didn't have access to my bank account anymore, but she did start her own account at the same bank. Of course she did. While this was convenient for transferring money to her, it also presented some problems, especially on the 1st of the month.

> **Holly**: I obeyed. It is past 8 am. When will maintenance money become available? I am not ashamed to be living on what you give me. It was your choice for our family. God has always been so good to me. He makes all the difference. In math, I would never be positive. In God it is all paid in blood. And He made me B+. Giggles for you, Silly Goose.

> **Alex**: I will be working it out with the bank today, will text when transfer happens. Martin will bring kids to you by 3, let me know where.

> **Holly**: My home at 3. Are you short the amount?

Somehow, I collected the funds and made the transfer by 3 pm. The kids made it to the visit, this time consisting of playing basketball at the athletic club and dinner at the local Mexican restaurant. That night, drifting off after some clever conversation with Nikki, I was awakened by the phone buzzing next to my bed. It was almost midnight.

> **Holly**: They will understand over time that it is okay for me to drive them. You just needed to wield control to defend yourself. Losing a cherished lover is worse that death. My driving was bad for a season. I had to work through your loss of love for me as your wife. Sadly, the children are left confused as to why you have control that hurts them and makes their life hard. I forgive you. I understand you. I love you.

# # #

April 11, 2010

The six-week period known as Birthday Season was nearly over. While convenient on the one hand, it took a toll on Alex. Birthday season put demands on all aspects of Alex's parenting: scheduling, recruiting help, sourcing gifts, keeping them hidden, maintaining some sense of equality and customized individual keenness, all with the idea he could somehow finance the entire operation. Alex routinely used his tax return to make it all happen, which totally sucked for Justin in August. With the five kids, he maximized his deductions to keep his withholding as low as it could go without tripping an audit. He still got money back from the IRS. I decided to help ease the stress normally leveraged on him during this time of year. Alex typically would go to the stores at night between birthdays in search of something cheap but meaningful to give to each of the children, sometimes opting for an item they needed but had learned to do without. This year, I was determined to help him shop.

Thankfully, Alex didn't object. It was a stranger experience than I had anticipated. Alex routinely found some cheaper way of getting something of lesser quality so that everyone got more of something. I was used to spending between $500 and $600 for my niece on her birthday. Alex spent less than that on all five. I convinced Alex to let me go in with him on a couple of the gifts for the kids. He was overjoyed, glad for the help. I felt a sense of pride knowing I had found a way to help this family through their very awkward situation. Plus, I was pretty sure Holly would figure out she was no longer the only female influence in their lives.

Birthday shopping soon evolved into grocery shopping. We found shopping to be fun together; we'd each push a cart and occasionally I'd throw in something to my cart that I planned on taking to his house. We never got kicked out for playing bumper cars but I'm certain we were the focus of the people behind the surveillance cameras. After making it through the checkout lines, we'd compare receipts. "I saved $3.61," I'd proudly announce. "That's eight percent on my total bill!"

"I saved $65.30; that's fifty-five percent," he answered coyly.

"That's because you eat crap."

"All tastes the same coming out of the Crock Pot!"

We headed off for the grocery store late Saturday afternoon intent on finishing the shopping before the kids came back from their mandatory visit with their mom. Today's scheduled visit included a whirlwind trip over the river to Stanwood where Holly's grandmother was in the process of dying.

Holly wanted the kids to see her "just one more time" in case she died soon. All of them were groaning and complaining before heading out in the Mitsubishi for the day. At least the court had limited the visit to only 7 hours due to Holly's continuing antics.

While at the grocery store, Alex pulled down some generic brand raisin bran on sale and commented, "Whoa! $1.99 for this baby!" I held back the puke in my throat when he put the cheapest loaf of bread in the basket. I couldn't take it anymore.

"That shit tastes like crap. Here, let's get you some 9-grain," I quipped.

Alex froze, staring at the fresh loaf of bread I put in his hands, then said distantly, "That's like two dollars more."

"And worth every penny," I said, grabbing his bread and pushing the cart forward out of his reach. "Today you're gonna get some regular food and not worry about the cost. What, do you think the kids will be mad?" I continued down the aisle with a bit of a dance in my step for effect.

Alex remained stunned. I knew I was crossing a line, but this was something easy for me and I wasn't about to turn it around. Up to this point, I had simply accepted Alex's manner of surviving, even with a high degree of respect. For a very long time, he could turn a pretty small paycheck into some form of happy survival for this struggling family. But today, I wanted to give him a taste of what life could be like in a dual-income home. I wanted him to know there was another life available to him.

"Wow," he said as he came out of his trance and caught up with me. "They'll be super glad. You know you don't have to…"

"Zip it!", I said, spinning around with my finger aimed at his lips. "You don't get to do all the blessing around here."

He smiled and relaxed. "Yes, uh, yes ma'am," he said with a Forrest Gump drawl. I was glad he didn't try to change my mind. He started to follow after me as I located the most expensive olives and cheese I could find. My phone rang, displaying a number I didn't recognize. I answered it anyway.

"Hello? Oh, hey Katherine! Yeah? I'm at the store picking up some amazing groceries with your dad. Do you like artichokes? You've never tried one? Ok, I'm making dinner for you guys tonight and you'll get to try it out; they're super good, you'll love them! Whose number is this anyway? Your mom?

Oh…okay. Uh, yeah, that's a good idea, good thinking. What was that? Yes, we will be picking you all up from your visit in the Mitsu-BEECH-y. Yeah, Mitsu-BEECH-y! Are you guys back from Stanwood yet? Oh, you're at a hotel? In Lynnwood. Got it. All good? Yeah? Oh. Oh, wow, Katherine. Okay listen, we will pick you guys up in a bit. Yep, regular time, I'll tell your dad. Bye!"

Alex was holding his phone out. "Dead. Glad she had your number…I wouldn't have known they were at the hotel. Is everything okay?"

"She sounded fine," I said, "maybe a little annoyed. Apparently they just got to the La Quinta Holly's staying at for the weekend."

"So did she say anything about the visit?"

"Yeah. Katherine said Justin was super upset with mom. She made him hold her dying grandmother's hand while she was already non-responsive. Justin was horrified. It's so fucking morbid! What person in their right mind forces a 15-year old to…"?

"Yeah, check your premise."

"I know she's not in her right mind, but how is this okay? She keeps doing these crazy things and the impact on her children is direct and horrifying!" I was on a roll, not about to stop. "And it keeps happening! There's got to be something we can do before she totally warps these kids. It's so messed up."

Alex was quiet. My concern was clearly his concern as well. And yet I could see the gears turning in his head as he did the math. Holly's crazy actions demanded someone do something about it. He had to protect the children from their mother while trying to maintain the capacity of the children to have a decent relationship with her down the road. Since his actions were continuously insufficient to curb the craziness, he continued to feel guilty for its impact on the children. I stopped the cart and held his hand. "Hey, we're in this together. I'm here for you, and for your family." I brought him close, embracing him briefly, then moved the cart forward. "Besides," I concluded, "I am the Yoda master prankster. Maybe it's time to fight crazy with some crazy." I held up a bunch of very green bananas and covered my face, raising my eyebrows.

Alex giggled. He rarely let on about his inner struggle to keep doing the so-called right thing. He never spoke badly of Holly despite all she did to make that a normal reaction. He was committed to his mission to take the high road at every turn.

So was I. Well, sort of. The struggle was real.

# # #

April 12, 2010

> **Holly**: Please tell the kiddos I love them very much. Especially repeat and show this to Evelyn. She will be most troubled by the absence of mommy. She spoke honestly last weekend about how she does not feel like she fits in anywhere. She is so special and needs reassurances and time to be cuddled even if she pushes love away. Please touch and speak encouraging words to Katherine. She is so beautiful. She pushes me aside because she believed you were the BEST parent. She continues to put me down and jokes about how I am weird I understand and swallow her negative opinion. She says she wants me to find a new husband in California or Hawaii. I stay here because, no matter how hard it might be, the kiddos do not recognize now, how essential having both of us near is. It will be harder when grandma dies and mom goes back. Never enjoyed aloneness.

"Hey Dad," Kevin yelled up the stairs. "I can't find my cup! Can I borrow yours?"

"You're out of your mind. Look in your dresser, Kev. You actually might have put it away." There was no way this was actually possible.

"Not possible!" he yelled back. "It's gone!"

The odds of Kevin putting an article of clothing away into a dresser was slim, but it was better than his older roommate brother. Sharing a room with Justin was necessary, but rather than benefitting from each other's strengths, Kevin and Justin were much quicker to glean from each other's depravity. Hard to believe Kevin would become almost excessively tidy later in life. It wasn't in the cards for Justin. Ever. Never, ever.

Kevin bounced up the stairs to the kitchen where I was cutting a Costco pot roast into smaller Crock-Pot sized hunks. "Dad, I'm serious, it's not there. Don't you have one?"

"You think for a minute that you'd fit my cup? Pretty ballsy, kid. Go look again in your stinky lacrosse bag."

Katherine moaned, complete with eye roll and slamming of textbook before taking her homework out of the kitchen. "Sorry, Katherine," I called after her. Growing up with two older brothers and one younger one put Katherine in the middle of an unavoidable testosterone sandwich. I hoped she would find the benefit of this at some point, but for a girl who was groomed by her mother to be a tea-sipping, prim and proper girly girl, she was going to have to cover a lot of ground before coming to a place where she would intrinsically enjoy sports, blood, and bad language.

Katherine was taught to always respect her parents, but Holly took it a step further, especially when brushing Katherine's long, thick blonde hair. We didn't have the funds to purchase any special conditioners or products to prevent the natural tendency of her hair to tangle. No matter, Mother would use whatever force necessary to get through the rats and recover the shine of smooth, beautiful hair. And force was always involved, despite the quiet objections, tears, and crying Katherine would emote. Occasionally, Holly would give up. "Here, you do it!" she would say before storming off. I learned to grasp Katherine's hair in bunches and run the brush using my hand as the anchor rather than her scalp, comforting Katherine's tired head and fear of grooming. I made regular effort to prevent these painful episodes, but Holly thought brushing a daughter's hair was a prerogative for both parents, so she made sure she stayed involved despite the obvious pains.

"She has thick hair, she'd better get used to it," she would say.

I couldn't exactly disagree, both because she had a point about life not being all easy, and also because disagreeing with Holly meant I wasn't being a supportive husband. This was the regular message any time I opposed Holly's idea of how to handle something, how to plan an event or a trip, which house to buy this time, and how to negotiate a mortgage. It tapped right into my own fears. I later reflected on all the pain I allowed to happen right in my presence by not speaking up. While I don't regret the marriage itself, or my efforts to preserve it, I do regret not standing up to her sooner. Damage was done, and I was afraid of the ridicule and harassment I would receive for suggesting so.

It wasn't until age 12 when Katherine herself finally spoke up to her mother, unleashing years of built-up frustration and anger during an episode of Holly's disdain for me and blame of her children. For almost a full hour in the fall of 2007, Katherine screamed at Holly, telling her that she was the one who had caused so many problems, who had made people afraid to confront her, who had destroyed her friendships and her family, who never took responsibility for herself. Katherine defended me, her siblings, her extended family, and the church staff all in the same flood of anger. The rage which came from the sweetest, most congenial 12-year old girl on the planet was completely unleashed and unhinged.

I was so incredibly proud of her.

Katherine remained Katherine, sweet, a little shy, uncertain of herself and her role in the family, but Katherine had done the thing I never had the courage to do.

"Found it!", Kevin proudly announced coming in from the garage, as if he had just solved a great mystery. This kid could probably hide his own Easter eggs and still come up short. Sort of a chip and block situation, I suppose. I was greatly relieved; I had no freaking idea where my cup was.

# # #

April 28, 2010

Another Thursday for the kids. After her latest eviction and two weeks living out of her car, Holly had just moved in with a guy who owned a large house in the northern ritzy part of town. According to Camille, the man had offered her some sort of employment; I hated to think what it might have been. I don't know how she finds these people. Alex had given me the address after he finally obtained it from Holly the night before. On our walk that evening, Alex explained he needed a hand getting the kids to the weekly visit. I told him I was happy to help but would need to use the family car as mine only had two seats. We made it to our favorite bench overlooking Puget Sound. "Okay, your mission, should you choose to accept it," he started.

"Yeah yeah, I know. Deliver the packages to the drop site at precisely 2:58 pm and get out unseen. I got this," I said.

"Don't take the bait, Nikki. She'll be looking for me in that car; when she sees it's you, I'm not sure how she'll react."

286

I leaned close to his ear. "I got this," I whispered, then took his earlobe in my teeth. He squirmed with nervous pleasure.

The following day, I got the available kids to their unfortunate destination with two minutes to spare and encouraged them to make the best of things. It was just the girls this time. Martin had not attended a visit since turning 18, Justin had his game at 6 pm, and Kevin arranged a ride with a teammate after his team's practice. As I pulled into the circle driveway in front of the large house, I spoke with a hint of authority. "Remember you guys, your mom truly loves you. I realize it's not always easy, but she does really love you. Don't forget that."

Katherine was quick to reply. "She always tells us that. I think she's getting better. She's only texted me twice today, usually something about how God loves me and she does too."

I smiled. "I'll pick you guys up at 7. Your dad will be coaching at the lacrosse game with Justin until around 8. Have a good time!"

Despite my best encouraging tone, Evelyn remained pouting with her arms crossed, slouching in the back seat of the Mitz, chin tucked to her chest. Katherine grabbed her hand to unfold her arms, dragging her passive body out of the car in a sisterly kind of way. "C'mon Evie, we gotta go! Mom said we can just come inside."

"I don't *wanna* go!" Evelyn protested.

"Evie," I said, "you can do this. Rely on your sister. She is stronger than you think! Go on, now. I'll be back before you know it."

As Evelyn held Katherine's hand and walked toward the front door of the house, I considered tossing a glare to the front windows before driving off, just in case Holly was watching. *Nope. Keep the high road*, I thought as I turned and drove away. This was killing me. This crazy, messed-up woman who had destroyed a perfectly good family for her own pathetic demands of a more perfect life was causing so much pain for children who barely understood why. *It's only a matter of time before they start to turn on each other.* It pained me to think of it. It pained me more to think that somehow, Holly may possibly never be held responsible. It just seemed so wrong.

By 3:25 pm, Katherine texted me saying they had to wait at the home since Holly wasn't back from a trip yet. A sudden rush of panic flew over me. *We don't even know this guy, or if he actually lives there!* I spun the Mitz around and started to speed back to the house. A minute later, Katherine sent another note saying it was okay, her mom had arrived. I pulled the car over to gather my breath, realizing the whirlwind I had just suffered due to someone else's lack of planning and communication. Alex deals with this shit all the time but it was new to me. My irritation only fueled my resolve to defend this family from the one person who was actually responsible for the pain: Holly.

# # #

April 29, 2010

Holly: Good morning. It makes me so sad that you choose yourself over our children. You pretend to be coaching the coach on how to coach. You chose to be at Justin's lacrosse game while Martin was home sick and your daughters put themselves to bed. I stayed at the game to see what mattered most to you. Kevin had my dinner, because he came straight from practice. Please stop the unkindness to our kiddos.

Holly: What in your heart requires that you be THE MAN ON TOP AND BETTER THAN OTHERS? You believing you are the better coach than the Head Coach was negative momentum for the team. To speak of his failings to another parent was ugly. Encourage him privately, he is a man. The spirit of our son was missing. Whenever I attend, I stand alone, so as not to confuse our children. I will not bring a mate to their activities. The Head Coach is a spunky fighter; he has never spoke a negative word about you or me. He sticks up for the team. During the last 2 games I paced behind the goal and prayed, at the end. Chiefs scored 2 more, both times. Please encourage Chiefs parents not to scream negative words to their sons.

Holly: "Let's go men!" Is way better than, "What happened?" And..."Man Up." You should be saying, "Show them what you can do men! You have the power! I believe in you." Does the team pray together? Of course, I choose to believe the Chiefs lost because Justin was not there. Please consider what may be taxing his immune system. Records prove that kiddos have been sicker the past two years. They have been in to see doctors more than over the past 6 years, since the decision was made to oust the heart of the mom. Consider getting his RA level checked and his thyroid levels. We know nothing about your birth parents. These are the real immune factors that are part of his heritage, as we know it. Of course, as promised I pray for you and the kiddos moment by moment.

Holly: I am gifted by God to encourage and exhort others towards love and good deeds. Take your question up with the God who gave me to you as a wife and help-meet. You got what you asked for. You knew all this before you bent your knee and made a covenant before God and man. I do not lie. I have received equal harassment and more hatred from you than any woman deserved, I believe in the man God desires you to be, not the sad boyish attitude that needs to MAN UP behind a pistol and power from position. I will be in Edmonds at 3 to 7 to love on our kiddos. I do all I do for GOD and my family. Press on towards godliness and sacrifice. The impressive example of both head coaches is that their families were there to encourage their teams. Youngest to oldest siblings and cousins were there. You left your children home to fend for themselves while you pursued YOURSELF. Shame on you for representing yourself as the best parent. I am documenting it all. Love the children GOD GAVE YOU...not others to bolster YOURSELF. I LOVE YOU...I HATE YOUR CHOICES TO BE UNKIND TO OUR CHILDREN. Truth hurts. Bow your knee and repent. Jesus loves a contrite spirit.

Holly: A perfect example of your constant correction over my every waking moment. Until lawyers make changes your choices harass my heart hopes every moment. You can bear a little correction. Btw. From your home to me the kiddos were 30 minutes late. Thank you and good night.

May 8, 2010

Holly: Hoping you marry Nikki so our kiddos don't have to deal with another loss of a woman you endear them to.

Nikki answered on the first ring as if she didn't know who was calling. "Hello?"

"Hey, this is me...is this you?"

"Oh, it's you. Ya coming over or what?"

"That depends," I said. "Did you hide the body?"

"Depends is a type of underwear."

She had me there. I mean when you hijack and define a grammatical variable, all bets are off. "Ok true, but what if I'm not wearing any?"

"Well," she said, "now *that* depends."

Touché. "Wait…what were we talking about?"

"Your lack of cereal. Shouldn't you be shopping or something?"

"I'll be right over." I peeked in on Evelyn to ensure she was asleep. This "peek" is defined as exerting ninja-like skills to enter the room undetected from the lightly lit hallway, avoiding the trigger spots in the carpeted floor carefully designed to sound daddy alarms, trusting there were no liquid surprises in discarded yogurt cups on the floor, utilizing night vision and acute sensory systems to find the child among the mounds of stuffed animals she had amassed over the past 9 years and insisted the company thereof surrounded her each night without fail, confirming breathing, then escaping without question or evidence. Which was going swimmingly until Kevin slammed the front door.

"What a great day!" he exclaimed, bouncing up the stairs.

"Daddy…is that you?" Evelyn sleepily inquired, eyes barely open.

Shit. "Yes, sweetheart." I bent down and kissed her head. "I love you so much. Go back to sleep."

"Love you, Dad. Nite. Mooey-mooey."

"Mooey-mooey," I replied softly, then closed the door. I turned my Dad-scowl look toward Kevin, who was standing frozen at the top of the stairs doing the math. "Dude!", I whispered loudly. "It's 9:30 at night!"

"Oh dang! Sorry Dad, I'm just a little giddy." He could barely contain himself.

"Clearly," I replied. "Wait, do we need to invoke the 24-hour rule?"

"How is that even a thing?" he laughed, looking both entertained and annoyed. I had made a deal—okay, a dictate—with the kids early on. Any time they kiss someone outside of family, they had 24 hours to tell me about it. The whole "it" was to be spelled out in solid detail. When Martin and Justin each had theirs, the youngers did all they could to try to be around to get the whole story. The sordid details of mushy romance, the desperate whims of juvenile love, the build-up, the first move, the awkward pull-away…all of it.

"It's my thing and your re-direct of the question shows I'm totally on to you, lover-boy."

"*You're* a lover-boy," Kevin quipped, using his go-to formula for answering any sort of challenge. His smile could not have been bigger, so proud of himself on every single front currently in play.

"Whatever," I said. "I'm headed out for a bit, so try to keep the frivolity down to a dull roar. What kind of cereal you want?"

"The big kind," he answered. "With tons of sugar to help rot my teeth and make you worry."

"On it," I replied. "Give me a shout if Evelyn wakes up or whatnot." I gave Kevin some perceived duty regardless of his actual readiness, hoping it would plant seeds of responsibility.

I quietly left, driving out of the neighborhood with an eye for any occupied suspicious vehicles. I was pretty sure Holly had made attempts to catch me leaving the home at night, despite the legitimacy of three well-qualified babysitting-aged kids at home to manage the fort. Once sure the coast was clear, I turned to Nikki's house in Lynnwood. The 12-minute drive was ample time to feel like a teenager sneaking out to see his girlfriend while his parents slept.

May 16, 2010

8:55 am

> **Holly:** Ok. Did a bunch of praying and thinking. I want you to give a picture of family to kiddos and Nikki. I am praying for her to come to a living and active faith in Jesus. God will use you to bless her. I bet Calvary Fellowship would be a better place for her than Faith.

May 19, 2010

8:54 am

Holly: Help Nikki. She is your new choice. You are the ghost in my life. Financial docs said you were deceased. It is true. You killed our marriage, and broke the hearts of our family. The kiddos need to see new support and the strength or their mom's faith

Holly: In God, carry my half of the family forward to their dreams. God is going to do it! He promised to give my family a hope and a future. Mock me if you choose. Call me names. I am proud to be a Fancy Nancy. Thankful the Lord helped me sing through my sorrow. He brought beauty for ashes. All this, is to bless the heritage of family. Women and children first. My captain is Christ. He holds me and the babes I bore.

Holly: My heart follows my words, at times. I did not believe Nikki was woman enough to take my man. Truth is, she can have the man that was not man enough to hold his commitment to marriage.

How? How does she do it? It boggles the mind to consider how fast she can use a flip phone to text things to me. And I know I'm not the only one she is pounding with her thoughts.

Since Katherine had an after-school activity and the boys had lacrosse practice until 6 pm, Evelyn rode the bus home with Chloe after school. On days like these, Evelyn would go to the nearby church's Awana club, a sort of youth group for elementary school kids who were borderline pre-teens. Evelyn didn't really enjoy Awana, it reminded her too much of her early days of catechism studies. She had been questioning everything in her world, including the existence of God, which precipitated more internal conflict when she went to youth events at church. She saw her mother as religious, which I figured made her all the more skeptical about any reality of faith. Still, it was worth getting play time with Chloe, and it meant I could actually work at least a full day at the office without scrambling to pick up kids.

It seemed like a good plan until around 5:30 pm.

Camille: Heads up Alex, Holly called me to announce she's stopping by.

Alex: Ok, thank you Camille. I'll just have Martin pick up Evelyn at 6 tonight and have her home.

Camille: I think that's a good idea. Holly is a little off her rocker lately.

Alex: Lately?

Camille: Maybe more than usual. See ya later!

We only lived three blocks from Camille, making the occasional after-school care very convenient. Camille never asked for anything from me, explaining Evelyn's friendship with Chloe was worth the world to her right now. Evelyn told me she liked being with Chloe since Chloe's life was mixed up like hers. "She's weird, but that means I'm not the only one," she would say. I didn't want to argue with her about her self-image, but wondered how deep that would set.

Camille, a little messed up herself, supplied the added benefit of keeping current intel on Holly. She kept communication open with Holly, partly from a big heart, partly from fear of becoming the next victim. Direct sources of information about Holly's latest plans to get custody of the kids or to right some social wrong in her world were rare, putting Camille in that awkward position of friend and informant.

Martin was on time as usual to pick up Evelyn and take her home. When I arrived home a short time later, I could hear the kids yelling at each other in the house. I opened the front door to observe Evelyn on her back at the top of the stairs with Justin at her feet and Martin at her head. Both boys were attempting to achieve the impossible: control of a wild 10-year old with ground advantage, fingernails, and a serious lack of remorse.

My entrance was the distraction they needed. I borrowed my work voice. "Evelyn, STOP!!!" She turned to plead her case, at which moment Justin scooped her up like a ground ball and tossed her over his shoulder, then carried her kicking and screaming - literally - to her room, where he deposited her on the bed and evacuated before she could throw a book at him. He had the combined look of pride and disgust. "You should have never stopped spanking her" he said, shaking his head.

Nobody could explain what had just happened. And only then did I notice Nikki at the open front door behind me. "Hi there…how's it going?" she asked with wide eyes, despite the obvious indicators.

"Just another day in paradise," I said. "Got a spare straight jacket?"

"Fresh out," she replied. "She gonna be okay?"

"Oh yeah. I'll circle back with her shortly."

Though a bit embarrassed, I secretly hoped Nikki would come in and go talk with Evelyn. Maybe she could magically turn her into a reasonable child, or perhaps she had some insight about these weird outbursts or how I was supposed to manage them. I worried this next level of exposure to my own world of chaos would break the camel's back and drive her away. Instead, Nikki gave me a much needed hug until my shoulders finally let go, dropping about three inches. I couldn't believe how much stress my body was holding.

# # #

I wasn't sure what I had just seen, but it was pretty clear Evelyn was having a "moment" and Alex was trying to figure out what to do. And while I'm pretty good at figuring out what makes people tick, I was categorically clueless about what to do with a kicking, screaming 10-year old. We didn't have a kicker in our family, nor the need of a big brother to haul us off like Justin did. It was as if he had done this before.

It was just after 6:30 pm and there was no evidence of dinner, so I made an executive decision and ordered some pizza from Papa Johns. Alex seemed uncomfortable but also thankful for another adult brain in the mix. It dawned on me that he didn't exactly have that with his ex, certainly not as the children grew and multiplied.

Alex went for a chat with Evelyn while the kids and I talked, waiting for the delivery. They clearly enjoyed being able to tell someone about their attempts to deal with Evelyn, airing all her dirty laundry in a matter of minutes. None of it was really bad, just a little riskier recently as she was getting bigger with that affinity to kick things. Especially brothers. And despite the complaints, it was clear they didn't hate their sister. In fact, there was no hate anywhere in the house, not to each other, not to their crazy mother, not to anyone.

# # #

20. HOOK

May 20, 2010

> **Terri**: Hey, you there? I think someone hacked your Facebook page. You better check it out.

I didn't really have time for this, but I recalled having digested an intelligence report about terrorists' use of military and law enforcement social media pages to wreak havoc on people doing the work of counterterrorism. I'd better check.

Surprisingly, the FBI didn't have a big hang-up about agents accessing their personal social media pages or email at work in 2010. The FBI did, however, get their proverbial panties in a wad about anyone accessing the Internet from personal devices inside FBI space. Several times each year, a small group of Men-In-Black types would show up unannounced with "sniffers," these futuristic-looking handheld devices which were rumored to be able to tell if anyone was selling secrets to the Russians or thinking bad thoughts. I figured it was like a polygraph: the device does nothing to detect truth, it only detects unseen anomalies in physical behavior. Either way, it creeped everyone out and we typically found some "field work" to do when the suits showed up.

But not today. I had been re-assigned back to the JTTF for 60 days due to the combination of an on-duty injury I sustained in a fight with a girl (oh, did I skip over that?), along with an uptick in overseas source reporting and activity around the globe, the last of which was the failed Times Square bombing on May 1st. After an early morning all-hands meeting, all remaining nine of us in the office had plenty to address. Faisal Shahzad had been arrested by FBI agents two weeks earlier for the attempted bombing, resulting in every terrorism squad across the country being directed to immediately re-work their sources for indicators of pressure cooker or propane tank bombs and components. We were on a short timeline for headquarters and I only had a few weeks to help before I got pulled back to patrol. New York division learned he had been in direct communication with elements of Al Qaeda, including the notorious and highly effective propagandist Anwar Al-Awlaki, meaning anyone else we were already looking at for similar connections to the English-speaking jihadist in Yemen suddenly had a heightened level of importance. And, like most places in the US, we had a few.

I switched the Black Box KVM switch from red to green, thoughtlessly clicked through the small print warnings of how I'd lose my birthday if I shared classified information (red) in the unclassified (green) environment, then navigated my way on the World Wide Web to Facebook. *"They're not gonna let us do this much longer,"* I thought. I logged in and found my latest post, strangely put up this morning.

"Nikki is the bomb!!!" it read. Funny, I don't recall typing the word *bomb* on the green side in a long time. There were already four comments and 12 likes, including a deer-in-the-headlights comment from Nikki herself coyly pretending to be flattered. *I love this gal,* I thought *I wonder if she's ever thought about going undercover for the Bureau.* Eh, probably a conflict of interest. I picked up my cell to text Terri.

> **Alex**: NICE.

> **Terri**: She's a good one, that Nikki.

> **Alex**: No doubt. If that's the way I get hacked, I'm good with it.

While texting Terri, I could see notifications of a little barrage of messages from Holly. Her flip phone broke up each one of her messages into several parts, amplifying the number and making it a pain to navigate. I checked the swarm from Holly to see if there was some new instruction for tomorrow's visit with the kids or something useful. More likely, it's another jab at me for dating someone. Holly had taken on the job of sending me daily emails from a self-help service aimed at helping Christians deal with divorce *the right way.* Only none of them included the possibility that one party was bat-shit crazy. It was all part of her pity-party which provided a constant reminder of her view that she was the victim, I was the bad guy, and the kids were suffering because of my choices.

8:59 am

> **Holly**: There will always be a mix of emotion towards you. I am thankful you were my choice of a spouse and friend. This is a hard week. Today, May 20th, is my wedding day. I still believe in my vow. Until you remarry, you are my choice. I would have done anything to save my marriage. I will do anything to be a close encouragement to you and our children. Hurts like hell, and thankfully God gives the

grace to see a bit of heaven every day.

Holly: Please forgive me for being sassy to you, today. I do not think I will ever get over being lied to in front of so many people. The Weird Al Yankovich song was the truth in your heart. I was only 'good enough for now'. When you sang 'Only God could love you more than I do' at our wedding, it was all for show. A center staged lie, just to shame me.

Holly: Who is available today? What is the available time with kiddos, on the weekend with me?

Holly: Do you understand how I still cannot hold a REAL job? I remain faithfully, Semper Gumby. If I shirk on any of my awarded time, you might use it against me. I can never be sure what you might do.

Well, that was fun, I thought as I shook my head. Switching back to red.

# # #

May 24, 2010

It always made me smile when I saw Sally's name pop up on the inter-office phone. I picked up the ringing handset with an abrupt, "Wanna blow this popsicle stand after lunch?"

"You read my mind, girl. Am I supposed to be doing something?"

We both laughed. "You're asking me?" I said with a snort, then laughed harder. Working at Rove Aerospace sounded important, but most of us could honestly accomplish our actual tasks in about a tenth of the time afforded. I finally recovered from myself. "Hey, can I ask you a question?"

"As long as it doesn't involve you commandeering my Facebook page," she quipped.

I gave my best fake gasp. "Why, I can't *believe* you would even *think*...." I changed tone to bring it back. "Okay anyway, so you have a religious background and I don't. But we get along swimmingly."

"As it should be," she said. "My faith is a big deal to me, but I made a commitment a long time ago not to be someone who used it against anyone."

"That's it exactly! Do you and Frank go to church?" Sally had never talked about that.

"Not really. Frank's coming along in his faith but he's not real interested in joining a church."

"Does that cause conflict? I'm asking for a friend…." I looked aimlessly out the window.

"It can, but it doesn't for us. We both share core beliefs but have different ways of showing them."

Sally was my kind of example of how a person of faith should be. Honest, caring, and consistent, all while not making people around them feel like they are lesser citizens. And while she was a little crazy, she was the good kind of crazy I liked.

I think it's the secretive hypocrisy of judgmental religious zealots that drives me mad. When people pretend to be better than those around them while putting on the act of humility, it is just wrong on all sides. The pastor preaching sexual sin but who has an affair, the priests who preach a culture of piety but who engage in horrible systematized culture of sexual abuse of children, the minister who advocates for the poor but steals thousands from his congregation while hiding behind his religion. It's not that I can't accept that people make crazy mistakes in judgment…I'm a long ways from a saint! But when these people push their own image of righteousness onto others whom they barely know, it boils my blood.

Alex connected with me on this point early on. He was deeply educated in his faith, yet somehow I never felt judged for not having the same depth of religious education he had. At the same time, I felt like he craved my strength of brutal honesty. I decided to make it my mission to help him figure out what he actually wants.

"I'll break for lunch at 11:30," I said.

"Perfect. I'll come by your office then. All this trying to work is driving me to drink."

And there it was. Typically, being in HR meant while I knew things about the company and everyone in it, I didn't make any actual bonafide friends at work. Sally was the exception. She had no interest in trying to leverage in to the confidential information I maintained for the organization. "You're the best, Sally. See you shortly." My cell phone started to buzz.

Alex: So, this just in from Camille…

Nikki: Oh, do tell.

Alex: Confirmed. Holly is on Match.com.

Nikki: WHAT??? OMG!!!

That little religious psycho. Here she belittles Alex for dating me openly while she herself is doing it in secret.

Alex: And…it's not going well.

Nikki: Oh there's a big surprise…

Alex: Yeah, Camille said she's talking to anyone who will listen, getting sympathy for being an abandoned wife of an abusive police officer husband.

Nikki: Uh-oh…

Alex: She asked to use Camille's computer last night and failed to log off when she was done. Camille looked through all the profiles and messages Holly has been exchanging with random men.

Nikki: Oh my God. Alex, that could be really dangerous.

Alex: Hey, she's on her own…there's some creeps out there.

My thumbs couldn't keep up with my brain at this point. I called Alex.

"Hey," he answered. I could tell he was stressed.

"Hey, so I don't want to alarm you or anything, but this could be really dangerous for you. If she gets some Bubba-freak who has it out for the police due to his own criminal history, then hears her so-called-plight, he may just choose to prove his love and dedication by coming after you."

Alex was quiet for a few seconds. "Yeah, I had not really considered that

299

angle." I had.

"Did Camille say anything about these guys she's talking to?"

"One she saw was a car salesman for a little dive dealership somewhere. It creeped her out."

Again? "Did she get the name?" I suddenly wanted nothing more in the world than to see who she had gone after…who was going to be her next victim.

"I don't know," he said. "I'm guessing Camille could figure it out. But there's something else you should probably know."

"You found another long-lost kid?" I asked.

"Yeah, no…" he paused again, getting more serious. "Holly sent me another blast of texts earlier this week. No surprise, but one of her comments was how she didn't think you were 'woman enough' to take her man. I think she may not like you."

"*Really*! You don't say?" The shit-eating grin started to take over with the feeling of *game on, bitch!* But then I became pissed off and my mind veered straight into Protection Mode. "Hey Alex, I gotta run, Sally has arrived and she looks hangry."

"Why are you still on the phone?" he asked. I hung up on him before he said phone. *He loves me*, I thought.

I filled Sally in at lunch, getting her take on the matter.

May 27, 2010

All week I began to be plagued with a dangerously crazy idea. For months, Holly had been meeting weird guys out of the blue. I wondered what kind of guys she was finding online. So…I went online. Between meetings at work, I created a fake email address on Yahoo and a faceless account on Match so I could check out her profile. Didn't take long to find her. Hmm…Hip Pretty Holly. HPH. Good Lord.

I wondered what her ideal soul-mate would look like? My analytical brain started firing on all cylinders.

I ran some technical tests on my little idea Thursday night.

May 28, 2010

By Friday, I knew I needed to check myself. I needed that one person I could trust to pull me back from the brink of disaster. I called Sally.

"Sally, let's do The Blazing Onion. I got something I need to run past you."

"On my way!"

For Sally and I, "lunch," as it was called, usually consisted of a well-intentioned salad followed by rounds of wine and French Fries which lasted well past any reasonable employer's idea of lunchtime. Today was to be no exception. I explained to Sally how Holly had been using a dating service on the Internet to troll for unsuspecting men. When I dropped my bombshell idea on her, Sally's immediate reaction honestly surprised me. I should have been able to predict that she would urge caution, circumspection, and strong warnings for the fallout on Alex. I should have known she would appreciate my creativity while then gently helping me realize the reality of harm I could be invoking on an already stressful situation. I should have guessed Sally would push back her last glass of merlot half-full and suggest we get back to work. But then I would have been wrong.

"Oh. My. God. *Let's do this*! I am so in." Sally bounced in her seat, barely able to contain herself. "This is so risky!"

True that. I told Sally how I had logged in to the corporate network from home via a VPN, then logged into a virtual machine located in Fort Lauderdale where one of our HR servers was housed. Fort Lauderdale was good; it was next to the water and fit the persona I was making. From the Florida server, I logged into my new Yahoo account and changed the profile name to something more in line with the scheme, then sent an email to my business email and to my personal email. I checked each of these on the receiving end to inspect the source data and…Bingo. Everything pointed to a Yahoo server in Florida. I had just laundered myself.

"As long as I follow my send-protocol through the VPN and the Florida server, I'll be safe."

"Remind me to never piss you off," Sally said with amazement.

Since lunch had already turned into Out of Office for the rest of the day, we ordered more wine and mapped out a basic cyber-operational plan worthy of Alex's security clearance: public Wi-Fi spots nowhere close to work or home, use of the VPN with encrypted routers and anonymized IP addresses, the backstopped source email address with activity in Florida, and more. I had used some of Holly's own verbiage on her Match profile to make her ideal man even more perfectly ideal. He had kids, was a single dad, a man of pleasant faith, successful, appreciative of his ex-wife, but struggling to see his kids needing an engaged mother figure at home while he traveled occasionally for business. Oh, and a business that works with non-profits to benefit children with disabilities. Ok, maybe leave the disabilities out. And the non-profit…I'm too clueless about those to make it work. Maybe a marketing company…yeah. I showed Sally the image of some poor schmuck in Chicago I had chosen who had no clue of his future virtual life in the Northwest.

"Most importantly," I explained, "I have to keep Alex in the dark. I'm certain he would not approve, and he'd need absolutely plausible deniability, just like in the movies. If this goes south, I need to be sure Alex in no way could be held responsible."

"Totally," Sally agreed. "That might be tough, keeping a secret from Mr. FBI."

Holly could hate me all she wanted and I wouldn't care a hill of beans. I even welcomed it at this point. But Alex had to be protected from my scheme. Still, I knew if I got caught, I could jeopardize our relationship entirely.

May 31, 2010

Monday was Memorial Day and Alex was busy carting the kids all over creation. I met Sally for coffee at a Starbucks in Mill Creek.

"So, have you decided?" she asked.

I grinned and nodded. We giggled with glee and terror like two schoolgirls shushing themselves in a boy's bathroom while hunched over the laptop. I put myself in Florida, then changed my Match profile pic to the Chicago dude. Poor guy, he had no idea what his alternate life was about to become. With one final look over our shoulders and a deep breath, I browsed to Holly's page and clicked the Button of No Return.

Wink.

We both sat back in silence for a minute, then placed bets on how long the dangle would dangle before she'd bite. Both of us overshot by 3 days.

She bit that very night.

21. Line

May 31, 2010

Match.com/profile

Meet Hip, Handsome Hank.

I'm an educated, hardworking individual. I own my own marketing business and love what I do so I feel lucky to say it really doesn't seem like I go to work every day. Having said that, the stress in my life is greatly diminished making me a pretty well adjusted, happy-go-lucky person.

I try very hard to take good care of myself. Eat right and exercise, don't smoke, and pretty much just keep it to a couple glasses of wine (good wine) here and there. I come from a large family; we love to cook, eat, and enjoy each other's company in the process. I definitely know how to have fun and can be easily classified as the life of the party. I'm "one of those creative types" so watch out! I enjoy life and live by a work hard play hard mantra. My perfect first date would be something in a social setting…coffee house, dinner, maybe even a beach day or something outdoors. Together we'll figure out something fun. If what you read interests you, drop me a note and let's see where it goes.

Holly winked back.

# # #

2:55 pm

Holly: Very concerned about our kiddos going on the church trip to Useless Bay with neither of us. They do not deserve so much rejection. They tell me almost every time we are together that they are lonely for what they remember as family. Katherine feels ugly and like she has few friends. She says her friend is TWITTER. Kevin is tired of going home to a place he does not want to be. Evelyn cries and says she does not really fit in anywhere. She pleads to be loved for who she is. She says you are making her play lacrosse, even though she does not want to. What have you taught them about how I make situations awkward by being present for their events when you are there with Nikki? They are just as much mine as yours. I will be at everything I can to love and support them. WHAT IS AWKWARD about that? Katherine tells me that she will sit with her "family" at graduation. Her family is BOTH of us. I will be asking Justin to sit with me. I am comfortable with anything.

The refrain was becoming more regular. "Dad, Mom's being weird again."

"I'm sure she means well, Kevin."

"I don't know," he pondered. "She made all of us get in a line and follow her up the hill at the park, and there were these big cameras there and some Asian lady who was asking us questions like if we liked to swim."

I needed to set aside my Friday morning brainstorm on how to get a team of French operatives to tail a Moroccan subject into the Basque region on his travel the next day in order to focus on Kevin's dilemma. "Was she wearing a bright yellow jacket," I asked.

"Yeah, and so was the guy with the camera. I think they were TV people or something."

Ah yes, the Yellowjackets of the King 5 news team. Holly had created relevance again by inserting herself into the tragic pending closure of the local community pool. Our kids had learned to swim there, become lifeguards there, heard their first coyotes there, and probably got a first kiss or two there as their adherence to the 24-hour rule waned.

Evelyn couldn't wait to chime in. "She made us walk like penguins," she complained. Evelyn looked like she was putting all her energy into making her face squint up like Kevin's.

"Go get dressed, Evelyn. I'll come brush your hair before I head to work. And Kevin, would you please throw away the empty boxes of cereal from the cupboard?" Kevin looked at me with crazy eyes, chomping his Cinnamon Life with an on-purpose drool of milk flowing down his mug with no chance of draining back into the bowl, and replied with his un-swallowed mouthful of food, "Shhhure ting, Popsh!"

"Oh good God. You're gonna clean that up."

"Look Dad, I'm a penguin!" Evelyn stupidly waddled across the kitchen toward the bathroom, pinballing herself through Katherine and Justin who had come to see the morning show.

"Dad, I need money for gas," Martin called out from the dungeon. I had made a deal with him: if he would handle taking the kids to school in the Mitz, I would pay for his gas, usually about $40 every ten days or so.

"It's in your account," I hollered back, then realized he had ascended the stairs and was standing behind me. The kid was sneaky. "Oh, sorry—I thought you were...."

"Downstairs?" he whispered.

"Yeah. Hey, what's the penguin thing?"

"Oh, that," Martin started. "Yeah, mom was making us all line up and walk like penguins for the cameras. King 5 is doing a story on the pool and how it's gonna get shut down if they don't raise more money for it. And you know mom, she can't let any good opportunity to show off her kids to the world."

"Evelyn didn't seem to be too happy about it," I said.

"Good one, Dad. We all were a little less than happy. Evelyn was pretty much mortified." The other kids all nodded in agreement with wide eyes, telling me they were together on this one.

I didn't know what to say. They were clearly uncomfortable about it, but I suspected at least Martin liked the idea of being on TV, whatever the cost. "Hey Evie, let's get that rats nest handled, I gotta take off in a minute." My phone dinged, because I didn't have enough to think about.

> **Holly**: I emailed Lauren Hughes, at King 5. She is going to get a positive outcome story, hopefully, Opening Day. Evie wants to make 'Hooray' signs, and Martin would be a great speaking voice. The city council will be getting details as to how Edmonds accomplished the feat. I enjoyed the "cheerleading" for funds. It is always great to hear a positive outcome from an outcry for help. "Ask not what Edmonds can do for you, but what you can do for Edmonds."

Good thing I got this info, I mused. Somehow I knew more was coming.

To: Alex
From: Holly

I would enjoy as much time with the kiddos, as you are willing to give. I have the weekend free for them. I am here at the Jacobs, until the 2nd of June. I have rented a spot, in a house in Edmonds, after that. It will be comfortable and easier to get to.

The address for my check is: 7514 58th Avenue West, Mukilteo, WA 98275

Thank you and God Bless,

Holly

# # #

June 4, 2010

7:00 am

To: Hank
From: Holly

Good morning! I am pouting this morning. I had quit Match several months ago. I saw you winked at me a few days ago. I winked back. Then, I saw someone had emailed. I took a big leap back to subscribing, in hopes that the email was from you. Now I am sad, it was someone else.

I am a very hopeful romantic. I thought that your profile name was so much like mine, that maybe you had chosen it purposefully, to match mine. Okay, this is where you laugh out loud. Call me absurd, but I wanted to believe it. The believing was fun. Darn it though, I think I was wrong.

So...I love that you know you are handsome. And, you got lots of private coos over the cutie pie in the photos with you. I am a mom.

I love loving so my kiddos are my hobby. They are cute, but do not like me saying so, in public...there is only one that is not a teenager.

I wanted to tell you the truth, so I did. You can think what you want. I value honesty, above all else.

;-) HOLLY

I literally ran to Sally's office. "Oh my God Oh my God! We got a live one!"

5:08 pm
To: Holly
From: Hank

Good afternoon! I love your romantic theory regarding my user name, however, in actuality I was browsing on Match and your user name jumped out at me because it is quite similar to mine. Your interests and photo peaked my curiosity further so I winked at you then promptly left town for a few days. I'm pleased that you not only winked back, you emailed me as well. I'd like to know a bit more about you if you're willing to share.

I read you have 3 or more children. What are their ages? I have one—he is the joy of my life and lives full time with me. He's turning five in July. I've been divorced for about two years. I struggled for about a year not having my life partner with me however I think I've adjusted well and have begun the search for that special woman that will walk next to me for the rest of our lives.

You indicated you are self-employed/entrepreneur. What do you do? I own a marketing company. Our core business is branding organizations and giving them media materials (print, TV, radio, internet, etc.) to let the world know what they are all about. I've spent the last 5 years building the business (hiring trusted principles) to work with me to ensure a legacy for my family. My company employs roughly 250 people world-wide.

Is your family in the local area? I come from a large family: 2 brothers and 2 sisters. Older brother 52 (has 3 children); I'm 45 (1 child); sister 43 (has 4 children and is expecting another in September); brother 40 (has 3 children) and my youngest sister is 34 (has 2 children but says she's "practicing" for more). Both of my parents are alive and extremely healthy and the best grandparents a child could ever ask for. My Mom is 72 and my Dad is 74. They travel a good bit however they make a point to always be home during the holidays.

I have maintained a decent relationship with my ex-wife to ensure my son has the opportunity to know her. She has moved to Florida and rarely sees him but I'm encouraging daily phone calls and am planning on going to Florida this summer so he can visit for a period of time.

I hope the holiday weekend treated you well. Please respond if you are interested in communicating more via email to enable us to ascertain whether or not we are compatible.

Sincerely,
Hank

June 5, 2010

7:00 am

To: Hank
From: Holly

Good morning! It's a beautiful day in the neighborhood...I am walking the waterfront. I was looking forward to communicating with YOU.

Ok, so the romantic thoughts are just part of who I am. Thank you for not spurning it. I wished after I pushed send, on the first note, that I had not been so giddy. Even the capital letters are in the same spots. :-)

Your return response was the longest one I have gotten, so far. I am a talker, so I loved your willingness to be so open. I will do my best to keep up.

I am the mother of five precious jewels. The first is a son of 18 years. He is charming and an observer. He loves what his senses can take in. He is graduating this month. The oldest has senior prom tonight. He is romantic like me.

My second was born not breathing. I begged God to not just keep him alive, but to make him a strong powerful man with a heart towards healing. He is a lacrosse star. His team just won the State Championship. He is being honored with Team Captain for the upcoming season. He is doing High School and College simultaneously. God is doing a great work in him.

My third is a beautiful songbird. She was welcomed with all the pink and frills my heart desired. She makes the best expressions and has a lovely singing voice. She loves love. She is lonely for the life she dreamed of. Divorce has set her back. She is trying out for Dance and Drill Team. A circle of friends combined with Christian fellowship will heal her.

The fourth is another boy, a redheaded wonder. He wakes up hungry for food and action. He loves people and sports. He is funny and fun to be with. He is a great public speaker and enjoys writing. He takes life by the horns and rides hard. I love his spirit.

My baby is 10. She is a golden fairy princess. She loves flowers, bugs, music, and stories. She is very outgoing. She was most wounded by our family split. She had been my little cheerleader for the older siblings. My hope is that she finds a special niche and gains true confidence in who God made her to be.

So that leaves me. I am a woman who loves family. I am a promoter by nature. I love experiencing life more than reading about it. My love language is touch. I believe that comes through skin and the soul embracing what God does to enlighten the eyes of our hearts. I enjoy taking in what is around me, with all my senses. I am the middle daughter of 3 sisters. My parents were divorced when I was 9. My mom remarried when I turned 16. She is a spunky accountant who gave us the love of learning and a courageous hope for the future. She lives in Equador and teaches. My stepdad is her longed-for soul mate.

My father loves me, but is distant in connecting. He is a sensual man that lives simply and loves nature.

I said I am self-employed because I am working on figuring out how to go forward. I loved being a wife, mother, and homeschool teacher. I graduated from C.W.U, with a degree in Family Studies. I have a strong belief that I am called to orient from home to my loved ones. I am still figuring out what to do next. I will be honest in saying, I was never my partner's lover. He cherished me as a friend and a mom.

I have a strong spirit and clear belief that the Lord has already forged my path. It has to happen with my children and I together. I have a mentor—his wife believes with me that the dreams and desires of my heart will come to pass. They are a part of World Wide Dream Builders. I am taking steps slowly, but with health, dignity, and beauty. I needed to heal in the process.

I have done some public speaking, cheerleading for the best in my children, growing in compassion for homeless women and children, a modeling job, some sales and service, and two years of cherishing myself...that was a new thing.

It makes me a little nervous to respond to such a strong confident man. I am looking for an equal that is sure of his gifts and can treasure his partner's talent and creativity. Mutuality and blessing one another so that the people close to us are blessed in the process is my hope and goal. I DO believe dreams come true.

Warmly,

Holly

#

"Get moving you freaks!" I yelled to the girls. "We leave in 20 minutes!"

Evie and Chloe shot past me on the stairs and out the front door. "Not yet—" It was futile. Odds were good they had already made it to the creek and were getting soaked. For no reason at all. *Kids.*

I finished my trek up the stairs with two baskets of clean laundry. I distributed the baskets to their respective rooms, then re-traced my steps to pick up rogue socks. Nikki pulled into the driveway. "What are you girls doing over there? Evie, pull your shirt down!"

I stayed inside, opting to grab a fresh cup of coffee for Nikki. She started up the stairs then called back to the girls, "the bus leaves in 15 minutes!" She was getting good at this.

"Is that for me?" she asked, making her way up the stairs.

Score. "Indeed it is," I grinned, followed by a kiss. "Are you ready for this?"

"As I'll ever be," she said. "Should we drive or walk?"

"Let's walk. Parking will be a bitch."

Somehow the girls got moderately dry and we headed out, hand in hand—all four of us. The Port of Edmonds Waterfront Festival was the community's declaration of summer. And while it normally rained like a tempest, today was 65 and sunny. Perfect. We spent the next three hours perusing the festival booths while trying to keep track of the girls. Evie drug us to a face painting booth and pulled out all the stops, demanding action.

"I want a star! Right HERE," she said, slapping her forehead. Chloe did the monkey-see-monkey-do thing, mimicking the leader. I'm not sure how they both didn't end up with bruises on their noggins, but at least we could cover them up with some blue paint.

Blue stars in tow, we headed for the food trucks where Nikki handed out $20 to each of the girls. "Go choose something and meet us back here at the table."

"Awesome!" they both squealed, skipping away.

"How 'bout a gyro," I asked.

"Sure. No onions. And I'll take some of those fries with feta cheese!"

Nikki kept her eye on the girls while I fetched the food. We gathered at the table and chowed down, watching the world go by.

It felt like family again.

On the way back, the girls used their leftover cash to buy a tie-dyed Frisbee. I only had to retrieve it twice from the road on the walk home.

# # #

I parked the black, shiny, massive Lincoln Town Car at 5 pm sharp in the taxi lane to drop off the overdressed teenagers on Martin's prom night. Julio had pulled some strings for me with his buddies and came through nicely with the car. "Get out," I ordered madly. Martin's dinner reservations at the Space Needle were at 6:15. No time to spare.

Martin laughed. "I only need five minutes for the photo," he called back as he struggled to gather up his camera equipment. Photography had become a passion of Martin, resulting in his collection of used but high-quality equipment. I had donated a remote trigger to the cause from my own collection of equipment, most of which remained stored away in my garage.

I watched Martin and his date disappear over the bluff next to the ferry dock. Cute. I called Alex.

"The package is at the photo booth."

"Copy that." Cop-like. Alex was bummed to miss out on prom night due to a mandatory graveyard overtime shift, but glad I could swoop in to help out.

"Martin is totally excited to get a shot down by the water. I offered to take the photos for him, but he insisted on doing it all by himself. Such a boy." Something in my rear-view mirror caught my attention. I glanced up and recognized Holly's pinched face in the driver's seat of a Kia. "Uh...Alex...gotta go. Call ya later."

I hung up the phone and slithered down in the driver's seat. *Thank God she doesn't know this car*, I thought. I watched as Holly traced Martin's path toward the water. As she disappeared over the hill, Martin and his date came running from the other end of the park. Martin had a tri-pod and his camera in one hand and his date dangling from the other as she struggled to keep upright in 5-inch heels.

They made it to the car and flung open the door. "Go! Go! Go!"

I stuck it in drive and stomped the pedal, tearing out of the taxi zone like Kasey Kahne exiting a pit-stop, but not before I got to see the pinched face round the far corner scanning for her lost prize.

"That was close!" Martin exclaimed. "I told her I'd send pictures and not to come."

"No worries," I said with a grin.

# # #

June 6, 2010

8:25 am

To: Alex
From: Holly

I hope you enjoyed your time helping our son have a wonderful night at his prom. I have learned that you are not thankful, but rather full of bitterness and vengeance. Only God can deal with that, when you choose to repent.

I love the man you are when God shines through the most. I love you even when ugliness is the first presentation. I have never hated you. You have given me too much joy to let the worst overshadow the best.

God Bless You and our children,

Holly

# # #

3:00 pm

To: Holly
From: Hank

My son and I attended the festival in Edmonds yesterday and today we went to the fish hatchery. We both thoroughly enjoyed it, face paint and all. Did you attend?

I would imagine having five children at home is quite taxing and I enjoyed your descriptions of all of them. What is the custody situation with the children? You indicated your "partner" in your response. I'm assuming you are divorced, please correct me if I am wrong. You referenced WWDB's. Are you active in Amway? You also said "...the Lord has already forged my path. It has to happen with my children and I, together", can you expand on this statement?

I know that I'm full of questions - it's my nature to explore and understand. Feel free to ask me any questions you may have - I'd be happy to share. I hope you enjoy today and I'm looking forward to learning more about you.

Hank

6:01 pm
To: Hank
From: Holly

Thank you, again, for the response. I did go to the festival, yesterday. I was sad to be there alone, so I came home. I did not have the kiddos, this weekend.

I do not mind answering your questions. Like I stated earlier, I treasure honesty, above all else. Yes, I am divorced. I would never consider chatting with a man on Match, unless I was. I believe in faithfulness.

Please have an open heart and mind on the custody issue. I ended up homeless and displaced, due to the separation. I had no means to gain the position of my ex-husband. He took advantage of my ignorance in court issues, and misused his authority as a law enforcement officer. HE HAS CUSTODY OF THE CHILDREN. It was a devastating and unkind divorce. I see the kiddos on a once weekly, and every other weekend schedule. As the kiddos request, and he approves, I can see them as much as they want.

For instance, some weeks, I spend time with one or more of them every day. This is why a personal business is best. I have gotten some criticism for not getting a regular J-O-B. I love being mom, and knew they needed me as available as I chose.

I love children. I taught Special Ed. Preschool, an International Outreach Preschool, kindergarten, and Pre-K, before becoming a mother. I also love people connections. I was a Youth Director of Activities, at church, while at C.W.U. And a leader in Fellowship of Christian Athletes, during High School, and College.

Are you a part of Amway Global? I am just getting started. I really believe in what the business offers. Just not skilled in sales yet. Glad you and your son had fun yesterday. I hit my limit. I had a great time taking photos of my son and his prom date, down at the waterfront. He was so handsome and she was very pretty.

I wondered if I would recognize you if I passed you, in public. Would I? Kinda was wishing to have a chance meeting. Do you attend a local church? I am still searching for the right place to settle on. My house mate is involved at Mars Hill. I am interested in there.

Okay...try to top the number of words in your response. I will feel best, that way.

Could you include why your ex-wife is not near her little man? Only say what does not demean her, while still speaking the truth.

Warmly,
Holly

8:57 pm

To: Holly
From: Hank

Let's see...if you saw a 40-something year old man walking around with a 5-year old boy sporting a blue star on his forehead (me not the boy), carrying a really cool Frisbee (spin painted) and sharing a gyro then you saw me. I'm fairly tall so I tend to stand out in a crowd so if you've looked at my photo the odds of you recognizing me are pretty good.

Prom night...Wow! I can't even begin to imagine what that day will be like for me when my son reaches that age. Where was his prom held? What a great idea to take photos at the waterfront. You indicated you'd hit your limit. Do you have a fun meter limit?

If you don't mind my asking what happened that you ended up homeless? What caused your separation? Where was your family during this difficult time in your life? Obviously your home situation has changed - is there any recourse to the custody arrangement through the courts?

My ex-wife relocated to Florida with her new husband about 6 months ago. The reason we are not still together is after having our son she realized she did not want that life—being a Mom was not her cup of tea. It was a hard realization for both of us – I loved her dearly but respect her decision to leave. I have a wonderful blessing from our marriage and I will never regret the time we spent together—we were married 13 years. How long were you married?

I am not involved with Amway Global. I hope that venture is helpful to you but remember no one makes money overnight and I often see people get into businesses such as these with the dream of instant success. The key to success is hard work and goals—which I'm sure you know.

My family attends Calvary Chapel Overlake. It's been our church for a very long time. My entire family has continued to attend CCE even though we are located throughout the Puget Sound area. I am thankful for this tradition because there are weeks when Sunday is the only day my son is able to see his grandparents and cousins.

Can you describe for me what a typical day is like for HipPrettyHolly? What kind of goals do you have for yourself (i.e. short-term and long-term). I'm looking forward to your responses.

Hank

11:03 pm
To: Hank
From: Holly

Before this proceeds, I need assurance that you are truthful, sincere, and trust-worthy. It would not be wise for me to take you into confidence without some sort of reality check. I know from a female friend that also is beginning to date, and on Match, that the gentlemen she opens up to are willing to share a website connection to their work. You are free to choose what the identifier is. I just need an element of security, at this point.

I hope you understand. I have been through a lot over the past few years. I am still learning how to guard myself properly and not trust too easily.

I want to continue getting to know you. I also need to use wisdom and discretion.

I will answer the question of where was my family during this season. I was very alone. The same time that the separation process was started by my ex-husband, my close parents relocated to South America, to serve.

Please be thankful always for the family support you have had. And as scripture teaches, "Do not begrudge the day of the little things." Your son will bring out God's best in you, as you humbly sacrifice for him.

Thank you again for the responses.

Warmly,
Holly

June 7, 2010

7:00 am

To: Holly
From: Hank

While I can understand and appreciate your caution the same holds true on the flip side for me. Because I am a successful business owner sharing any identifiable information with someone I'm still trying to determine would be a good fit for me is not advised. I've had one experience that, quite frankly, I will not repeat. The beauty of online date sourcing is the autonomy and please accept my apologies if my questions were too invasive. I wish you luck in your search and hope you find what you are looking for.

Sincerely,
Hank

# # #

I was half way through my grande drip in a venti cup when Sally called. "Nikki, can I come to your office? I just read through the saga…"

"Door's open," I replied. She was there faster than normal. She shut the door with careful speed, eyes ablaze.

"Just…wow! Amway? Seriously?! I bet she doesn't write back. When was Hank's last letter to her?"

"This morning," I said. "I predict she'll think about it and continue the conversation with him. I mean really, what if she's missing out on this really great guy?"

"True, Hank is a catch," Sally said as her eyes drifted up to that place of total fantasy. I let her drift. Sally snapped out of her daydream back to the other…daydream. "She actually seems smart enough to realize that if she did share everything, Hank would run for the hills. It is interesting reading through what she wrote knowing her situation and mental state. I found it odd she described her stepfather as being very 'sensuous.' Isn't that an odd adjective for a parent?"

"Well, yeah," I said. "Might have had something to do with his attempted sex change. I loved the comment about taking pictures at the waterfront. Of what? The kids running from her? Oh hey wait-wait…this just in!"

Sally scrambled to my side of the desk as we read the email together.

11:06 am
To: Hank
From: Holly

I hope and pray you remain successful and content. I did not wish to take anything from you. I gave you a lot of answers into myself. I understand that you need to guard yourself, also. So on we run, as single parents that have been forsaken by a lover. Jesus will not treat you like that.

Press on. The prize has already been won for you and your son. I am happy to continue to communicate. You did nothing wrong.

I need to work hard and go forward strong for my children. We all need encouragement. It makes me sad that someone hurt you so that your heart has to be extra cautious.

Remember that abiding in Him will bring you LIFE IN THE PARTY. Celebrate what God does for you. And...be the example your son needs to direct him to Christ, the true lover of his soul. I will pray for the emptiness your son has in a missing mommy.

Warmly,

Holly

"Man, she sure likes to use Jesus to control the conversation," I quipped.

Sally agreed. "And clearly she wants to keep the dialogue going."

"I'm gonna make her wait for it," I said. I'll answer her tomorrow on my way to work."

June 8, 2010

7:02 am

To: Holly
From: Hank

I appreciate your kind words, understanding and prayers. I am thankful for all that I have achieved and grateful I'm able to give back to the community in ways I never dreamt possible.

I am thankful God has blessed me with a wonderful wife for 13 years (I am a better person having known and loved her) and the sweetest son imaginable. My caution comes not from my ex-wife but from an over-zealous potential date. She showed up at my company after exchanging a handful of getting-to-know-you emails. I took the incident as a lesson learned. I'm still new to the online thing and I'm hopeful we can get to know one another better and forge a relationship at some level. Whether or not that is a dating relationship remains to be explored.

I hope you are able to enjoy the weather today. I think Matthew and I will play hooky this afternoon ;)

Hank

To: Hank
From: Holly

A big happy heart leap! I thought your closing on the last note was a farewell forever. You are a star! Thank you for hanging in there with me. I was going to try again this morning. I am glad you beat me to it.

I understand your caution. FYI...I am zealous, but would not show up at your work. You gave me all I needed in today's note. Matthew is a great name. My oldest son's middle name is Matthew.

My children's names are: Martin, Justin, Katherine, Kevin, and Evelyn. The sons have Biblical middle names. The girls have their grandma's middle names. Their dad's name is Alex. I am the incomparable "Holly," there is no-one just like me...LOL.

In answer to your question of recourse for better custody: Yes. Gaining equal footing in court will take God helping me to prosper finances. Seeking how to be a professional mom, I was led to Seattle Midwifery Institute. I took a course to become a doula. I love how it encompasses my desire to help women to be overcomers and not simply survivors. The birth process and thoughts around mothering, coupled with the power of choices, are very empowering. I know that if I would have lost my cherished lover and not had my children, I would have not gone forward well. This is very personal. I mean no judgment on your former spouse.

I am taking this week to document and put a timeline to the events over the past two years. Several attorneys will receive them. I am praying for justice, not vengeance. The court scene was really frightening for me. I was not ready for the fight. I love the children's dad too much. I will not treat him the way he treated me. The truth needs to be known and dealt with in a way that confronts, and also heals our family. Alex has made a choice for someone else. I could not so quickly. For my children's sake and my own I need to take this battle on, in God's strength, and pray for freedom to love openly and practically, again.

Amway Global, and promotion of the Vision House project, Jacob's Well, are sideliners. My mentors believe the business is a means to make extra cash by doing what you are already doing, just differently so that you are earning from your spending. I did not know what they did to earn. I knew their character and the strong children they pour so much into. Their son was my son's encourager, as team captain, on his lacrosse team. This coming season, my son will be honored with the same title. God is very good.

So my turn...tell me something about your childhood.

I look forward to your response,

Holly

Leaving for a walk on the waterfront...IN THE SUNSHINE

Have a fun hooky afternoon, with Matthew.

Astounding. Holly seemed completely incapable of having an outside view of herself to know if her own actions were potentially or actually hurtful or offensive to someone else. And yet she stopped herself in talking about her own divorce, realizing it may be interpreted as applying to Hank, then calls it out saying she means no judgment on him or his ex.

This verified what I had suspected all along. Her behavior was a choice. Holly was capable of shutting off her manipulative behavior. Although…wait. She's doing it *right now*. She's manipulating Hank! Funny…he doesn't even exist.

12:11 pm
> **To: Hank**
> **From: Holly**
>
> Lunch break, so here are the answers to your other questions. I do not have a fun limit. It was my sad meter that reached it's limit, at the festival. We would probably have to settle for a tie, in being the life of the party. I would let you win, as long as you gave me credit for the surrender.

Goals are simple. I have a week to focus on getting some very painful documents sorted and written up for an attorney. They are like Kryptonite to my soul. Very disempowering to look at. I know it is right to do. Some dear friends have come alongside me. By the end of this month the weight of the heaviest part will be lifted.

On a daily routine, I keep to a "kindergarten" schedule, with adult additions. I wake with a song in my heart, so I sing it, plus a few more praise songs, that fit my thoughts. I read my Bible, then pray specifically for my children and myself. I am a constant pray-er. As I go through the day, I pray for others and needs as they come up. I love a walk outside, if it is sunny, or some exercise indoors if not. I favor breakfast over the other meals. Do not like to skip it. Sometimes have breakfast fixings for dinner. My kiddos really like that. I network and keep myself available, most days. I do most of that from my phone. Thus, you may catch grammar errors. I try to swim, during the week several times. I am still recovering from a bicycle fall. The swimming is very restorative. I love the hot tub, afterwards. I catch lunch, and a recess, by getting outside. The focused stuff, comes between lunch and dinner. I am doing textbook reading for my doula certificate, and some self nurturing reading to encourage my faith. I am looking for a part-time job so I do online searching and applying. Again, I remain flexible, due to the kiddos. Often, they call and want "mommy" time, other than the scheduled residential time. I like to cook, do crafts, and play. So on their weekly visits I bake, cook, and prepare for a game of something that makes a memory. I love family time around the table. We have a tradition of telling our "best and worst," then we close the day with thanking God and making our worst stuff a prayer request. I like them singing together. We had habits that I do my best to keep. I think it is crucial. I stay busy until I sleep. I always close my eyes with forgiveness of myself and others. Miss the closeness of someone beside me. I have felt very "held" by Jesus. I sleep better now than I have in years. PRAISE GOD.

I am known for being SEMPER GUMBY, always flexible. Have to work around other's schedule to remain available. There is equal strength in the oak tree and the bruised reed that beds under adversity and challenges, but remains intact. When oaks fall over from storms, it is messy.

I love weekends. Sunday always has church and refreshing activities. I am kinda strict about laboring into rest and resting in my labor. I treasure a Sabbath. I trust God knew what He was doing by setting a day aside for worship and relaxing.

This is my best shot at answers. Did I miss anything?

Warmly,

Holly

Uh, what was the question? Ho-ly shit. I might have to quit my job to keep up with this!

June 9, 2010

I realized bringing Alex a donut for his birthday was inappropriate, especially on duty. It was probably even borderline offensive. And that, for some unknown reason, made me want to do it all the more. I was on a roll.

I met Alex at the heavily wooded and under-utilized Maplewood Park with a cup of Starbucks and a bacon maple bar before heading to the office. "That's mine," I said, nodding to the bacon maple when I opened the bag. "Yours is the Old Fashioned. It's under mine."

"Right where I like it," he said.

Alex had a rule about public displays of affection while in uniform, but that didn't prevent me from getting a rise out of him. It literally only took staring at his pelvis for a few seconds.

"Stop," he ordered. I failed to comply. Shocker. Unable to focus on his donut, he playfully shoved me out of my trance.

"Help!" I pleaded, like a damsel in no distress whatsoever who wanted nothing more than to be grabbed, spun around, handcuffed, embraced, and roughed up a bit. "Police brutality!"

Alex broke his own rule. No handcuffs, but for the next minute or so it was a good thing there was nobody around. I had nothing to do with it, I swear.

Eventually, I broke away and brushed my makeup off his uniform. "I gotta run," I said. "I have a meeting with Sally this morning."

"Do try to get some work done today," Alex said.

After getting settled in at Rove, I forwarded the latest to Sally. She came down the hall an hour later.

"What the heck is she talking about the messy oak trees falling and 'Semper Gumby'? The only thing that did make sense was her comment about her kindergarten routine."

"I know," I said. "This one is going to be hard to respond to."

"Good time to ask about the ex-husband's new girlfriend. I bet she'd open up on how she feels."

2:13 pm

To: Holly
From: Hank

I hope this note finds you well. We had a fantastic day yesterday. The lake was so beautiful. Grandpa, Matthew and I decided to take the boat out and fish a bit. We spent the rest of the day with my sister Mary, her two daughters and my folks at their home (Medina – west Bellevue). It's the home I grew up in, and I must say a wonderful comfort to be able to visit. We have an entire wall dedicated to photos of everyone throughout the years – I added a photo just yesterday.

As a child I was the curious one of the group of five. Always probing, analyzing, questioning and reasoning. My father always hoped I'd follow his path of profession. He was an attorney and has since sold his practice and retired. My Mom worked until I came along. She retired from investment banking and put her family first. In hindsight what I respect the most about her is while she was our rock, our home base, she also had interests outside the home. She was on the Board of Directors for a couple of charities and really instilled community service into all of us. She is the master organizer.

I attended New York University and received my undergraduate in Marketing. I went on to obtain a MBA at the UW before entering the workforce. I got my feet wet in a large marketing firm, invested right (thanks to Mom) in real estate and before I knew it I was able to open my own firm. It sure has been a blessed path and I continue to be thankful for all that I am and can be in the future.

I'm sorry to hear of your struggles regarding custody and your relationship with your ex-husband. It's unfortunate when children are involved and the adults can't come to a mutual agreement. My father represented some pretty high profile custody battles – the stories he would tell us only affirmed our commitment to doing the right thing for all parties involved. You indicated your ex-husband is remarried—how long have you been divorced? I hope this week's tasks are accomplished and that you draw strength from the activity.

Tell me more about how you get certified to be a Doula and what a typical work day would be like. It sounds like a very rewarding profession. About the life of the party thing…I will share the title but only if you sport a blue star on your forehead for a day, heh heh. Semper Gumby! Wow, you just took me back 20 years to my Latin class. I appreciate that you are a "pray-er". I should probably do more of that. I, like you, enjoy the weekends. Sunday is the best day of the week for me. Family.

I'd better get back to the proposal that is sitting on my desk. Enjoy the rest of your day, you will be in my thoughts and prayers.

Hank

2:55 pm
To: Hank
From: Holly

Many grins as I read your note. Today has been very busy. This is my day with my kiddos. I will respond with a detailed note, at the close of the day.

So glad you had an afternoon, on the water with family. Hope your proposal gets completed and you are content with what God puts in your day.

Praying for you,

Holly

P.S. I would wear a big blue star. Like I said, I love promoting what

I believe in. :-)

# # #

Kevin led the parade into the house from the Mitz after the Thursday visit. "Dad! Mom's gonna be a karaoke DJ!"

Evelyn followed. "And she wants to have other people's babies."

Justin. "How is that even a thing?"

Katherine. "She's too old to be a surrogate anyway."

Martin. "And old enough to know better. Oh wait, that would require a non-crazy brain. My bad."

They each scattered to their rooms before I could respond. Except Evelyn, who had planted herself on the couch, chin tucked into her chest, arms folded, brow furrowed. I sat next to her for a minute, then put my arm around her and drew her in. Her tears started to fall.

"It's like we aren't good enough for her," she cried.

# # #

11:00 pm
To: Hank
From: Holly

I wanted to honor my word. I am very sleepy. I had a friend offer to give me a small business. He wanted to talk about it tonight. I just came home from the meeting. It is something I consider a great opportunity. I did not expect the day to be so full.

I had a blessed day. I wanted to tell you that I am really enjoying your emails. Feeling a little nervous that I may be lesser status than you are seeking. Actually shed a few tears asking God to help me share some things with you...not sure how much caution to use.

Holly

11:30 pm

To: Holly
From: Hank

I'm glad your day was full and that you were presented with an opportunity. Those are the types of days I cherish. I hope you rested well.

I'm glad you are enjoying our email exchanges and I hope that by sharing my past, present and future you aren't intimidated by my successes and failures. All those events make up who I am and what I will become. I believe we are all equals regardless of financial, community and/or family status and that our current and future actions are what matters the most. Our pasts are exactly that...the past. It is the past that creates the experience and opportunity to serve others. Please forgive me if I've made you uncomfortable.

(Climbing off my soap box!) My hope for you, us, is that we can be transparent in our thoughts, hopes and dreams. From the first communication with you I got a sense of reality from you. You think it, you say it, which is so refreshing. So! All I ask is that if we continue this process of getting to know one another you share with me as much as you feel comfortable sharing. While I am looking for someone to spend the rest of my life with I am patient because I know when we find one another it will be forever.

Hank

22. SINKER

9:02 am

To: Hank
From: Holly

It is a beautiful morning, at the waterfront. I really want to share a few things with you. I am a bit nervous that they will cause you to pull away. My choice would be that you hold on and be compassionate.

I lived my whole life with extra hope, with my eyes fixed on a dream I am convinced God gave me. The hopeful expectation carried me through some really rough storms. I am not letting go. I believe God puts desires in our hearts and bids us to have faith in His calling.

My heart longed for the kind of family life you grew up with. I did not experience it, in reality, although I envisioned it and continued to experience peace that it would come to pass. The first 2 men I honestly loved, had families like yours. The parents and 1 of them remain my dear friends. They are hopeful and also sad that divorce was part of my journey.

You asked how long I have been divorced. Our official separation occurred in March 2007. He dissolved the marriage August 2007. The divorce was signed by he and the attorneys, January 2008. Alex is not remarried, he has a girlfriend that spends nearly everyday with he and our children. Our marriage took a dark turn, about 5 years before the separation.

Like I said, there was someone I loved before I was married. He was a soul mate. He carried a love for myself and another young woman he had grown up with. We dated for nearly 3 years. He was a best friend with some kissing and cuddling mixed in. We were involved in Youth ministry together, and Fellowship of Christian Athletes. His family was very encouraging and Christ-centered. They believed in my hopes and dreams. There came a point where he needed to make a choice between the two lovers. The other woman had loved him from childhood. He actually came to me and said he wanted me. I sensed that he would have been happy with either of us. I did not feel as if he really just wanted me above her. Also, I could not imagine her not being his wife. She would have been crushed.

I told him rescue her heart and focus on her. He married her 6 days after I was married. I was there. It was very sweet. They projected a little paper letter she had written in early grade school, "Dear Donnie, I love you and I want to marry you." They are still happily married with 3 sons. He is still serving youth, as an elder, in a church. He and Carrie serve on the worship team. They are partners. I am grateful for their dream come true.

At that time, back in college, my pastor met with my ex-husband who had expressed an interest in me. He took a fatherly role, due to my estranged relationship with my dad. The pastor told Alex that he knew how hard it had been for me to wait for Don, then to let him go. We met for premarital counseling and the pastor explained my heart's desires to Alex. I loved serving in the church and wanted a partner that would do so alongside me. That could have been through a job or actually in a formal ministry. I am very evangelical. I hoped for a very old-fashioned large family that had an open door policy to welcome others in. I desired to live frugally enough to carry no debts and be able to give as God lead. I dreamed of either homeschooling our children or being very involved in a Christian school. I did not want a separate career so that I would be available for my husband, children, and then whomever the Lord wanted us to welcome. I had travelled overseas on a trip during college and had a heart for missions. Alex promised all these things.

Just two years into our marriage Alex chose law enforcement as a career. I was very supportive and active as I could be in spousal connections. We joined a very dry church where he became a deacon. He remained evangelical in his work, although I was separated. He loved our family life and we did our best to remain open and welcoming to others. His job became him. I prayed for his success. He has done very well in it. I delighted in serving he and our children. His hopes changed. I was not his partner, rather his subject. He wanted me to think his thoughts and became abusive. He threatened that if I told his commanders about the pushing around that he would lose his job and I would have no means to go forward.

I lost my lover, but believed in the strength of commitment and covenant. I struggled for a long time. I saw counselors, sometimes with his participation. It was very painful. In the midst of family struggles the past childhood hurts surfaced as well. Alex dealt with me in a very commanding manner and I crumpled. I had some very wise counselors that held on tightly and encouraged me. Alex wanted out. He was very defensive and has yet to repent. I dealt with some bitterness and anger that had not been characteristic of me. My family did not know how to love me through it. My young heart flew to God and dreamed of being loved and never forsaken.

Still makes me cry. I have no real memories of the time before my dad and mom separated. My mom prayed with us nightly, as children. We became a part of a church, shortly after, their separation. The Lord built in me the desire for family through His adoption and His Son's marriage to my soul. I have never doubted His faithful love.

Life over the past two years has been a wild ride. I have seen and experienced so much. My prayer has continually been, "Lord give me a heart of compassion, and make me a shelter of comfort." I had to go through ALL of this to be what He wanted.

The questions you ask about career goals are hard, because I never dreamed I would be doing it alone. I am a great planner and organizer and am not afraid to take things on. I want to remain a connected mom as I go forward. And...very honestly, I want a partner that comes alongside me to make the dreams a reality. I do believe two are better than one.

So there you have it. The lover, advocate, and friend named Holly had to love herself enough to share her heart. Scary. I hope you will understand. I am totally worthy of someone like you. My course has been hidden with Christ. I have faith, like Noah, that my family has been sheltered through this storm. I see a rainbow every day.

Like you I have always been one to challenge everything. I am bright and spunky. I have not backed down on my hopes and I have been very blessed. My investments were not material, rather deposits into the character of my children. My gifts and talents are equal, but different.

Hoping you do not run away,

Holly

Sally ducked in and slammed my office door. "What the?!" Her eyes were even wider than normal. "Yesterday she's not worthy and now she's claiming abuse!"

"I can only guess it has something to do with the men her mom dated after her divorce from the guy who wanted a sex change. You know, dear old Dad."

Sally was impressively keeping up. "Maybe Hank should share a personal moment from back in college when his girlfriend or true love broke up with him and he thought about ending his life. That could be when he became a Christian."

"I like it," I said. "I'm going to tell her a story about being arrested for drunkenly disorder back in college, or whatever it's called. I'll be sure to do the girlfriend thing too."

Sally laughed. "Oh, Lord. Maybe when it gets a little further along you can do the Jerry Springer treatment and tell her that you looked up her record online because you couldn't consider meeting someone if you didn't do a background check. Then you can let loose on her about her arrest record."

Good thinking. "Yeah, the only problem is I'd need to have her last name to do so and I can't ask for it or she'll want to know mine. But you betcha…If she divulges her last name, it will be my quick, cutting, destructive out!"

"Oh right, Hank doesn't know her last name," she replied. "Bummer. Can't wait to see how this eventually ends. It's so crazy—you could completely crush this person, but instead you're doing something good. She may finally get the help she needs."

Eh, maybe.

"On the other hand," Sally continued, "she'll just keep playing the victim more than she already does and find someone else to manipulate into feeling sorry for her."

"By the way," I said, "I want to call bull on her story that someone wants to give her a business."

"Didn't you know? It's one of those "self employed" businesses. You stand on a corner with a card board sign saying "will work for food... God Bless." She's probably getting her own corner."

"I'll get her a Tin Cup."

"This new corner plan has potential too," she said. "I can stake out her corner and alternate between sending Christie and Julio by to freak her out!"

"Stop following me!"

Sally ran out of my office, pretending to scream. "Stop following me!" She called less than a minute later.

"Oh my God," she laughed, "I had to close my door on that one! The guys next to me probably think I'm a little crazy myself. HA!"

"Start sucking your thumb and rocking…It works every time."

3:15 pm
To: Holly
From: Hank

Thank you for sharing these very difficult items with me. One thing you will learn about me is I am compassionate to a fault. I am an advocate for good people in general but especially children and I'm taken by the story of your childhood. I really was privileged in a storied childhood that less than 2% of the population ever experiences. A fairy tale of sorts, which, for all intents and purposes, is extremely difficult to achieve. Have faith that the past experiences will drive you to succeed. Where did you grow up? Forgive me if I've already asked that question.

Like you, I've been in love twice. The first was a high school girlfriend that ended shortly after I came home from my first year at college. The distance between us was just too great for our young relationship to withstand. Honestly, she was my fun buddy. We got into and out of trouble together, we entertained each other through our love of adventure but ultimately we couldn't sustain our love over distance.

The dissolution of my marriage to Dedra was by far more difficult to overcome. The last 2 years of our marriage was peppered with marriage counseling sessions that she didn't want to be at, one trip to the hospital because I feared she was going to hurt herself and arguing over symptoms of the real problem: she didn't want to be married or a mom. She suffered through a depression that would cripple most humans. Just last month she told me she was very grateful I was by her side during that dark time in her life. We remain friends today not only for my son's sake but for ours as well. I can't stop loving a person because they grow a different way than I and I'm thankful she has found a man that shares her goals and dreams, loves her and our son for all that they are and will be. I hope you and Alex can come to a mutual understand on how to do what's best for the children and each other.

I have a couple of questions for you. What is your most cherished memory from your childhood? From your years in college? As a married woman? I'm really looking forward to the response and I hope you have had a great day and an even better evening.

Hank

I grabbed my keys and headed out my office door. Sally was doing the same. We walked side by side in silence, like a pair of Charlie's Angels who just swindled a CEO out of some compromising evidence. She gave me that look, the one that knows things.

"You are diabolically brilliant," she whispered.

I giggled. "Who's crazy now?!"

"Maybe me," she said. "I'm gonna have a hard time explaining to my sister this weekend why I can't put my laptop down while we sit by the pool. Even right now I am headed to one of our vendors and I can't wait to read more! My boss thinks I am leaving the office to address some urgent issue. Hahaha!"

"By the time you make it to Ohio, I'm sure there'll be plenty to digest."

I was multitasking like a mother. Dear, God. Dinner with Alex in 30 minutes in Edmonds. No way I was gonna make it on time to pick up Alex at his place. I suddenly recalled what it was like to date 3 men at the same time. *Wait, I'm the one with the simple life, right?*

# # #

My commute home was precisely a 7-minute walk, which meant I was only going to be 17 minutes later than I wanted on account of a late arrest. Why people insist on getting drunk and crashing into their own damn garages at 5:00 pm on my Friday will forever be a mystery. I was taking Nikki to dinner. Okay, let's be real: she was taking me to dinner. The Loft was a swanky little joint on Main Street run by a Greek-ish couple who had an aura of "don't mess with me" about them. Theo and Polly prided themselves on their success and being a cut above the average. Their white Land Rover and black Mercedes made it clear, as did their lack of tolerance for loud-mouths and idiots. This provided some nice little corners for a romantic date, especially when my favorite Colombian, Alonso, was performing.

As I rounded the corner of 7th and Daley, her voice caught me by surprise. "Hey, handsome. Need a ride?"

My God she was beautiful. "How'd you know?" As I reached for the door handle, Nikki gunned the turbo, skipping up Daley Street and out of view in a hot second.

Brat!

I finished the final 30 seconds to my house and found Nikki standing at the top of the porch stairs with her arms folded, staring at her white gold watch. "What took ya?" I gave her a smug glance and pretended to ignore her as I walked inside to put on a fresh shirt.

We made it to the restaurant by 7. Theo was in his full gregarious mode. "Alex, my buddy! How you doin?" He gave me that handshake-half-hug combo, minus the European cheek-kiss, thank God.

"Theo, this is Nikki Myers."

Theo stared, then slowly extended his hand to take hers, bringing his lips to her knuckle. "The pleasure is mine, to be sure," he said. "Come, your table is ready." Theo led us to a private seat in the upper, well, loft.

"Well," Nikki said, "he's sure Greek, ain't he?"

# # #

9:55 pm

To: Hank
From: Holly

I had a great day. I spent the evening with an attorney, that is also a great friend. I shared with him my profile on Match. He is concerned that I gave out too much identifying information. I think I told you that I had been off Match, and only subscribed again because I saw your wink. So glad I did, because I am really delighted to get to know you. He quickly listened to some parts of a few of your messages. I asked if he thought you were for real He said yes, and that you are as romantic a spirit as I am. I have been wondering if perhaps your messages are God's own doing, just to meet my heart where it needed some hope.

So I am sleepy, but happy. I may need to change some of the info. To be safe. Just letting you know.

Night night,

Holly

10:03 pm

To: Hank
From: Holly

Forgot an answer...I grew up in Grandview, WA. Moved to Maple Valley when I was 12. We lived there while I started college at Pacific Lutheran University and finished up at Central Washington University.

I've attached some pictures of my beautiful precious jewels, along with a link to a special song in my heart.

Holly

She really did. She sent six photos of her children to a man she never met. A man who didn't exist.

June 11, 2010

2:00 pm

To: Holly
From: Hank

Good afternoon! Today has been filed with chaos. Good chaos, but chaos none the less. Thank you for your note. I really enjoyed reading about you and your travels through life. It helps me to put things in to perspective. The photos of your beautiful children were a wonderful surprise. You are very lucky to have so many treasures.

I will write you later this evening or tomorrow morning. I'm leaving for NYC Monday morning for a short business trip. I'm hoping to be back home by Thursday morning.

The video/song was beautiful. Thank you for sharing it. I had not heard it before—I can't wait to share it with Matthew. I hope your day has been pleasant and productive and ends with a song in your heart and a smile on your face.

Hank

7:00 pm

To: Hank
From: Holly

I want to whisper something in your ear...just imagine standing next to me. We are at the beach barefoot. I take your pinky in my hand and lead you to a piece of driftwood. I step up on it, put my hands on your shoulders, lean close to your ear..."I like you."

We exchanged notes that read...I, like you, have...When I read them, I smiled and thought, I really do like him. So I just thought I would tell you.

Reading your responses makes me feel like you are close by. Today, I felt a little sad knowing you will be so far away, over the coming days. Do you travel very often? What does Matthew do while you are away from home?

I am glad your busyness was good, today. Was your proposal received the way you hoped it would be? It is great to have the sun out, this afternoon. My friend's son graduated from UW, yesterday. I did her grocery shopping for their weekend celebration party. I was up late, with an attorney, getting documents sent off and a letter written. I normally wake up by 6. I slept longer, this morning. The song I sent you was running in my head. I loved the photos that went with the one I chose. There were so many stages of life represented. My college studies were focused on how every stage of life is impacted by the events and people we interact with.

Have you read A. Milne's little book, When We Were Six(five?)? He is the author of Winnie The Pooh. It is very dear. Matthew would like it. Pooh's favorite two words were, also, 'thank you'. My most cherished time with my children was stories read aloud. We worked ourselves   through   hundreds.

My second son and I are having dinner together, here in Edmonds. I need to run and get ready. Oh...guess what? Last night I ran into the woman that lead me to Seattle Midwifery. She is 70-ish, and is a doula...that is Latin for birth companion advocate. She said there is an organization called Open Arms, that helps ladies get their certification and then support women that have no partner. That is exactly what God had laid on my heart. The Jacob's Well project is also for single moms in transition, just a different kind. It is for homeless women and children. My hopes and dreams are borne out of my own life experiences. So thankful for my children and really have compassion for a mother's need to go through difficulties as empowered by her choices.

Treasuring the thought of you,

Holly

9:01 pm
To: Hank
From: Holly

I am not sure when you leave. If you are here tomorrow morning, there is an extreme low tide. If Matthew has ever seen the taffy puller at the Seattle Center, explaining that the sun and moon pulling cause the tides to shift and change. The will be full moons. The tide will be several feet out farther than normal. This means that really cool critters can be seen. Like...hermit crabs.

Just a bit of info.

I had a nice dinner with my son, He walked me through the World Cup recent games. He wants me to watch the USA play England in the morning. He works at the pool, so he thought I could get the details for him. We have a Lacrosse Family Celebration tomorrow. Please pray for me to keep my chin up. Alex is a coach and he comes with his girlfriend. I was the only single mom without a partner this year. Our sons are very valuable players.

Sleep well and I will be praying for your trip to be enjoyable as well as productive. And...I hope God keeps you safe while you travel.

Sweet Dreams,

Holly

9:07 pm

To: Hank
From: Holly
Forwarded Email

Hank,
I get these each night. I thought you might be blessed by them. It hurts to know that Dedra wanted away from you and Matthew. I am glad you had your family and the Lord's strength and mercy to support you. Forgiveness not only heals our relationships with others, it also heals us. Just before our separation our family with another family read aloud The Tale of Despereaux. It was a great analogy of the healing power of forgiveness.

Thinking of you,

Holly

One Day at a Time' from DivorceCare
365 days of healing and encouragement

Forgiveness Is Not Pretending You Weren't Hurt

Day 294

Laura Petherbridge says, "Forgiveness is such a complex issue during divorce because it appears as though you're letting the other person get away with the offense. If you forgive, it feels as though you are saying, 'My wound isn't real. This stab to my heart and the pain of rejection isn't significant.'"

Your wounds are real, and they are important to God. He never wants to see you hurt. You do not need to make excuses for your feelings or pretend to other people that you were not hurt that badly. This behavior does not solve anything. Be honest. You were hurt, and it's lousy. But physical and emotional wounds should not keep you from forgiveness.

"How do you forgive when you've been hurt so badly?" says Jan Northington. "Forgiveness comes in knowing the facts and being willing to let them go. Forgiveness is the only thing that allows you the kind of peace that will turn your mind from injustices in your life toward God."

When you forgive your former spouse, it does not release your former spouse from being responsible for his or her actions. It does release you from orbiting around those hurtful events.

"But I say to you, love your enemies and pray for those who persecute you" (Matthew 5:44).

Lord Jesus, I hurt so much. Why did this happen to me? Help me to be honest about my pain, but willing to learn how to forgive. Amen

----

P.S. I am smiling

P.S.S. I just caught that you were here for the weekend. Enjoy your blessings.

#

June 12, 2010

11:45 am
"Ludicrous is leaving the station in t-minus ten minutes!" Martin announced,

proud of himself as he ran the show. He had agreed to take the gang to the Saturday visit with their mom, despite the fact he was outside of the parenting plan as an 18-year old. Martin knew by doing the driving today, he would ensure they could attend the end-of-season lacrosse celebration at the head coach's house. It started at noon.

Nikki zipped into the driveway, top down and shiny. She lay on the horn. "Let's go, Alex! The potatoes are gonna get cold!"

"All right already!" I ran down the steps, giving Martin $20 for gas and a quick pat on the shoulder. "Thanks for doing the run, Martin."

"I got ya covered, pops."

We made it to the coach's house in seven minutes and parked at the only available spot in the cul-de-sac, right square in front of the place. Nikki carried her amazing Cake Balls while I hauled in the forty pounds of Killer Potatoes, the dish containing four pounds of butter, six pounds of bacon, and three pounds of cheese all baked into a beautiful pile of love. She quickly became the talk of the moms, every one of them wanting the recipe.

"That's classified," she'd say, implying some connection to my secret work world.

The kids arrived a few minutes later and all scrambled to the back yard where an un-supervised trampoline was in full swing with kids bouncing everywhere, usually for distance, occasionally into the bushes.

Twenty minutes into the food, Holly made her appearance. I'm guessing she was shooting for the glam-look on a Goodwill budget. Nikki couldn't hold back.

"Holy shit, Alex! Do you see that?"

"Trying not to," I said. It was borderline disgusting. Holly had dyed her hair flaming maroon-red. She had drag-queen red lipstick pushed past the corners of her mouth and was wearing a floral jumper straight out of *Little House On The Prairie*. She was carrying four plastic bags full of day-old buns which I recognized from one of the front-porch dumps she had made from the food bank.

It wasn't that the lacrosse moms created instant space to avoid her, it was more like they just didn't shorten the distance. These lax-moms (as they liked to call themselves) had experience with Holly, experience which taught them to steer clear of her. They were cordial, even compassionate at times, but all had learned not to engage with her drama lest they become the next victim. Holly made her rounds nonetheless, ensuring her relevance to the occasion. Until, that is, the awards started.

As the team began to gather for the awards, parents began to drag their little ones from the trampoline. Since this was technically Holly's residential time, I tried to pay no attention to the kids, giving Holly her space to be the parent in charge. Holly caught up with Evie at the edge of the trampoline, pleading with her to come off. "Evie, you need to stay close to momma or you could get hurt!" Evie held still with Holly's hand grasping her arm, saying nothing.

The coach took control of the moment. "Let's gather around for a few awards, everyone!" The next twenty minutes was full of long-winded speeches and accolades for each player and some volunteers. "And a huge thank-you to Assistant Coach Hill and to his beautiful lady Nikki for stepping in to help out wherever she was needed." He handed Nikki a massive bouquet of flowers while I did all I could not to glance at Holly.

The goalie made his way over to Nikki and hugged her. "Thanks for those amazing Cake Balls, Momma Nik!"

Evie managed to break free right then and ran to Nikki. Holly started to go after Evelyn, but steered away as Nikki locked eyes with her with a Texas-style smile. The lax moms were loving this. Nikki gave Evelyn a quick hug and sent her away.

"Isn't this fun?" Nikki whispered beside me. I gave her a quick, hidden elbow, causing both of us to giggle and turn away.

As we carried the empty dishes to the car, Nikki couldn't stop laughing. "I thought she was gonna blow a gasket! She was more concerned about you and me than she was about the kids."

"You're just jealous of her lipstick." Nikki looked at me like I was the crazy one. We burst into hard-core laughter as she handed me the keys. "Oh my God, you drive. I just can't!"

As we pulled away from the house, I caught a glimpse of Holly in the rear-view mirror. Right where she belonged.

2:00 pm

Holly: There is a constant theme of spoken words, "Dad is cool," and "Mom is not." Many times Evelyn says I treat them like babies. They use many adult comments with adult-repeated words. Please do your best with the adults around you to not speak dishonorably about me. The paralleled affection for you and what you offer is not healthy for our divided family. When it is my time with the children please quickly tell them to stay with me. What you ignored at the lacrosse celebration was not helpful. If we are at events during my time, please do not hoard time to yourself. I mean all these thing as encouragement for what is best. Thank you.

#

4:04 pm

To: Hank
From: Holly

I hope you had a great day enjoying the sunshine. The awards ceremony went well. This is my day with my kiddos. I have just moved. I was blessed that two of my kiddos felt comfortable inviting friends. I stopped and asked the Lord to give them creativity and constructive interactions. The boys played hoop and are now watching a lacrosse game. The girls watched just one show and are now making a fort with cardboard boxes. I am very grateful. Hopeful to include the friends in some sort of devotions, before they leave.

I would like to ask for a favor. This is a new process for me. I believe communication is essential in all relations; family, co-workers, friends, and possible forever mates. We learn by living. It would help me grow stronger in people skills if you would remain open and honest. I may say more than you are comfortable with or ask for something you do not wish to answer. I would like to understand either one of these. My experience so far with other people that have gone through divorce, has taught me that walls and vulnerability are difficult to balance. I am willing to recognize mistakes and learn from them.

You had mentioned these issues earlier. I hope your openness was not jeopardized by my questions or blissful imaginings. If so, I welcome your honesty. I respect your encouragement and welcome counsel. I do lean towards sensitive, and am not ashamed to admit it. It has helped me be compassionate. I know that it is not best to make negative assumptions. I believe these are absolved by keeping communication flowing.

All that said...I hope to stay connected. If I crossed a line that made you uncomfortable, please say so.

Hopeful,

Holly

10:00 pm

To: Holly
From: Hank

Forgive me...The mayhem has continued from Friday and while I enjoy an active lifestyle the last 2 days has been way more than I expected. Friday night Matthew and I had dinner at the Loft. I really like that little restaurant and so does Matthew. Have you eaten there yet? I saw the Taki Tiki right across the street and thought of you. We went to the movie The Karate Kid and really enjoyed it. We both stayed up way past our bedtimes—he was delighted and I was exhausted. This morning I woke to a kiss on my forehead with delightful giggles as Matthew played with my ears...at 6AM! We planned to spend the day on the Sound and he was so excited to get going that he thought I'd had enough sleep. Hence why I didn't email you this morning – I didn't even get my typical cup of Jo from Starbucks – travesty I tell you! I am just now slowing down to relax and will hopefully pass out the minute I hit the send button.

You asked if I travel often. Before Matthew, I traveled regularly for business and pleasure. For the last 5 years I've minimized my travel and take Matthew with me when possible. I have an Assistant that helps when Matthew is able to come along on business trips however the majority of the time he prefers to stay with Nana and Papa. This year I have traveled 4 times all within the US. I have NYC on my calendar, Miami later this month (with Matthew) and in August we'll be heading to Montana for a week.

The proposal looked good and we're about 70% positive the client will accept the campaign. I love the creative process when an organization finally realizes they need a brand image to promote themselves to the next level of greatness. I can't begin to explain how rewarding the feeling is.

We have not read A. Milne's little book. Matthew would absolutely love it I'm sure. He is an avid reader/listener and loves words. I'm glad your day with your children and the lacrosse celebration went well. I get the sense it is difficult for you to attend these events where your ex-husband and his girlfriend are attending. Is that a fair statement? It was difficult for me at first when Dedra was dating Michael. It actually took Michael and I sitting down over a beer and having a conversation. Were you able to spend time with all your children? You indicated you have just moved. Are you still in Edmonds?

Favor granted! If there is one thing I'm really good at it is communications. You will find out soon enough that I am a life coach. I have the ability to coach and counsel with respect and transparency. Without open and honest communication, we will have a difficult time moving forward. I love the phrase "you live some you learn some". Nothing you have shared with me has offended me or crossed the proverbial line.

There is another full day on tap for tomorrow so I'd better retire. Here's to little boys sleeping until at least 7 am and Holly having wonderful peaceful dreams. I hope your Sunday is full of love and kindness.

Hank

June 13, 2010

6:00 am

To: Hank
From: Holly

I was right when I told you that you felt close by. Friday night you and I were across the street from one another ;-) Justin, my second, and I had dinner at A Very Taki Tiki. Justin was an extra special child, from birth. He came most easily, but was not breathing. He was kept alive and near me by the healing power of God and my heart's loud cry of faith that God would heal him, and not just give him breath, but make him into an amazing man. God spared him and I praise

Him for keeping him close. He is my most determined and most busy. He also was my most sensitive, although he has such strong character traits, a few words of encouragement bring double blessing. I have faith God gifted Justin with healing and vision beyond what is normal. We have a unique endearing bond.

I need to interject something critically important, before I say anything else...THANK YOU, your note of response cleared an ugly storm, in my heart. I carry a fear of abandonment that can be crippling. Truthfully, that fear often holds the hand of rejection. This is why TOGETHER is my favorite word. The phrase I LOVE YOU is God's unforsaken promise that holds me when the fear becomes too much to bear. The world was formed with words and I am amazed at the power they possess, both for good and evil. You blessed me more than I can communicate in words, with your response. No forgiveness needed to be asked for, but I willingly give it.

I have been to The Loft. I will find the courage soon, to explain a circumstance that keeps me from returning. I zealously over-reacted to a man's sexual desire for me and it lead to a painful learning process that I am mostly over, but still processing. I hope you will be discerning about this.

Yes, there is pain whenever I attend events with Alex and Nikki. Yesterday had a segment that affected the rest of the day. The girl goalie, spoke these words, "I want to thank Coach Alex for yelling at me and getting me to do what he wanted me to, he is great at that." I had to quickly walk away. Something remained unsettled and dark, until after the kiddos and I left. I did the best I humanly could to manage it and had to keep praying that the effect would not hinder the rest of the visit. My unsettled emotions hurt my youngest. At the celebration she spent more time with her arms around Alex, than she did near me. He is always capable of gaining public honor. My advocate soul that successfully enlivens the best in others, longs to be given the same in return. Ok. So I know this just enlightened your understanding. I know from your letters that you are gifted in this realm.

Your comments about Matthew are endearing. I can feel how much you love your little man. Karate Kid looks like a great movie. I loved the first one. It was a great story of branding and believing in success. I am glad the two of you had a special time together. That makes less sleep worth it. I have very fond memories of waking up to my children's eagerness to "seize the day." I am geared the same way. I love mornings. They are a new beginning. I wrote a beautiful letter to the Edmond's Enterprise editor that expressed the importance of sandwich boards and advertising in downtown Edmonds. You would learn a little more of my heart by reading it. My waterfront walks are a hopeful inspiration.

I am impressed at how you do not miss details. You catch and respond to nearly every comment or question I send. Thank you for the kindness of communicating so well. It is such a refreshing blessing.

I moved back to Edmonds. I was staying with my friends that owned and operated On The Way Gourmet. They believe I can take it over and be successful running the company. My only hesitation is that my personal hope for an income-earning profession, was becoming a Doula. I drew a logo and chose a business name a year ago. This hope was borne out of my circumstances. It is hard to imagine letting go. I cannot do both simultaneously. Babies do not wait when their arrival time comes. I thought this desire was perfectly suited for me. The chosen name is Beyond Conception. The logo has a little pea-pod-shaped newborn nestled in the arms of a mother's heart. I believe mothering involves a hopeful vision for life that goes beyond what our eyes and minds can ever conceive. A mother's love, even if she is absent, affects the whole child.

The moment my grandma passed on to eternity, the truth of my belief became a reality. I held my grandma's face and saw her peace as she took her last breath. She was such a beautiful believer in the capabilities of the people she loved.

I should stop. This has been a big window into my soul. I will be praying for the eyes of your heart as you take in the landscape. I am more hopeful this morning, than last night. I love church. It feels like home. I am closing with a smile.

Happy to have Hank communicating,

:-) Holly

12:01 pm

To: Hank
From: Holly

Ok. They say two are better than one. I am choosing to follow that proverb. Note two is keeping up with your details. I got in self exposure mode, first, this morning. I want to thank you for making that comfortable.

I am grateful you enjoy the creative process of seeing a campaign reach its greatest potential. So do I. I will admit that I am more the cheerleader than the coach. I do respect the coaching role. Every player or team worth cheering for has a good coach.

So thankful to know that Matthew gets to stay close to either you or your parents. It was a wise and loving choice to be near to him in these shaping years.

Your senses are accurate. I am uneasy and feel my position as mom is threatened by Alex's quick insertion of a woman in his life and the home life of our children. Getting settled with so little resources and so many raw emotions and hurdles has been difficult for me. Nikki is not a strong believer and was married with no desire for any children. She seems to be my opposite, which confirmed that Alex wanted a family, but could not cherish me as his lover. This is why I had to let go of hoping for reconciliation. Hard to understand the issue of wanting him when he did not really want me.

No, I did not see all my children. I miss time with Martin. He is busy getting ready to graduate. He has a darling girlfriend and is very friendly. A bit sad that I cannot provide much to celebrate this transition. He is my best at assuming the best. He has a solid positive spirit that soaks life in. He is peace in a package. He opened the door to motherhood for me. I love him to the moon and back a google times.

Thank you for being on board with my favor request. I do trust that you are respectful and feel I can be genuinely transparent with you. I hope you do, too.

As far as wonderful and peaceful dreams go, I will be day dreaming today. Thank you for starting my day with love and kindness. I will keep my heart open for more throughout the day. I hope Matthew granted your wish to snooze until 7. If not, I hope you gain a restful demeanor as you go along. That is cute that he plays with your ears :-) It is great that he feels so close to you. Make the most of his trust and touch his little heart in ways that will bring great rewards in his life campaign. I will be cheering for you.

Joyfully,

Holly

1:58 pm

To: Hank
From: Holly

Kinda a slow daydreaming day. Hopeful expectation that forward looking is right where I should be. Since I do not really get to see you, would you send a photo? Please and thank you. :-)

Holly

# # #

6:00 pm

Holly: The comments from the girl goalie, about how you yell and made her do what you wanted, did not set well in my spirit. That, tripled with the fear of blame, and Evelyn cozying with you during my visit was more than I could wear a fake smile through. I am real.

Maybe they didn't set well with your spirit because your spirit is just a wee bit twisted. Maybe.

8:00 pm

Holly: Is Evelyn up for a steamed milk, before bed?

Yep. Twisted.

# # #

11:03 pm

To: Hank
From: Holly

Would you be willing to do some business banter? This is a new realm for me. I believe I am capable. I spoke to another business owner and an attorney. I am concerned about L.L.C. Being given and liabilities associated with turnover.

I know you are traveling and may be limited in availability. I hope I get to hear from you. Did you have an enjoyable time with your family, today? I snuck into your world and listened to a sermon at the online site for Overlake. Have you gotten to know the pastor?

Please know that I am really honest and would rather have you ask hard questions than wonder about issues. Theo, the owner of The Loft, and I have had open communication. I stumbled but kept walking towards God's best.

I am one to be boastful. I am flattered by a little recognition I got. Did I tell you I was asked by a modeling company to do a photo shoot and an audition for a commercial? The filming was such a blast!

I will be praying your trip goes well and that you travel safely. I will also remember to pray for Matthew to enjoy time with his caregivers, and not miss you too much. He is very cute. Did you say he is 5? If so, is he starting kindergarten this fall? The delight is learning at this stage is so fun.

Enjoying the thought of you,

Holly

June 14, 2010

6:05 am

To: Hank
From: Holly

Thinking of you. I am singing along with Amy Grant this morning. Enjoy the things God gives you to do. There are some historic catechisms written by Westminster Divines. One of the first questions is: How do we glorify God? Answer: We glorify God by obeying Him and enjoying Him forever. John Piper wrote, "If we do not enjoy Him, we are not obeying Him." He believes that we can get lost in doing our best for God, with the goal to please Him. Instead, our goal should be to be pleased with all that GOD DOES.

I agree!

Have a great day.

:-) Holly

6:35 am

To: Hank
From: Holly

I stopped in to the Tiki after a walk, last night. Just as I finished my pineapple juice, a group of gentlemen came in. There was one that I thought might have been you. Any chance It was?

:-) Holly

I had to admit it. I was addicted. My essential morning routine had been altered. Every morning I reached for my phone to drink in the latest, even before I touched my coffee. Some would consider this a problem.

Sally: Hey Nikki, my sister and I are poolside and just went thru the Hank/Holly saga. Karen would like to thank you for taking us along on this journey and she also would like to hire you first as her therapist and also to find her a Hank!

Nikki: I'll keep that in mind. Would she prefer someone normal, or with a side of crazy?

6:30 pm

To: Holly
From: Hank

I wish it had been me at A Very Taki Tiki because that would mean I didn't spend my evening yesterday packing. I'm in Manhattan staying at the Palace. I just got back from dinner at Sushi Samba. I love the sashimi! Funny you say that about having someone glad you came home. My sister was thinking I needed a dog. She claims no matter how long you're gone, 5 hours or 5 minutes, they have the same level of enthusiasm when you come home. I told her I preferred a human. She has a wonderful sense of humor. I also gave the names of the books you recommended to my Mom. She was excited to get them for Matthew—I'm sure they'll be reading one of them tonight.

I haven't been able to view the video. I dorked up my video/sound player on my laptop and need my IT person to fix it. I can really be technically challenged when it comes to that stuff—that's why we employ experts! I would be absolutely willing to banter about business types. Sole Proprietorships, Partnerships, Corporations, Subchapter S Corporations and Limited Liability Companies (LLC) are the 5 most common business types. There are several things you should consider before making a decision:

What is your vision regarding the business?
Will you be involved daily in the business?
Vulnerability to lawsuits—what do you have to lose?
Do you expect profit (or loss) of the business?
Do you need to reinvest earnings into the business?
Do you need access to cash out of the business for yourself?

Once you have answers to the questions above the business type will most likely present itself. But, be sure to include a financial advisor, tax accountant and an attorney in your decision making process.

WOW! A commercial! That's big time! Do you have plans to continue a talent career? I read the letter you wrote in the Enterprise as well. I searched the Enterprise with Holly and "sandwich boards" and was able to find the letter. It was well written and definitely came from the heart.

I'm lucky to be able to call Rowan (Pastor) a close friend. He and his wife Janet have been a wonderful inspiration and their children are absolutely delightful. He's been our pastor for I'm guessing 12-13 years and is a very talented man. We had our typical routine today and took in the wonderful weather in the afternoon at my parent's home. I just got off the phone with Matthew. He and Nana had a fantastic day today. He's such a joy and I am so thankful I have the family foundation to ensure his safety and care. Matthew will be starting Kindergarten in the fall. I'm looking at a couple private schools. I'm really torn with whether or not public school will be an option when he enters the first grade.

I'd like to say you shouldn't worry about your motherhood being threatened. Has Alex or Nikki given you cause to feel that way? What I find interesting is you say Nikki has no desire for children yet she's involved with a man that has five. That's a bit odd. What would have forged reconciliation with Alex? When did you realize reconciliation was off the table? I know rejection can be a blow to the heart and ego but I would imagine you are happier now than you were five years ago.

I've met Theo and his wife (I can't for the life of me remember her name). I am quite impressed with the amount of business that little place does and how they are able to control the flow of patrons. It's amazing. I was there about a month ago with a couple of friends, got a seat on the patio and listened to a wonderful Flamenco guitarist. It was really incredible, thoroughly enjoyed myself. I think we closed the place down for the evening!

I'll be retiring to my really comfortable bed soon. It's difficult for me to get on east coast time but I'll get over it—probably on Thursday when I arrive back home. I hope your day was full of adventure and hope.

Hank

7:15 pm

To: Holly
From: Hank

I forgot to attach a picture so here it is. I'm a bit leery to send this because I had my Mom send it to me and I can't open it (those pesky IT issues) to see exactly what picture from Saturday she picked. So if my shirt is off, please forgive her and me—she just really wants me to find a special someone. I could also see her sending a baby picture of me or from my high school graduation since she knew I was having computer difficulties. So here's to trusting mothers!

Hank

8:02 pm

To: Hank
From: Holly

So I bit my bottom lip and closed one eye, pushed the enter button…Oh, my goodness you are VERY handsome. You look great in that color of blue. You did have your shirt on. Thank you for sending it.

I think you are VERY handsome. Please do not change your profile name, though. I want to stay in the running, as a possibility. I bit my lower lip and raised my eyebrows and sighed. I am very fortunate to get to connect with you.

You had a blue shirt on. It is a great color choice. The blue sky was the backdrop. Thank you for asking your mom to take one and please thank her for sending it. She can be trusted. Shirt off or baby photo would have been okay, also.

I think you can use your phone to take a picture, then choose to send it via email to the talkmatch.com address. That is what I did. I use my phone for all my emails. Pretty fast with my thumbs. Feel free to send anything that sparks your interest. I enjoy sharing.

Holly

11:08 pm

To: Hank
From: Holly

Your letter was the best part of my day. I had a couple of hurdles present themselves. I choose to end every day with slow and endearing activity. I will tell you more about business stuff, in the morning.

For now, I want to say…I am delighted that you are keeping up the connection. Thank you. I am flattered that you told your mom about the books. It makes me happy that you trusted me. I am honored that Matthew and your mom will share a special memory that I shared with my children.

I hope you find someone that will remind you everyday that the best part of life is being together. You are a special man. I, like you :-), would prefer a person being glad to see me, over a pet.

Would you ever consider a partner that wanted to make a "career" of putting you and your desires for yourself and your son, as a first objective in her daily goals? It would be like going back to the "fun buddy," with many years of wisdom added. If you did the same, other goals would get accomplished. It could mean that Matthew would be able to come to where you were, whenever it was convenient. And since he is so close to your parents, the partner could travel with you.

Kinda musing...must be sleepy.

Thinking of you and smiling. :-)

Holly

# # #

June 15, 2010

7:30 am

Holly: Have you heard anything about seating and best time to arrive, for Graduation, Saturday? How do I get my ticket? Yes, life transitions are expensive. Thank you for bearing the financial expenses. I pray God blesses you as you provide for the large family you desired. I will be at my home, tomorrow, to enjoy our kiddos. haven't heard.

Alex: Ticket? I don't know. Martin will arrange that with you.

Holly: Ok. I will contact him. Hope and pray you did not put Nikki before the mom, on this one.

# # #

8:58 am

To: Hank
From: Holly

I hope you slept well, despite a time warp. I am praying you time there is productive and that your creative coaching gifts are a blessing to whatever you invest your efforts in. When your "work" is completed, I hope you end the day with something refreshing and relaxing. This morning while I had to confront some feelings of desperation, I settled myself with the joy of knowing "God did not give me more than I can handle." I was presented with a letter from the homeowner that I rent a room from, that he wants me to find something different by the 30th. I just moved here the first of this month.

The security I had in his word of supposed helpfulness towards my family, was shattered. I need to get into something that feels comfortable as "mom's place." What he did in changing his mind and getting angry was confronted by a deacon, at his church. Instead of choosing compassion, he wants to terminate the agreement. It has been very confusing. I was asked to date a check for rent a month back so that a loan modification proceeding was met. I did as he wished. Now, he is very back and forth. There were supposed to be two other tenants. I was uncomfortable, from the start. I have to focus on this housing hurdle today. I did speak to the owner of On The Way Gourmet, this morning.

There are some questions in likeness to yours for me, that remain unanswered. I am thinking of you. Need to do some practical business. I will look forward to giving attention to the details of your last letter, at the close of the day.

Enjoy your busy-ness, :-)

Holly

10:00 pm
> **To: Hank**
> **From: Holly**

I really enjoy your letters. They are full of details that are forming a frame around who you are. I have been more places abroad than across the U.S.A. I have not travelled very far east. Will you be in Manhattan for the whole trip? I like sushi, also. I had several Asian gals live with us. Tried lots of interesting dishes with them. Not real fond of chewy squid and too slimy, but I will try anything. I agree with you on preferring humans being glad I am present. I have not met a dog yet that can give an embrace that comforts the soul, much less a kiss that assures you that you are cherished. Again, thank you for the honor of sharing the book recommendations with your mom. I hope she and Matthew enjoy their story time.

I could benefit from an I.T. Helper, also. By the way, I thought you thrive on challenges. I am relieved to know you have some limitations. There is greatness in recognizing you cannot do everything. Learning to ask for help is a strength. Here's hoping your laptop is un-dorked up.

Thank you for the shaping business questions. The one I was asked to run is now in limbo. There has been an assistant running most of the business. All involved are burnt out. If the assistant is not willing to consult for the first 3 months, the business will die. The owner is my friend. I am encouraged by his belief in my capabilities and hate to see his dream die. The assistant is unsure about growing forward. She has not been paid from the business for many months. Her compensation was to date the owner's son. My first decision would be to 'pay the lady a deserved wage'. The owner and I spoke today. He would not yet disclose financials, not until the assistant commits. I am praying and waiting. I was grateful for your input.

The commercial was so fun to do. I felt like a star. It was a great esteem booster. It was filmed by Focus Films and Productions, in March. There were many staff and stage crew. I had my make up and hair done by a woman on the set. "Lights, cameras, fans..." It was a blast. I was told not to give out that I was a newbie, that also meant I did not know not to sign anything without asking my agent. I signed away residuals. I would love to do more. The agency offers talent seminars. I need to go back for more portfolio shots. You will find that I do lead with my heart. The article in the Enterprise was a fine example. I am blessed by the continual reminders of God's favor and faithfulness, as portrayed in nature. It cheered me to think of you searching and discovering it. You are good at follow through.

I agree that your pastor is very talented. He is also a deeply studied pastor. He connects scriptures well to the hearers. I met his son in high school. I am glad his family has inspired you. You must have a good role model for a father. You have displayed a delight over being a dad. The solid foundation you had will be a blessing for generations to come. Do you have a special day planned for this Sunday? It is Father's Day. I want to amen your decision for private Kindergarten for Matthew. Spiritual nurturing is so important as they take in so much in the early stages of schooling. I am blessed to have been so close to my children. They taught me so much about purity of vision. I have no regrets for the many years of serving and enjoying them in such sweet communion. I will pray for you as you make educational decisions. Remember that his reception to everything has everything to do with the presentation. Loving learning has to be the primary goal.

Thank you for easing my concern about motherhood being threatened. Yes. Alex and Nikki have done things that cause me to feel this way. They want to win their affections and trust. Alex has told my children that the divorce was all my fault. Nikki tried to pull a restraining order that would have allowed her to be next to Alex at events, which would have alienated me. Several of his commanders stopped that process. There are countless numbers of circumstances that could be used against Alex. It was a misuse of the power entrusted to him. Many of his co-workers have told me to rise in formal complaint and litigation. It is indeed odd that Nikki is his chosen partner. I am praying for her. We are opposites. Her father's nickname is 'Sarge'. She is accustomed to an authoritarian. Communication would have forged reconciliation. I asked him to come to an appointment with a counselor we had seen for over a year, last fall. Alex stated that he had no interest in reconciliation. My stepdad will not speak to Alex unless he repents. Not a pretty picture. My mom and I try to advocate for what we have seen of Alex's best qualities. He did not have his mom (adopted) near him as a child. His father fought and won custody, also. His dad frightened him for most of his growing up years. He has become softer. His dad did not become involved in the divorce issues. His mom and sister were ugly to me.

I let go of the hope for a reconciled marriage last fall when Nikki tried to get the restraining order. Their togetherness against my efforts towards our children was a painful blow. They support each other. I am praying they both grow deeper in their compassion openness to the Holy Spirit. I hope he honors her with marriage.

Theo's wife is named Polly. She is a strong woman. We clashed. I did honor Theo for defending her. She called me a "fuckin' bitch" in front of Mayor Pope. I defended the rights of a female bartender that wanted to quit. It did not go over well. It was best not to be there. I was vulnerable and naive. Singleness was shocking. They do a fantastic job with the establishment. I bet the guitar player was Alonso. He and Alex are friends. I was also there until closing many nights. I enjoyed the place and the people, just not a best place for a pretty single woman with morals to be hanging out. I have a soft and welcoming spirit, it was misread and I was mislead due to a lack of experience.

I hope you are sleeping well in your comfortable bed. I am sleeping okay. I am hopeful and my adventures are kind of thick with tall grass. God has a way already cut. I will press on.

Blessings to you,

Holly

June 16, 2010

I called Sally while my computer took its sweet time booting up. "Alex just found out she will be homeless again. I guess she was hysterical last night. The landlord didn't even give her until the 30th. Cold."

"My sister says Hank has worked way too hard to get to this place *not* to break it off before graduation. We feel Hank should push the button on Friday."

12:13 pm
To: Holly
From: Hank

Good afternoon! This trip I'm spending all my time in Manhattan, SoHo, Greenwich Village and the Financial District. Last night I enjoyed my favorite Italian restaurant in SoHo. I rarely venture in to the Bronx, Queens or Brooklyn. I really enjoy NYC in the fall. The foliage in Central Park is wonderful, not to mention upstate NY. My favorite town up north is Potsdam. It's a quaint little university community. The Clarkson Inn is a wonderful hotel with a bed and breakfast feel.

It's disappointing to hear about the business opportunity and your housing situation. I'd be concerned how the legacy business has been run based on the woman being compensated by dating the owner's son. Very odd and hopefully I read that wrong. I didn't think those things happened in modern times. It's even more of a reason to do your due diligence looking closely at potential liabilities. Your landlord didn't give you any indication or reason for the eviction? You are protected by the Washington State Landlord Tenant Act. It would behoove you to obtain a copy of the act so you are clear on your protections. I'm sure it's online.

It's unfortunate to learn about your ordeal at the Loft. You indicated you were sexually harassed at the establishment. Were there two incidents? I do know Theo's wife is a protective woman and she has always been very delightful to me. Again, it's regrettable you had this experience.

It sounds like you know Nikki quite well. Was she in your life prior to your divorce? What caused her to seek a restraining order? How long have Alex and Nikki been together? At one point in our conversation you indicated you could never honor Alex in the way God intended and you came to that realization when you were troubled about the pending separation. Why did you entertain the thought of reconciliation? I can guess at the answer but I don't like to presume anything.

We do have a special day planned for Sunday. The entire family will be gathering at Mom and Dad's house on Sunday, then church, then—weather permitting—we will enjoy each others company all day on the shores of Lake Washington. These types of gatherings are my favorite. It's very relaxing. How will you be celebrating your father(s) on Sunday?

To answer your question about what I think my partner's life work will be, I really don't know. I feel how ever someone spends their time is entirely up to them. Whether that's with a full time career, a housewife, a mother, philanthropy activities…it's entirely up to them. I would only become concerned with activities that are not ethical, legal, or in the spirit of grace. So! With all that said…Yes ;).

I'll be glad to be heading home tomorrow afternoon. I hope your day is full of achievement.

Hank

# # #

9:12 pm

Holly: So Katherine told me that the second round of tickets were obtained, today. I kindly, with no negative tone, asked "who were the first round of tickets for"...Answer: "Dad, Nikki, Grandma, and another relative". It is a grief to me that you continually have not paid me the honor that God would have you do.

# # #

11:02 pm
To: Hank
From: Holly

Good Night! So before I nod off I will respond to the questions in your letter and give you a glimpse into my day. It started out gray and rainy here. I did home stuff, instead of an outside walk. The moisture makes me feel extra chilly. I have to rely on the bus for transportation, mostly. My friend lets me use her car for grocery trips and laundry. Today another recently single mom and I went shopping together (that word I love). Her birthday is this weekend. A very special man is taking her away for the weekend. We got her some special treats. It was fun. I am caring for her daughter while she gets away. I will enjoy extra time with my special little friend. :-)

My friend told me about some of the places you mentioned. I am glad you treat yourself to favorite spots. You are definitely not dull. I have been told by many that upstate is lovely in the fall. My mom is a Bed and Breakfast enthusiast. They treated us to many memorable stays. I do believe she has been to The Clarkson. The place she went that I envied most was Prince Edward Island. I am an Anne of Green Gables fan.

What I said about the assistant is not alarming. She had been forsaken by her husband. She has been with the company for 3 years. She has only dated their son for less than a year. She actually lives at the business owner's home. They closed it down last month. She is tired and wants to pursue other interests.

Thank you for the compassion about housing. I did get a copy of the Tenant Act, a week ago. His letters have all been taken to an attorney. He wanted to view all my documents regarding issues over the last two years. I told him firmly that having known him only a week that I did not want to disclose my business to him. He got angry. He really wanted to be helpful. We both spoke things we should not have. He will not forgive and move forward. He chooses to be cold and not speak to me unless there is something he wants me to do. The deacon that tried to help told me to seek legal advice. I will do my best to find something that is my own. This will be best for myself and the children. They need a space that feels like just ours, for a little while longer. God will provide.

I agree with you that Polly is protective. She does treat the male customers very well. They have done very well with their businesses. Yes, the issue would be considered sexual harassment. I was involved in one incident with Polly. In truth, there were two incidents involving two different men. One was a friend of theirs. He is a local businessman that wanted more than I would give him. His tactic was both dishonorable and rude. I think he was tipsy and also struggling because he was at the end of a divorce proceeding. I denied his advance and he was later very embarrassed. The other incident was a painful choice that resulted in a very personal issue surfacing. It was a "one-night stand" that he stood proud. I fell down, and it took me over a year to recover from the impact. I will tell you more about it, as I feel comfortable. It was a good decision for Theo to not allow me back, for a season. The openness and less cocky crowd at the Tiki is better for me. Both the owner and manager are very understanding. When I was hostessing a karaoke gig there, Theo assured me he was supportive. The bar scheme has a specific personality. I had to learn who to trust and how to trust myself.

I did not know Nikki during my marriage. She and Alex met at Starbucks at the beginning of our separation. That is the story from one of my children. I told her that spending so much time with my children so quickly after their loss was not healthy and that it only added to the reality of Parental Alienation Syndrome. I said it hoping that she would consider the children. She felt threatened. She and several people tracked me the next week and followed me. When I stopped at my destination, a person in the car with her tried to hand me a document. The person standing next to me intercepted it and later shred it. The following week, a woman came up behind me and tried to shove an envelope into my coat. The police responded and tried to locate the woman. Later that evening when I was meeting my son and some friends at the Tiki, the same woman tried to approach me again. I quickly left out the back. The manager later shredded the papers. The police officers were called back. When I was contacted they told me what the papers were regarding. They were given the information from Alex. I did not ever receive them and the envelopes were never opened. They were intended for me and asking Alex about them was a wrongful breech.

I hold so much real evidence against Alex and the department. I was told by a very strong and honorable attorney at the very beginning of this that it was a misuse of power and would likely be considered a Federal offense.

I must have miscommunicated about when I felt I could no longer honor Alex as God intended. I did not come to that conclusion until after he signed the change to dissolve our marriage. The answer to the question involving reconciliation, is...I believe marriage in God, is forever...and I love Alex...I always will. It took me a very long time to understand the pure truth that God meant the divorce for my good. He wanted me free from the marriage. He has a better plan.

I respect the answer about who you would consider for your next marriage partner. It was the answer I was hoping for :-). Yes or no are equally merited answer, although "yes" feels so good when you hope for it. The element of honoring her choices as long as they were in keeping with proper boundaries and kindness showed me the strength of your character. I will add that gracefulness in any endeavor make it a worthy effort.

Let me see, I am getting very sleepy. Okay I missed something. I am volunteering all weekend, except Saturday, at the Edmond's Arts Festival. Some old friends are the directors for the Children's Creative Area. I will be there Friday evening and all day Sunday, after church. I will send my dad a special card, walk down the pier where people go fishing, and call him. He does not want me to spend money going to see him. He knows finances are tight and wants me to focus on myself and my children. I drove there last year and went to dinner with him. It means a hotel stay and a day's travel. He is very worth it, but has always been content with simply communicating that I love him.

Knowing these words get read with kind consideration is worth the effort. Thank you for the graceful communication. It actually is healing.

I still like you. No imagining or whisper necessary :-)

I was with my friend when the little email icon appeared on my phone. I said..."oooo, I hope it's Hank"...then "Oh, Camille, it is him." She said, "Holly, I love you, you're so open-hearted and real."

I achieved all I hoped for today, plus extra smiles. My youngest kissed me so sweetly when she said good-bye. She called as she was falling asleep to pray together.

I will be praying you close your trip being thankful for what you achieved and very glad to be coming home.

:-) Holly

I do know, ultimately, the answer to any heart longing is God's love. I would not be on Match responding to a man with a child and a beautifully creative spirit, if I had not been convinced that singleness was my destined future. Ok. I am done. Whew!

Holly

June 17, 2010

12:00 pm
To: Hank
From: Holly

I want to risk a possible emotional investment that may get rejected. It is a long-hoped for desire, that would be difficult to let go of. I want to preface the question with you being mindful that I would let the hope go if the empty space was filled another way. So here goes.

Although it may seem crazy, my profile states that I definitely want another child. There was a promise and a plan that was broken by Alex, for our family to add one more treasure. During premarital counseling he promised to never ask me to do anything permanent to cut off fertility. After Kevin, he changed his mind, thus there is a larger gap between the fourth and fifth. He did not want Evelyn. Six weeks after she was born, I had a tubal ligation. It was offered free of charge, by my OB-GYN. I surrendered my will to his.

My doctor here ran tests and did scopes and talked with other doctors about the possibility of a reversal. The money set aside for it was spent on sending all the children to a private school. Alex also chose to sell our home and move our family in with his parents. They were financially unstable and dishonest in their tax dealings. I did not want to do it. His mother told me there that she wished her son would not have married me and that I should not have had more than three children. His parents asked me to lie for them about their financial situation. I would not do as they wished.

My mom begged Alex to stop making me cower to his wishes. He would not back down. The night he told me the money was spent that we saved from equity, I confronted him with the lies, he got pushy and threatened me. I called my mom. She has a document into court that was never read. It was a very true declaration of his abuse.

There is the backdrop. Painful as the letting go was. My doctor thought that I would be a perfect candidate for becoming a surrogate for a family that could not carry their own child. We did tests and found out my eggs were still viable. This increased the options for prospective couples. Seeing another couple blessed with what I let go of, would have been a beautiful gift to give. I talked with an attorney in Brooklyn. Found out that living in Washington made working with their agency impossible.

The choices around our births were mostly Alex's, in the practical aspects. He was given up for adoption, at birth. He was too afraid to have a home birth. We had five very different deliveries together. I enjoyed every moment focusing on a life to love. This is part of my hope to become a doula. The power of a woman's choices effects so much of the endearment to her child.

We settled with the choice to adopt rather than reverse what had been done. The core missing link was that my hopes were not Alex's. I had to let him walk away. He wanted so badly to be a father, unlike his own. He is very pained about how similar their choices are.

So...there is so much real attraction to your love for Matthew and your love that let you free Dedra to pursue her choices. Do you think that having a loving spouse who would cherish my nurturing heart would fill the definite longing to be the parents of a TOGETHER child, be it naturally, or by adoption? Or do you think Matthew and a career of being the advocate for other women would fill that longing?

I think I am thinking so much about it because my firstborn is on my heart this week in a special way. He graduates Saturday. He is very cherished. I could not have asked God for a sweeter entrance into motherhood. He is very confident and took in the things before him, with all his senses. Did I tell you...I love my children? :-)

Well, I am guessing this question may cross a proverbial boundary, because you have been through a hardship that I am sure still brings up real sorrow at times. I also think I know that you will say, the answer would have to be my own, but babies and the creating of family is not an alone adventure.

I am blubbering...so would you be willing to enlighten me, from your side?

Thank you for bearing with me,

Holly

2:40 pm

To: Hank
From: Holly

Good afternoon! I am wanting to tell you something romantic. I keep going back to look at your pictures. My favorite one is the side view with you leaning over a delighted Matthew. So when you asked forgiveness in case your weekend photo would be shirtless, and said your mom really wanted you to find someone special...I had a secret hope that it would have been revealing. Someone special should be a woman who wants YOU as a man, not only a dad. Thinking right now that being in my favorite photo in Matthew's place would be awfully nice. Just a little afternoon delight. ;-) Holly...I felt it, I said it, I meant it.

Holly

At this point I recognized it was time to end the virtual relationship. Getting a little creepy. *Next I'll get a va-jayjay pic or some overdone cleavage.*

I sent a well-crafted break-up email to her that Thursday afternoon. Much to my shock, for the first time the Match proxy service failed to filter my email, resulting in the break-up letter going directly from Hank's email address to Holly. Now she had a direct email...with direct source information, the IP address of my workplace, and the name Pencke which I had chosen for Hank. Oh God...she could figure out her virtual boyfriend works at Rove Aerospace. She could actually show up at the door and ask for Hank! Okay, breathe. Being in HR was never quite so beneficial. I started searching the network. How many Hanks work here? Howards? I'm probably breaking some sort of rule.

Eh, screw it.

# # #

23. Cut Bait

6:07 pm

To: HPencke
From: Holly

To whom it may concern,

This email address began appearing when communicating with someone I thought only sent and received through a "blind" connection network. If it does not trouble the receiver, who, may I ask, does this email address belong to?

(Name withheld)

Shit! Shit! Shit! I can't ignore this one or she'll keep digging. Time to come clean. Well, time for *Hank* to come clean.

6:19 pm

To: Holly
From: Hank

The message is from me, Hank—as indicated by the closing line on the email. The last email came from my yahoo email account.

Regards,
Hank

6:30 pm

To: Hank
From: Holly

Good evening. I hope your trip home was smooth. I am sure you received a happy welcome :-). Thank you for letting me know about the email. It was just received as an unknown contact.

I am enjoying dinner with my son, at Hamburger Harry's.

Gotta focus on him.

Holly

She has no clue about the break-up! I pulled up the original letter and resent it through the Match server. This time it went through.

7:30 pm

To: Holly
From: Hank

I've grown concerned regarding the way you are answering questions which prompted me to do a little digging. Your attorney friend was correct. You have given enough identifiable information about yourself for me to research who you really are. The letter you wrote for The Enterprise (Sandwich Boards Important to Community) was by far the riskiest because it identified your last name. With that said I won't rehash the past 2 years with you regarding the numerous restraining orders, trespass items and evictions that have been or are currently levied against you, notwithstanding an arrest due to a violation of one of those orders. I was also taken back by who has restraining orders granted against you—you have lied to me several times as I have attempted to validate your "stories" verses court documents. FYI: When you are served papers (whether or not you read them is entirely up to you) twice it's a pretty good indicator there is a judgment against you. I am a firm believer in our legal system and think that 99.99999% of the time they get it right. Holly, I believe the courts have gotten it right with you based on the public records I've reviewed.

While I can appreciate individuals that must work through their emotional struggles I would suggest you begin by taking some responsibility and accountability for yours. Based on my review of your repetitive civil and criminal record I don't think this is occurring. If you aren't currently seeking help through a therapist I would highly recommend it to work through those memories that you claim are hindering your ability to move through life and behave in a manner that is acceptable in our society, not to mention for the sake of your children. I'm sure they would like their Mom to be able to communicate with others without making a scene in public which is what it appears you do frequently. I pray they have not witnessed any of your past/future digressions.

In addition, I'm sensing your faith is reactive rather than proactive. I say that from the standpoint I think you react to uncomfortable situations (for whatever reason) in a way that is not indicative of a good Christian but you repent asking for forgiveness with all that you are and for you that is acceptable. My faith is proactive. Every action, communication and expression is made with the end in mind. I don't believe we are equally yoked in this regard and while I am not perfect I am also not a disruptive or a mean-spirited person.

Holly, I have way too much to risk and I know there is a kind, loving, honest, stable, God-loving woman out there for me and at this time I don't believe you are the one. As I said when we first started this journey I'm looking for a partner I will spend the rest of my life with. Good luck in your search for God and a soul mate. Should you see me in public please do not communicate with me.

Regards,
Hank

June 18, 2010

12:58 pm

To: Hank
From: Holly

Forgive me for saying more than you were comfortable with, if I did. Shopping with my lady friend for her special date, sitting through a pedicure and massage, thinking lots of loving thoughts about my son, and...I lost my journal when I moved :-). I hope I did not offend you.

Holly

1:08 pm

To: Hank
From: Holly

An attorney and I will be coming to a mutual agreement on how best to respond to you. I have not lied to you.

Holly

Together we searched under H. Penskey, and have not located a male voter in either near counties.

Well, no shit, Sherlock! *Because he doesn't freaking exist!* But even if he did, you *still* spelled his name wrong.

1:24 pm
To: Hank
From: Holly

Who I am is not found in a stack of papers. I am not a problem or a risk.

Believe what you will. I have never been one to judge with grace and all the facts. Criticize and tell me what you think I should do. Again, choices are expression of a heart. I choose to rise above the locked arms of law enforcement and being berated by others. I am here to love mercy, seek justice, and walk humbly with my God.

Enjoy your weekend celebrating fatherhood.

I made myself known and vulnerable to you. I have no regrets.

Gracefully,

Holly Lynnette Hill (maiden name: Henderson)

I am honest to the core, and walk about without shame or a spirit of condemnation.

Holy shit. She's of the rails! I wondered if Alex was getting bombarded with text messages.

1:30 pm
To: Hank
From: Holly

Janet Anderson and I had a long conversation this week. She spoke at the church when I attend the Women's Retreat. Her encouragement was very helpful. I am working myself through issues of the past.

Like I said, you are a man of status and value. I am not a worthy partner. I hope you and Matthew are blessed as you go forward.

Holly

2:41 pm

To: Hank
From: Holly

Hank, or whoever you are:

I was only asked about incidents at the Loft. If you researched well, you should be able to obtain the judge's remarks. Also, there should have appeared a Sexual Assault report from April 2008. The incident that caused The Loft to ask me not to be there, was with a man named John Jones. He is the store director at the Edmonds QFC store. He frequented The Loft and Daphne's. His store also provides liquor and food to the establishment. His words to me went, "I want to ^%$$* you so hard, do you like to feel my balls pounding against you?" His reputation was guarded.

Judgments are heard best when the one speaking them judges by a standard he understands through diligent study. Your questions opened a door. I chose to answer them. I am as free as you are to offer advice. You being a professional investor know the importance of research to meet potential investors or buyers needs intelligently. I think I remember the stated words, due diligence, from your encouragement to me. Please consider the spirit of judgment you apply yourself to in the light of the spirit of grace. I know it is fair to ask for this because it is what you stated you hope for.

As to you having the final word, by shutting down contact. I know that this tactic alienates people. I do not treat people that way. If you ever want to say anything else to me, you are welcome to.

I was happy to communicate. I was real with you. I hope you invest many efforts into keeping Matthew closely connected to his mom. She chose to give him to you. She is just as essential to his character development as you are. I learned much from living out an honest and open communication with you.

"Only in God is my soul at rest, in Him comes my salvation, He only is my strength, my song, my stronghold, my Savior, I shall not be moved."
-Psalm 62

Crying,

Holly

3:12 pm

To: Hank
From: Holly

I hope your mom did not teach you that "sticks and stones can break your bones, but words can never hurt you." It is not true. I am really hurt by your words. I feel like you wanted an open door into my hopes, dreams, and heart. I believed by the things you said that you could be trusted.

I trusted you because of the words you wrote about compassion. I find nowhere in my responses that I lied to you. I think it strange that you write to me as if I am your child. I do not think you would be honestly proud, if I behaved you. I did make a mistake, when I told you.

Holly

3:25 pm

To: Hank
From: Holly

Mistake when I said my son's graduation was Saturday. It is tonight. I will be attending with my son Justin. My children know the truth about their mom. They are not ashamed to bear my likeness.

I will rise above the opinion that your soul mate will be a better woman than I am. I will choose to work through how disheartening your words were, today. I stand in my integrity; not proudly, but humbly, in the blood of Christ alone.

I will try to show no emotion and will say nothing to you, if I should ever see you in public. Your request will be honored. I promise.

Holly

4:23 pm

To: Hank
From: Holly

The criminal trespass was cited because John did not want the person he hurt to be close. The documentation was created after Edmond's officers arrested me, to cover what they did. Check your research more deeply. What time did John sign his first court document? What time did I get booked in? There was not anything written that said I could not be at the store. The documents arrived at the jail after I had been taken into custody. Police were mortified by John's behavior. I plead guilty to the offense, so that I did not have to sit in court anymore. I continued to volunteer at the Senior Center and the Edmonds Food Bank, as I was already doing, before the charges. My choices to not seek litigation to vindicate myself were to guard my children's opinion of their father. I believe forgiveness and love are my strongest defense.

You can believe in the near perfection of court documents. If you ask your father, he will tell you that litigation is very tainted to benefit the one with the larger stack and most believed attorney. I did not have an attorney to represent me, until the day of our trial. She signed in as my representative, that day. I prayed for nearly a year that Alex would not go through with his offense.

Every other thing you dug up is in regards to a family law case. There is a reason the documents sat in the attorney office. I spent every penny given to me on my children. The eviction came without proper notification. It was not easy living on my $1,000.00 a month maintenance. Meals for six, in Edmonds, at restaurants is expensive. I took responsibility. I paid for the majority of last summer's vacation, that my children went on with Alex. I did not have one myself, and did not want to disappoint their hopes. I paid for the summer pass at the pool, and volunteered at their swim meets. If you want to keep looking, check out King 5 Community Stories, Yost

Pool, with Lauren Hughes. You will see my children and I there. We earned much of the weekend drive's funds to match Mayor Pope's plea for residents. I created the gift giving table at Petosa's Grocery, and stood there all weekend talking to people. I was part of a community support for the South County Senior Center, with a little citizen band on a television show, last July. Do you want credentials?

An attorney would be happy to give you a compassionate perspective. My responsibility was to my children, since I did not have a spouse. I did above and beyond what was required of me. I did see a therapist that was assigned to me after the sexual assault. I saw her weekly. I was responsible.

Let me see...if I took every word you say I am not, I could give you evidence that I certainly am the positive side. In lacrosse we call this a "face off". I would be more than your equal. My team of five and I are fixed on the goal to win. As God is my witness, I did not lie to you. If you would have asked questions in regards to what you dug up, I would have answered you with the truth.

If you think a woman should back down to your challenges, you are right, you need a weaker woman than I. I challenge everything to get to the truth and the heart of the matter. Keep challenging, I will keep meeting your challenges. I will not be accused falsely.

I will find time to respond to every other thing you used to form your opinion, after I honor my son, at his Graduation.

Holly

4:49 pm

To: Hank
From: Holly

You read everything against me. Would you be willing to share the messy side of yourself? I am confident my failings are no worse than yours. You have yet to humbly admit anything questionable about yourself.

Unlike Dedra, I will always stay near my children. I care more about them, than anyone's opinion of me. I have a sound mind, a strong spirit, and a love for my children and their father that triumphs, over the messes of the past.

Holly

###

We had arrived at the high school stadium two hours early hoping to ensure a central spot in the lower rows of the grandstands. I thought this would provide Holly with the vast majority of the seating area to chose from and not encroach on the rest of us, especially since Nikki and her sister were with the gang.

Of course, I was wrong. I tried not to look directly at her as she walked up the steps and plopped herself three rows back and two seats to my right. I shut my eyes and shook my head.

"Seriously?" Nikki said.

"There's 1,500 seats available, and she has to sit within earshot of us," I said quietly. Unreal. My annoyance was soon distracted by the giggling kids cracking inappropriate jokes with each other. "Hey Kevin," I interrupted, "Here's some cash. Go grab us some popcorn from the concession stands." Food was regularly useful for controlling his behavior, and we had an hour to go before this thing got started.

Nikki seemed distracted. She couldn't contain herself; she kept looking back at Holly every ten minutes or so. "Just ignore her," I said. "It's clearly an emotional thing for her with her oldest son graduating." She snickered and focused on her phone in between tossing in her own two bits to the inappropriate jokes.

Before the ceremony began, Justin got up and sat next to Holly. After he gave her a hug, I could hear her voice, that familiar stressed voice with intensity on the rise. He lasted a minute or two before retreating to the line of siblings in our row. He glanced at me. "I tried," he shrugged.

"You're a good kid, Justin," I said. "I don't care what they say about you."

###

6:02 pm

To: Hank
From: Holly

We found Carol, Katie, Molly, And a Michael Douglas with the last name matching yours. Attorney looked in law directory database, no one in Washington with his bar.

I am very careful because anything I say and do can be used against me, and my time with my children. I will not come where you are. We just are hopeful you did not draw out my information to use it against me.

Janet Anderson says she does not recognize the name Hank. She does not think there is a large family with a son and grandson, that attend Overlake Calvary Chapel. I do not understand why you would be playing with my mind.

Holly

7:00 pm

To: Holly
From: Hank

Holly,

Please stop badgering me with your nonsensical emails/texts and enjoy your son's graduation. You have no idea what my last name is. I am thankful that the process of determining whether or not we were a good fit is over. Again, I wish you luck in your search.

Hank

# # #

Evelyn was snuggling up with Nikki, who was giggling to herself but not about the kids. "What's so funny?" I asked.

"Oh, nothing, just some funny work emails." The band kicked off *Pomp and Circumstance* at 7:00 pm sharp, saving Nikki from any further explanation.

# # #

Well that was fun! I couldn't believe I made it through graduation without being found out or spilling the beans to Alex that I was posing as a man on the internet trying to break up with his ex-wife during their oldest son's graduation. Surely greater minds have attempted things like this.

And still I craved more. I opened up Hank's email. Oh, goodie—another one!

9:02 pm

To: Hank
From: Holly

Pastor Rowan and Pastor Janet will be looking forward to you introducing yourself on Sunday since neither of them said they recognized you from your picture. Please prove yourself a gentleman. It would be sad to remember you as the predator-type.

Keep your focus on the hope of a forever family. Think, I love you, of Matthew, every waking moment. Keep a forward-looking vision.

Remember that the perfect soul mate is Jesus. You will never find another Lover that meets your every need.

Holly

Ok, even I know when it's gone too far. Holly's attempts to search Hank were giving me the serious heebie-jeebies. Hank agreed—he told me so himself.

9:30 pm

To: Holly
From: Hank

First let me start by saying based on your response I have made the correct decision. Your subsequent actions are in line with what I ascertained from public records and I'm grateful you have no idea what my last name is nor what church I currently attend.

As I said to you from the beginning the anonymous nature of online date sourcing is by its definition suitable for me. Good luck in your search on Match.com.

Hank

In all of three minutes, I blocked Holly on Match, made a formal complaint to the site administrators and made Hank's Yahoo account invisible where all the emails were being received, with a little promise to myself to put it away for a while. None of that curbed the anxiety I began to experience over my one exposure to my employer's web server. Hank's Yahoo account email, the associated IP address and the related web server name were all findable. Which meant, ultimately, I was findable.

I started to think I may have a lot of explaining to do to Alex. *Oops.*

# # #

June 19, 2010

Camille was in that awkward space between freaked out and burdened with compassionate angst when she called. "I just couldn't understand it," she said.

"So were you planning to have her over tonight, or did she just stop by unannounced?"

"She called at about 7 and said she had some flowers for me. You know, I thought 'Okay, she's trying to be kind, so might as well go with that.' But when she got here, it quickly turned into a total meltdown bitch-fest."

"Doesn't sound like you, Camille," I said.

She laughed. "Oh, believe me, I can bitch it out every now and then! But Chloe was getting visibly scared as Holly kept ramping up. She said how she hated Nikki and called her a fucking bitch. I couldn't understand where all the anger was coming from."

Neither could I. Although if I did the math, Nikki had won the affections of the children, the same kids who were regularly reluctant to spend time with their mom. And despite Holly's comments of challenging Nikki to be 'woman enough,' she had endured a year and a half with me. She wasn't a flash in the pan or some sort of rebound relationship. From Holly's point of view, Nikki actually stood in the way of getting her family back.

What else could it be? It's not like they've even talked outside of the lacrosse field encounter.

June 20, 2010

8:54 am

> **Holly**: Happy Father's Day! I will be thinking and praying for you, in a more devoted way, throughout the day. I love what Evelyn said, "Daddy would not be a daddy without you." She is right! I could have chosen anyone to give me children, I will never regret that YOU are the best choice, I could have made!
>
> :-) Holly

June 22, 2010

I worked a metric shit-ton of overtime ahead of Nikki's birthday to fund a surprise dinner at The Metropolitan Grill in downtown Seattle. I was specific with my lie, telling her I was taking her to The Keg in Lynnwood at 6:00 pm for a little birthday dinner. She didn't ask any questions when I headed south on I-5 to Seattle, causing me to wonder if somehow she knew all along.

Julio and Sally joined us along with their significant others for an evening to remember. Julio's new girlfriend was a stunningly gorgeous thirty-something who fit right in. Sally's husband Frank was familiar with the finer things in life with some serious Chicago flare. The six of us ate and drank like kings, finishing it all off with The Met's famous Bananas Foster table side presentation. Lots of fire.

I sat there in pure amazement. Nikki was absolutely beautiful. She was the most honest person I'd ever encountered. Her friends were the most excellent of people. They had become my friends without hesitation despite knowing I had a bit of baggage in my sphere. All my days pouring out love to others, striving to encourage and strengthen my family and friends, and serving my community at my own risk were suddenly in the background. This woman, this incredible woman…she had taken my upside-down world and flipped it more right-side-up than I'd ever known possible.

I'd gone beyond appreciation and gratitude, beyond respect and admiration. I finally started to feel free.

Free to love again.

June 26, 2010

10:50 pm

To: Alex
From: Holly

Why did you continue to deny Evelyn? She asked and also asked why. Shutting her down hurts her and leaves her confused. She enjoys her time with me. Are you planning on tainting her relationship with me, for all the rest of her childhood? She does not need to be brought into your negative attitude towards me.

We are all so hopeful for things to get better. Please allow the hearts to thrive. Whenever you rule this way, the kiddos feel it. It will not hurt to let go and release the control. It would be so good to see you with an easy-going spirit.

I DID NOT MEAN TO MAKE YOU ANGRY OR CONFUSE YOU. I WISH I HAD A PERFECT WAY OF KNOWING WHAT YOU ARE THINKING AND EXPECTING. I do not. Please do not restrict Evelyn or the other kiddos out of your own misgivings and disappointments. It does not and will not bless their souls.

Enjoy enjoying our children's delights and openness to both of us. I do care and wish I had not crossed you. Wipe the anger away and know you are deeply loved.

Holly

# # #

June 28, 2010

To: Sally
From: Nikki
Subject: Saga continues!

So here's the scoop! She sent a text to Alex regarding her Saturday time with the kids. She then told him she no longer lived in

Edmonds. "People in Edmonds have hurt me. I stood up to the commanders (Edmonds PD) and it upset them. They aren't helping me. I now live in Lynnwood. It's a cute farm with goats."

So! It appears the fun is just beginning. This poor guy who just kicked her out called Alex yesterday. He's already filed suit and obtained a restraining order and plans on going after Holly for slander and failure to pay rent. He called her dangerous, likely to hurt somebody, and a master manipulator. Can't wait to hear about how his serving of the papers goes!

Nikki

To: Nikki
From: Sally
Subject: RE: Saga continues!

Oh my God! This is too crazy! Wait—don't YOU live in Lynnwood? Do you have goats for that massive lawn of yours?

Sally

I ditched all manner of productivity and snuck into Sally's office. She was expecting me.

"I can't believe she is able to find so many people willing to help her," Sally said. "Don't these new landlords ever explore how many times she's been evicted? Ever heard of a background check?"

"Life must be easy when you're always right and everyone else is always wrong," I said. "I just told Alex I'm going to write a book about all of this...won't he be surprised about certain things."

"Oh yeah! Perhaps that can be how he finds out about Hank."

"I think it may be time to bring Hank out of hiding," I said.

"What? You're gonna tell Alex?"

"Oh God, no. I was worried Holly was going to figure out Hank was me. That appears to be unlikely, so I think I'm safe. And he has some emails he never answered, so we could pick up right where we left off. Just like old pals."

"You're nuts," Sally said. "DO IT!"

This would not only buy me some time for things to settle down, it would give Alex a good reason to see past any misgivings he may have about my more recent behavior. After all, I never used it for evil, only for good.

To: Holly
From: Hank

If you took any of the prior communications negatively or as criticism that would be a good indicator you're finding it difficult to take responsibility for your behavior/actions—I'm sure you've heard this before. There is a big difference between criticism and observation. Why would I speak unkindly of you to others? Maybe there is a disparity in our definition of what constitutes unkind behavior.

Upon reading your last email I was struck by how you sound so much like a victim of your own circumstance. There are programs for individuals that need mental health assistance—the key here is the individual needs to want to get help. If what you receive as support is not enough to live on why not go get a job? With a job comes health insurance, money to buy groceries which, in my opinion, would ultimately give you more quality time during the scheduled visits with your children. I can't think of an employer that would not accommodate your schedule to allow you to see your children during these times.

Again, Holly I wish you no ill will and thank you for attempting to understand what my wife and I have gone through in the past. Counseling for me and my family has been a big part of why we are so well adjusted.

Hank

#

June 30, 2010

8:42 am

To: Alex
From: Holly

I love the man that you are. I will not go forward as God intended, until our friendship in reconciled. We are not one in marriage. We are one as parents of five beautiful children. I hope and pray daily that you will have a change of heart. I am here to walk through the process with you. I will not hold things against you. I chose forgiveness, over a year ago. You mean more to me than our children. They need to see the wall down to learn how reconciliation and open love and encouragement works.

I believe in your advocate spirit, and I believe in my own as well. We were meant to have a close partnership for our children's sake.

Loving you always (Someone lied to you when they said I hated you. I hate divorce, not Alex),

Holly

July 1, 2010,

9:05 am

Holly: Alex, I am still hoping for a joyful restored friendship with you. Would you be willing to let Evelyn and Katherine, and Kevin stay the night? Any or all of them are always welcome, wherever I am.

Holly: Did you know that the kiddos want to spend the 4th, with me, the first part of the day? We decided on the parade...but...there is a fun run to help pay for the fireworks. I will pay for the shirt and registration for any kiddo that will do it with me. ;-)

Holly: I will meet Evelyn and Kevin where I planned, for today. After this visit, you are responsible for all transportation to and from my time with them. The times are to be met. I am worthy of every moment and more. Thank you.

Katherine: Dad, Mom lost her phone at the bus stop. The first bus stop after Claire's Pantry on the right hand side of the street going south. She needs someone to go and get it for her.

4:11 pm

> **Martin**: Dad, Mom left her phone somewhere, I picked it up and
> left it on the piano. Can you bring it with you when you get the kids?

By now, I had it figured out: things tended to work themselves out if given
enough time. The challenge was deciding which things fell into that category.

# # #

24. Fireworks

To be fair, I knew full well that I was going to poke the bear. But my goal in this entire operation had changed: I wanted Holly to hear what the world around her actually thought and believed about her behavior. Everyone was being kind, pleasant, even cordial with Holly, then would talk amongst each other complaining of the ridiculousness of it all. That wasn't helping. I realized I had a seriously amazing opportunity: Holly respected Hank for his stature, his looks, his family...everything. And even though she didn't like what he had to say, she would actually pay attention to it and address it. Over, and over, and over.

This could really work to help her. And that would help Alex and the kids.

With my mission re-defined, I set out to accomplish yet another impossible task. I was going to help Holly become aware of her impact, then get her the help she desperately needed, both for her sake and for the sake of her children.

To: Holly
From: Hank
Subject: Closure

Please read this note in its entirety before you delete it. Since I sent you the email by where I informed you that we were not a fit I have felt a bit uneasy. I'm mortified by your behavior of attempting to track me down through the church I indicated I went to. As I said from the beginning, being anonymous is a part of this process that works well for me. The Pastor and his wife are correct when they told you they didn't think I attend their church. I am considering contacting them to apologize for your behavior and for me leading you to them. While I did attend that church in the past (roughly 6 years ago) I do not today. I ask you the question of why would you contact them? What were you attempting to accomplish? Did you wish to confront me for not wanting a relationship with you? These are questions that have been plaguing me since the incident occurred. Please do not feel obligated to answer them.

I have not been truthful with you about many things: my name, name of my ex-wife, the church I attend, the Universities I've graduated from—all items that could lead someone to my identity. For this I'm sorry however the safety of my family is first and foremost my priority.

I get the sense you are in a really bad place in your life right now. Tormented is a word that comes to mind. Please accept my apologies if our interaction caused you any consternation, it was never my intent. I hope you continue your pursuit for a life partner and explore all the items in your past that are impeding your path. I will pray for you and your children.

Regretfully,
Hank

10:45 am

To: Mr. Hip and Handsome
From: Holly
Subject: RE: Closure

Thank you for the note. Please reconsider the subject line. Instead of "closure," there is a better word. It is reconciliation. What happened between you and I was foreordained. You wanted me to hold onto your accusations, and let them hurt me. I will not. It is clear to me that God has helped you identify your own pain. Trust me, there is more strength in admitting a wrongdoing, than to hide it or run from it. So from me to you...I forgive you.

Okay, from the start until now, I have not lied to you. So in answer to your question about calling Overlake Calvary Chapel, I thought that if you attended there and if I had anything that would hinder me from being a suitable partner, then that would be where to go for complete healing. I was walking one morning and was prompted to call the Women's Ministry phone number. The woman who answered was very compassionate and referred me to Janet Anderson. Later that day, Janet called me. I openly shared my heart with her. She wanted to know who had questioned me and opened me to wanting to make the call. I told her it was a man that I had communicated with on a confidential dating network. She asked what I knew about you. She did not recognize anything you represented to me. She was very concerned about me. She then asked Rowan and the staff involved with young children. We communicated over the following week. She encouraged me to not let myself be so vulnerable on anything that allows a man to open my sensitive spirit. She and Rowan could not identify you as "real." I was very hurt.

I felt sure that you were "real." I still do. You said I throw forgiveness around. You are absolutely mistaken. I shoot it right on target. Forgiveness given, hurts like hell on earth, when it is not received. My job is not to make sure others are healed by forgiveness granted. Forgiveness heals me. The goal would be full reconciliation. My pastor, when John Jones took what I had to give and called me a problem in public, prayed over me asking God to give me a spirit and will to forgive him. What he did is forgiven. How Edmond's City Police used him as a puppet, is forgiven. What Alex did to our family, is forgiven. What my family did to isolate me, is forgiven. Why? Because forgiveness is for me. It is received readily from Jesus. It is given to others because Jesus is my Perfect Husband, He wants me to walk close to Him. I could not continue to pray and hope my prayers would be answered if I shamed my vow to Jesus.

I have an honest and clear conscience. I walk about in integrity of spirit. I am an amazing woman who has been gifted with beautiful strength. I get mad when treated in a way my Heavenly Father hates. He did not want you to open my wounds and throw alcohol on them. That may get the irritant to leave, but there are more compassionate means to heal a wound.

Do you remember the words that I told you John Jones said to me? He had said his wife did not want him to touch her. I understood that kind of rejection. After he had proved for himself that someone beautiful did want him to touch her, he was peaceful. Then he had to deal with the falseness of his choice. I had told him I was not any man's toy and he promised to not treat me falsely. I stood my ground. He pulled back in defense. He lied on his police report. I told the entire truth. I asked for a restraining order, also. I was denied. I was falsely arrested. I spent the days in jail praying for John and Alex.

When released, I chose not to defend myself. I put in community service hours at the Senior Center and the Edmonds Food Bank, and paid fines. Why? Because Alex had taken me to court and won everything. I do not like what the legal system did to me and to our family. I fought his charge of breaking a restraining order, at over 10 court appearances, had 3 attorneys represent me. I won. The issue at the Loft was written off by Judge Glenn. He saw it for what it was. Polly protected Theo and the gentlemen who pay their mortgage.

If I would have fought the Criminal Trespass charge, I would have had to go through at least 6 more appearances, and a jury trial. I decided to plead guilty, instead.

Guilty of believing John: I was blessed in the process. You may not understand this, but I had prayed for someone to help me work through the issues tied to my sexuality. In a profound way, God sent John. He was affectionate in a way my ex-husband had never been. He was passionate. He, as God uses the word, "knew" me. My response to him, was something I had never experienced before. He woke up the woman inside me. I had been treated only as a girl, and a mom, until then. It has the beautiful mix of pleasure and pain that God is using to heal my bruised spirit. The memories it brought back needed to be dealt with. This beautiful mix is what we all need to let in. It is like the story of The Velveteen Rabbit. The rabbit becomes "real," by being loved until he believes he can become "real."

I may never know who you "really" are. I woke up this morning thinking about you. I did a few duties, exercised, then looked at my phone, the little icon, let me know I had an email.

I would not have come to your workplace. I learned a very hard lesson...if a man does not "really" want a woman, he can be used by, or use systems against her, and win. I am considering going to a grief and loss women's group that starts next week, at Overlake Calvary Chapel. I had decided to wait until I knew I would be safe from your presence. I have no desire to hurt or harm you or your family. I meant to be helpful.

I am not sure I answered all your questions. My little phone does not let me see your letters while I respond. I will tell you two last things. THANK YOU for the note with honesty of heart. Feel free to be a compassionate coach...I am actually more than a pretty cheerleader. We both coached each other. We won the game of honesty, ...TOGETHER.

I want you to know that John Jones, told me that my insecurity about my desire for him was all tied to my "choice". I do believe the power of a person's choices determine how they navigate life. I chose Alex as my first husband, no regrets. I chose that night with John, no regrets. I chose to share myself with you, no regrets.

Enjoy Independence Day celebrations.

Happily,

Holly

PS: I figured out how to go back to your message and then get back to mine. Specifically answering the question about what my intention was in figuring out who you were through a Godly church...that is where Janet wants me to confront MY past, present, and past. I would not have confronted YOU. You were a blessing; why would you be ashamed of wanting to explore the possibility of me as a match for your soul. Churches are the best place to meet a soul mate. I met Donald at a Christian Fellowship. I met Alex at a Christian Fellowship. I met John at a bar...so what does that tell you? Don and Alex would tell you the real answer...Holly Hill chooses to love whoever God puts in her life. I think you are so hilarious. I guess you could call and honestly tell Rowan that you had an attraction for an honest woman that thought she could love you even though you thought you were too good for her. You choose. Now...giggle...it is good for your soul.

11:23 am

To: Mr. Hip and Handsome
From: Holly

Why do you think about mortification and confrontation? Those are related to death and condemnation. I will be praying you think more about life and being totally loved for who you are. That is my gift to the people God puts in my life.

I am totally free...to live, to dance, to love.

Holly :-)

12:35 pm

To: Mr. Hip and Handsome
From: Holly

I have no need for you to apologize for my behavior. That is very silly. I taught my children to tell the person they wronged that they were wrong. After confessing they were wrong to hurt someone, they were told to ask forgiveness. If they asked and were forgiven, I rejoiced. I do not believe I did anything wrong concerning contact with Janet Anderson. She wanted me to be protected. You have not wronged anyone there. I will encourage you to not open another heart, unless you are willing to take responsibility for hurt it causes the woman when you choose to shut her out. You did that. I think you are all clear.

I have two questions. Are you John Jones? I already promised him I did not wish him any harm to his job or family. I keep my promises. Did you read the return emails when I was mad at you? I am always honest. I unloaded a big defense of myself on you. If that hurt you, I did say I was wrong, and please forgive me.

Aaaccckkk...my teachers always said I was talkative. I work it out in words. I am quiet if the intended hearer is responding. Okay, so there are three questions. Last one: are you hearing me and believing me?

Holly

# # #

2:01 pm

Holly: Alex, I just picked up the Parenting Plan from an attorney. It states that you are responsible for the kiddo's transportation.

Alex: Read it again. All statements about transportation are about getting the children to your HOME for the visit. What you do with them during your time is your responsibility and yours alone.

July 2, 2010

5:59 pm

> **Holly**: So...I am at the bank. Unable to cash your check.

> **Holly**: There is a hold on the check you wrote me. Please call the bank, ask for Lindsey.

"911, what's your emergency?"

"Hey Cheryl, Alex here. I just finished my shift but was told to call dispatch." Cheryl Baxter was the work-version of Terri, a great person and a trusted friend. Cheryl could read through someone's bullshit faster than anyone while also managing to calm them through their crisis and help them focus. Not today.

"Oh my God, Alex, what's the deal with your freaking ex? She called 911 screaming and demanding a supervisor go to her location at Wells Fargo Bank because they won't cash your check!"

"Seriously? It's after 4 pm so they likely put a hold on the check until the next business day since her account is so whacked, or maybe because the date was changed. Or maybe because she's so...anyway, did a supervisor respond?"

"Sgt. Arancio called her and had a conversation which apparently didn't go very well. She called back here yelling at the call-taker, something about how she's not talking out of her butt. Not sure what she meant."

"Okay, wow. Thanks for the heads up. Let me know if it continues to be a problem and I'll see what I can do."

"Thanks. We're all getting to know her pretty well up here fielding her crazy calls, not to mention all the calls from businesses in Edmonds who have kicked her out. She doesn't seem to be getting any better, huh?"

"Nope. Thanks again, Cheryl."

Somehow this woman is going to get me fired.

#

July 3, 2010

6:08 am

To: Hank
From: Holly

Good morning. I would like to go back to what made you and I want to communicate. It was simple. I thought the purity of your desire to love yourself and your son was very attractive. I thought how you spoke of your joys and desires were beautiful. I enjoyed reading your letters and answering your questions. I felt sure that you would not torment me if I told you the truth.

I believed you when I got nervous about some of your stated accomplishments. I openly told you that I may not be a worthy partner. You assured me that my past was just that. We exchanged several letters after that. Then you got nervous about me. You researched my past two years and decided I was not a worthy partner. I wanted to hold onto what you had said previously. I wanted to deal squarely with your concerns because I felt like you believed in my spirit.

I was not trying to track you down to confront you with a reprimand. I was trying to come under the counsel and shelter of something you trusted. If I enjoyed and believed you why would I have a reason to hurt your reputation with your friends and family? I truly am a lover, friend, and advocate by God's design. My gifts are helps and encouragement with a bit of admonishment towards what is true mixed in.

I will honor your wish to remain anonymous until you are comfortable meeting. Will you please honor my wish that you remain as open and honest as you can be? You stated that open communication was essential and that you would not shut down. I would like to share your desire to be proactive rather than reactive.

A big part of my scenario is that you viewed what papers showed. You characterized me as an embarrassment and shameful. This did cause me some consternation. I was encouraged by a wise attorney to let Alex be caught in the trap of his own actions. She asked me to patiently pray for my children and let his character prove itself. I love Alex and my children. This choice was very painful. I now hold many documents and proof that he abused the authority given to him.

Edmonds City Police upheld them. I took a lot of criticism. The anger and strength of my will got projected wrongly because I chose not to blame Alex. I needed my children to be healthy enough to form their own opinions. Once I was confident that I held all their hearts as before the separation, I decided to pursue litigation.

This litigation will not be against Alex, personally. I learned how painful that can be. It is to confront the institution that encouraged that decisions. The Assistant Chief is my friend. He supports this decision. Being proactive in conjunction with The Washington State Criminal Justice Training Panel is the goal. Power and control in Law Enforcement should not lead to domestic violence and Parental Alienation Syndrome. It did, in our marriage. I want to help reduce the percentage by making others aware and help other marriages thrive and families be healthier. My personal issues may become public, that is okay with me. I do believe that I am not just a survivor, I have overcome my past.

My children need the truth. I need to direct my efforts and emotions towards health and strong virtue for my sake and for theirs. I was hopeful that you could muster the courage to coach me from the sidelines. I could tell from your letters that you had the heart, fortitude, and wisdom to be worthy of this hope.

There you go. I thought it, I wrote it, I meant it.

I have continued to both wake up with a song in my heart and fall asleep with one also. Thank you for praying for me and my children. I am praying for you and yours, too.

Honestly,
Holly

P.S. I am going to send you the songs. Just say no more, when you have had enough. Yes and no are equal answers. I value both.

# # #

Holly: Hello. On Thursday, Evelyn wanted to stay overnight. I told her there was probably not enough notice. I sent you a text, to inform you that an email had been sent. I have not received a reply. Evelyn called this afternoon and requested to stay overnight. She also requested to stay overnight last Saturday. Could you please not deny her requests?

Holly: Please have the kiddos take chairs down to the end of your street, tonight. Near the little park, next to the track would be nice. They want to watch the parade. I will meet them there at 11:30. I see that other folks do the same thing. Kevin decided to not do the Fun Run. I am still available for fireworks and any help you need for Evelyn. Thank you.

Alex: I'm not having the kids take chairs down, sorry. Kids are available any time after 8, 10 is better. They'll meet up with you whenever you are ready. Overnight may continue per the order, possibly next week if things are getting a little settled. Kev and Evie have plans Sunday evening after 3 pm. I don't mind if they hang with you until 4ish, whatever works well for them. Martin and Justin will likely spend time with you after work tomorrow.

# # #

8:31 pm
To: Hank
From: Holly

Could you just entertain the thought of being a responder to the very hopeful romantic Holly? Please. I know it makes you nervous, but I promise to not intentionally cause you embarrassment or pain. Haven't you ever wanted someone to think you were so totally awesome? I promise to get happy every time I see you took the time to send an email. Even when you have strong words that cause consternation, I will assume it is for my best, and that you have a positive intent. And if you just want to spew something out that you are not sure someone else would receive and still hold you in high regard, I will take it.

Will you tell me something you delighted over the last couple weeks? I missed your letters. I still promise not to say anything to you if I see you. Do faces of cheerful acknowledgement count? Do you even look like those photos? That could have been made up, too.

If you just have to say no, maybe you could get a friend to do it...LOL. I would probably figure it out. Btw. You do not have to fuss over grammar. And if you flip flop words, I will know you are just a step ahead of yourself, or outside a pragmatic role.

I REALLY WISH YOU WOULD.

Holly

Oh my God! I've become her actual imaginary friend!

July 4, 2010

8:09 am

To: Hank
From: Holly

Happy Independence Day! YOU ARE FREE...TO LOVE, TO CHOOSE, TO DANCE, TO SING, AND TO BE ALL GOD INTENDED FOR YOU TO BE. Have a great day with your family and spoil yourself in the process.

Holly

PS: Morning song: I AM FREE. Last night's song: Tonight You Are Mine (Carol King). She is my range...my mom listened to her. I sing her songs...I am singing this one to my next husband, just before the honeymoon, in front of everyone present. For now, I am just Held By God.

I had to remind myself Hank had already broken up with her. Sitting at a coveted 2-top table at the downtown Edmonds Starbucks, I was deep in thought debating with myself on how to respond to Holly. Alex pinged me.

Alex: Coffee?

Nikki: Already there and have a table!

Alex: Enrouting.

I handed him an americano as he walked in the door. "Thank you, love!" He gave me a lean, which was all the public display of affection he was allowed while in uniform. He handed me his phone. "Check out the latest." I read.

Wow. Not only was Holly freaking out with Alex, she was spinning with Hank at the same time. It was interesting to analyze how she was handling the break-up with Hank while simultaneously badgering Alex.

"Hey, yoo-hoo…Earth to Nikki?" Alex said.

"Oh, sorry," I said. "It's just so crazy, all this instability she introduces to everyone." I knew I had to focus or I'd blow Hank's cover.

# # #

5:04 pm

Holly: Justin and Martin ignored me when I brought a picnic lunch for them at work. Evelyn was very disagreeable today. Katherine spoke over me and commanded the day, as you do. I tried to speak and was corrected by both girls, almost every time I spoke. Katherine said she had to be home by 3 to do laundry. Stop using the children as your personal maid service.

Holly: I made every effort to celebrate. There was a lot of complaining and put downs. Our family needs continued counseling.

# # #

6:26 pm

To: Hank
From: Holly

Do you understand that Janet Anderson and I spoke, before you said that we were not a good fit? I spoke to her about other things, as well as our interaction. She asked about you to guard me. I forwarded your photo. She and Rowan chose to ask others about you and Matthew. Please do not take this so hard. You know so much more about me. It is no shame to be considering the hope of a life partner. I do not think that hiding and doing so without Christian people aware and a part is best, for me. I enjoy fellowship and togetherness. I quit match.com. It has proven to not be the best means to my desired end.

I am continuing to pray for you and your family.

Holly

9:21 pm

To: Holly
From: Hank

To say I was surprised to see the volume of email you've sent me would be an understatement. I hope my email did not encourage false hope for you. As I said before we are definitely not a match and your response to me was all I needed to validate my choice. When you asked if I received all the angry emails, I can't honestly answer that question. I read several however upon realizing they were coming from a very troubled soul, I elected not to continue. The latest emails have me baffled wondering what you are talking about. If you are not currently seeking professional psychological assistance please, for the sake of yourself and your children, consider it.

The title of the email was appropriate: reconciliation is not something I'm considering as it relates to us. Good luck, Holly.

Hank

# # #

Nikki had two blankets spread on the field in a perfect location to watch the fireworks. I found her just as it was turning dark. "Take a seat, mister," she said.

"Gladly." I'd been on my feet for a good 14 hours by then.

All of us were there together, watching the stars as they began to shine through the night sky, listening to the pre-show music celebrating America. The fireworks show brought the ooh's and aah's from the crowd of 30,000 people. A few minutes before it was over, I leaned over to Nikki and violated some department policy.

25. Breaking Up Is Hard To Do

July 5, 2010

8:17 am

Holly: Good morning. I would like to spend an hour with EVELYN, today. Is this okay with you?

Alex: Thursday at 3.

Holly: I will pray hard for her bruised spirit. I will be at my home. Transportation will be your responsibility both directions. Justin did not make contact for our split holiday. I will be in town to see him, today. Thank you.

Alex: Justin had to work July 4th, so he didn't go to your home or to the fireworks.

# # #

2:09 pm

To: Hank
From: Holly

I was wrong. Please forgive me. I will not trouble you.

Holly

2:28 pm

To: Hank
From: Holly

Please will you not shame me by speaking unkindly about me to others. Your stated negative opinion and words of criticism were painful. This would honor my children and me.

Thank You,

Holly

# # #

July 6, 2010

5:57 am

To: Alex
From: Holly

A Reason to Reconcile: Heritage Day 318

There are several reasons you should consider reconciliation. We will discuss eight reasons over the next eight days. The first reason to reconcile is because of the valuable heritage that you already have together.

"Once the separation occurs," says Dr. Jim A. Talley, "there begins to be a loss of all the positive memories and all the positive heritage, and an accumulation of all the pain and all of the negative. In order to get back into a balance and to really consider reconciliation seriously, you have to go back and remember some of the good things that happened. Every family and every relationship has a heritage that is valuable to be passed on to the children and to the grandchildren."

Alice shares, "We had always been each other's best friend, so we had a lot to build on if we could bring it back together."

When you think back to the time you were first getting to know your former spouse, the dating and the early part of your marriage, you likely have many fond memories. You have been through good times and bad times together, and the memories and traditions you have built together are your heritage. It is an important part of you.

"Indeed, my heritage is beautiful to me. I will bless the LORD who has counseled me" (Psalm 16:6-7 NASB).

Lord God, help me to remember the good times and not let the negative memories take over. Amen.

Holly

# # #

To: Hank
From: Holly

Good morning. I hope and pray you continue to grow in compassion for women and children. If you knew the details you would not have been so stoic and judgmental. I trust that if you are really as stable and gifted at seeing a campaign succeed and continue to prosper, then you know that that requires resources.

I give myself wholly to nurturing the souls and bodies of myself and my children. The $1,000.00 a month maintenance that I receive from Alex is difficult to survive on. I barter for my groceries by mowing lawns and doing housecleaning. My medical care is granted in exchange for filing documents and lab reports. I am home for every opportunity I have to spend quality time with my children.

You should know I am training for a mini-triathlon with a very kind gentleman friend I met at Overlake where I continue in Christian fellowship with the Women's group. I get the help I need. Paying for professional counseling is not in my budget.

Do not tell others what they need without first considering their means to obtain them. I am fully capable and able. I would like you to consider a humble look at why your first wife wanted to not be married to you and why she would choose to live away from her beautiful son. After you have the answers, then seek professional help to overcome your own issues. I suggest you remain in counseling for a solid 5 or 6 years. It would also be wise to have BOTH you and your next mate remain seeing a life coach. Two strong people that want a successful marriage need coaching more than a professional sports team. Families that last are constantly seeking, asking, and finding positive game plans to win victories. Let your losses teach you how to play better.

Better than you think,

Holly Hill

# # #

July 8, 2010

Holly: Why are you keeping Justin from me?

Truth was, I had nothing to do with keeping Justin from his mom…he did that all on his own. Despite my ongoing encouragement for him to spend time with Holly, Justin took advantage of his work at the community pool, along with his occasional outing with friends, summer lacrosse games, practices, and driver's education classes, to conveniently get in the way of the scheduled visits with mom. I had told Holly of these self-directed interruptions and indicated I'd encourage him to seek out time apart from the scheduled visits to go see his mom, but these largely fell on deaf ears. Justin easily found ways to avoid spending time with his mom. It worried me: Justin's heart was supremely tender underneath a dragon-like skin, and family was important to him. Justin witnessed much of Holly's malfunctions over the years, especially when her malfunctions were in full swing, so while it wasn't surprising that he would avoid embracing more of the drama, it worried me that his own future relationships with women could be scarred before they had a chance of being normal.

Either way, I wasn't about to explain to Holly that her son was avoiding her all on his own. I was gonna take the hit either way from her.

3:00 pm

Holly: Will Evie be here soon? Will Justin be coming?

Alex: Yes, she should be there any minute. Justin is working, may come later for a bit. I'll find out.

Holly: Will Justin be coming?

Alex: Justin won't be coming today; he has drivers ed.

One of the benefits of working patrol is the 4-on, 4-off, schedule. The 12-hour days are long, but the weekends are four days long, sometimes during the middle of the week. It's a fair trade for hours but certainly a benefit in terms of actual days off. So much so that when I'd show up at the downtown coffee shop on an off day, I'd regularly endure a solid pound of ass-chewing from the local retired muscle-car enthusiasts asking me when I was ever going to work again.

On this particular day, having the day off meant I could go over to Nikki's house after the kids made their way to visit Holly and before Nikki got home from work. I stopped at the grocery store and picked up a $10 bouquet of flowers, then made my way into the depths of Lynnwood to her rambler. I laughed thinking about the B-52's song, *Love Shack,* along the way. *Man, I'm weird.*

I found a vase in a cupboard, cut the bottom inch off the stems, and planted the flowers in the wide-mouthed glass. It was awkward, but I figured the effort would count for something. I'd brought home flowers on numerous occasions during my marriage, usually to some elementary level of satisfaction by Holly but never for the purpose of gaining some real favor with her. I just figured it was a good husbandly thing to do, especially on certain holidays, regardless of her reception.

Nikki arrived home in time to see me engrossed in mortal combat with the overgrown grass in her back yard. The thick mix of clover and dandelions was all the 5-horse Briggs & Stratton could handle. Just as the machine bit off a little too much and gagged a quick death, I caught Nikki out of the corner of my eye. "Hey there," I offered.

"Hey! Whatchya doin?" She didn't really need explanation…it was pretty obvious. I let it pass.

"Eh, I was thinking we could barbecue some lettuce."

"You're really gonna cave, aren't you?" she taunted. I had previously laughed at the ridiculous notion that romaine could be prepared on a hot barbecue. I was calling her bluff.

"You're on, baby."

"As long as you don't call me 'babe.' My ex called me babe."

"Duly noted," I replied. I wasn't sure if I'd called her Babe or Baby, but apparently it mattered. Maybe I'll go with 'hun.' *Wait—what the hell am I doing?* I'm already having discussions about pet names for her and we don't even live together! Here we were about to embark on a delightful evening of blissful barbecue, cooking fresh grilled ingredients in the heat of a Western Washington July evening while I was discussing the finer points of reference for a girlfriend in my head. Pathetic.

"No worries, lady. 'Babe' is out of the vocab."

"Good," she said. "You like artichokes?"

Never had 'em. "Yep!"

Nikki fired up a pressure cooker from her selection of pots with a bay leaf, a solid tablespoon of minced garlic, and sufficient water to steam for fifteen minutes. The garlic gave me hope. She snipped the tops off a pair of Costco-sized artichokes and set them on the steamer tray in the cooker, sealed the lid, and set the timer. Within a minute, the contraption was threatening to blow. All I could think of was abu-Farouk. "Don't let the feds know you cook with that thing," I quipped.

"I know a cop," she said, as my phone started to buzz. It was a bit of a buzz-kill.

> **Holly**: Katherine showed me photos of your home. She is not your maid. Stop using her to meet your needs.

We managed to ignore the nonsense and enjoy the evening together.

When the kids arrived home, Katherine told me she looked through some pictures on Holly's phone. "Mom went ballistic. She got all upset that I was looking at her photos, even though she let me use her phone a lot. I saw a few of her photos, nothing weird or whatever. She just got super mad." Katherine clarified Holly was very angry when the kids wouldn't sing along with her to *Who Let The Dogs Out*, then complained about the divorce.

Kevin chimed in. "She was so mad, I thought she was going to hit us!"

Evelyn nodded along with him. "I wish Martin was still coming with us to these. He always kept mom from getting mad."

# # #

July 9, 2010

Nikki: I sent you an email…Happy reading!

Sally: YEAH! I was so hoping to hear from you today. I've missed Hank!

To: Nikki
From: Sally
Subject: RE: Ok…Here's the latest

Wow. It's troubling seeing the time stamps on all of her obsessive emails…I re-read all of it and the one where she asks Hank if he is John Jones. Her next line worries me a bit: "I already promised him I did not wish him any harm to his job or family. I keep my promises." Knowing now how her mind works it's obvious that she is trying to find Hank and his son. I have no doubt she showed up to services at that church looking for him in addition to walking the streets of Edmonds searching. What worries me is if she's capable of violence. I keep picturing a boiling bunny on the stove for some reason…

Proceed with caution, my friend.

Sally

# # #

July 11, 2010

Police Officers have long known the need to separate the job from personal matters. The days of going home and kicking the dog has long since passed as even remotely acceptable behavior. Police agencies in the Pacific Northwest were leaders in this field in some senses, but when the Chief of Tacoma PD went home one day and murdered his wife, we all knew some updated training was headed our way. With it came my own renewed dedication to being an excellent father and, hopefully, ex-husband.

Somehow this didn't prevent my arrest stats from looking a little awkward. Fifteen of the last eighteen arrests for domestic violence resulted in the female half going to jail. I had to take a hard look at myself and ask if I had been taking out my own anger with Holly on the general public.

The results were in: there were just a lot of crazy women around here. Must be the rain.

I parked my patrol car at the QFC parking lot in Edmonds after releasing a shoplifter from the Goodwill store. I'm not sure how else to explain that. Writing my report, I heard my name being hailed from somewhere in the parking lot by a woman's voice. I turned around to see a woman standing there smiling at me. I racked my brain trying to place her but couldn't figure it out in the 1.6 seconds it took her to cross the parking lot in her heels. She extended her hand. "Alex Hill? Tina Babineaux. We've met briefly before…through Holly."

Tina Babineaux, attorney at law. That name came with a certain sultry reputation noted by more than a few officers, mostly of command rank. Her jet-black hair, fair complexion, defined lines, and propensity to get physically close made her hard to miss. "Right…hi, Tina. How are things?" I was still drawing a blank on ever actually meeting her, but at least I had the adequate heads up. I smelled a rat.

"So…what's up with Holly?" She was trying to draw me in. "How long has she been having all these problems?"

Everyone asks this. Everyone wanted to know what happened to Holly, someone who seemed so nice, so kindhearted, and so, so charming. They would hear her story of the difficult situation she is in, then they'd want to help, then they wouldn't do what she wanted, then they'd get targeted for harassment, a rash of false accusations, and targeted blame for her own circumstances. It was like one of those commercials that keeps repeating itself during the NFL pre-season games, over and over, with really bad actors making you feel bad for having the wrong kind of phone. Holly's apparent breakdown probably started in a minor way a long time ago but took more obvious shape around the literal turn of the century. The major mental eruptions came in 2005, starting the full-tilt roller coaster until she finally left in 2008.

"You know," I said, shaking my head, "I'm not really sure. It sorta snuck up on all of us."

"It's just crazy," Tina continued. "If she would just admit that she has mental issues and get some qualified help, it could really help her."

"I think you're right, but that's the hard part with her condition, whatever it is...she doesn't think she has any problems. It's always someone else's problem, then someone else's responsibility to fix it."

"It's like a personality disorder," she said. "One minute she's super nice, then the next minute she's like super evil. She's all over the map! So, why can't she drive anyway, did she get in an accident or something?"

It seemed like Tina may have been starting to skirt her attorney-client privilege, but the topic of driving made me think Holly had already primed the pump. "Several, especially between 2001 and 2008, after which she hasn't driven much at all. Still, when people ride with her they independently call me saying, "Holy smokes, I was scared to death!!" She might do fine by herself, I don't know. But when she transports kids, especially her own children, she is very distracted. Lots of close calls, lots of reports of severely distracted driving, and yes, numerous crashes. The Guardian ad Litem determined it was not safe for the kids to be in a car with her if she's driving."

Tina looked concerned. "I had her babysit my daughter last week, thinking maybe if she spent some time with a child it would do her some good. Yeah, I'm never doing that again. Her call to 911 for a combination of burnt toast with my unreasonable 11-year old, along with her blowup with the responding officer were enough to seal the deal."

I'd heard the shift supervisor respond to the disturbance call, but he never told me Holly was involved until the following day. "Best to steer clear of that address, Hill," was all he said. I knew what he meant.

"So Tina, Holly projects that you are one of her attorneys who is going to bring about my downfall and get the kids back."

Tina involuntarily flipped her hair to the side. "Oh, no," she said, shaking her head, "I have tried to stay out of the middle of all that."

I still wasn't entirely sure. I also wasn't entirely sure that I wasn't being hit on. In broad daylight. Saved by the bell, I heard another officer requesting backup over my portable radio earpiece. Or maybe I didn't, but that's what I told Tina as I quickly got into the patrol car and raced out of the parking lot in the nick of time. None of it stopped me from hearing the timely ding of my phone.

Holly: I am praying for you. Let the SPIRIT lead you. Justin told me that you are not attending Calvary Fellowship. I would like to be where my children are. I will be there for the evening service.

Well ain't that a relief! Good God. Holly always complained Calvary was too groovy for her. Likely it's just another attempt to find resource on her part, or maybe a new victim.

# # #

July 12, 2010

1:52 pm

> **Sally**: Is there a Hank/Holly update to get me through this long Monday afternoon?

> **Nikki**: She's mad at Hank I think. But rest assured…She can't keep her mouth shut or her thumbs still for long.

2:44 pm

> **To: Hank**
> **From: Holly**

> You were unkind to me. It makes logical sense that if you freely shared your negative opinions with me, that you may also share them with those you are in physical contact with. Your words revealed your heart. The wise people that read your emails, also took them as negative and critical. I am a critical thinker and challenge nearly everything. I do not fault you for being critical. I am not finding it difficult to take responsibility for my behavior/actions. As I said, I chose counseling for the last three years of our marriage. I went to weekly counseling from the week after the sexual assault occurred. I remained in counseling, until two months ago. To be honest, no person was as firm and confronting, as you were. Your observations lead you to conclude that I was not a suitable partner.

> I am truly thankful for your straight-forward frankness because you were equally sentimental. You are very balanced and have a strong spirit of encouragement. I do think the compassion you choose to hope for started to wane when you observed what you believed to be the truth of my character. I did not want you to find out anything from someone else. I chose to be straight-forward in truth telling.

> I am a victim of domestic violence and sexual abuse. My

circumstances are my choice. I am reading, learning, and choosing to go forward without a "job" because my children need a healthy mom. I have a plan for my campaign. I will go back to school at Bastyr University, when my children go back to school. I needed healthcare, and chose to barter for what I needed. I am a hard worker. I also am a determined lover of my own soul and the souls of my children. I am committed to be their advocate. Their dad does not believe in counseling. This means I spend time researching and being prepared to counsel and encourage them through this stormy season.

I recently moved into a sweet little place of my own. It is a slice of heaven. It is a beautiful little farm property. I had my first real childhood memory, when I entered the apartment. It is just where God wanted me to be. Some lady friends that are involved with Vision House's Jacob's Well, are surrounding me with support. I am very blessed. I am not ignorant of my need for counseling. A comfortable and safe dwelling came first. A car is being prayed for and worked out. A career is just around the corner.

I wish you would tell me what specifically from one of the last letters made you sure you should pull away. We had agreed to be totally honest in hopes of helping each other. You had said you would not shut down without clarity of why you would choose that. Was it that litigation would be started to bring an end to injustices?

You are very welcome for the attempt to understand what troubled your heart. I agree that counseling helps people adjust well. I did not walk forward without it.

Holly

3:18 pm

To: Hank
From: Holly

I do not want to attach motives to your intent. I want to believe that you meant no unkindness. To me, there was no mutuality of honesty. I chose to be completely honest. You claimed I lied to you. I did not understand how. When I asked, there was no answer. Obviously, I was nervous about answering your questions. I told you I was, before I chose to be.

I do want you to know that your probing was instrumental in leading me in a good direction. My new spiritual family at Overlake will be instrumental in my path forward. I do take responsibility for the choices of my past. Those choices are helping me understand what needs to be addressed and worked through.

Please will you tell me how you believe I lied to you and what you meant by "throwing forgiveness around"?

Thank you,

Holly

# # #

Holly: Is it permissible for me to send FACEBOOK messages to our kiddos?

Alex: It is considered the same as text. Responses are great. Please don't initiate.

# # #

July 13, 2010

4:18 pm

To: Holly
From: Hank

I'm glad our interaction has helped you in your journey. I'm sure you will be triumphant over your circumstance. What surprised me the most was how many restraining orders are currently in place against you. I'm of the mind set we all do things we're not proud of every once in a while but over the course of the last 2 years there appears to be a habitual behavior. At some point in our conversation you indicated either your ex-husband or his girlfriend had attempted to get a restraining order (forgive me I don't recall which one) to keep you from your children. The fact is both of those people have orders currently against you.

I don't believe I said "throwing forgiveness around". I was referring to how, based on the documents I was able to review, you behave in a manner that is not generally acceptable in our society then ask God for forgiveness and that makes it ok for you. What concerned me the most is the apparent path of destruction you leave in your wake and I cannot afford to this type of risk involved in my personal life.

I truly wish you the best. I hope your new friends at Overlake and the Washington State resources I sent you will help you through this difficult time.

Hank

8:09 pm

To: Hank
From: Holly

I am socially acceptable. A bitter husband and girlfriend are not the determining forces for what is acceptable in society. I am thankful that you chose a better path for your family law case. I am not restrained from my children. Again, the unkindness is the shame you push for. There has been a clear desire for you to unveil and expose me, in order to dishonor me. No circumstance has taken my honor.

No person can condemn in hopes that I change to conform to what they believe is acceptable.

Your answer was not connected to anything I told you. It was connected to public record. You infer that I use my faith to cover my deeds. That could not be further from the truth. I am completely redeemed and give God the glory for justifying and sanctifying me COMPLETELY. There is not a court on earth that can remove a guilty sentence COMPLETELY. I am washed and free. I hope you walk about in your freedom, with compassion that blesses you, your son, and the people God places in your path.

I will pray for tender-hearted mentoring successes, kind compassion, honorable communications, and wisdom for you. Press on, but do not press hard for what YOU want, fight for the prize of reaching

God's best for you. I do hope that as you walk along there are songs that encourage your heart, sweetnesses that make you praise God, and delight that makes you want to dance.

Sincerely,

Holly

July 14, 2010

I started formulating a reply in the body of her note:

> **To:**
> **From: Nikki**
>
> Hank,
>
> I am socially acceptable. **2 days out of 7 isn't too bad.** A bitter husband and girlfriend are not the determining forces for what is acceptable in society. **What can I say…I'm bitter.** I am thankful that you chose a better path for your family law case. I am not restrained from my children. **Oh honey but you are…a total of 12 hours over a 2-week period, I'd call that restrained.**

Nope. It was honestly horrible and went straight to the trash. I realized I was becoming angry; it was so unbelievable how Holly continued to misrepresent facts and pretend she had no culpability in her own circumstances. Mental illness sucks. For everybody.

I started over.

5:03 pm

> **To: Holly**
> **From: Hank**
>
> It appears I have upset you and that was not at all my objective. I only meant to answer the questions honestly and if that distressed you please accept my apologies. I've pasted the excerpt from your email where you indicated Nikki had attempted to get a restraining order. This is where I concluded you were not being entirely

transparent with me:

"I let go of the hope for a reconciled marriage, last fall when Nikki tried to get the restraining order. Their togetherness against my efforts towards our children was a painful blow. They support each other. I am praying they both grow deeper in their compassion and openness to the Holy Spirit. I hope he honors her with marriage."

I only hope as you move through this challenging time in your life your beliefs and practice of those ideals become proactive.

I've pasted a link to the Washington Department of Social & Health Service website http://www.dshs.wa.gov/mentalhealth/. The organization has programs that can assist you that are free of charge.

Sincerely,
Hank

# # #

July 15, 2010

Alex: I was called in to work today, so I will arrange a ride for kids to your place. Let me know if you'd rather meet them in Edmonds; either is fine w/me. Thanks.

Holly: It is your responsibility to bring them to me. I will see them here at three.

Alex: Like I said, I will arrange a ride for them.

Holly: Yes. You will. I will stand strong. My defense is coming. Your divorce was the ugliest choice. Beauty is the choice I MAKE.

Alex: Please stop the harassment with texting. I was only verifying plans for today.

Holly: It is not harassment. I do not need to heed your demands. Use a stop sign on the streets, not on my phone.

July 16, 2010

Holly: Good morning. I was telling the truth. An attorney is plowing into a defense for the children and me. It will benefit many...even you. Divorce and it's ramifications will always have a painful sting. It was not GOD'S choice or mine. You will be comfortable because it was your choice. I know you understand this.

# # #

July 18, 2010

11:38 am
To: Hank
From: Holly

I appreciate your continued attempts to be helpful. I was transparent with you. I did not know until last week that there was a restraining order that applied to Nikki. I have never seen it. I never received a document. I did not know that it could become served and processed without me ever seeing the documents. They were thrown away by the manager of TIKI, when a friend of Nikki's followed me through town. They were shredded by an owner of a car lot that she and 3 people followed me to.

I have been honest.

Holly

You are so full of shit! "I have never seen it..." *My ass!* Funny how she can quote the order to Alex demanding clarifications, but then has never seen...Oh, bullshit.

High road, Nikki. Take the high road.

5:30 pm
To: Holly
From: Hank

Holly,

I would have thought one of your attorneys would have informed you of the restraining order(s) and the legalities behind attempting to avoid service. It is not looked at favorably by the courts. Service avoidance really only happens in the movies. Just FYI…Often times the Petitioner is present for the serving of documents because it eliminates the person serving from having to establish if indeed you are the person because a visual is done by the Petitioner.

I hope you and your children are doing well and that you are able to enjoy the wonderful weather that has blessed us as of late.

Hank

July 21, 2010

To: Holly
From: Alex

I will be taking the kids for a week of camping starting August 14th to Birch Bay. More details to follow, just wanted you to be aware ahead of time.

Alex

9:14 pm

Holly: Could you please ask Justin to call. No call yesterday.

Holly: I have not heard from Justin. Evelyn does not want to feel like she is making you mad by not choosing to play the sports you coach. My children are not your maids. Please do not make them 'muscle' through your demands. Hickies are bruises. My son should not be sporting pain inflicted by a girl. Our children are more precious than this. Kevin is not enjoying being left in charge of Evelyn. You have a big heart. Let it shine

Holly: What I really want is to be a cherished woman and dearly beloved wife and mother. The day of my birth does matter. Public shunning was not what GOD wanted for me. Could you please explore why Justin has not called. My mom and I MATTER. Plans for celebrating DO MATTER.

# # #

I checked Hank's email before going to bed and was surprised to find an audio file attached to an email from Holly. The high-pitched, chirpy voice was all I could bear.

9:20 pm

To: Hank
From: Holly

Transcription of .wav file attachment:
"Hey Hank, I want to say something to you. My children matter more to me than boxes of paperwork. I've put the lids on them, and I went forward advocating for the souls of my children not for what it was about myself that I felt like I needed to uphold. Okay? So you know more about me than I ever knew about myself as far as what is represented in documents that the public eye can see. I've put it on a back burner. I've put my children first. That seemed to be the thing that was attractive to you in the beginning. Until you peered into what could be seen the other way. So. I am doing something about it, but I've chosen not to…yet. My kids matter more."

July 22, 2010

To: Holly
From: Hank

Holly,

That was really impressive, a voicemail via email! I appreciate your words and can certainly respect them. Remember, your children do follow by example. I think it's good you've taken the high road. I hope you enjoyed your time with your children yesterday. You are correct: the initial attraction was due to your maternal aura, love of God and your children. I hope that you are able to overcome all the obstacles that have influenced your journey.

I see your birthday is coming up this week. Do you have any extraordinary plans?

Hank

# # #

July 25, 2010

6:00 am

Holly: This is the time of day that I was born. I came early. This year I will be dishonored by my mother and my husband. I am alone. My children will celebrate with me. The two people GOD chose to cherish me and shelter me have despised my soul and robbed me of the love and companionship I desired. I pray that you both discover the answer of why you sided together against what GOD intended as a beautiful blessing. For now, I am deeply grieved by the weight of your choices to cast me aside.

# # #

July 30, 2010

To: Hank
From: Holly

Again, you accuse me falsely. I believe you are the one who needs further counseling. I did not avoid service. It was deemed improper service. Like I said, an attorney was appointed the same day as the trial. I did not have legal counsel. Alex being a Top Security Detective for the FBI limited who wanted to touch the case. The D.V. Coordinator I was working with at Edmond's City Police and I both attempted to secure an attorney, to no avail.

Your original letters were kind and compassionate. Your last ones all focus on legal logistics. If you want an attorney for a lover, you are on the right road. If you are looking for a woman to cherish your soul and the soul of your son, I suggest the cold-heartedness be warmed up a bit.

I am enjoying the sun, for my birthday week. This is also the week of my grandmother's birthday. My children and I are enjoying the close company of my parents. They are back from Equador. We are having delightful family visits.

I am seeing a musical with my daughter and her friend, this evening. I had lots of hugs and kisses, from my family. I am registering for continuing education courses. I am earning a free computer for volunteering to help others do the same. I have secured an attorney to fight on my behalf. I enjoyed being involved in supporting a gentleman friend of mine, Tony Milano, who is a beautiful man of God with a passion to uplift people. I found the perfect job.

I hope and pray that over time you will step aside from criticism to value the person behind the words. With whomever you choose to pursue, they will appreciate the wise counsel. Touching a soul and then slapping the mind with a critical spirit, did not seem to be your original intent. Once I have funds to invest in property, maybe you will choose to reveal yourself. I would be happy to pay you to do what you do best, which is obviously not loving and advocating for compassion. If you want money, like Alex, and supposed fame for being a single dad that is better than the mom, YOU WIN!

Be the life of the party at some other woman's expense. You have done very little to encourage and strengthen this beautiful woman. Ride your high horse and proclaim your power and trust in God. I do not like the way you treated me. So unless you can find a way to be truly kind, please do not communicate with me any longer.

Happier with people like you not trying to pile condemnation on me,

Holly

I honestly thought that was the end of it. And while I was relieved on the one hand, I knew the absence of this steady stream of information would leave a vacuum and keep me guessing. Probably best.

The end of it? Yeah, that turned out to be a pipe dream.

26. The Girl Next Door

July 30, 2010

12:52 pm

To: Hank
From: Holly

I have spoken up about some past pain that influenced my mother's choices. This year, for the first time in my life, my mom chose to not remember me with singing to me on my birthday. My children gave me their presence and kindness. My friends hosted a dinner with all my favorite things. I was given flowers and a movie date with my 16-year old. My oldest son bought me a massage.

I had a delightful birthday, although my heart yearned for my mom and for a partner that has always remembered me. I am doing the best I can.

Man, I read this one after I responded to the first one. Positive that I am real and very honest. I am not just a mom, Hank.

Holly

1:18 pm

To: Hank
From: Holly

I do have to say, you are far more admirable when you are positive. Didn't your counselor tell you to keep the negative away from people you care about, unless you are willing to suffer the consequences. We have never met, and possibly, never will. Why do you feel like someone closer than you are? The consequence for questioning my intentions and virtue was that you brought up a myriad of emotions and a defense of my character. You are not God, therefore, I really do not have to answer to you. I chose to.

Having said that, I will take the sting away since I do not enjoy it myself. Could you tell me something sweet about what you have been doing, without making yourself too vulnerable? How is work going? How is your son? Does your mom enjoy the recommended books? What is bringing a sparkle to your eye, lately?

I want to tell you about my job. A very special family has asked me to carry a child for them. I had prayed about this desire at the beginning of my separation. I am confident it is God's calling. It is the grandparents that will be supporting the child. A little unconventional, but perfectly, Holly. I have been asked to provide the other half of the genetics. I went through the testing. So, the pretty lady of 44, with 5 children, and pregnant with no spouse, in Edmonds, that will be me and my very special child. It is the best investment.

I do cherish the soul behind your words. I do not understand why you were so critical. Do you know that I plead guilty to the charges in Edmonds so that I would not be in the court room. I preferred community service and the special time with my family. I fulfilled all my obligations and the charges are being removed from my record. The restraining order from John Jones expired. Alex has been unable to pay my alimony. He is in contempt of court. His restraining orders all expire in less than a year. An attorney is working to overturn all false allegations. I live up to my birth sign. I am a lioness that protect her pride.

My mom and my grandma taught me by example to keep fighting and keep loving my children, no matter what. My dad taught me to cherish things unseen, and to make sure my children knew that it is not words, but actions, that are most helpful and most harmful.

Hopeful,

Holly

Oh my God. *Oh my GOD!*

1:23 pm

To: Hank
From: Holly

You might want to try a little more compliments for the beauty of the woman you pursue. Just a little hint...most women like to be thought of as pretty, not just a good mama. Try it on your next date, like, "you have pretty eyes, I like the way you giggle, your hand is nice to hold in mine." We come to the world without children. Try to separate out the woman.

Holly

3:14 pm

To: Hank
From: Holly

These are the pretty flowers from Justin. Hank, keep your promise to be truly YOU. It makes me sad to see you represent yourself as less. Thank you for the remembrance of my birthday. I would wear the number of blue stars, to match your age, for your whole birthday. My favorite perfume comes in a blue star-shaped bottle. I tell my children they are stars. They bought me the perfume the MOTHER'S DAY, after the divorce was final. It is called ANGEL.

Ok...did you know that very intelligent people make connections well?

Holly

4:21 pm

To: Hank
From: Holly

I am as bright as you are. Did you know that it is not lawful to have a family member serve a legal document? The woman that tried to serve me the document from Nikki, was in fact her sister. I avoided service because two Edmond's officers sided with me and told me to. There are also documents to prove that Nikki knew how to find me because the sister asked Alex. This was a misuse of power because it crossed my right to privacy. At the time I was not Alex's wife. I learned a lot by being alongside Alex. Documentation is everything, and I am an excellent information, verbalization, and communication specialist.

You wait. You watch. You will see my transformation. I will be the advocate for women and children that God gave me the desire to be. I plan to promote Vision House-Jacob's Well, and be an advocate for successful marriages with The Washington State Law Enforcement Training Center. Watch me, you coach.

My turn in litigation has begun. I am totally prepared and have an amazing Civil Rights attorney taking my case. I am a very sensitive and real soul. I foresaw the turn of events. I remained faithful to the whispers of the Holy Spirit, and I trusted that the dreams I was dreaming came from God Himself. I am doing very well. My children are doing very well.

I hope you are doing very well.

A very hopeful,

Holly

P.S. Praying for a song to be in your heart (careful singing in public, people love labels), and that your love in being shared. Happy daddy helps have happy son. I hope your ears are getting tickled and you are enjoying many delights with Matthew.

# # #

August 3, 2010

Holly: Can KEVIN AND EVELYN CAMP OUT OVERNIGHT WITH ME, ON FRIDAY? Then I would get them back to your home by 3, on SAT. I have a tent and everything. We can just set up right on the lawn. It makes accommodations pleasant.

Neither Kevin nor Evelyn wanted anything to do with an overnight with Holly at this point. Hell, I still didn't even know exactly where she lived. I ignored the request rather than attempt to explain that and endure the subsequent wrath of another response.

# # #

7:18 pm

To: Hank
From: Holly

Your words are distant because you have chosen to believe I am represented by paperwork. It makes me sad that a soul as connected to your mind and heart would choose this. I want to say that I hope your search for a soul mate finds its end in a woman completely worthy of what you represented in our beginning communications. I felt like I had to defend myself and your questions felt controlling and unkind. I know that was not your intention. I believe you wanted me to explore the way you thought about my circumstances. I believe you meant to be helpful.

I would rather be found than to do the searching for someone to match my soul. To me it is a picture of how I was saved and drawn to God. He knew I had a need of Him. I stood amazed at the love and shelter the Lord was to me. I am confident that for me, I do not want to push my heart to be comfortable or push for someone else to be comfortable. I have learned through life's experiences that the epiphany effect is what my soul longs for. It will just feel 'right'. Please forgive me for making you uncomfortable, if indeed I did.

Thank you for the helpful shaping questions and answers around a career choice.

I hope and pray all is well in daily pursuits and with your family.

God Bless,

Holly

August 4, 2010

To: Holly
From: Hank

Good afternoon. It sounds as though you've been busy. Something joyous in my life…that's an easy one! Today is my sister's birthday.

We are hitting the town in Edmonds in honor of her early this evening. Not only does she turn 44, she is expecting a precious baby girl any day now. Her due date is around September 1st but we all think it's going to happen sooner rather than later. I'm very excited for her. Matthew can't get enough time with her—it's delightful for me to witness.

I opted for a weekend at the Salish Lodge in Snoqualmie for a birthday gift for her (and her husband). The place is amazing. After she delivers her newest addition to her family she will absolutely need massage therapy and a nice get-away. Matthew has already offered to baby sit should she ever need it. Maybe in 10 years!

Mom promptly found and bought the books you had mentioned and has been reading them to Matthew when he's been in her care. He really loves story time with Grandma. Thank you again for the recommendations.

The surrogacy you mentioned sounds exciting for you. Before I say this please know I'm not being negative. I know you just had a birthday…aren't there increased risks due to age? It has been an issue for my sister pretty much throughout her pregnancy. When is the planned due date?

I was talking to my younger sister yesterday and she indicated there are programs that she is involved in with the community for displaced homemakers. She spoke highly of them and sent me these links. One is to the actual legislature that diverts funding to the programs and defines who is eligible to participate. The other is a life transition program through Washington State Board for Community and Technical Colleges and assists with education/training to help women that have experienced a life change such as you an opportunity to establish a career outside the home. I thought the information would be helpful to you.

http://www.sbctc.edu/college/s_lifetransitionsprogram.aspx

http://apps.leg.wa.gov/RCW/default.aspx?cite=28B.04

I took a look at the website you sent me. I'll be honest, I'm not a big fan of direct marketing. It's just an opinion, take it for what it is. If I were you and set on a direct marketing product, I would select something like MaryKay, Avon, Isagenix, etc. These are well known companies that have a great reputation for service and product satisfaction. The products cater to you and would really sell themselves.

I hope your week is going well.

Hank

August 5, 2010

4:13 am

> **To: Hank**
> **From: Holly**

> I wish I could talk to you.

> Holly

August 9, 2010

9:43 am

> **To: Hank**
> **From: Holly**

> There is a VACATION BIBLE ADVENTURE happening at Community Christian Fellowship in Edmonds, this week. Matthew would really enjoy it. I hope your heart is happy.

> HOLLY

6:20 pm

> **To: Hank**
> **From: Holly**

> Good afternoon again. Yes, I have been busy with a lot of forward-moving plans and connections. I love your joyous descriptions. We had some similar shared joys. It is very precious that Matthew is already wanting to be the caretaker of his little cousin. It is very thoughtful and kind of you to think of your sister solely, and her

time with her husband with gifts to nurture their souls and bodies. I get to go for my birthday massage from my oldest son, tonight. I am looking forward to it. I am very grateful my sons know how to cherish a woman.

My mom is a storybook lover. She encouraged my love of learning. I have had an awakening of my lost childhood memories that happened right near my birthday. Mom and I sent texts back and forth for a day as I remembered portions and she filled in the blanks. I started reading aloud to my children this summer. It was difficult for them at first. I had a book running at all times when we homeschooled. They are still struggling with the mix of what was and what now is.

I love how the kiddos are becoming more and more transparent with me. I brought them up with the value of freedom of speech. I have always told them to remain open and to know that I would rather receive negative emotion than have them split off. They are also very joyful as well.

I spent most of last week in appointments with the Washington State Worker Retraining representative and the Displaced Homemaker Program counselor at Edmond's Community College. I am finishing all the paperwork this week. The Career Counsellor thinks Business Management and Public Relations would be a great tract to start. Coincidentally, my Grandma was an Avon Lady and I was a MaryKay Beauty Consultant during college. Grandma had those darling lipstick samples in her purse for my sisters and me.

My great-aunt was a model. I spoke to the talent agent that landed me that commercial today. There is a director-producer coming on the 21st for a day of training for commercials and film. He offered a great deal for me and my two kiddos who are also interested.

Let me see...I am not nervous about the sweet baby carriage. Process is planned to begin this month. I spoke to my children about it. We are all in agreement that it has been the desire of my heart for a long time. If the Lord wants it to be a success, then it will be. The anticipation has me feeling blessed and hopeful. None of my pregnancies ended in miscarriage and Alex told so many people, "Holly is definitely called to motherhood, she glows and is healthier being with child than at any other time." I love the process. It is a beautiful gift.

I'm grateful you set aside the legal issues. Legitimate shame is a reality of our depravity.

Thank you for the gracious communication.

Joyfully,

Holly

# # #

August 10, 2010

To: Holly
From: Alex
Subject: Vacation reminder

Hi Holly, just a reminder. I will be taking the kids to Birch Bay August 13-20, meaning the kids will not be available on the Thursday of that week. The trip will not affect your time on your Saturday, the 21st. I've been trying to plan ahead but the details have only finalized recently.

# # #

To: Hank
From: Holly
Subject: Thank you from HOLLY

I signed up for AVON. It was my choice to treasure the memory of my Grandma. I went to an AVON meeting this morning with the kind woman that helped me get started. I enjoyed learning about the business. The best part of the day was connecting with someone who believes in me.

Holly

# # #

August 12, 2010

Holly: Good morning. Will you please get a check to me before you leave for Birch Bay, with Nikki and our kids?

Alex: What's the mailing address?

Holly: 616 LOGAN ROAD, LYNNWOOD, WA 98036. Be faithful to the kiddo's souls. God hates divorce. They are all sensitive to the fact that you replaced me so quickly with a woman so unlike me. It was not a picture of love for anyone but yourself. I miss the things we did together. I long for my family. I will always be truthful.

Holly: Until you tell the world that I was and am not what you wanted in a wife, I will not totally give my life to another. I cannot be dishonest. You were my choice. I believe in the power of GOD to reconcile, redeem, and restore. I am HOLLY HILL. I bear your name, I bore your children, and I AM STILL HOPING IN A PROMISE. I cannot lie.

Shit. I tried to reach Nikki several times on her phone but no luck. 616 Logan Road was literally three doors down from Nikki's house. Had Holly moved there knowing where Nikki lives? I had to let her know as soon as possible.

Alex: Call me ASAP.

I was planning to meet her after work so at least I could tell her then.

#

I pulled in my driveway half expecting to see Alex's car there. No such luck. After closing the garage door behind me, I opened the front door for some fresh circulation. That's when I found it.

On my front door knob hung a pink advertisement for Avon with a personalized hand-written note on the back. Now I have fond memories of the Avon ladies in my own family's history. My grandma had an attic full of every car-shaped cologne bottle, glass poodle, bracelet, necklace, and that little locket they sold with the perfume cream inside, which gets rancid after enough time. My gut reaction to the hanger on my door was rather pleasant at first. It turned to the tragic movie moment, complete with the Dun-Dun-DUUHNNN as I read the note.

> *"Hi! I'm your new local community Avon beauty consultant, and I live just down the street! I noticed the pleasant decor in your window and your fondness for flowers in your beautiful yard. I would welcome the opportunity to help you with your Avon needs! Sincerely, Holly Hill."*

Oh, shit! Shit-shit-shit! She found me. Wait, she didn't just find me—she moved into a house just down the street! Down MY street! Has she been playing me this whole time?

I snatched the flyer from the door, secured every imaginable lock, and snapped the blinds shut. *I gotta call Alex!*

I ran to the kitchen. Not there. Wait—the bathroom. Nope. Pockets—I don't have pockets...purse...*where the hell's my phone? Ok, wait—should I even call him? Oh crap, I'll have to come clean! Maybe she doesn't know about Hank. Where's my fucking phone? Wait—the car!*

I scrambled out to the garage. Yes! *Oh shit—six missed calls.* This was not going to be an easy conver—

The doorbell rang.

I froze. *Fuck! Fuckity-fuck-fuck! It's her! Wait—maybe it's Alex. Why doesn't he just come in? Shit—I locked the door!* Unsure, I called Alex from the garage, hiding in the corner like the boogey-man was gonna get me. "Alex!" I whispered.

"Nikki!" he whispered back.

"Where are you?"

I snuck back into the house and looked out the window. Alex was trying to look at me through the blurry top pane in the door.

"Why are we whispering?"

I flung the door open, grabbed Alex by the collar and drug him inside. He started first.

"Nikki! You're never gonna—"

"—O my God, Alex! Crazy—"

"—believe where she—"

"—put a note on my door!—"

"—lives three doors—"

"—*My front door! THIS DOOR!*"

"Wait… *what?*"

27. PLAUSIBLE DENIABILITY

Alex looked at the flyer. "That's definitely her handwriting," he said.

"Alex, do you think she knows where I live?"

Alex looked out the front window toward the other houses in the neighborhood. "Looks like she dropped flyers on every house," he said. "It's possible she doesn't know. I hate to think she'd find a place and move there just because it's close to you—doesn't seem like her style. I know she's not really happy that we are together, but I can't figure out why she would want to get closer to you on purpose."

I knew the time had come. I had to tell him.

"Alex, I need to let you know something. Something I'm not entirely proud of."

He looked confused, then pivoted his head to the side. "What have you done?"

I took a deep breath.

"I'll understand if you are not happy about this, but I promise you I only did it to protect you and the kids, and I never used it for evil, only for good. I was really worried Holly was going to hook up with some dangerous cop-hating type when she was doing the online dating thing."

Alex was starting to look impatient.

"Two months ago, I made an online profile on Match of a guy who would be a perfect fit for Holly."

I hadn't been sure if my activity constituted a crime or was just questionable conduct, but the look on Alex's face suggested the bomb I'd just dropped might go beyond bad manners. "Are you serious?"

"At first it was just a way to steer her toward a good kind of guy and hopefully away from the train-wrecks she had been entertaining. But then she started to really like me—I mean, Hank, the guy I invented. Who was really just me. I'm Hank."

Alex started pacing the room with one hand on top of his head. He stopped abruptly. "Wait, so do you think she figured out what you've been up to?"

"I don't think so, but I did have a communication with her when I slipped up and didn't mask my IP address."

"She's not tech-savvy at all," Alex said. "How many communications are we talking here?"

"I saved them all, let's see here." I opened my laptop and scrolled through the messages. "A couple hundred, maybe?"

Alex staggered backward a step, his head shaking. "Holy shit!" He leaned in to look at the list of messages.

"I didn't tell you because I knew it was risky, and I didn't want you to have any chance of getting in trouble for it. I don't think it's illegal but this is all on me, and I would totally understand if you think it's too much or if you don't want to continue our—"

Alex grabbed me in a hug and buried his face into my neck, his heart racing. Pulling back, he held my face in his hands and looked directly into my eyes. "Nikki," he said squarely, "I can't believe how freaking brilliant you are."

Wasn't expecting that.

I explained my technique of covering my tracks, how I chose Hank's details and picture, how the conversation with Holly started out, and how we'd never met. "Remember when we were at Martin's graduation?"

"Yeah?"

"That was the first time I tried breaking up with her."

Alex stared, wide-eyed. "You can't be serious!"

"She wouldn't let go! I tried to end it like three times but she just kept coming back."

"I remember sitting there and you kept looking back at Holly—you were on your phone—oh, man." Alex looked perplexed. "So it's still going on?"

"Well, yeah...sorta. But it's different now. She might hold on to some distant hope of riding off into the sunset with Hank, but she's mostly just telling him about her daily business ideas and sharing her favorite spiritual songs. But the best part truly surprised me."

"Which is?"

"Hank has been giving Holly really good advice on how to move forward from her broken relationship with you and get the psychological and educational support she needs to be stable for her kids."

Alex looked bewildered. "So you had the power to completely screw with her, and instead you're helping her navigate through her difficulties and get better?"

"Yep."

He shook his head. "Unbelievable. Do you realize the power you have here, Nikki?"

"Oh for sure. Which is exactly why I kept Sally in the loop the whole time. She kept me on the high road."

"Sally knows about Hank?"

"She's in on it! Why do you think we had all those liquid lunches?"

"Well you little shits!" he said.

"For a long time I couldn't understand why a woman would use religion and the convenient excuse of mental illness to cover her bitchy behavior. But I really can see now that her mental illness is a real thing. Alex, she's caught in the trap of her own mind: she thinks she's totally well, which is exactly why she won't listen to anyone who tries to tell her she's got a problem. But for some reason, she listens to Hank. She even sought out a new psychologist and got herself into a post-homemaker educational program."

"That was Hank?"

"Yep. And while she's still no less risky and no less responsible for her refusal to address her own behavior, I can kinda see why she has such a hard time getting the help she needs."

Alex flopped to the couch staring straight ahead. He was re-thinking everything.

"Alex, you still made the right decision. You didn't have a choice—she was destroying your family, herself, and you in the process. She's still doing harm to the kids by her manipulations. She has the power to fix herself if she just listens to someone other than herself. Maybe now she can at least start to find her way forward."

"I know I did everything I could to save the family," Alex said. I'm doing it still, trying to keep the kids from rejecting her, speaking well of her to the kids. I know the risks of a child being estranged from their mother, so I never wanted to cause that. Even if it's necessary, like it was in our case, that estrangement can do it's own kind of harm."

"You aren't responsible for that harm, Alex." I said. "It's just the way it is."

"Right, but she never gets it. All these accusations of Parental Alienation while I'm doing everything I can to protect the kids from her damage while promoting a good attitude about her." He sighed long, then stood up. "So many times, I thought she was going to die, Nikki. We all did. I thought she was going to drive off a cliff into Puget Sound, or step in front of a train or something. Every time I go on a suicidal call at work, I was haunted thinking it's another glimpse into how Holly's life would end." Alex looked desperately grieved. He sighed again. "But now," he said, "Hank, who isn't even real, is convincing Holly there is the chance of a good life ahead of her. This is just amazing."

"Alex, I have been able to see the way she twists actual events and reports them to Hank in a completely different reality. She lives in a complete fantasy land. She told Hank she moved into her new place because it was cute and had goats for the kids, not because she was evicted again. I Googled all over Lynnwood for a goat farm but came up empty."

He looked at his phone and opened up a message I could see was from Holly. "Well…only one thing left to do," he said.

"Which is?"

"Let's go find some goats."

We piled into the Mitz and drove north past a couple homes and around a slight curve. I pointed to a fence post with the numbers 616 on it next to a long driveway. "That's the address," he said. "It must be down there."

I looked and saw a pleasant two-story house with a detached garage on the far side of a rolling iron gate at the end of the driveway. The property was hard to see from the road, so we drove by a couple more times all inconspicuously to piece it all together. Even the little pasture with a pair of goats.

Back at my house, Alex had formulated his thoughts. "I'll stay out of the loop regarding Hank," he said. "But Nikki, you know you're gonna have to shut it down. The risks here are huge for all of us."

"I agree," I said. "But Alex, there are a couple things you'll need to know about."

"Whatever it is, launder it," he said. "This is the nature of intelligence work: find out information through covert means, then find or create a path where the same information can be discovered in a more legitimate way. Sometimes that means creating situations where the information gets revealed naturally. But like you said, it's best to keep me in the dark about your little undercover operation." I nodded in agreement.

"Oh, and Nikki?"

"Yes?"

He pulled me close again. "I'm more impressed with you than ever before. A little scared of you, perhaps." He grinned. "But I believe you when you say you only used it for good and never for evil. Because that's precisely who you are. I know you understand how important it is for the kids to have a decent relationship with a healthy mom. You've shown here that your compassion for a messed-up person will supersede your disgust for their behavior. That means the world to me."

I hadn't thought of it like that. In spite of the five kids, Holly was the only thing that made my relationship with Alex actually stressful. If she became more stable, maybe she would turn her energy toward an actual good guy other than Alex. The kids, Alex, and Holly would all benefit, maybe even to the point Holly could have more time with the kids. I wasn't sure if Holly would hold up her end of the bargain, but at least I could look back at the end of the day knowing, like Alex, I had done everything I could to help this fragmented family find their way forward.

August 15, 2010

I knew if I was going to shut off the Hank op for good, I'd have to find a way to have successful closure. The only way to guarantee that was to make it her idea. How do I do *that?*

The answer came in a golden moment when I opened Hank's email that evening.

> **To: Hank**
> **From: Holly**
>
> Thank you for the coaching! Things are coming together. I want to share something with you about a kind gentleman I've met. I don't want you to feel awkward based on our relationship but I do value your opinion. Would that be okay?
>
> Hopeful,
>
> Holly

Yep. That'd do just fine.

> **To: Holly**
> **From: Hank**
>
> Yes, you can share it with me. If there is anything I would hope for you, it would be that you find peace in your soul and someone to share it with. That blesses everyone.
>
> Hank

August 16, 2010

> **To: Hank**

From: Holly

Thank you for being so understanding. Tony is…. Tony Milano is a deacon in training at Eastlake with a pleasant face and kind demeanor. He has a 13-year-old daughter who loves her daddy and has had him all to herself for the last 5 years. I met her recently and found her to be a lovely and brilliant child. She is insecure about my presence. She is not ready for a change this drastic. I'm very concerned for her teenage years but I am confident God will help me overcome the conflict.

Tony provides financial and emotional support to his ex-wife all while keeping a good mutual relationship with her. He is a financial planner with an apartment in Kirkland and a condo in Olympia. This allows him to stay near his daughter when she is at her moms.

So I thank God for you, Hank, for bringing Tony and I together. Unfortunately, it will now be best for us to stop our communications as God would not have me torn between two men. I hope you find your perfect soul-mate someday. That someone could have been me. It's regrettable you couldn't let your guard down. Next time try to look through God's eyes and see the best in others rather than serving judgment.

I offer you nothing but love and mercy. I pray that you will daily walk in the steps of Jesus your Savior and be blessed with wisdom and discernment.

Hoping in the Heavenly Husband,

Holly

Well, I'll be. God works in mysterious ways, to be sure. This certainly calls for a celebratory liquid lunch with Sally. I sent a quick reply to Holly congratulating her for the new direction and assuring her that I would honor her request to cease communications. I put the Hank account into hibernation.

# # #

November 1, 2010

After learning Tony and Holly started dating in late August, the regular slew of texts and emails rapidly declined. The kids came home from visits with stories of Tony which painted him as a genuinely good guy. Their resistance to visiting their mom was evaporating. Tony helped with transports, he was open to communicating directly with me, and he provided the missing stabilization Holly had needed. It wasn't that Holly became suddenly well or that all the stresses went away, but the direction was promising.

By mid-October, Holly announced she was engaged to Tony. She sent me a text asking me if I would walk her down the aisle. Ignoring that part, I congratulated Holly and wished her the best. As Nikki and I sat on a Sunset Avenue bench overlooking Puget Sound during our walk that evening, Nikki couldn't resist putting in her own two bits.

"You should really reconsider her offer. I could be the flower girl. Or—hey, Hank could be the man of honor!"

I just shook my head and grinned, watching the sun slowly disappear over the Olympic mountains, lighting the scattered clouds on fire with streaks of pink and orange. "You know, if this sticks, I won't have to pay the $1,000 maintenance each month any more. I could actually cut my overtime need in half." I was relieved at the thought.

"And," Nikki suggested, "Hank could find out every now and then how Holly is getting along with her latest love interest."

I held firm, saying it was better to find out naturally and only deal with things as they came. "There's a great advantage of knowing somebody's secrets," I said, "but it also means you have to constantly avoid revealing the fact that you know. Trust me—it can drive you crazy."

My hand had involuntarily found its way into the front pocket of my coat feeling the edges of the solitaire diamond through the velvet drawstring pouch. I knew Nikki was the one, which is why I had stopped at the jewelry store earlier that day to pick up the ring. It was a beautiful evening at the end of a beautiful day.

"I suppose you're right," she said. "Just this once. But it sure was great being one step ahead of her. Now I'm not gonna know who she picks for a flower girl. Whatever--marriage after 40 is just so unnecessary."

My hand reversed course. For now, anyway. *All in good time,* I thought. "Hey Nikki?"

"Yes?"

"Do you know the definition of a secret?"

"Enlighten me."

"Something you tell one person at a time."

She was unimpressed. I felt like a complete dork. "Hey, Nikki?"

"Yes?"

"I got a secret."

Nikki turned and looked at me, raising an eyebrow, then turned away, looking out to the expanse of the water. "Everyone has a secret, Alex."

Everyone.

ACKNOWLEDGMENTS

First and foremost, gratitude is overflowing for my wife Kristen, an incredible woman who has believed in me and in this project from the beginning. Without you, none of this is even imaginable. You know who you are, which has given me the freedom and permission to be the odd person I am.

To my children, I cannot begin to describe the love I have for you all. You have given me the great and unique privilege of happiness as a dad, something I'll never take for granted. I love you.

I am also grateful for those in my law enforcement career who have mentored, encouraged, and trained me for not only the nuts and bolts of a challenging profession, but also given me insight into the nature of this work and the things which drive it. Rich Myers, Mark Nelson, Julie Olson, John Cameron, Steve Harbinson, Tom Smith, Steve Dean, Clair Walker, and so many others. To the members of the Edmonds Police Department who provided incredible insight and support for this book, you are dearly loved and appreciated for your friendship, for all you do on a daily basis, and for your dedication to something far beyond your own personal benefit.

To my family of faith who remained alongside me through the valleys of doubt and grief, and who helped me remember what was truly important, you have all my love.

To my friend and literary mentor, Robert Dugoni, thank you so much for your willingness to take a man with major baggage and help him become an author with a purpose. And to Kimberly Hughes for your tireless, tedious, and sometimes ruthless insistence for commas, you have all my thanks.

For those who face the undefinable combination of mental illness and malice in a loved one: I hope this book provides some hope of a future and the acceptance of your own judgment, perspective, and path. There is no perfect way to navigate that space. "How did you get through it," they'll ask. I promise, you will never have what it takes to face your greatest challenges—until you are actually in the moment itself. Do good, and remember to care for yourself. Those who love and need you will benefit from it. You are not alone.

CPSIA information can be obtained
at www.ICGtesting.com
Printed in the USA
LVHW080146100719
623417LV00009BA/153/P